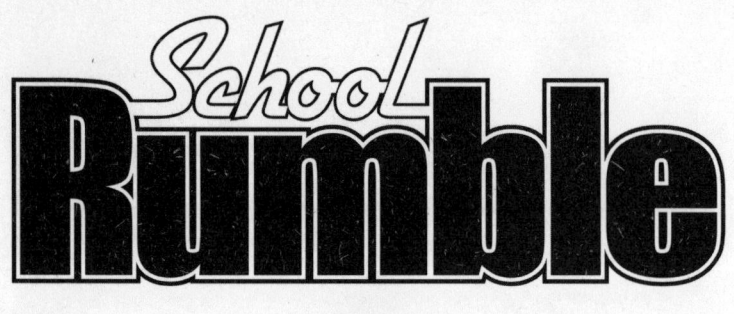

School Rumble

1

Jin Kobayashi

TRANSLATED AND ADAPTED BY
William Flanagan

LETTERED BY
Dana Hayward

tanoshimi
LONDON

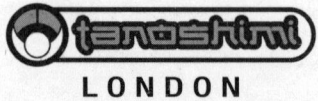

Published in the United Kingdom by Tanoshimi in 2007

5 7 9 10 8 6 4

School Rumble, Volume 1 is a work of fiction. Names, characters, places and incidents are the products of the authors' imagination or are used fictitiously. Any resemblance to actual events, locales, or persons, living or dead, is entirely coincidental.

Originally published in Japan in 2003 by Kodansha Ltd., Tokyo

Published by arrangement with Kodansha Ltd., Tokyo and with Del Rey, an imprint of Random House Inc., New York

Tanoshimi
The Random House Group Limited
20 Vauxhall Bridge Road, London, SW1V 2SA

www.tanoshimi.tv
www.rbooks.co.uk

Addresses for companies within The Random House Group Limited can be found at:
www.randomhouse.co.uk

Random House Group Limited Reg. No. 954009

A CIP catalogue record for this book is available from the British Library

ISBN 9780099506263

The Random House Group Limited supports The Forest Stewardship Council (FSC), the leading international forest certification organisation. All our titles that are printed on Greenpeace approved FSC certified paper carry the FSC logo. Our paper procurement policy can be found at: www.rbooks.co.uk/environment

Printed and bound in Germany by GGP Media GmbH, Pößneck

Translator and adaptor – William Flanagan
Lettering – Dana Hayward
Cover design – David Stevenson

Honorifics

Throughout the Tanoshimi Manga books, you will find Japanese honorifics left intact in the translations. For those not familiar with how the Japanese use honorifics, and more important, how they differ from English honorifics, we present this brief overview.

Politeness has always been a critical facet of Japanese culture. Ever since the feudal era, when Japan was a highly stratified society, use of honorifics—which can be defined as polite speech that indicates relationship or status—has played an essential role in the Japanese language. When addressing someone in Japanese, an honorific usually takes the form of a suffix attached to one's name (example: "Asuna-san"), or as a title at the end of one's name or in place of the name itself (example: "Negi-sensei," or simply "Sensei!").

Honorifics can be expressions of respect or endearment. In the context of manga and anime, honorifics give insight into the nature of the relationship between characters. Many translations into English leave out these important honorifics, and therefore distort the "feel" of the original Japanese. Because Japanese honorifics contain nuances that English honorifics lack, it is our policy at Tanoshimi not to translate them. Here, instead, is a guide to some of the honorifics you may encounter in Tanoshimi Manga.

-*san*: This is the most common honorific, and is equivalent to Mr., Miss, Ms., Mrs., etc. It is the all-purpose honorific and can be used in any situation where politeness is required.

-*sama*: This is one level higher than "-san" and it is used to confer great respect.

-*dono*: This comes from the word "tono," which means "lord." It is an even higher level than "-sama," and confers utmost respect.

-*kun*: This suffix is used at the end of boys' names to express familiarity or endearment. It is also sometimes used by men among friends, or when addressing someone younger or of a lower station.

-chan: This is used to express endearment, mostly toward girls. It is also used for little boys, pets, and even among lovers. It gives a sense of childish cuteness.

Bozu: This is an informal way to refer to a boy, similar to the English term "kid".

Sempai/senpai: This title suggests that the addressee is one's "senior" in a group or organization. It is most often used in a school setting, where underclassmen refer to their upperclassmen as "sempai." It can also be used in the workplace, such as when a newer employee addresses an employee who has seniority in the company.

Kohai: This is the opposite of "sempai," and is used toward underclassmen in school or newcomers in the workplace. It connotes that the addressee is of lower station.

Sensei: Literally meaning "one who has come before," this title is used for teachers, doctors, or masters of any profession or art.

Nee-chan/Nii-chan: Older siblings are not commonly called by name but rather by the title "older sister" (*nee-chan*) or "older brother" (*nii-chan*). These honorifics can also be used with someone unrelated, when the relationship seems like a sibling relationship.

[blank]:   Usually forgotten in these lists, but perhaps the most significant difference between Japanese and English. The lack of honorific means that the speaker has permission to address the person in a very intimate way. Usually, only family, spouses, or very close friends have this kind of permission. Known as *yobisute,* it can be gratifying when someone who has earned the intimacy starts to call one by one's name without an honorific. But when that intimacy hasn't been earned, it can be very insulting.

Cultural Note

To preserve some of the humor found in *School Rumble*, we have elected to keep Japanese names in their original Japanese order—that is to say, with the family name first, followed by the personal name. So when you hear the name Tsukamoto Tenma, Tenma is just one member of the Tsukamoto family.

WHAT THE HECK IS *LOVE?*

SMILE FOR ME!

A DREAM...?

I WANT TO BE WITH YOU ALWAYS.

I KNOW.

BECAUSE I'M STRESSED OVER IT.

I'M SO HAPPY!

IT MAKES ME SO MAD!

I'LL SAY IT, AND THEN YOU'LL SEE!

IT'S LIKE YOU'RE NOT AFRAID OF ANYTHING!

IT JUST GIVES ME THE CHILLS!

I WANT TO RUN AWAY SO BAD!

THAT'S WHAT THEY CALL FOOLING YOURSELF!

IT WAS USELESS FROM THE START.

I JUST DON'T UNDERSTAND BOYS!

THAT'S THE FIRST TIME I'VE HEARD THAT!

THIS REALLY HURTS!

DO YOU THINK I'M PRETTY?

I BELIEVE IN YOU, YOU KNOW!

AH HA HA HA!

IDIOT!

I CAN'T SLEEP.

OHH, NOO! WHAT'LL I DO?!

WAS THAT AGAINST THE RULES?

IT JUST COMES INTO MY BRAIN.

JUST ACCEPT IT!

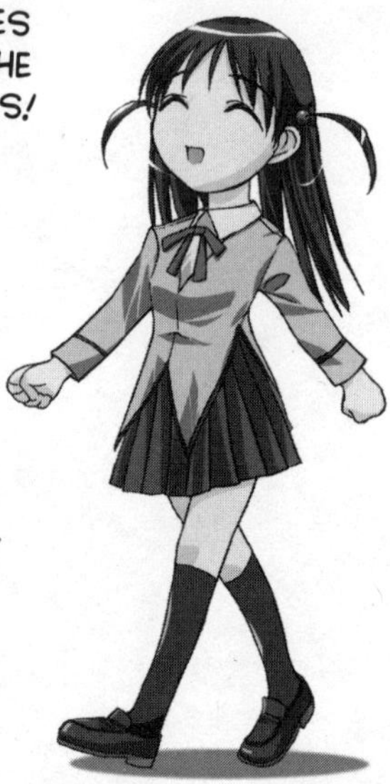

THIS JUST ISN'T LIKE ME!

AND YOU CALL YOURSELF A LADY?!

School Rumble

1

Jin Kobayashi

IS THAT A STAB IN THE BACK?

IT ISN'T AN EXCUSE!

JUST TAKE A LOOK AT YOURSELF!

I LOVE YOU!!

I'M THE ONE WHO SHOULD BE CRYING!

I'M GIVING THIS MY BEST!

Are there feelings that you can't feel?

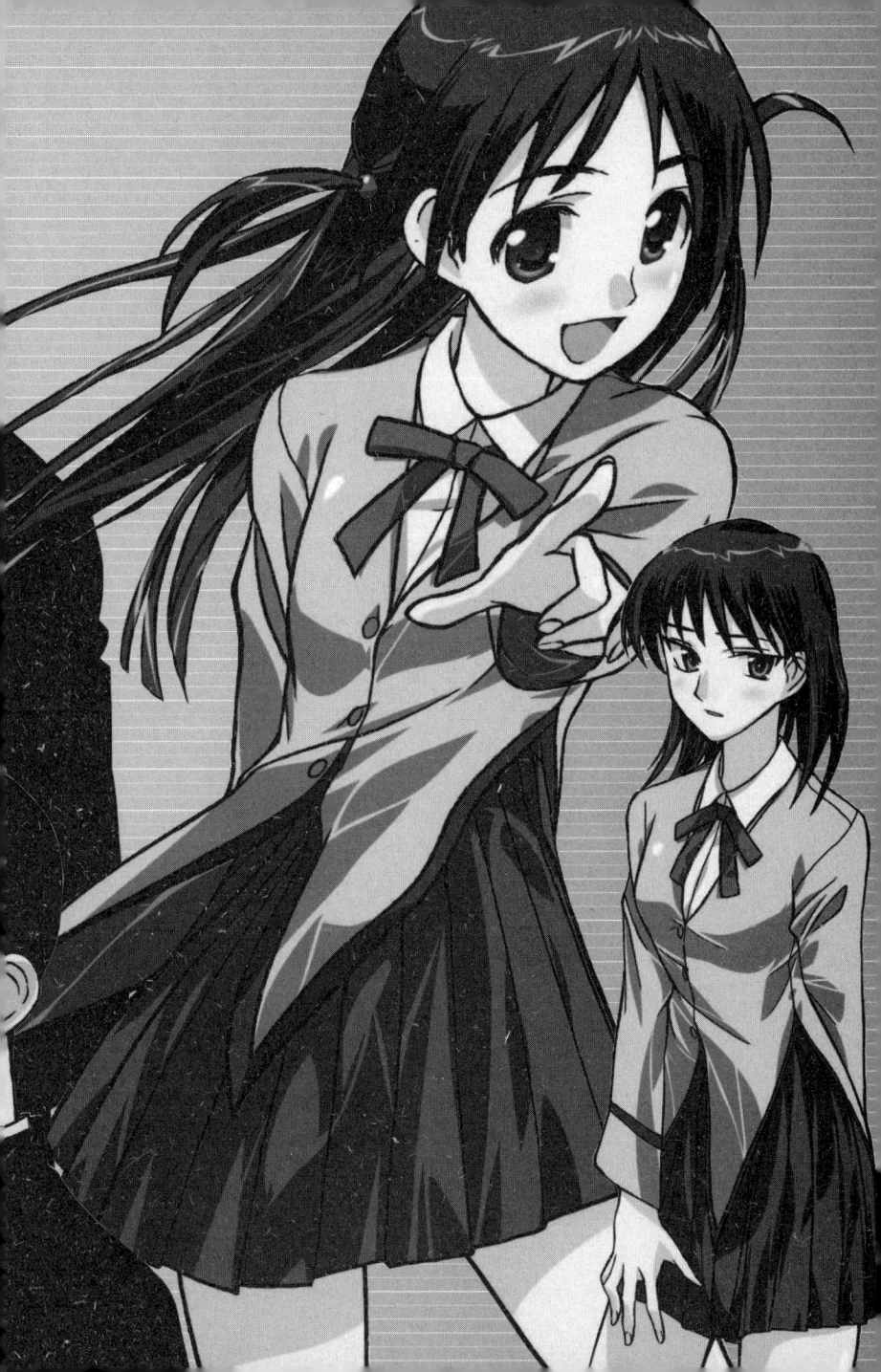

School Rumble

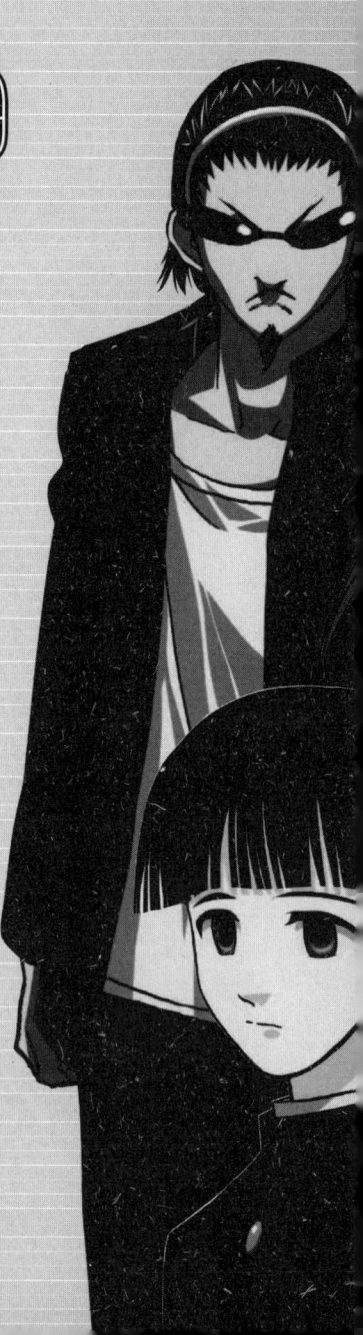

Contents

ONE DAY
I'LL SAY
IT...

THAT
YOU'RE
THE
REASON
I'M SO
HAPPY!

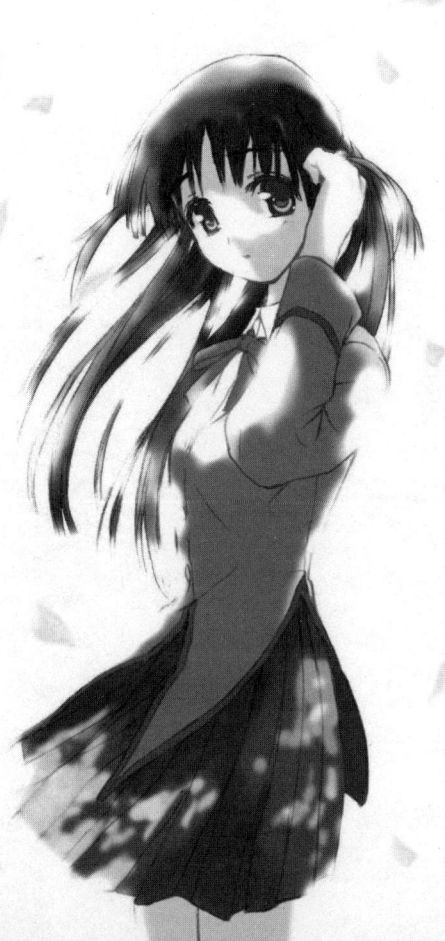

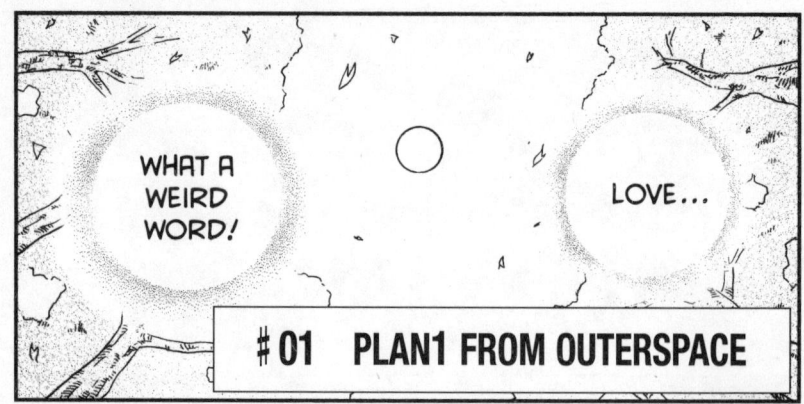

WHAT A WEIRD WORD!

LOVE...

#01 PLAN1 FROM OUTERSPACE

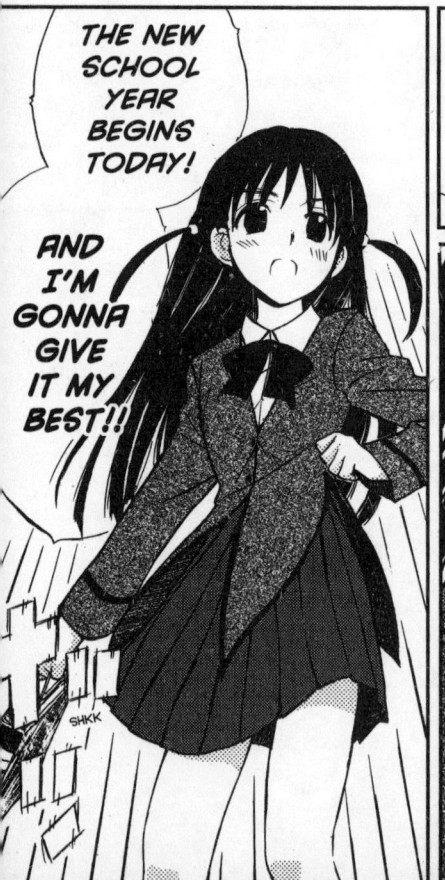

THE NEW SCHOOL YEAR BEGINS TODAY!

AND I'M GONNA GIVE IT MY BEST!!

SHKK

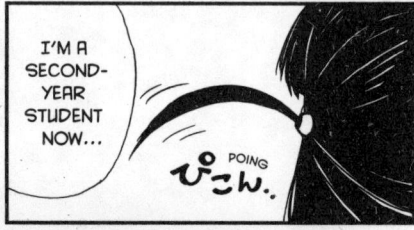

I'M A SECOND-YEAR STUDENT NOW...

ぴこん.. POING

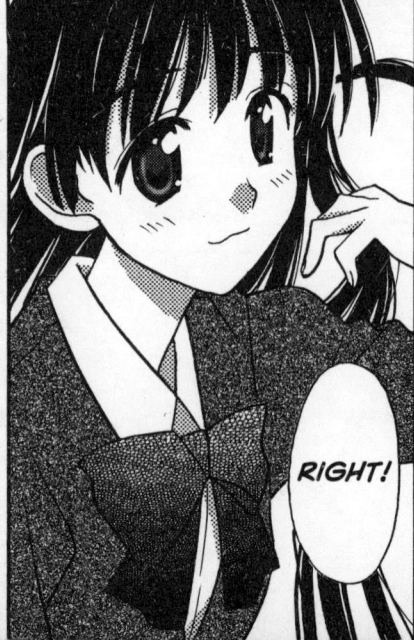

RIGHT!

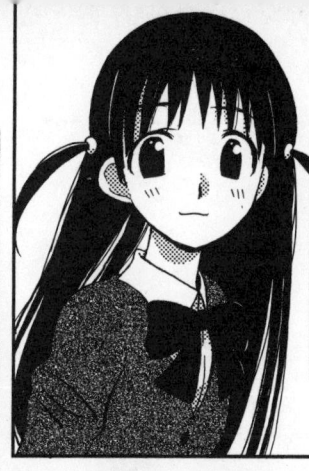

Her name is Tsukamoto Tenma.

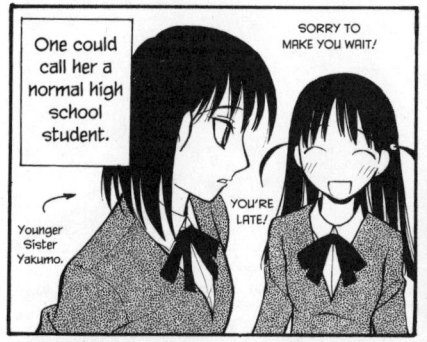

One could call her a normal high school student.

SORRY TO MAKE YOU WAIT!

YOU'RE LATE!

Younger Sister Yakumo.

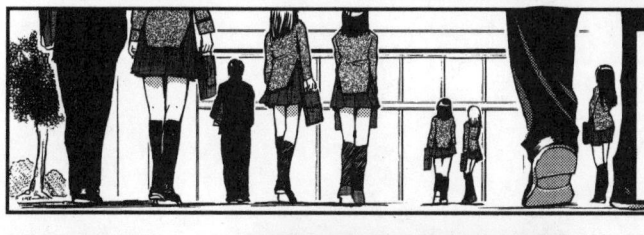

And like so many other girls around her age...

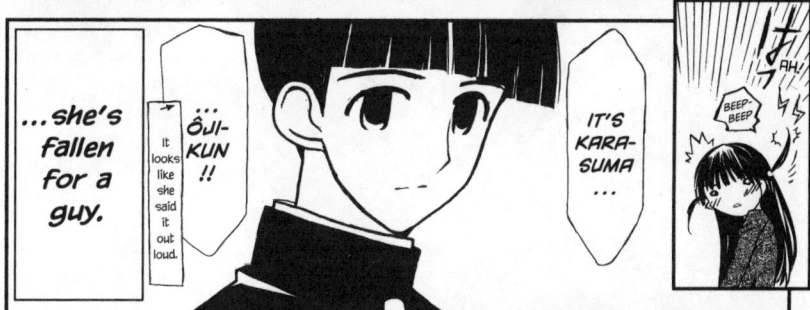

...she's fallen for a guy.

ŌJI-KUN!!

It looks like she said it out loud.

IT'S KARA-SUMA...

AH!

BEEP-BEEP

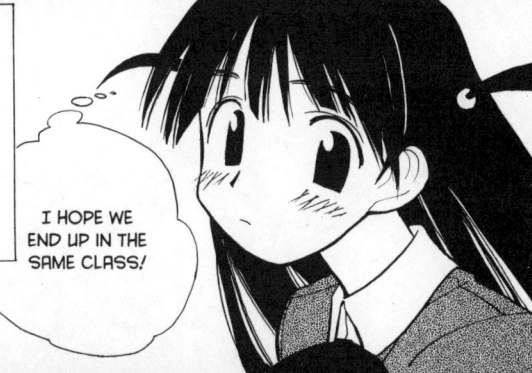

Today is the day that class assignments come out, so for Tenma, this is the pivotal day on which her destiny turns.

I HOPE WE END UP IN THE SAME CLASS!

CLASS ASSIGNMENTS

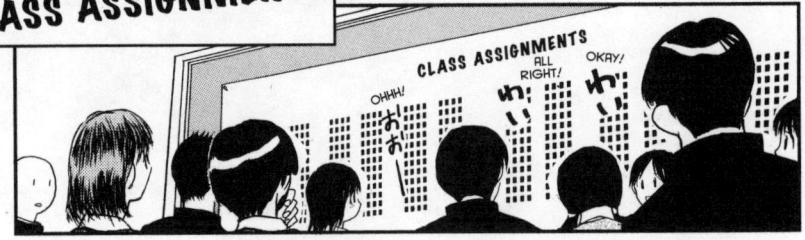

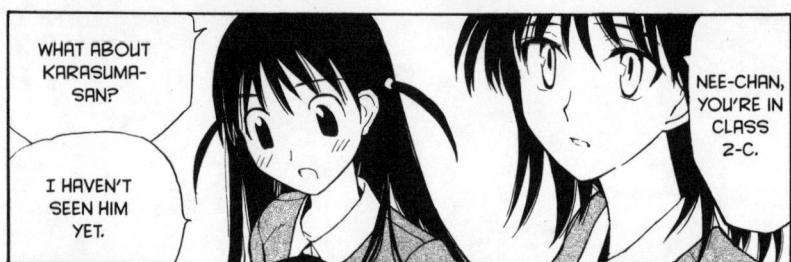

WHAT ABOUT KARASUMA-SAN?

I HAVEN'T SEEN HIM YET.

NEE-CHAN, YOU'RE IN CLASS 2-C.

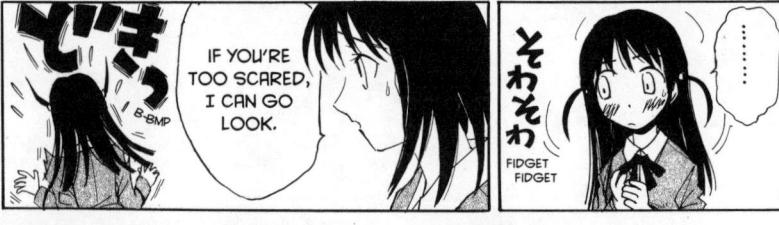

IF YOU'RE TOO SCARED, I CAN GO LOOK.

B-BMP

FIDGET FIDGET

......

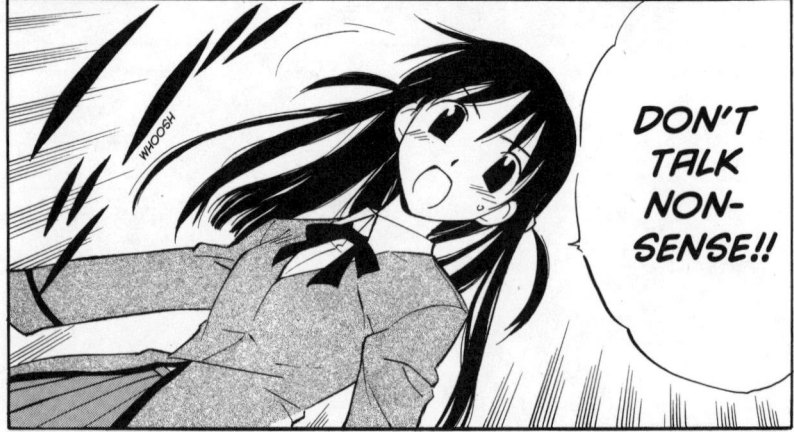

WHOOSH

DON'T TALK NON-SENSE!!

烏丸大路

Karasuma Ôji

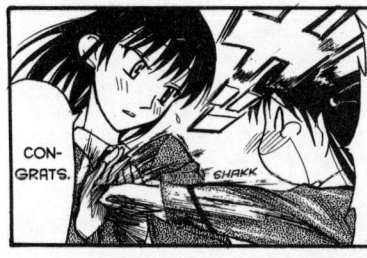

WE'RE IN THE SAME CLASS!!!

ALL RIGHT!!

CON- GRATS.

SHAKK

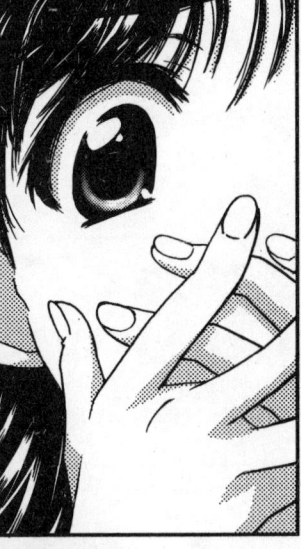

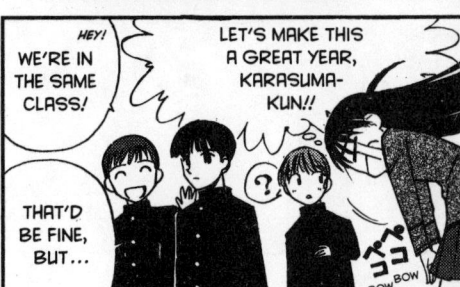

HEY! WE'RE IN THE SAME CLASS!

LET'S MAKE THIS A GREAT YEAR, KARASUMA- KUN!!

THAT'D BE FINE, BUT...

ペコ ペコ
BOW BOW

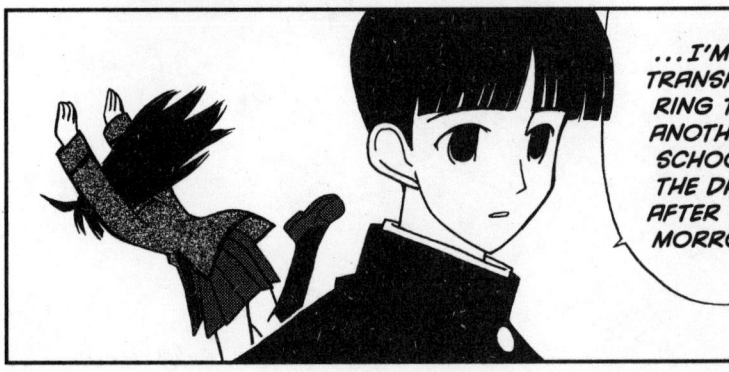

...I'M TRANSFER- RING TO ANOTHER SCHOOL THE DAY AFTER TO- MORROW.

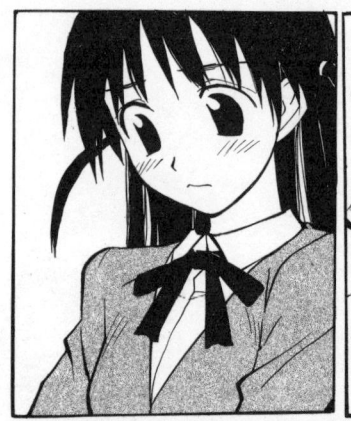

I'LL MAKE IT WORK OUT!!

THAT DREAM DIDN'T LAST LONG.

YOU'RE STILL AT IT?

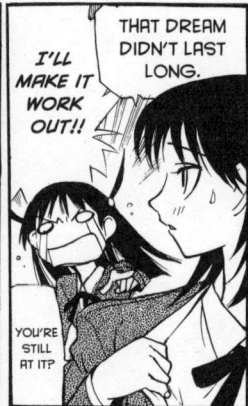

Tenma's House

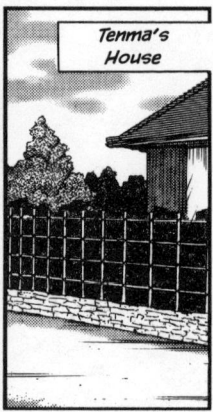

FIRST I'LL START CLEANING. THAT'LL CALM ME DOWN.

VWOOOM

うぃーん

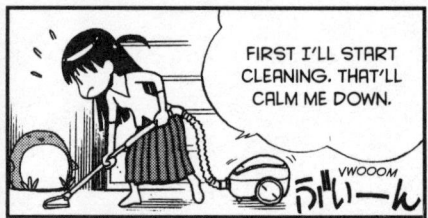

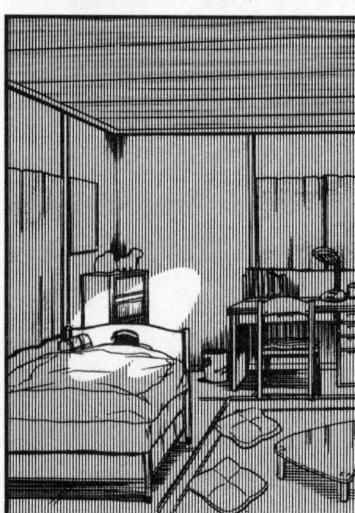

THEN I'LL WASH DISHES!

5 hours later.

3 hours later.

THEN I'LL DO LAUNDRY AND CONSIDER MY OPTIONS!

KLONK KLONK

ゴゥ ゴッ

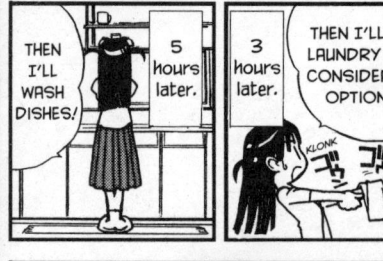

I'LL JUST SLEEP.

OH, HECK!

I CAN'T THINK OF ANY-THING!!

8 hours later.

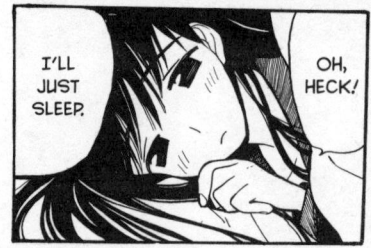

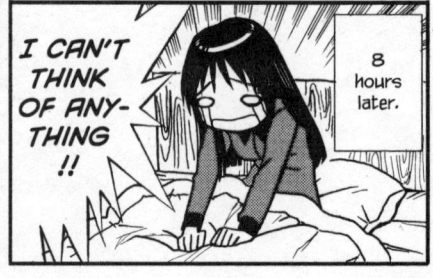

— 9 —

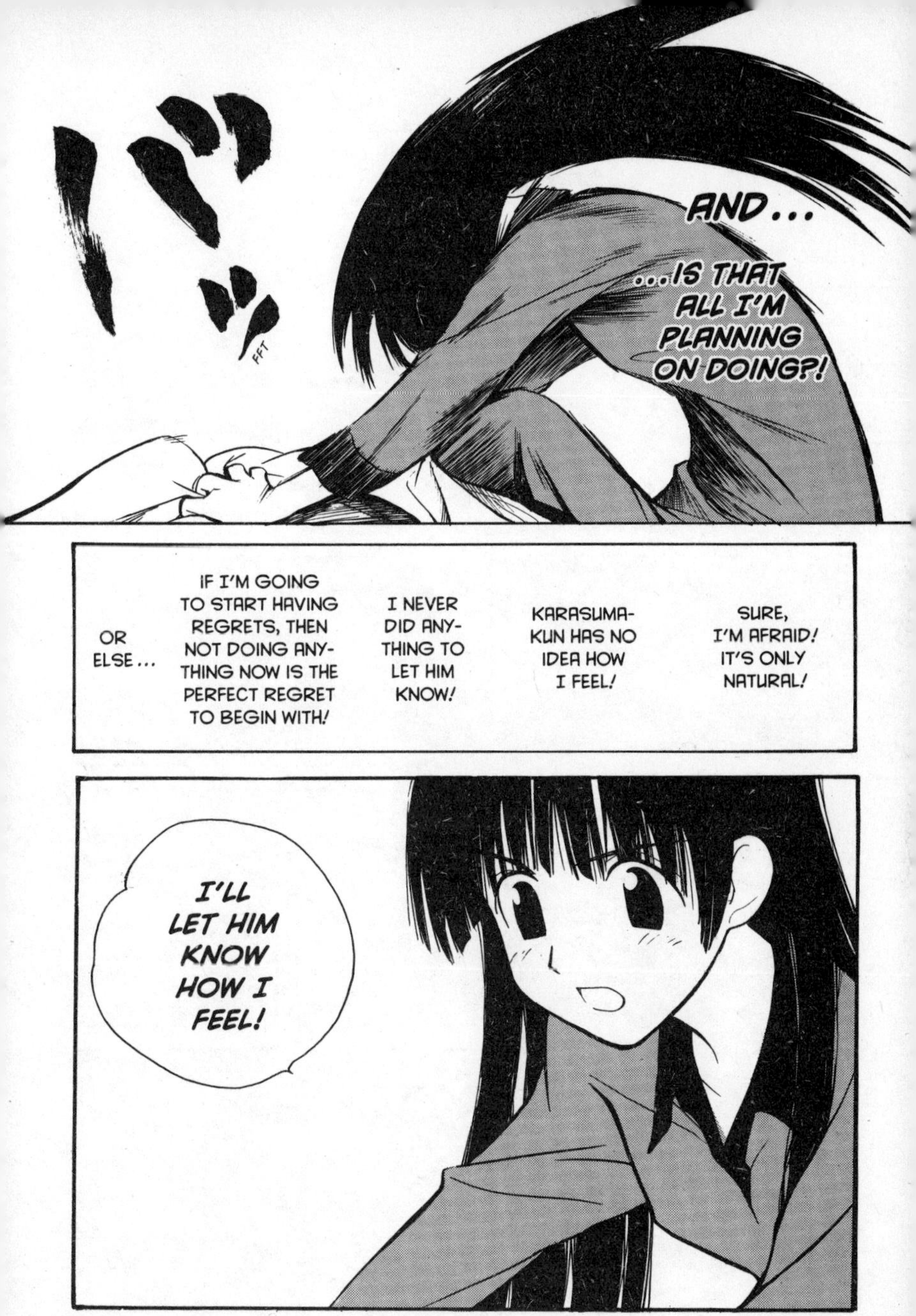

AND...

...IS THAT ALL I'M PLANNING ON DOING?!

FFT

OR ELSE...

IF I'M GOING TO START HAVING REGRETS, THEN NOT DOING ANY-THING NOW IS THE PERFECT REGRET TO BEGIN WITH!

I NEVER DID ANY-THING TO LET HIM KNOW!

KARASUMA-KUN HAS NO IDEA HOW I FEEL!

SURE, I'M AFRAID! IT'S ONLY NATURAL!

I'LL LET HIM KNOW HOW I FEEL!

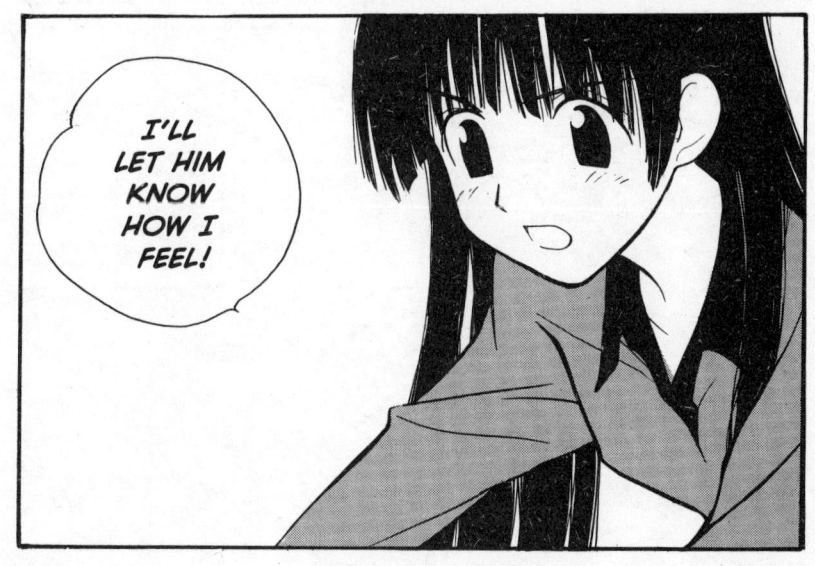

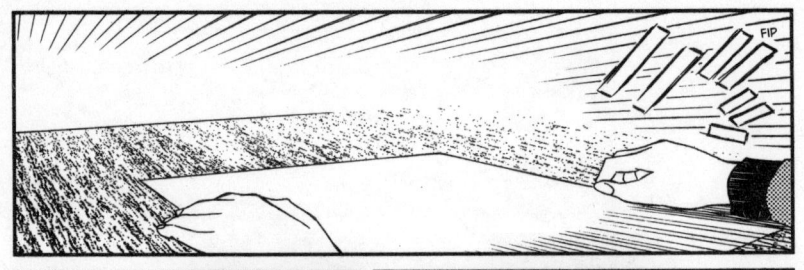

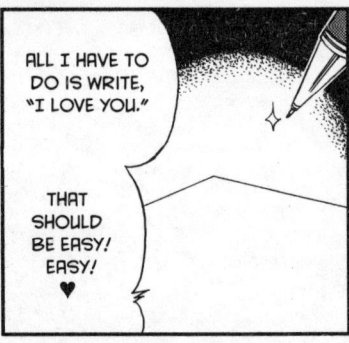

ALL I HAVE TO DO IS WRITE, "I LOVE YOU."

THAT SHOULD BE EASY! EASY! ♥

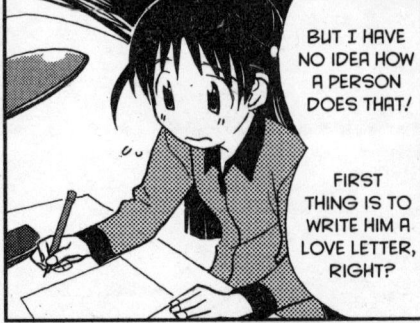

BUT I HAVE NO IDEA HOW A PERSON DOES THAT!

FIRST THING IS TO WRITE HIM A LOVE LETTER, RIGHT?

...LOAD MY STUFF TO GO INTO THE MOUNTAINS TO WATCH YOU SKI!

WHAT THE HECK AM I WRITING?!

POFF.

ZLOOM ZLOOM

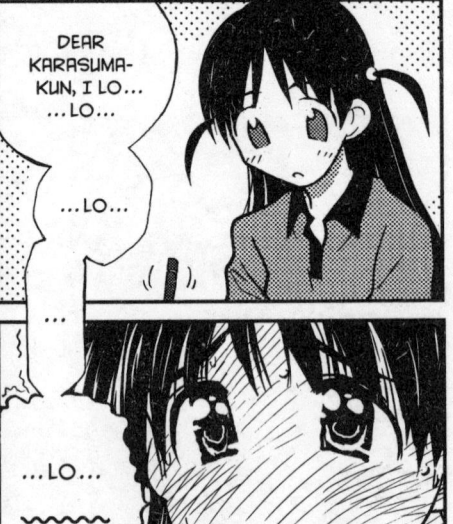

DEAR KARASUMA-KUN, I LO... ...LO...

...LO...

...

...LO...

~~~~~~

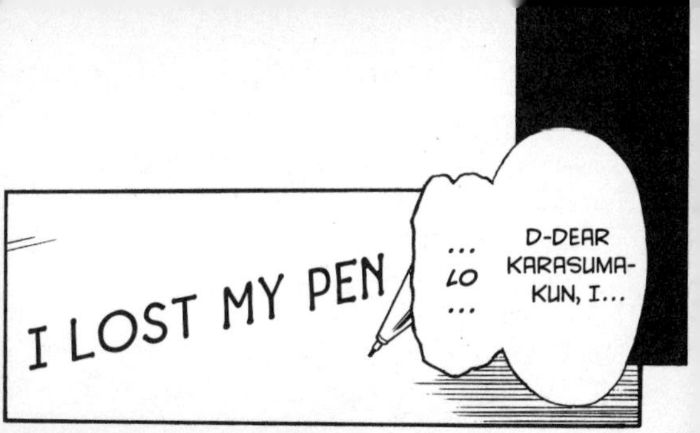
D-DEAR KARASUMA-KUN, I...
...LO...
I LOST MY PEN

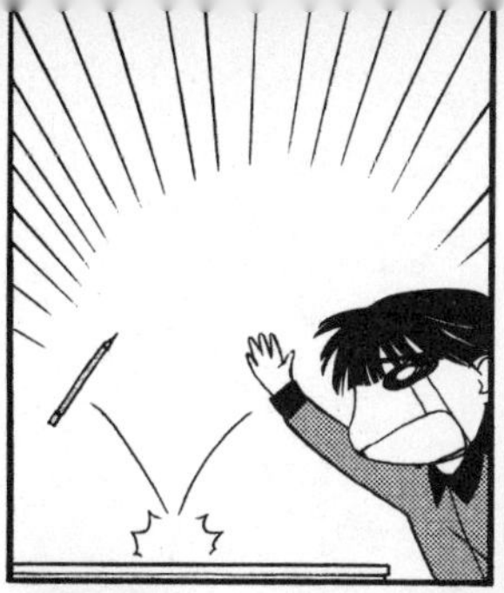

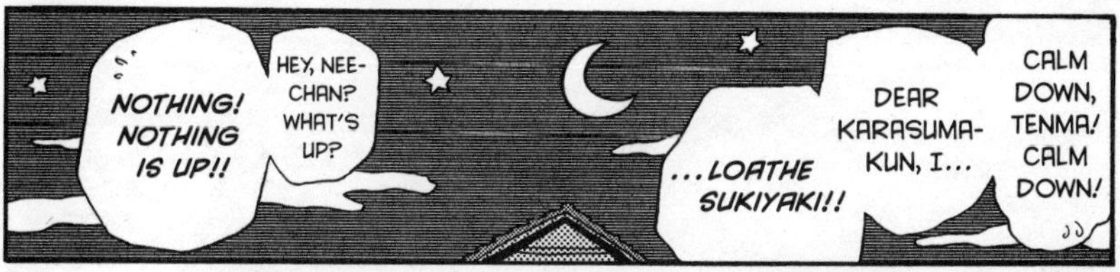
CALM DOWN, TENMA! CALM DOWN!
DEAR KARASUMA-KUN, I...
...LOATHE SUKIYAKI!!
HEY, NEE-CHAN? WHAT'S UP?
NOTHING! NOTHING IS UP!!

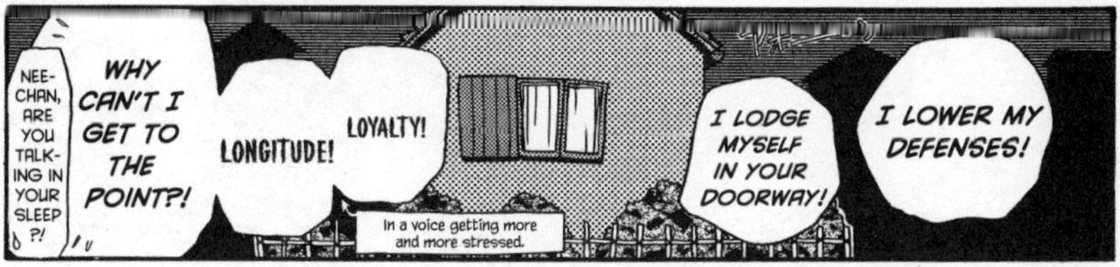
I LOWER MY DEFENSES!
I LODGE MYSELF IN YOUR DOORWAY!
LOYALTY!
LONGITUDE!
In a voice getting more and more stressed.
WHY CAN'T I GET TO THE POINT?!
NEE-CHAN, ARE YOU TALKING IN YOUR SLEEP?!

The next day...

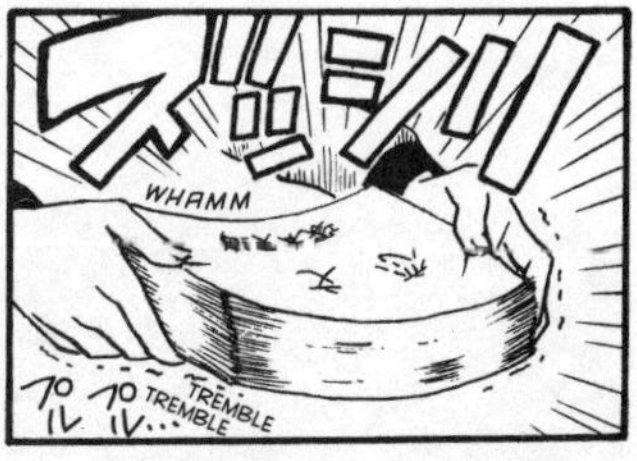
WHAMM
TREMBLE TREMBLE...

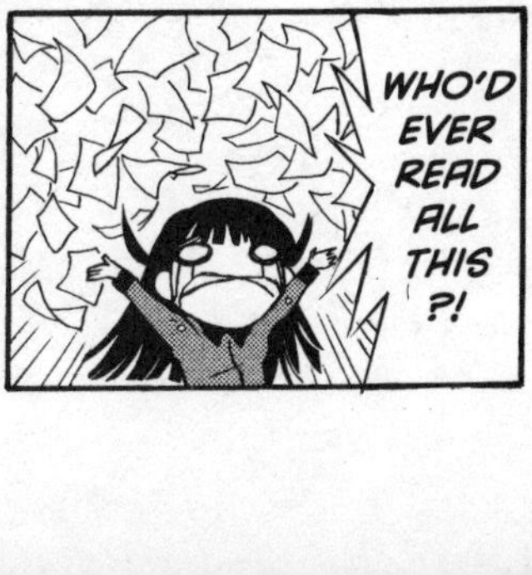
WHO'D EVER READ ALL THIS?!

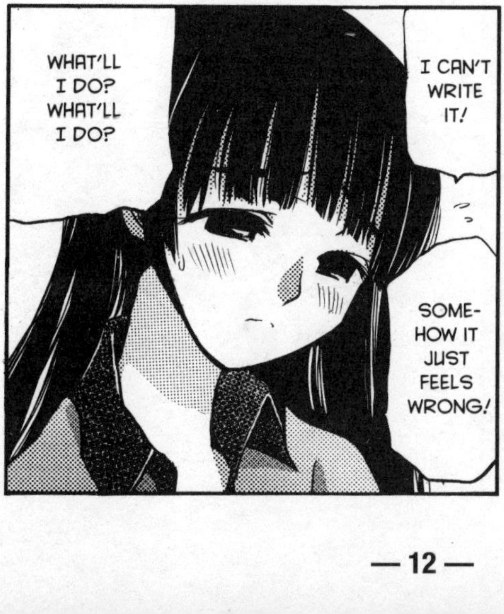
I CAN'T WRITE IT!
SOME-HOW IT JUST FEELS WRONG!
WHAT'LL I DO? WHAT'LL I DO?

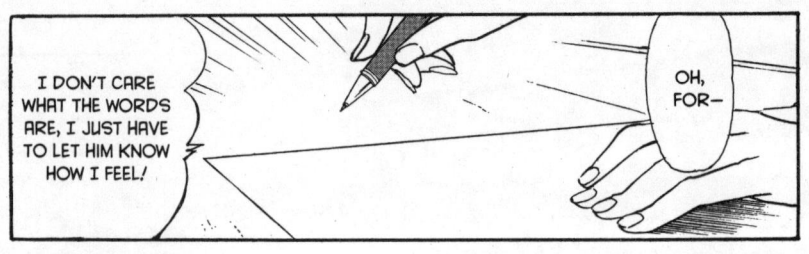

I DON'T CARE WHAT THE WORDS ARE, I JUST HAVE TO LET HIM KNOW HOW I FEEL!

OH, FOR—

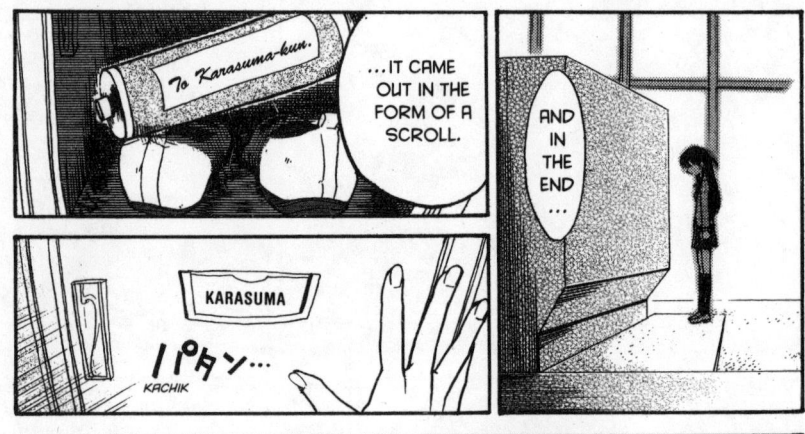

...IT CAME OUT IN THE FORM OF A SCROLL.

To Karasuma-kun.

AND IN THE END...

KARASUMA

パタン...
KACHIK

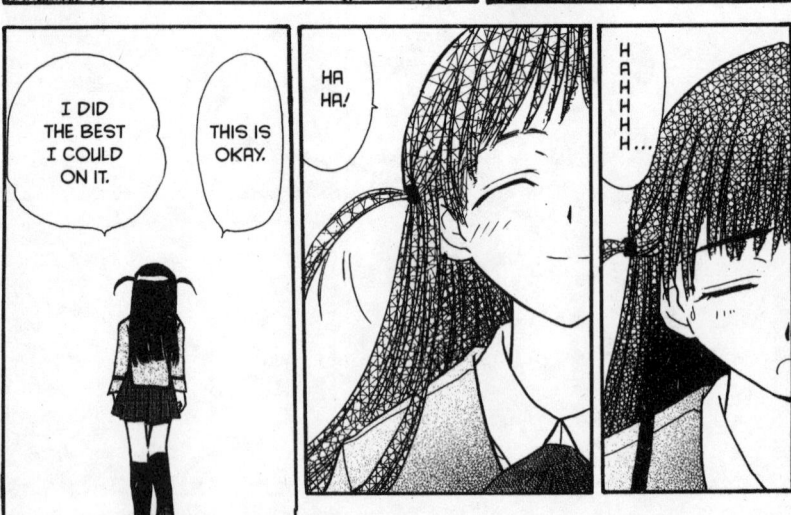

I DID THE BEST I COULD ON IT.

THIS IS OKAY.

HA HA!

HAHHHH...

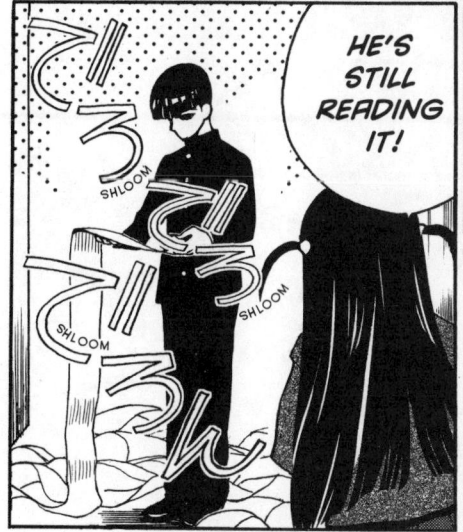

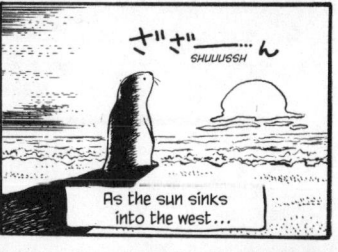

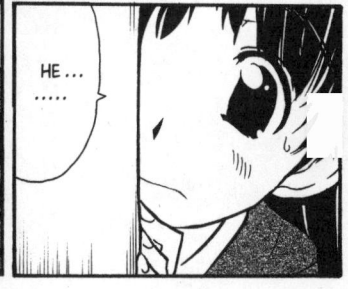

After school...

SEE YA.

CHATTER

SORRY, I HAVE MY CLUB RIGHT NOW.

CHATTER

HE'S READING IT!!

HE...
.....

HE'S STILL READING IT!

SHLOOM

SHLOOM

SHLOOM

SHUUUSSH

As the sun sinks into the west...

HE...
.....

— 14 —

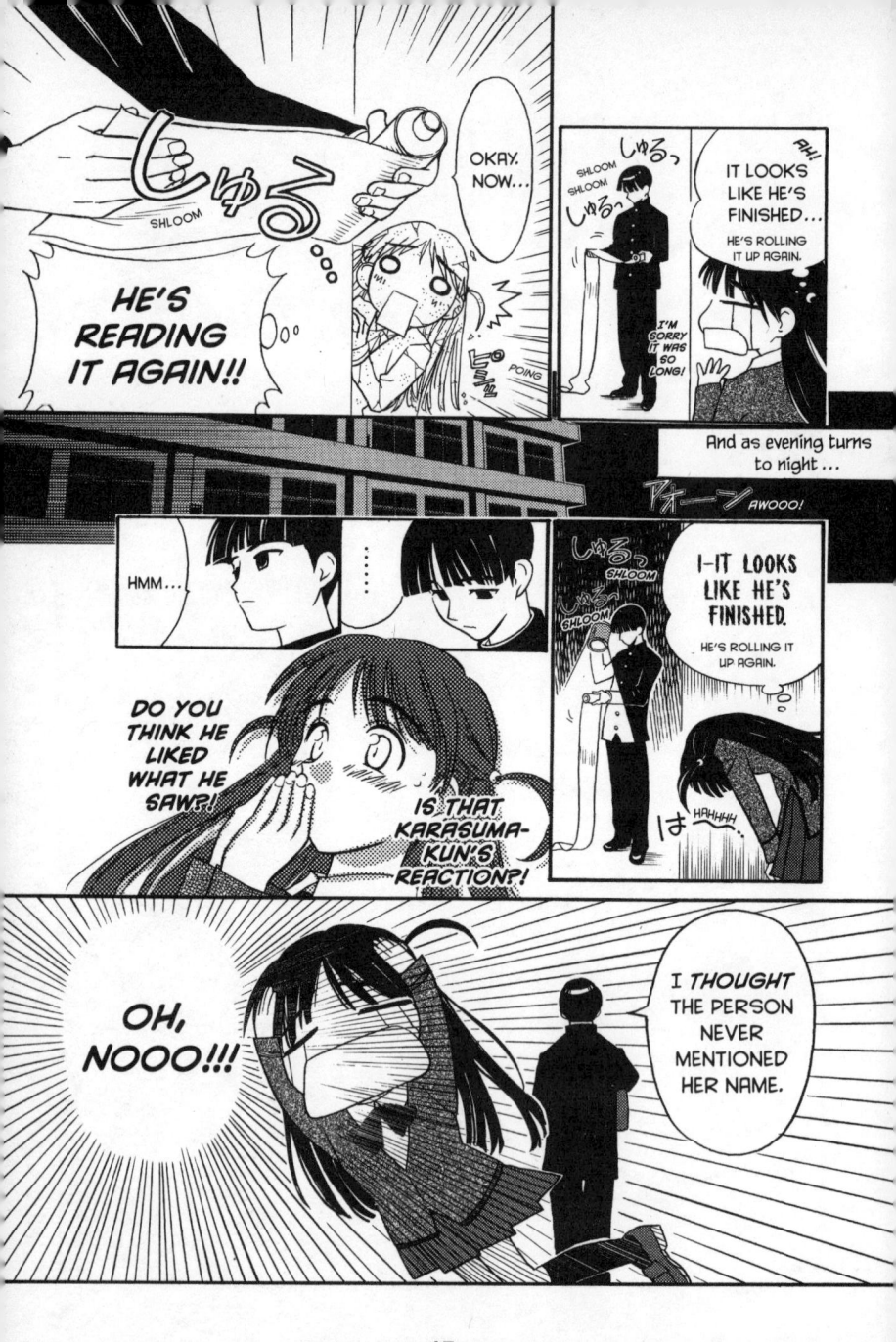

SHLOOM

OKAY. NOW...

HE'S READING IT AGAIN!!

POING

SHLOOM SHLOOM SHLOOM

AH!

IT LOOKS LIKE HE'S FINISHED...

HE'S ROLLING IT UP AGAIN.

I'M SORRY IT WAS SO LONG!

And as evening turns to night...

AWOOO!

HMM...

· · · · ·

DO YOU THINK HE LIKED WHAT HE SAW?!

IS THAT KARASUMA-KUN'S REACTION?!

SHLOOM

SHLOOM

I-IT LOOKS LIKE HE'S FINISHED.

HE'S ROLLING IT UP AGAIN.

HAHHHH...

OH, NOOO!!!

I *THOUGHT* THE PERSON NEVER MENTIONED HER NAME.

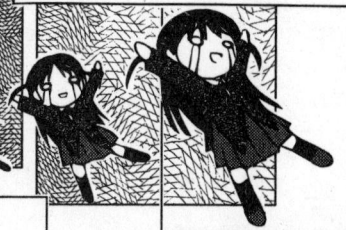

IT'S OVER...

MY FIRST LOVE...!!

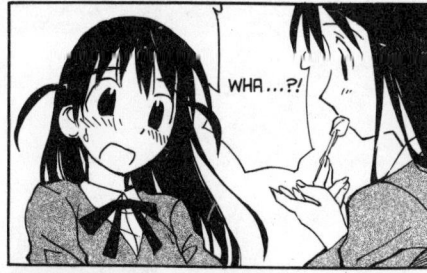

WHA...?!

DO YOU KNOW THAT GUY, KARASUMA-KUN?

THEY SAY HE DELAYED HIS TRANSFER.

But soon...

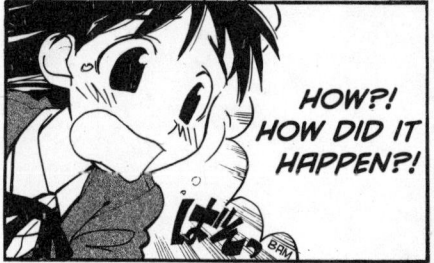

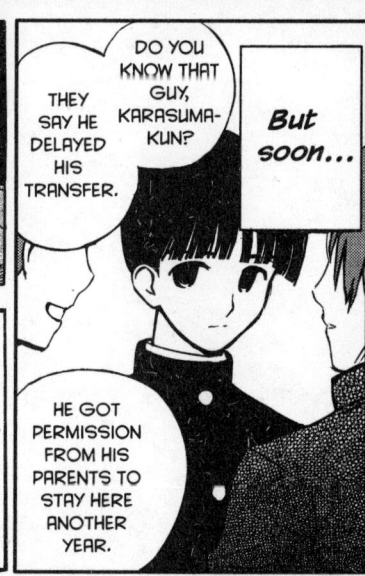

HOW?! HOW DID IT HAPPEN?!

HE GOT PERMISSION FROM HIS PARENTS TO STAY HERE ANOTHER YEAR.

...I HEARD THAT SOMEONE ASKED HIM TO STAY.

Don't go away! Please, don't go!

I DON'T KNOW MUCH ABOUT IT, BUT...

I DON'T KNOW.

♯ 01 . . . . Fin.

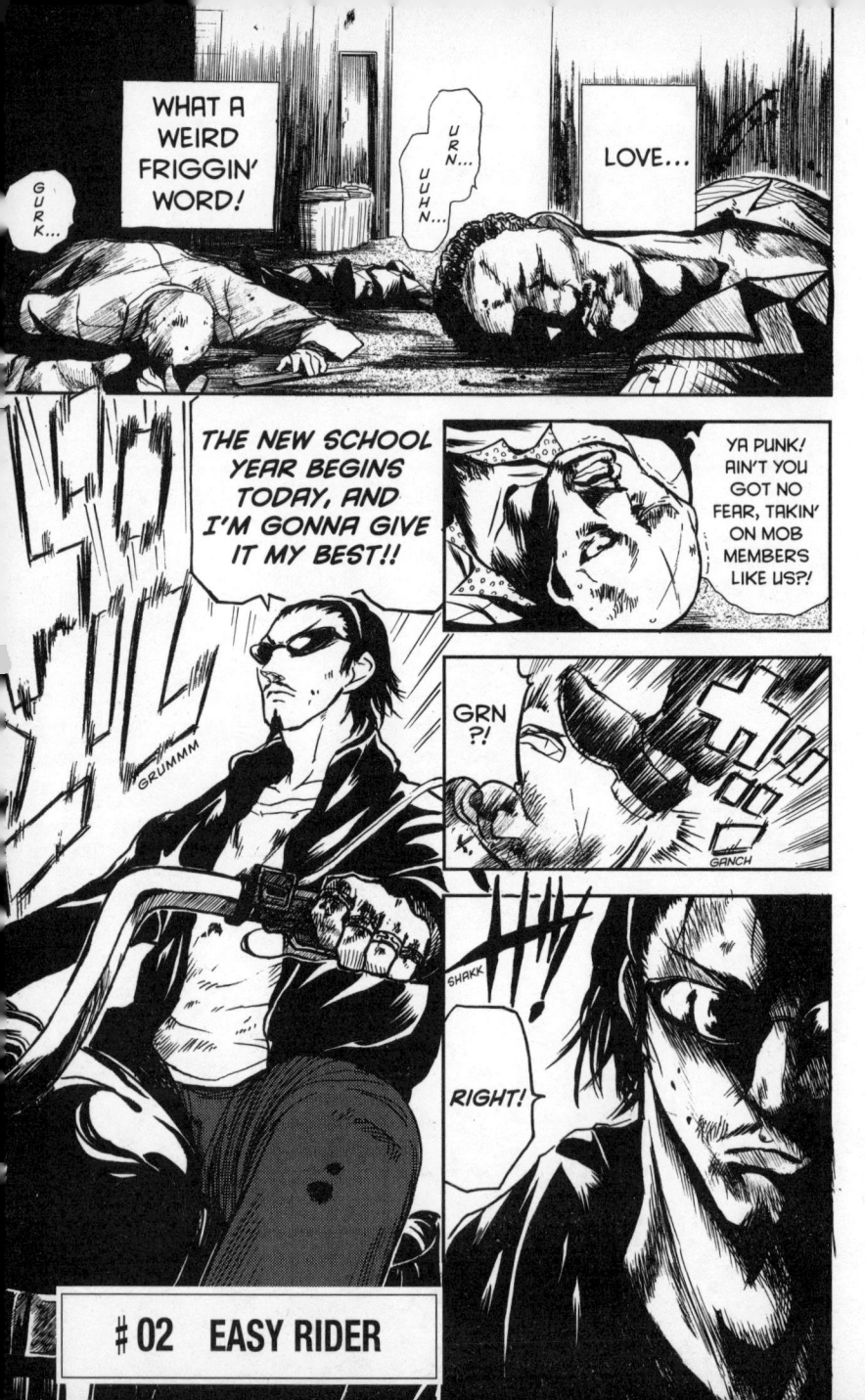

02   EASY RIDER

GLANCE

I'M JUST WHAT I LOOK LIKE, A JUVENILE DELINQUENT HIGH SCHOOL STUDENT.

MY NAME'S HARIMA KENJI.

I CAN'T BELIEVE IT'S MORNING ALREADY!

IT'S TSUKAMOTO TENMA-CHAN!!

Harima Kenji: *A Man Who Loves From Afar.*

Yet another one who is in love.

SKRA
THONK

HARIMA! HOW DARE YOU COME TO SCHOOL DRESSED LIKE THAT—

I WANT HER TO BE IN *MY* CLASS!

A newly hired teacher.

HEAVEN TO HELL

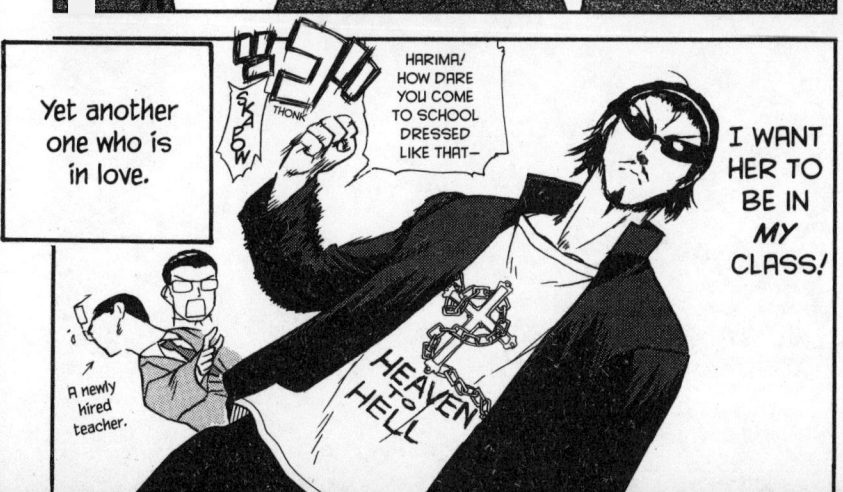

CLASS ASSIGNMENTS

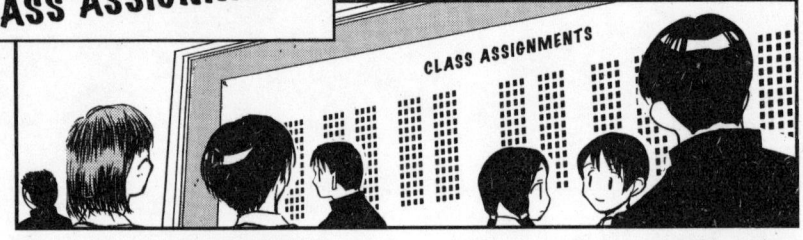

CLASS ASSIGNMENTS

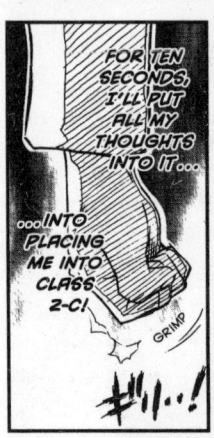

FOR TEN SECONDS, I'LL PUT ALL MY THOUGHTS INTO IT...

...INTO PLACING ME INTO CLASS 2-C!

GRIMP

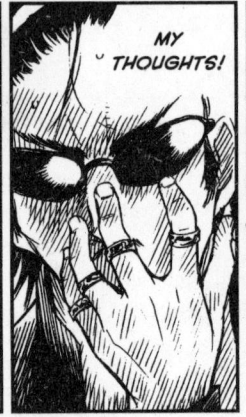

MY THOUGHTS!

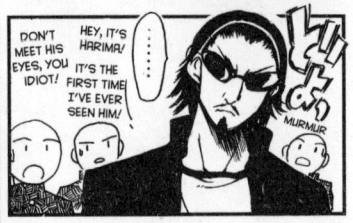

DON'T MEET HIS EYES, YOU IDIOT!

IT'S THE FIRST TIME I'VE EVER SEEN HIM!

HEY, IT'S HARIMA!

....

MURMUR

Takano Akira

Tsukamoto Tenma

Tonami Yoshiko

TENMA-CHAN IS...

...IN CLASS 2-C!!

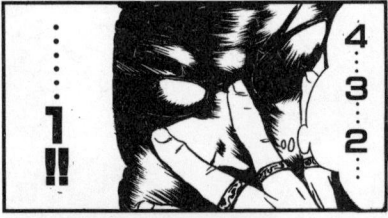

....

1!!

4
3
...2...

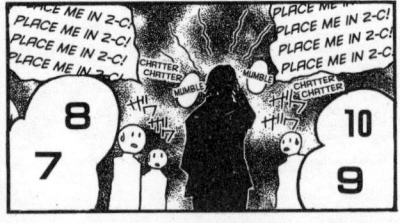

PLACE ME IN 2-C!
PLACE ME IN 2-C!
PLACE ME IN 2-C!
PLACE ME IN 2-C!!

PLACE ME IN 2-C!
PLACE ME IN 2-C!
PLACE ME IN 2-C!

CHATTER CHATTER

MUMBLE

MUMBLE

CHATTER CHATTER

8
7

10
9

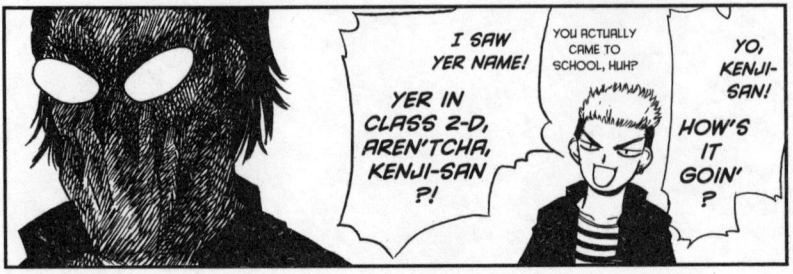

I SAW YER NAME!

YER IN CLASS 2-D, AREN'TCHA, KENJI-SAN ?!

YOU ACTUALLY CAME TO SCHOOL, HUH?

YO, KENJI-SAN!

HOW'S IT GOIN'?

—19—

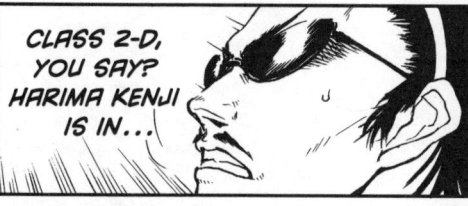

CLASS 2-D, YOU SAY? HARIMA KENJI IS IN...

Hamada Tosh...
Harry McKenzie
Hakunara Ruiko

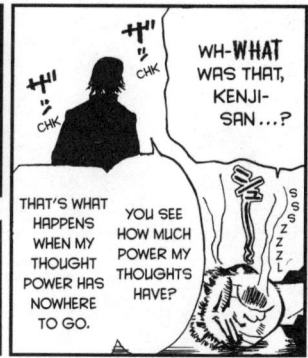

WH-**WHAT** WAS THAT, KENJI-SAN...?

THAT'S WHAT HAPPENS WHEN MY THOUGHT POWER HAS NOWHERE TO GO.

YOU SEE HOW MUCH POWER MY THOUGHTS HAVE?

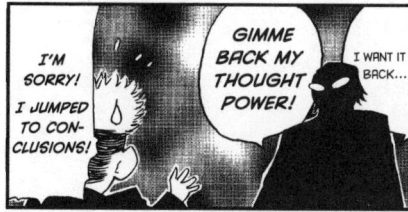

I'M SORRY! I JUMPED TO CONCLUSIONS!

GIMME BACK MY THOUGHT POWER!

I WANT IT BACK...

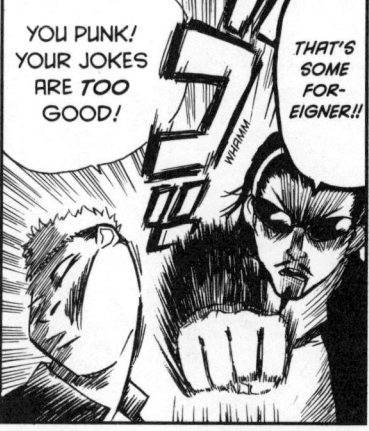

YOU PUNK! YOUR JOKES ARE *TOO* GOOD!

THAT'S SOME FOREIGNER!!

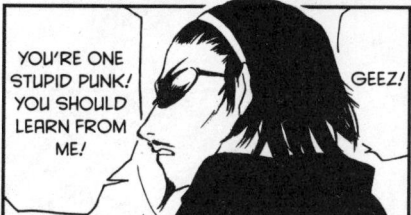

YOU'RE ONE STUPID PUNK! YOU SHOULD LEARN FROM ME!

GEEZ!

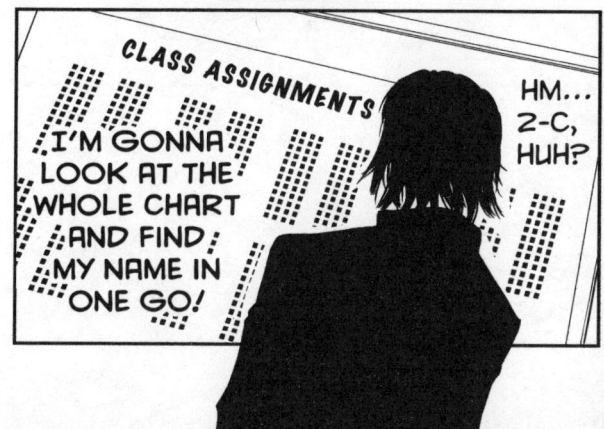

CLASS ASSIGNMENTS

I'M GONNA LOOK AT THE WHOLE CHART AND FIND MY NAME IN ONE GO!

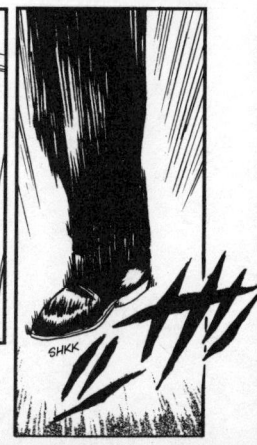

HM... 2-C, HUH?

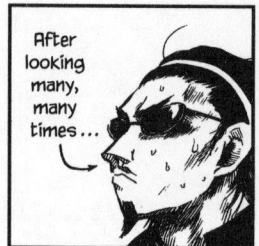
After looking many, many times...

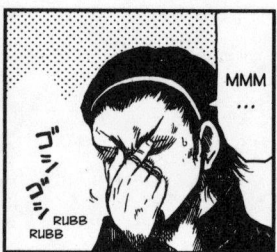
MMM...

RUBB RUBB

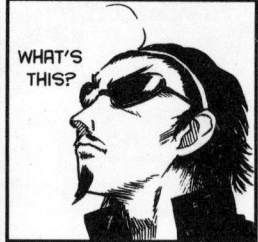
WHAT'S THIS?

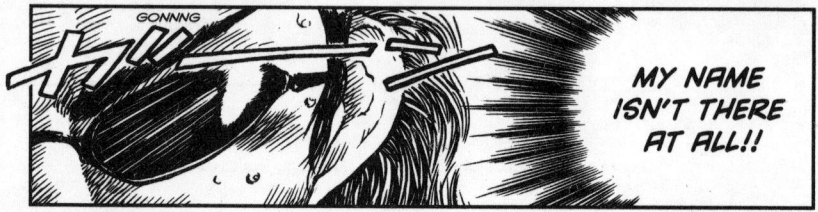
GONNNG

MY NAME ISN'T THERE AT ALL!!

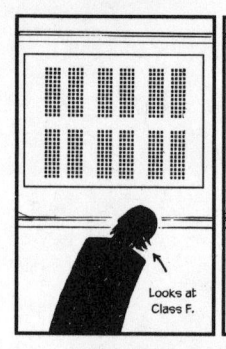
Looks at Class F.

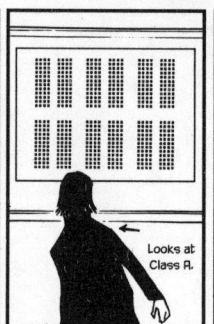
Looks at Class A.

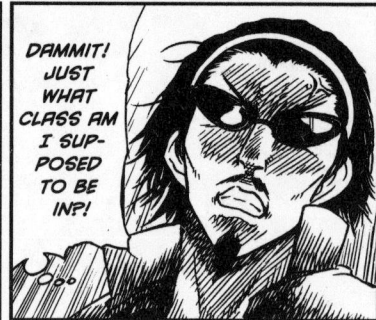
DAMMIT! JUST WHAT CLASS AM I SUPPOSED TO BE IN?!

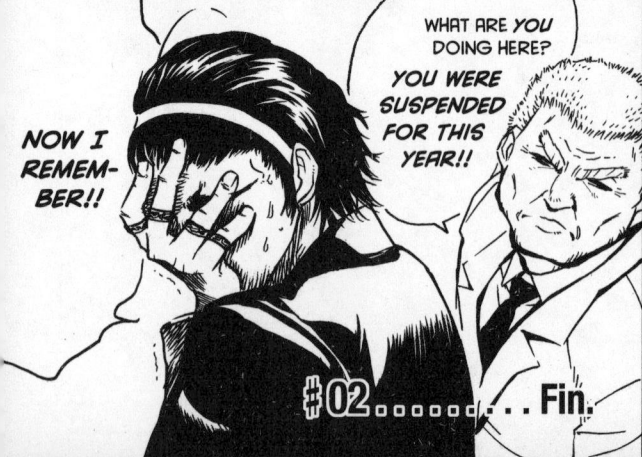
NOW I REMEMBER!!

WHAT ARE *YOU* DOING HERE?

YOU WERE SUSPENDED FOR THIS YEAR!!

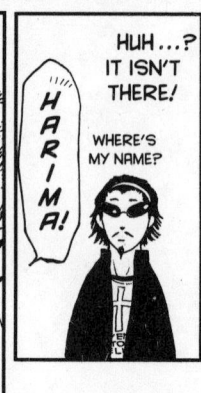
HUH...? IT ISN'T THERE!

HARIMA!

WHERE'S MY NAME?

#02 . . . . Fin.

#03 DEEP SPACE NINE

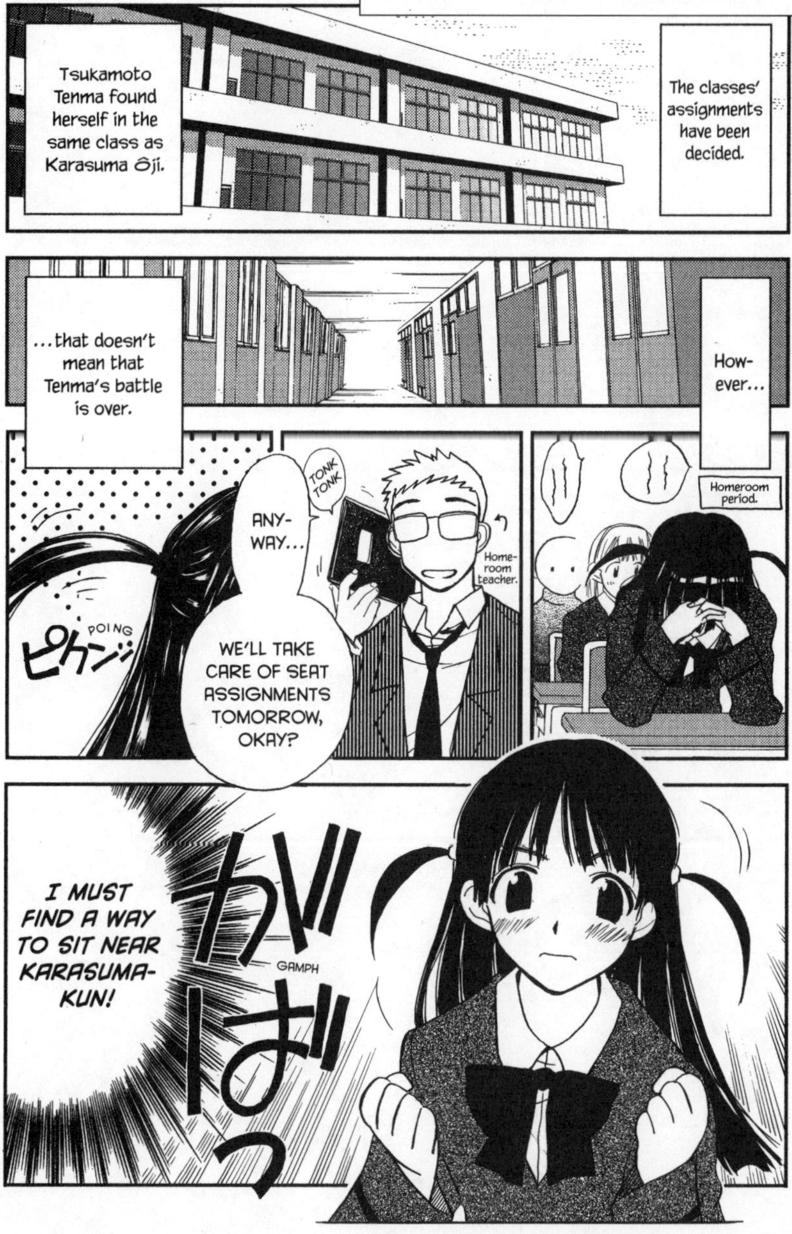

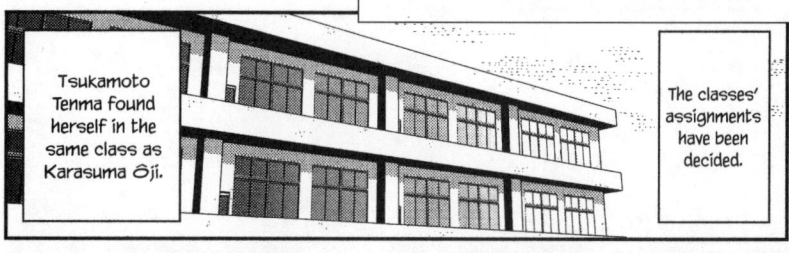

Tsukamoto Tenma found herself in the same class as Karasuma Ōji.

The classes' assignments have been decided.

...that doesn't mean that Tenma's battle is over.

How-ever...

Homeroom period.

ANY-WAY...

TONK TONK

Home-room teacher.

POING

ピクンッ

WE'LL TAKE CARE OF SEAT ASSIGNMENTS TOMORROW, OKAY?

I MUST FIND A WAY TO SIT NEAR KARASUMA-KUN!

カッ

ばっ

GAMPH

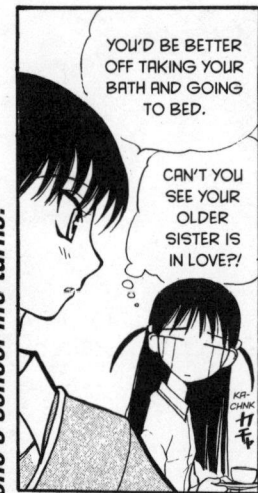

YOU'D BE BETTER OFF TAKING YOUR BATH AND GOING TO BED.

CAN'T YOU SEE YOUR OLDER SISTER IS IN LOVE?!

KA-CHNK

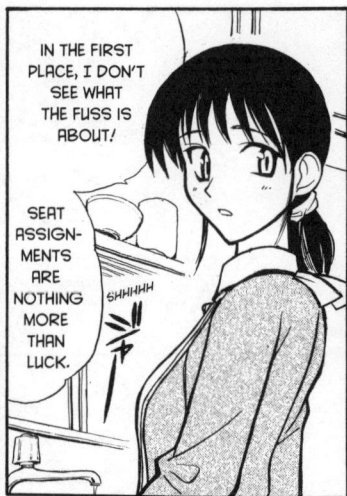

IN THE FIRST PLACE, I DON'T SEE WHAT THE FUSS IS ABOUT!

SEAT ASSIGNMENTS ARE NOTHING MORE THAN LUCK.

SHHHHH

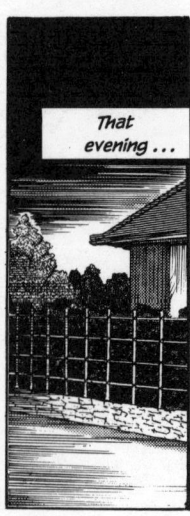

That evening...

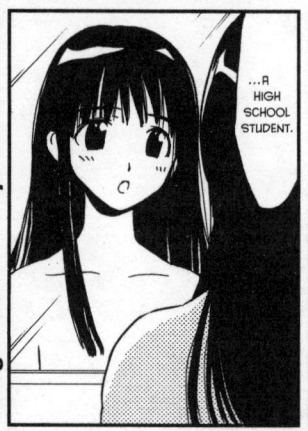

...A HIGH SCHOOL STUDENT.

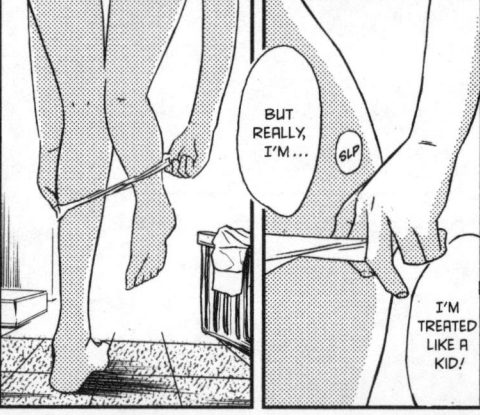

BUT REALLY, I'M...

SLP

I'M TREATED LIKE A KID!

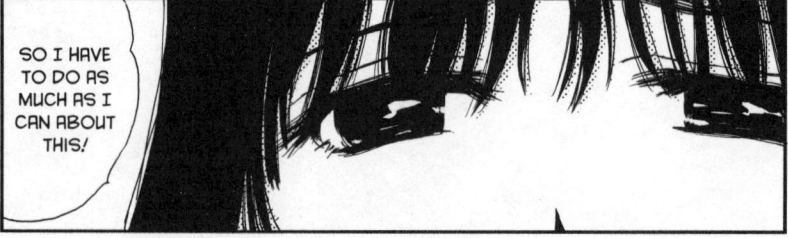

SO I HAVE TO DO AS MUCH AS I CAN ABOUT THIS!

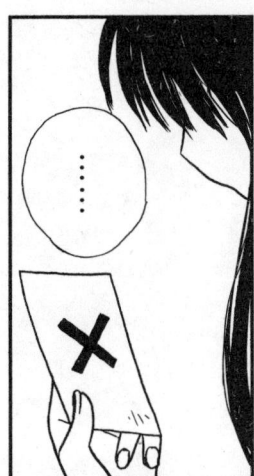

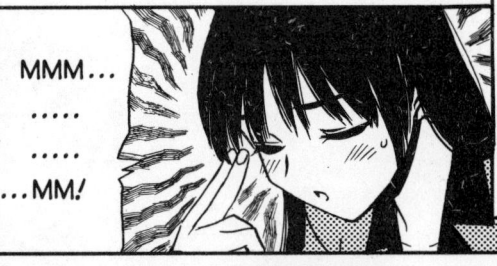

MMM...
.....
.....
...MM!

So...

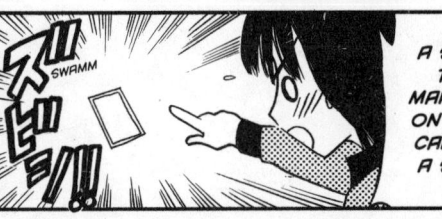

SWAMM

A STAR!!
THE MARKING ON THAT CARD IS A STAR!!

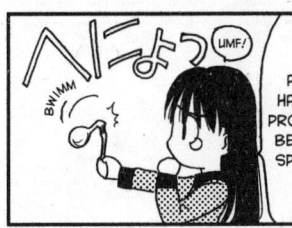

UMF!

BWIMM

AND I HAVE NO PROBLEMS BENDING SPOONS!

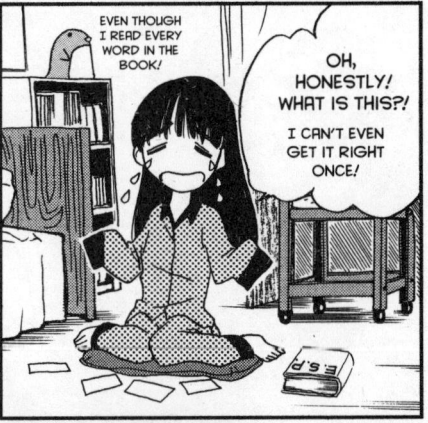

EVEN THOUGH I READ EVERY WORD IN THE BOOK!

OH, HONESTLY! WHAT IS THIS?!

I CAN'T EVEN GET IT RIGHT ONCE!

E.S.P.

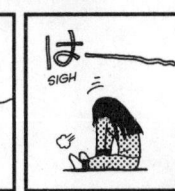

KARASUMA-KUN!

SIGH

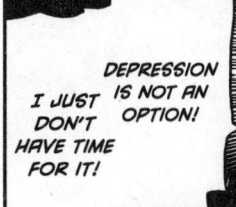

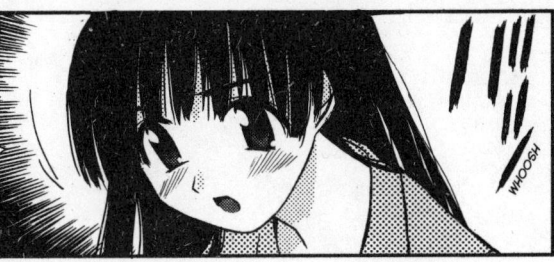

DEPRESSION IS NOT AN OPTION!

I JUST DON'T HAVE TIME FOR IT!

WHOOSH

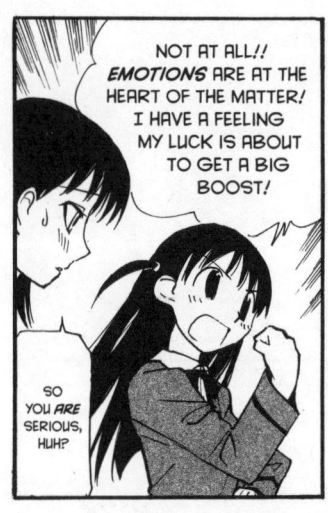

NOT AT ALL!! *EMOTIONS* ARE AT THE HEART OF THE MATTER! I HAVE A FEELING MY LUCK IS ABOUT TO GET A BIG BOOST!

SO YOU *ARE* SERIOUS, HUH?

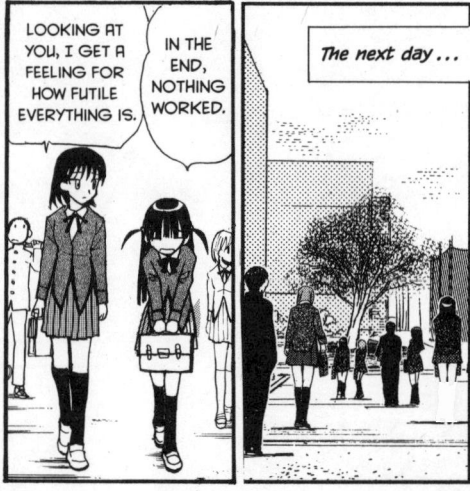

LOOKING AT YOU, I GET A FEELING FOR HOW FUTILE EVERYTHING IS.

IN THE END, NOTHING WORKED.

The next day...

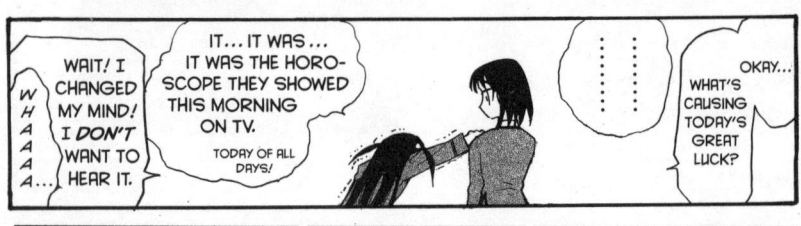

WHAAAAA...

WAIT! I CHANGED MY MIND! I *DON'T* WANT TO HEAR IT.

IT... IT WAS... IT WAS THE HORO-SCOPE THEY SHOWED THIS MORNING ON TV.

TODAY OF ALL DAYS!

: : : : : :

WHAT'S CAUSING TODAY'S GREAT LUCK?

OKAY...

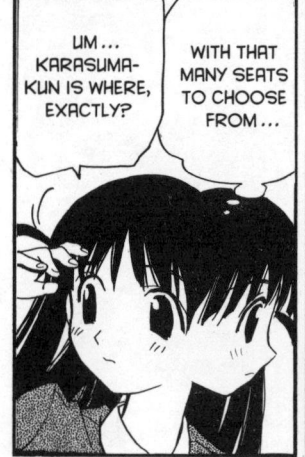

UM... KARASUMA-KUN IS WHERE, EXACTLY?

WITH THAT MANY SEATS TO CHOOSE FROM...

2 - C

RIGHT... FOR THE SEAT ASSIGNMENTS...

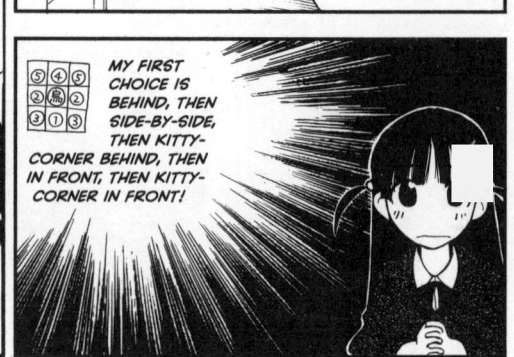

MY FIRST CHOICE IS BEHIND, THEN SIDE-BY-SIDE, THEN KITTY-CORNER BEHIND, THEN IN FRONT, THEN KITTY-CORNER IN FRONT!

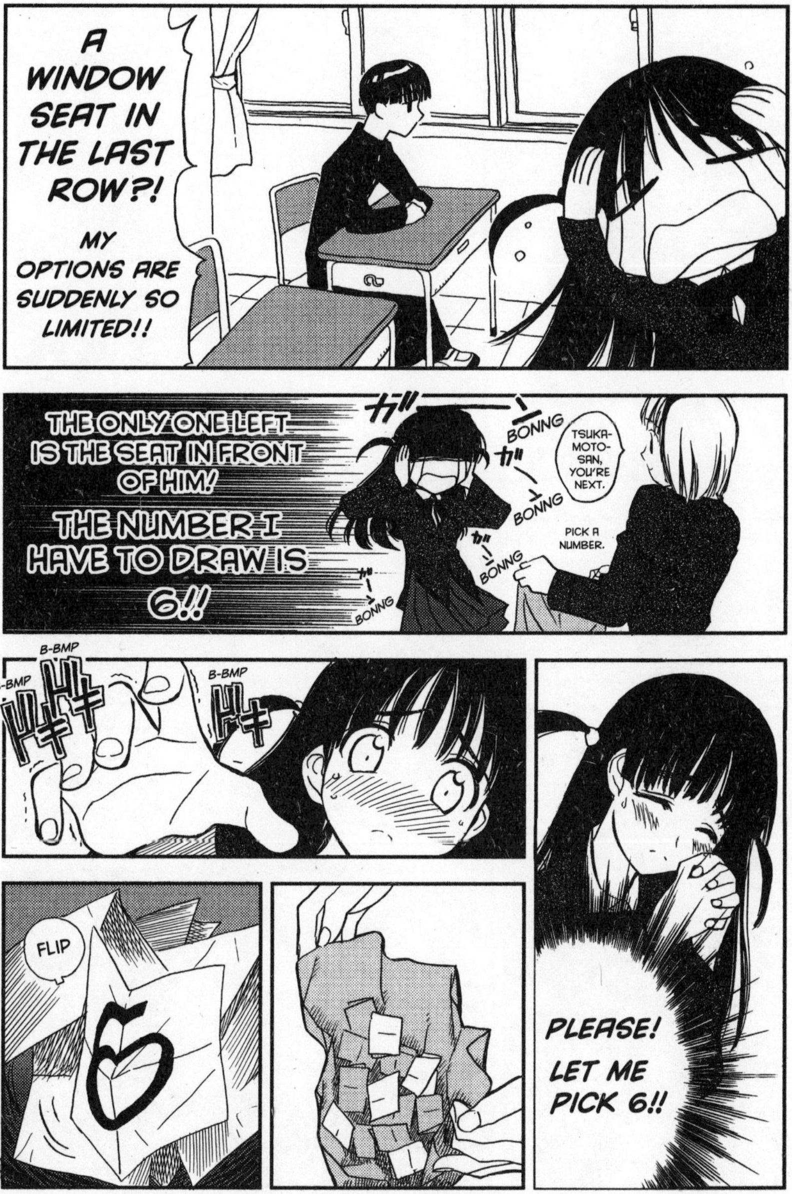
A WINDOW SEAT IN THE LAST ROW?!
MY OPTIONS ARE SUDDENLY SO LIMITED!!
TSUKAMOTO-SAN, YOU'RE NEXT.
PICK A NUMBER.
BONNG
BONNG
BONNG
BONNG
THE ONLY ONE LEFT IS THE SEAT IN FRONT OF HIM!
THE NUMBER I HAVE TO DRAW IS 6!!
PLEASE! LET ME PICK 6!!
B-BMP
B-BMP
B-BMP
FLIP
6

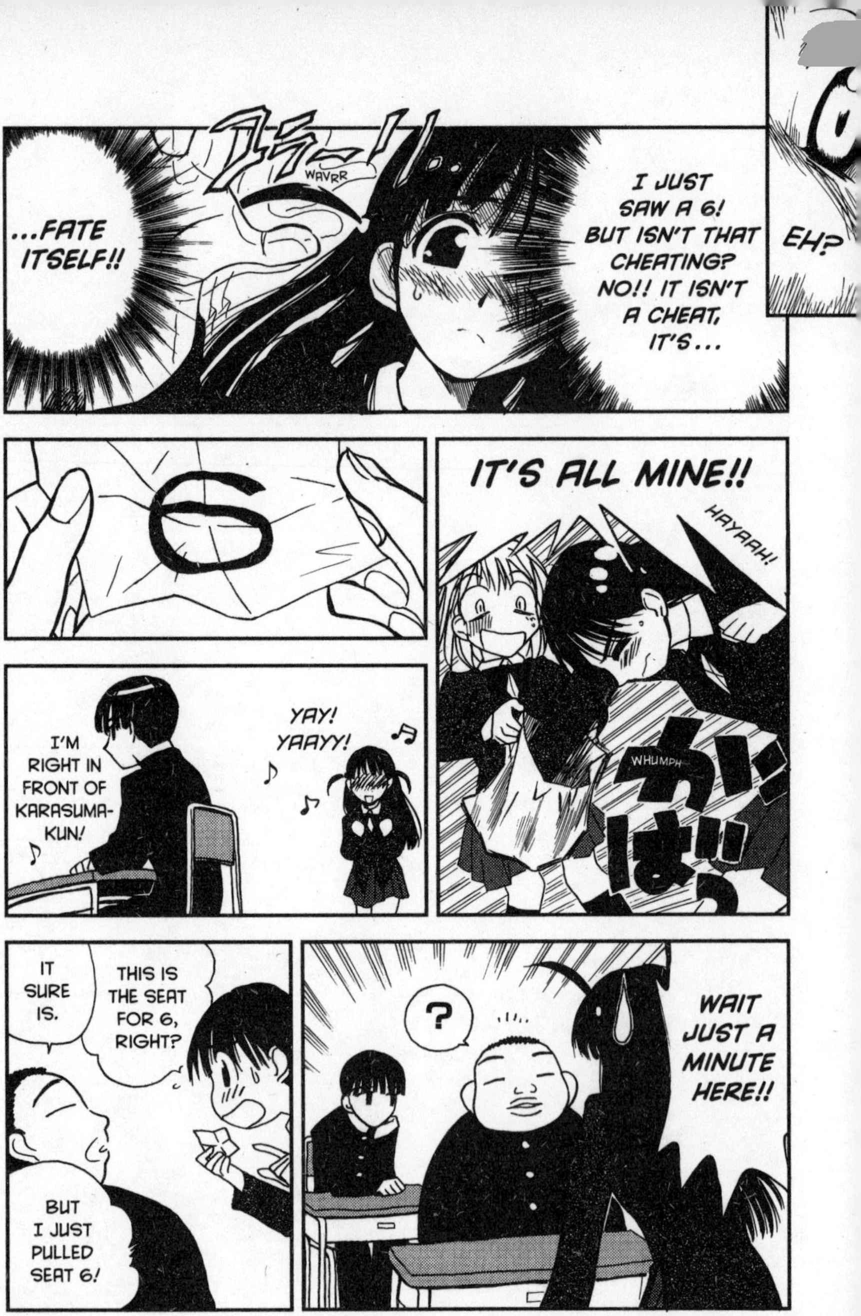
EH?
I JUST SAW A 6! BUT ISN'T THAT CHEATING? NO!! IT ISN'T A CHEAT, IT'S...
WAVRR
...FATE ITSELF!!
IT'S ALL MINE!!
HAYAAH!
WHUMPH
YAY! YAAYY!
I'M RIGHT IN FRONT OF KARASUMA-KUN!
WAIT JUST A MINUTE HERE!!
?
THIS IS THE SEAT FOR 6, RIGHT?
IT SURE IS.
BUT I JUST PULLED SEAT 6!

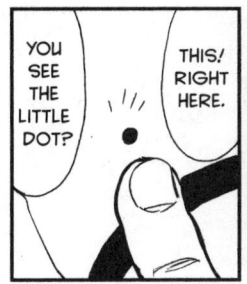

YOU SEE THE LITTLE DOT?

THIS! RIGHT HERE.

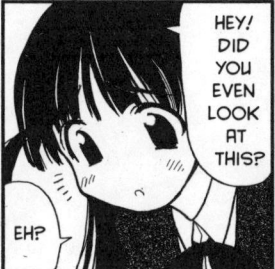

HEY! DID YOU EVEN LOOK AT THIS?

EH?

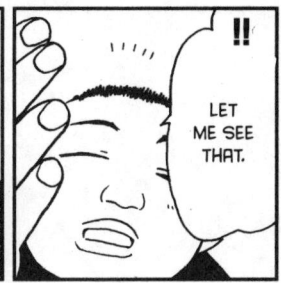

!!

LET ME SEE THAT.

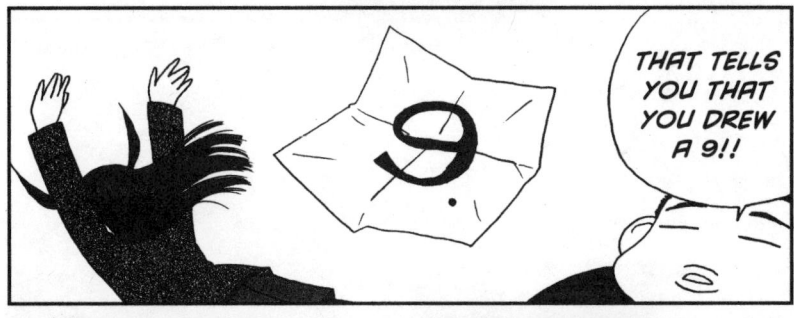

THAT TELLS YOU THAT YOU DREW A 9!!

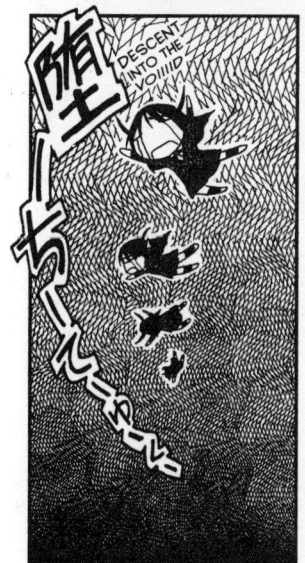

DESCENT INTO THE VOIIIID

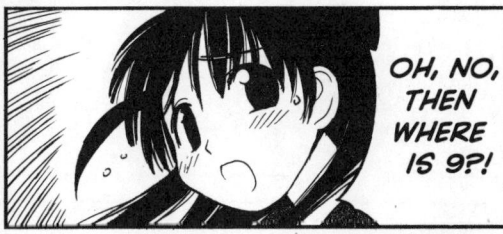

OH, NO, THEN WHERE IS 9?!

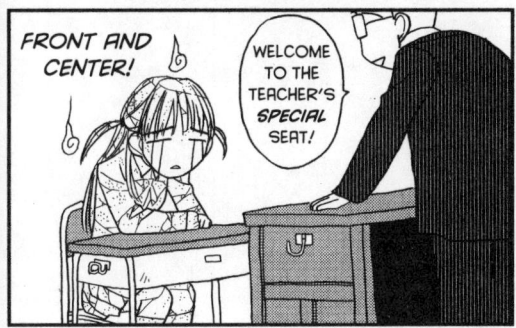

FRONT AND CENTER!

WELCOME TO THE TEACHER'S SPECIAL SEAT!

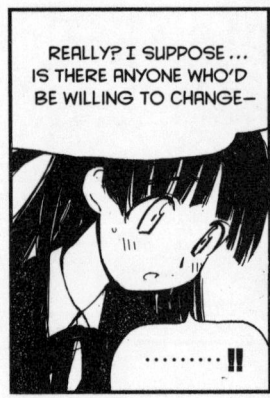

REALLY? I SUPPOSE... IS THERE ANYONE WHO'D BE WILLING TO CHANGE—

..........!!

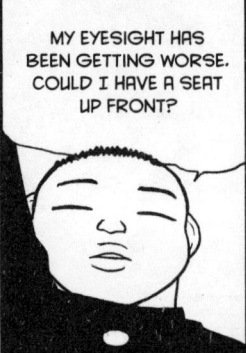

MY EYESIGHT HAS BEEN GETTING WORSE. COULD I HAVE A SEAT UP FRONT?

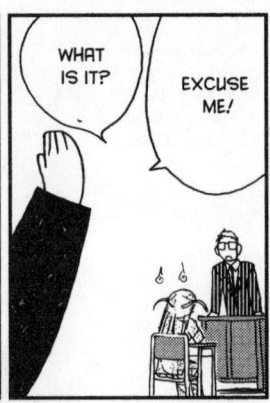

WHAT IS IT?

EXCUSE ME!

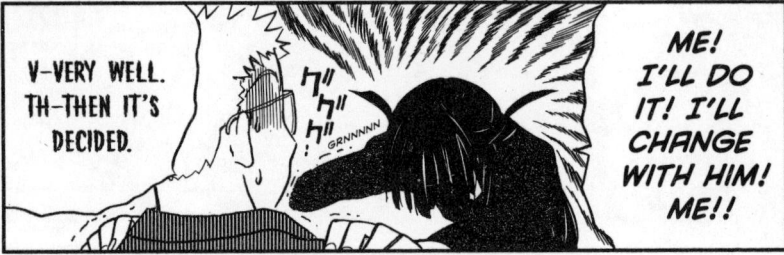

V-VERY WELL. TH-THEN IT'S DECIDED.

GRNNNNN

ME! I'LL DO IT! I'LL CHANGE WITH HIM! ME!!

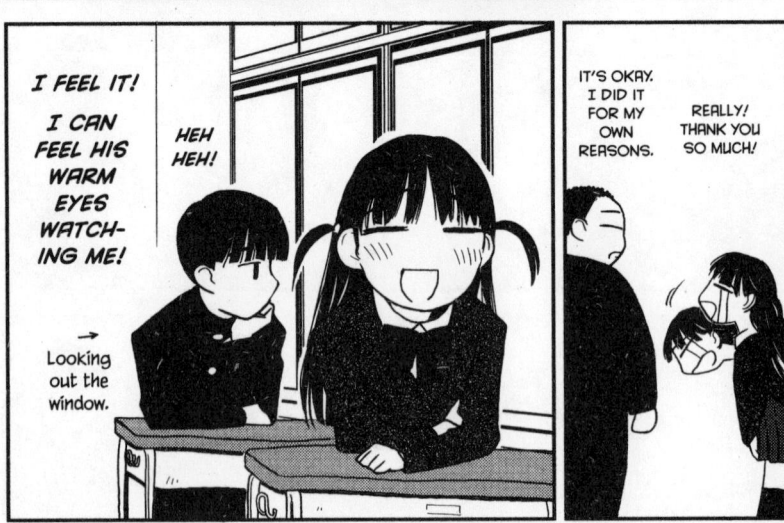

I FEEL IT! I CAN FEEL HIS WARM EYES WATCHING ME!

HEH HEH!

→ Looking out the window.

IT'S OKAY. I DID IT FOR MY OWN REASONS.

REALLY! THANK YOU SO MUCH!

03 .... Fin.

BONUS!

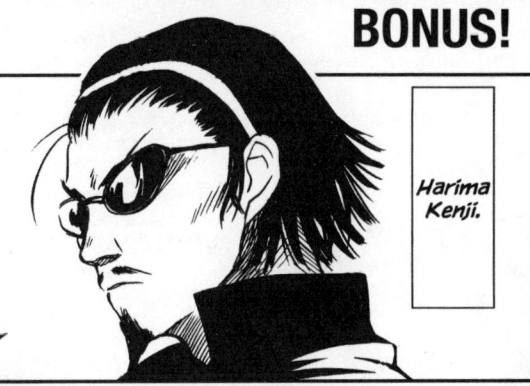

He was suspended for this year, but they made a special exception and allowed him to advance.

Harima Kenji.

Not only that, but they put → him in Class 2-C also.

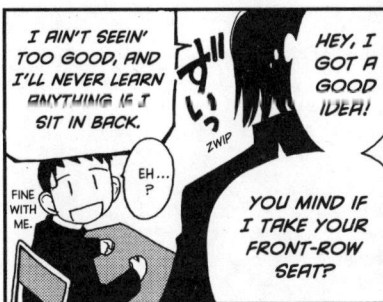

I AIN'T SEEIN' TOO GOOD, AND I'LL NEVER LEARN ANYTHING IF I SIT IN BACK.

ZWIP

HEY, I GOT A GOOD IDEA!

YOU MIND IF I TAKE YOUR FRONT-ROW SEAT?

EH...P

FINE WITH ME.

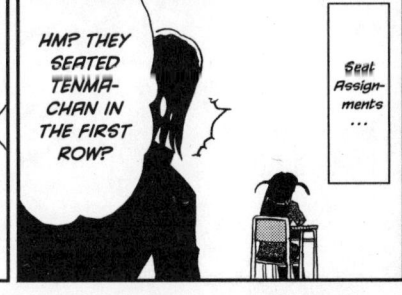

HM? THEY SEATED TENMA-CHAN IN THE FIRST ROW?

Seat Assignments...

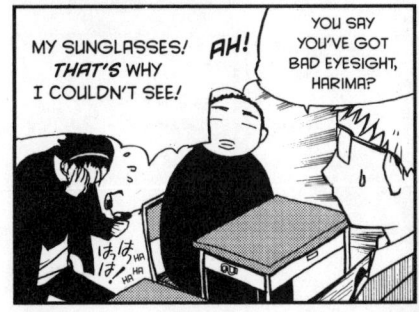

MY SUNGLASSES! *THAT'S* WHY I COULDN'T SEE!

AH!

YOU SAY YOU'VE GOT BAD EYESIGHT, HARIMA?

HA HA! HA HA

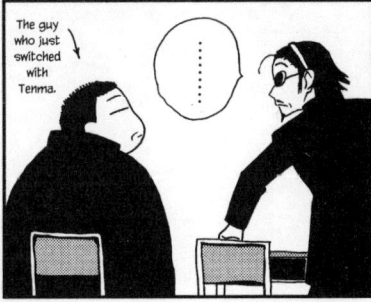

The guy who just switched with Tenma.

....

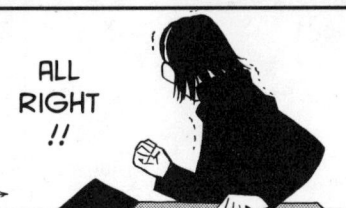

Kenji promised himself he wouldn't cause any trouble...

ALL RIGHT !!

Kenji's assigned seat is → right next to Tenma.

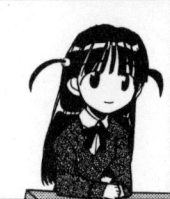

.....

03 BONUS . . . . Fin.

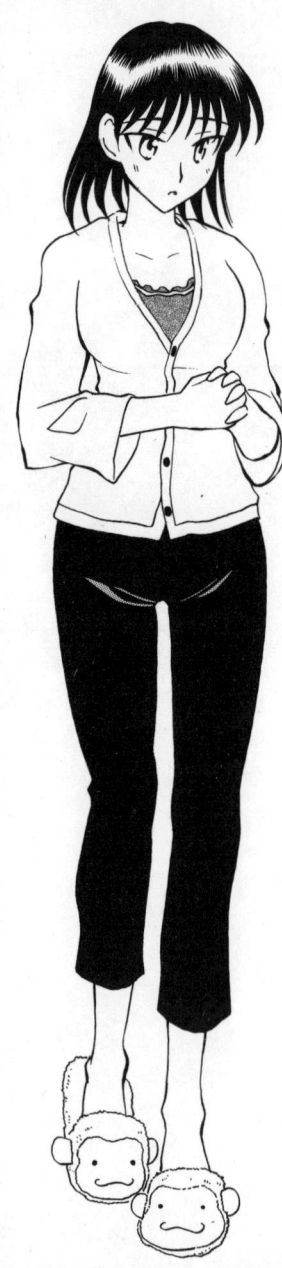

NEE-CHAN,
YOU REALLY
SHOULDN'T...

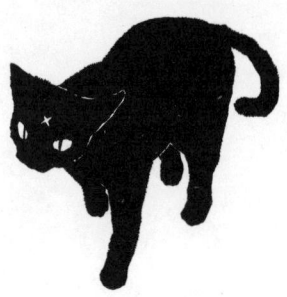

TSUKA MOTO YA KUMO
塚本八雲

STATS:

Height: 166 cm (5' 5")
Favorite Thing: Sister
Least Favorite Thing: Dogs
Favorite Place: A bright, sunny veranda
Special Talent: Cooking, taking care of her sister
Hardest Thing to Live With: Will fall asleep anytime, anywhere
Notes: Can read the minds of people who have feelings for her

By the way, her cat's name is Iori.

#04 BOOK OF LOVE

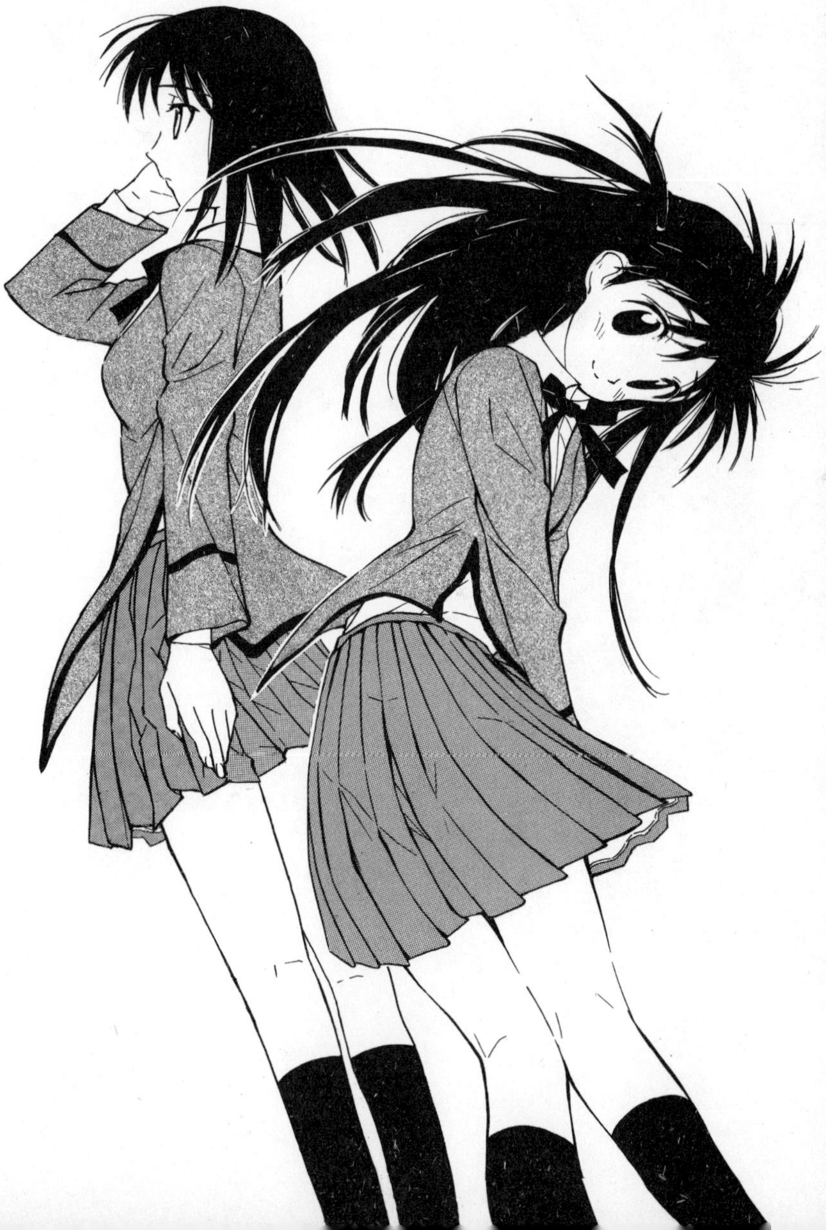

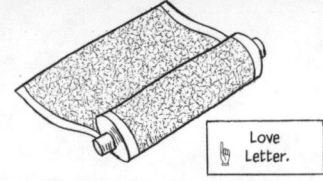

Love
Letter.

Realizing how precarious her situation is, Tenma composes a love letter addressed to her intended boyfriend. Unfortunately, despite the extensive message, her plan resulted in failure. (She neglected to identify herself as the sender.)

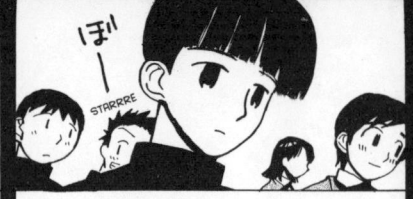

STARRRE

Class 2-C. Karasuma Ôji is the object of Tsukamoto Tenma's affections. However, it is revealed that he is committed to transfer to a scholastic institute in America.

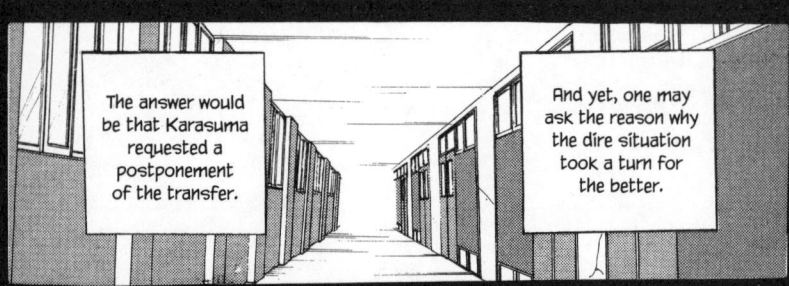

The answer would be that Karasuma requested a postponement of the transfer.

And yet, one may ask the reason why the dire situation took a turn for the better.

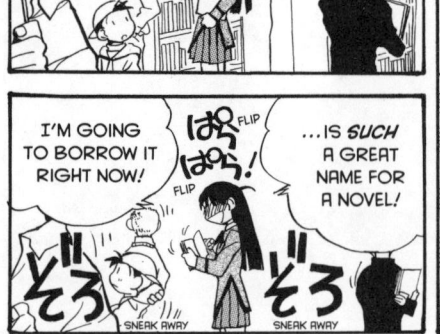

The Library . . .

I'M GOING TO BORROW IT RIGHT NOW!

FLIP
はら！
はら！
FLIP

. . . IS *SUCH* A GREAT NAME FOR A NOVEL!

そろ
SNEAK AWAY

そろ
SNEAK AWAY

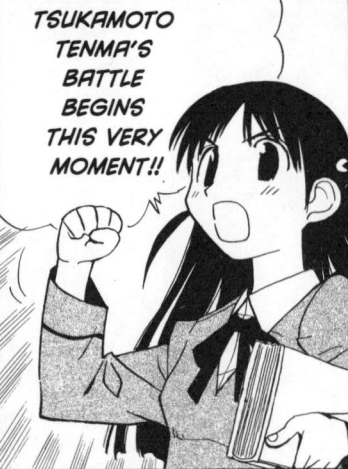

TSUKAMOTO TENMA'S *BATTLE* BEGINS THIS VERY MOMENT!!

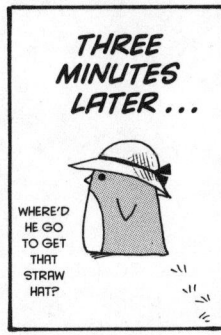

THREE MINUTES LATER...

WHERE'D HE GO TO GET THAT STRAW HAT?

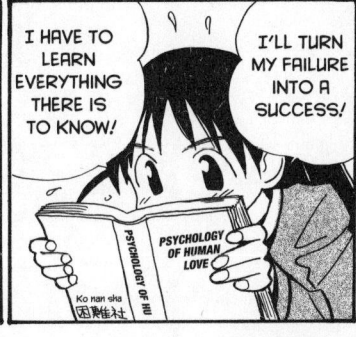

I HAVE TO LEARN EVERYTHING THERE IS TO KNOW!

I'LL TURN MY FAILURE INTO A SUCCESS!

PSYCHOLOGY OF HUMAN LOVE

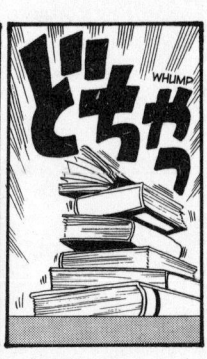

WHUMP

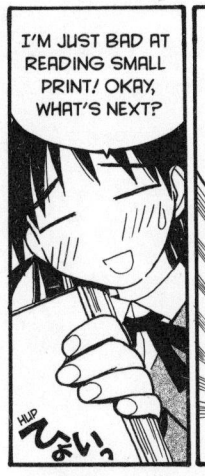

I'M JUST BAD AT READING SMALL PRINT! OKAY, WHAT'S NEXT?

HUP

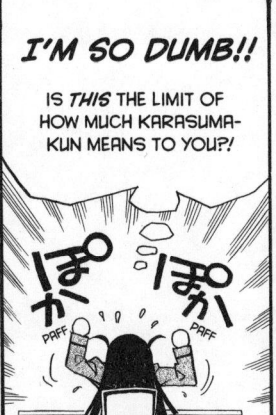

I'M SO DUMB!!

IS THIS THE LIMIT OF HOW MUCH KARASUMA-KUN MEANS TO YOU?!

PAFF   PAFF

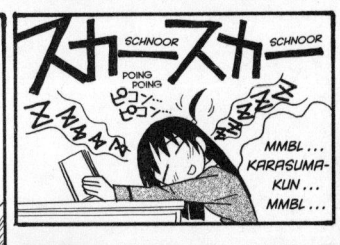

SCHNOOR   SCHNOOR

MMBL... KARASUMA-KUN... MMBL...

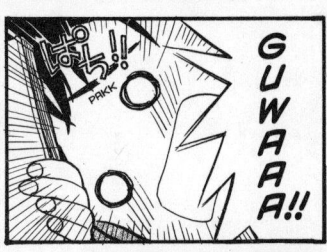

PAKK

GUWAAA!!

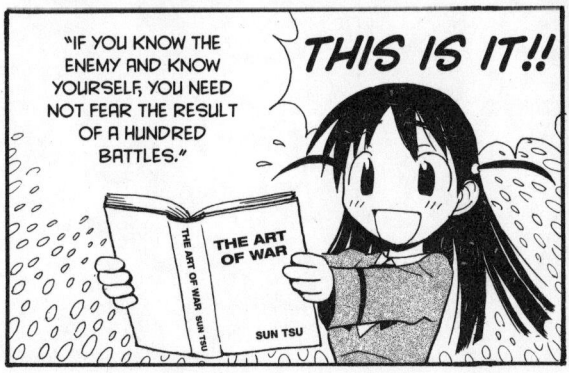

"IF YOU KNOW THE ENEMY AND KNOW YOURSELF, YOU NEED NOT FEAR THE RESULT OF A HUNDRED BATTLES."

THIS IS IT!!

THE ART OF WAR

SUN TSU

ASIDE FROM ROMANCE NOVELS, WHAT ELSE CAN I... OH!

Tsukamoto Tenma: 16 years old.

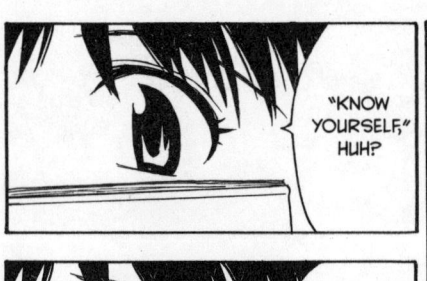

"KNOW YOURSELF," HUH?

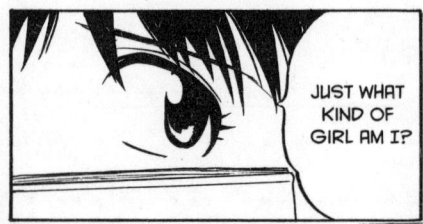

JUST WHAT KIND OF GIRL AM I?

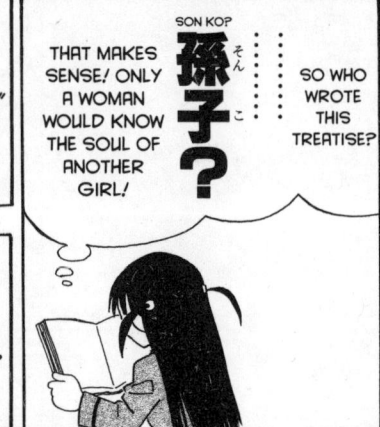

SO WHO WROTE THIS TREATISE?

孫子？

SON KOP

THAT MAKES SENSE! ONLY A WOMAN WOULD KNOW THE SOUL OF ANOTHER GIRL!

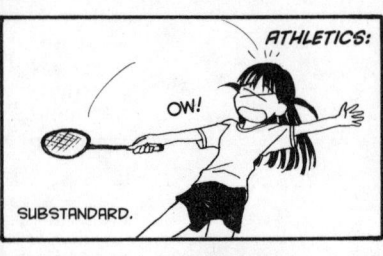

ATHLETICS:

OW!

SUBSTANDARD.

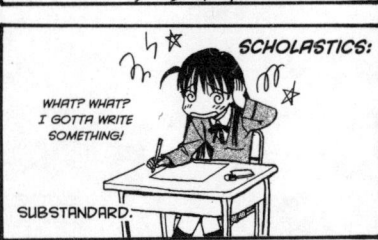

SCHOLASTICS:

WHAT? WHAT? I GOTTA WRITE SOMETHING!

SUBSTANDARD.

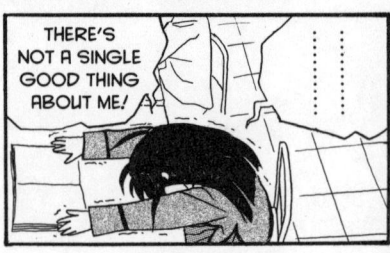

THERE'S NOT A SINGLE GOOD THING ABOUT ME!

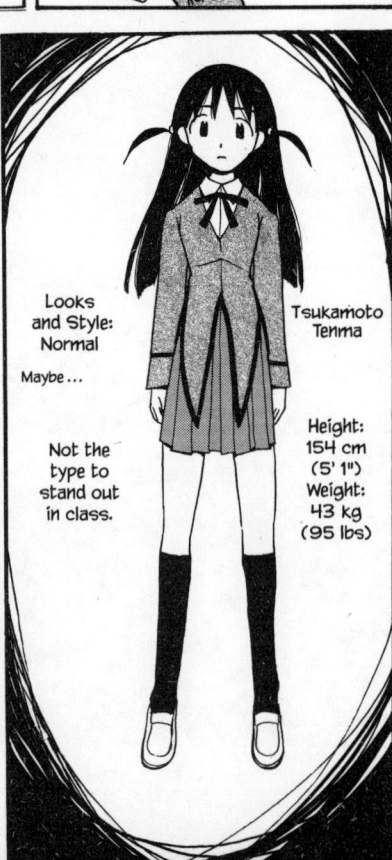

Tsukamoto Tenma

Looks and Style: Normal

Maybe...

Not the type to stand out in class.

Height: 154 cm (5' 1")
Weight: 43 kg (95 lbs)

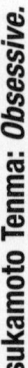

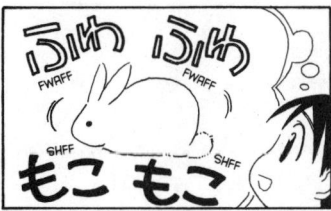
ふわ FWAFF ふわ FWAFF

SHFF SHFF

もこ もこ

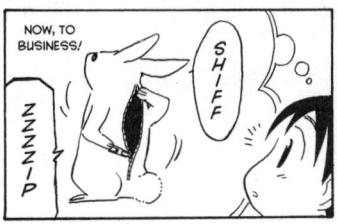
NOW, TO BUSINESS!

SHIFF

ZZZZZIP

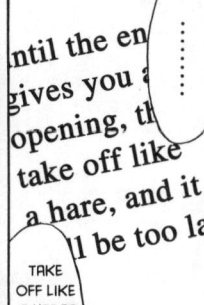
ntil the en
gives you
opening, th
take off like
a hare, and it
ll be too la

．．．．．

TAKE OFF LIKE A HARE? TAKE OFF WHAT LIKE A HARE?

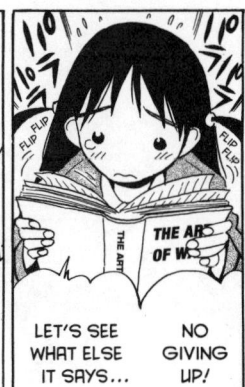
LET'S SEE WHAT ELSE IT SAYS...

NO GIVING UP!

THE ART

THE AR OF W

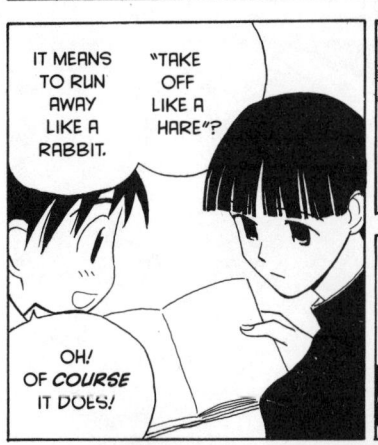
"TAKE OFF LIKE A HARE"?

IT MEANS TO RUN AWAY LIKE A RABBIT.

OH! OF *COURSE* IT DOES!

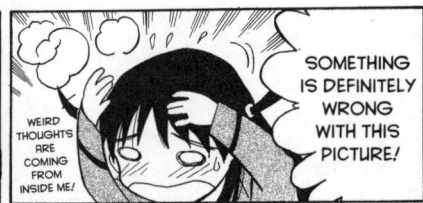
WEIRD THOUGHTS ARE COMING FROM INSIDE ME!

SOMETHING IS DEFINITELY WRONG WITH THIS PICTURE!

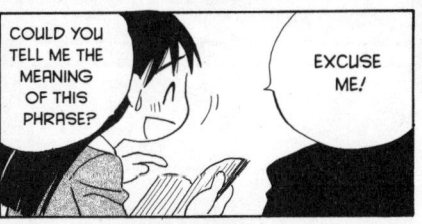
COULD YOU TELL ME THE MEANING OF THIS PHRASE?

EXCUSE ME!

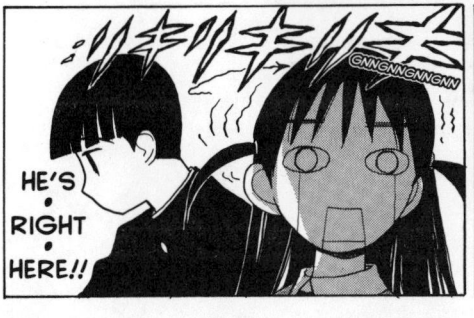
GNNGNNGNNGNN

HE'S RIGHT HERE!!

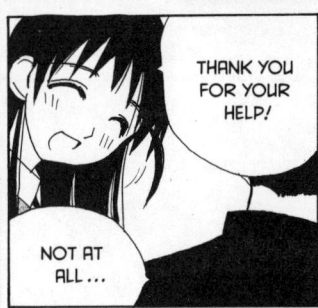
THANK YOU FOR YOUR HELP!

NOT AT ALL...

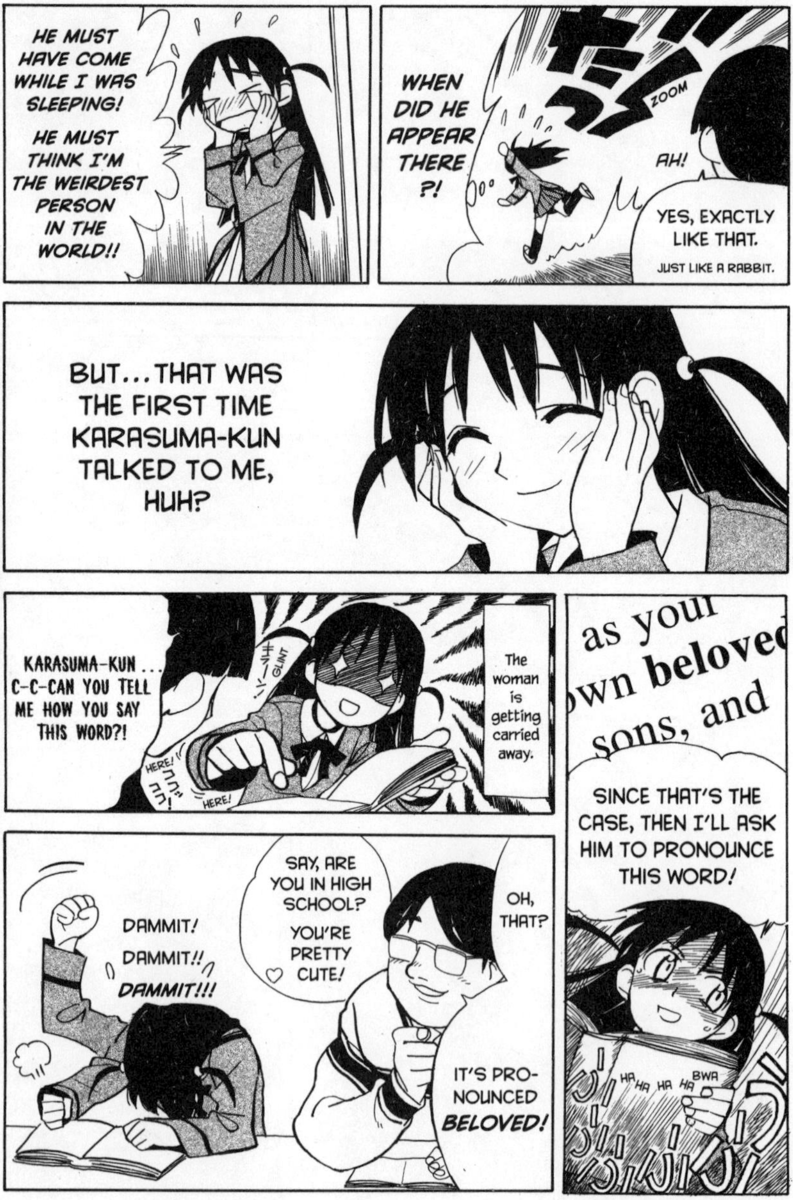
ZOOM
AH!
YES, EXACTLY LIKE THAT.
JUST LIKE A RABBIT.
WHEN DID HE APPEAR THERE?!
HE MUST HAVE COME WHILE I WAS SLEEPING!
HE MUST THINK I'M THE WEIRDEST PERSON IN THE WORLD!!
BUT... THAT WAS THE FIRST TIME KARASUMA-KUN TALKED TO ME, HUH?
as your
wn belove
sons, and
SINCE THAT'S THE CASE, THEN I'LL ASK HIM TO PRONOUNCE THIS WORD!
BWA HA HA HA HA
The woman is getting carried away.
GLINT
KARASUMA-KUN... C-C-CAN YOU TELL ME HOW YOU SAY THIS WORD?!
HERE!
HERE!
OH, THAT?
IT'S PRONOUNCED BELOVED!
SAY, ARE YOU IN HIGH SCHOOL?
YOU'RE PRETTY CUTE!
DAMMIT!
DAMMIT!!
DAMMIT!!!

Tsukamoto Tenma: ***Something of a dolt.***

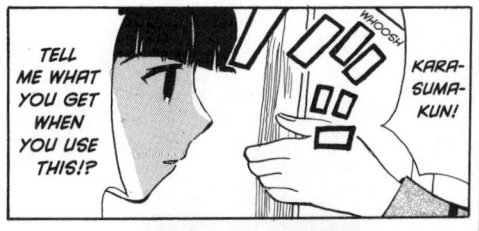

TELL ME WHAT YOU GET WHEN YOU USE THIS!?

WHOOSH

KARA-SUMA-KUN!

MAYBE I CAN ASK HIM WHAT A BEE-KEEPER'S EXTRACTOR IS FOR AND GET HIM TO SAY "HONEY"!

FLIP-FLIP

Doesn't know when to give up.

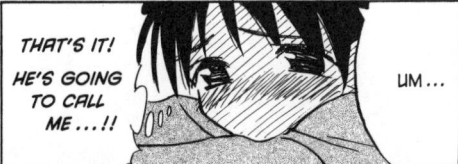

THAT'S IT! HE'S GOING TO CALL ME ...!!

UM ...

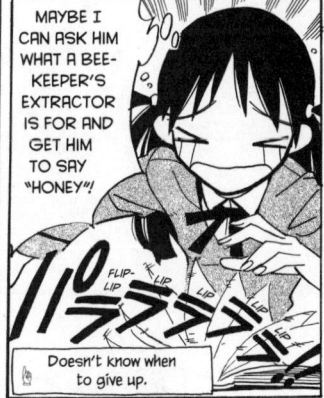

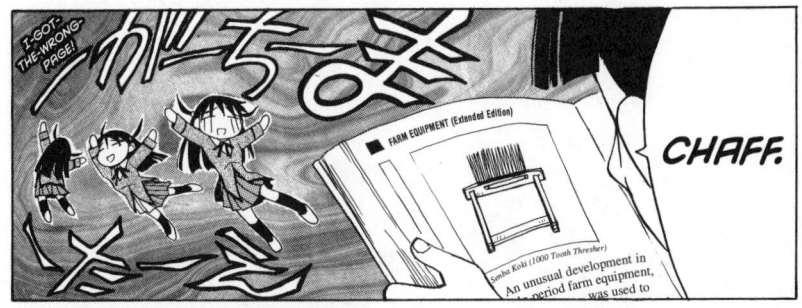

I-GOT-THE-WRONG-PAGE!

FARM EQUIPMENT (Extended Edition)

Senba Koki (1000 Tooth Thresher)

An unusual development in ...period farm equipment, ...was used to

CHAFF.

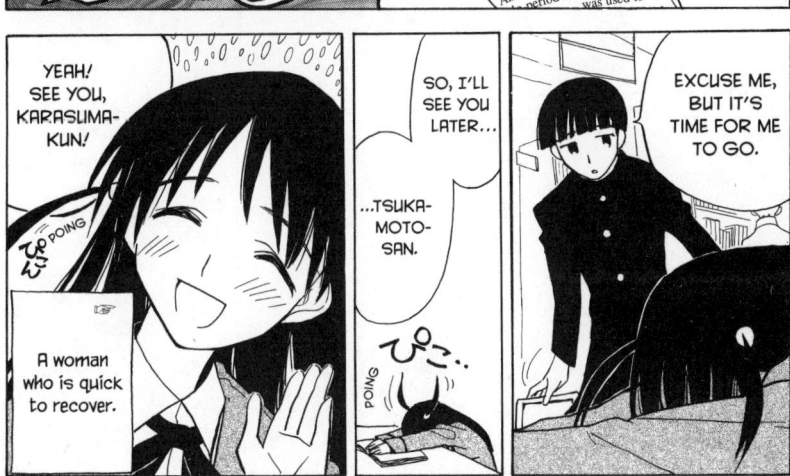

YEAH! SEE YOU, KARASUMA-KUN!

POING

A woman who is quick to recover.

SO, I'LL SEE YOU LATER...

...TSUKA-MOTO-SAN.

POING

EXCUSE ME, BUT IT'S TIME FOR ME TO GO.

04 .... Fin.

#05 ENTER THE DRAGON

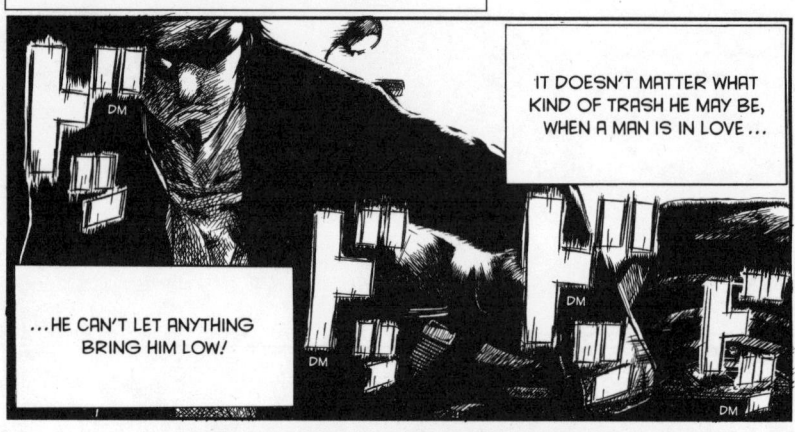

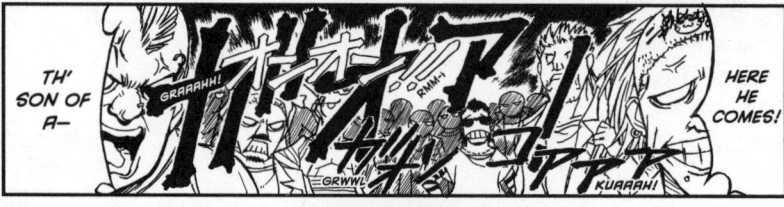

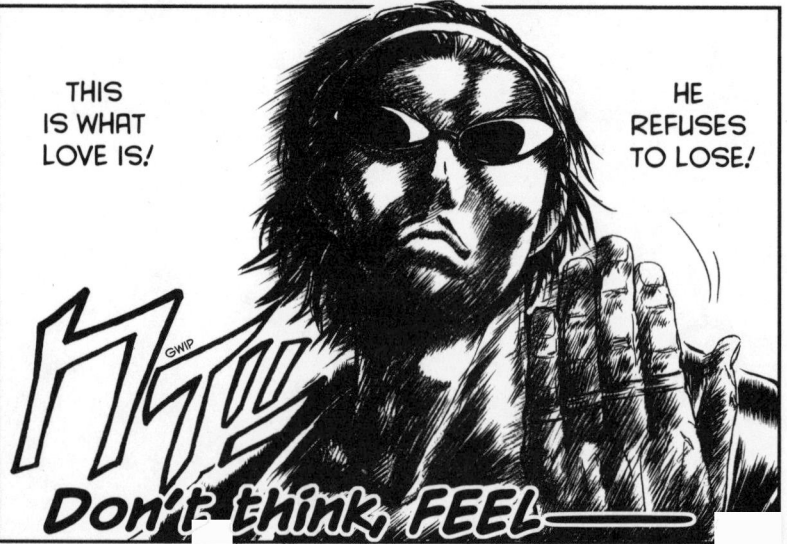

WRONGO

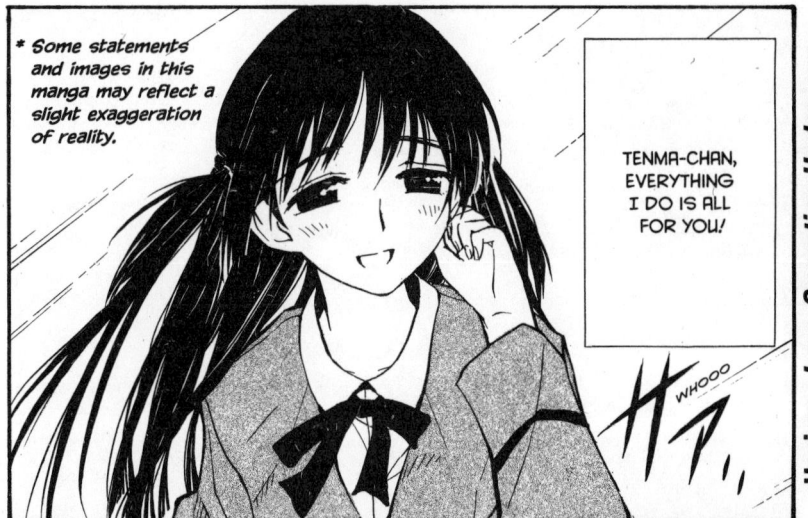

* Some statements and images in this manga may reflect a slight exaggeration of reality.

TENMA-CHAN, EVERYTHING I DO IS ALL FOR YOU!

WHOOO

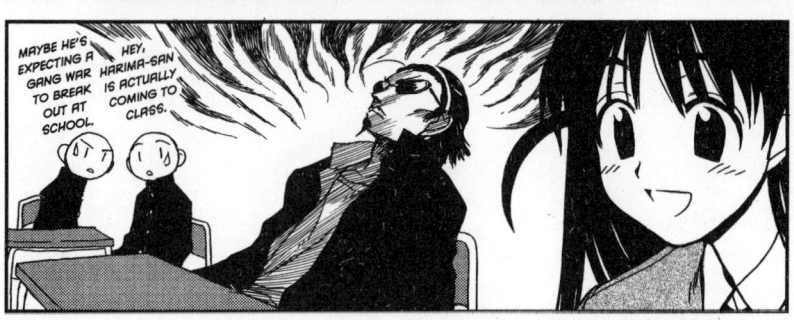

MAYBE HE'S EXPECTING A GANG WAR TO BREAK OUT AT SCHOOL.

HEY, HARIMA-SAN IS ACTUALLY COMING TO CLASS.

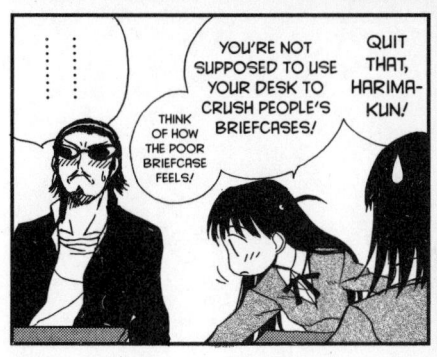

∴…

YOU'RE NOT SUPPOSED TO USE YOUR DESK TO CRUSH PEOPLE'S BRIEFCASES!

THINK OF HOW THE POOR BRIEFCASE FEELS!

QUIT THAT, HARIMA-KUN!

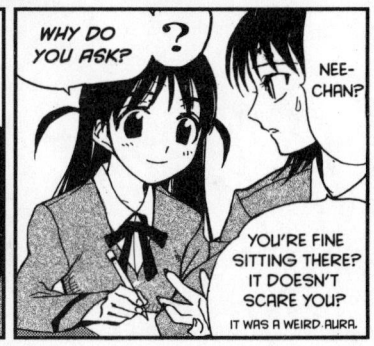

WHY DO YOU ASK?

?

NEE-CHAN?

YOU'RE FINE SITTING THERE? IT DOESN'T SCARE YOU?

IT WAS A WEIRD AURA.

Tenma-chan forgot her bento lunch box, so her younger sister Yakumo-chan came to deliver it.

— 40 —

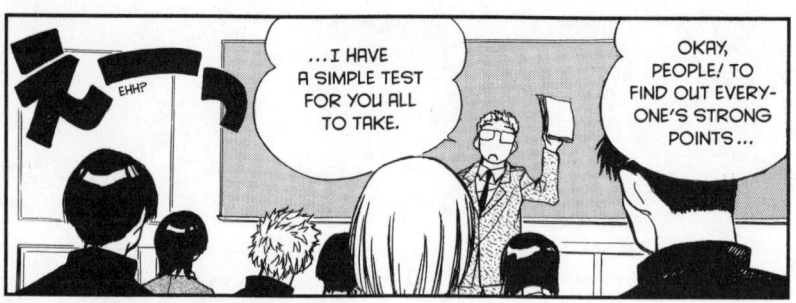

OKAY, PEOPLE! TO FIND OUT EVERYONE'S STRONG POINTS...

...I HAVE A SIMPLE TEST FOR YOU ALL TO TAKE.

EHH?

Harima Kenji: Juvenile Delinquent.

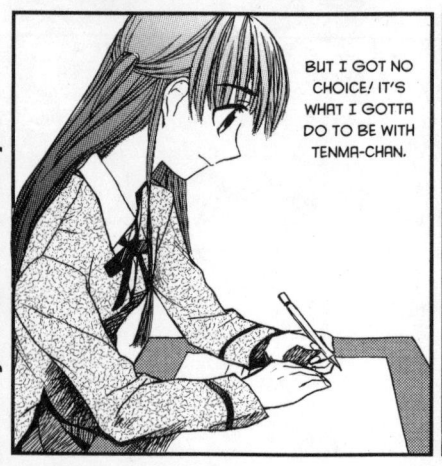

BUT I GOT NO CHOICE! IT'S WHAT I GOTTA DO TO BE WITH TENMA-CHAN.

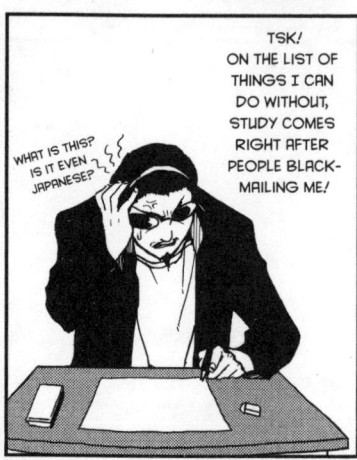

TSK! ON THE LIST OF THINGS I CAN DO WITHOUT, STUDY COMES RIGHT AFTER PEOPLE BLACKMAILING ME!

WHAT IS THIS? IS IT EVEN JAPANESE?

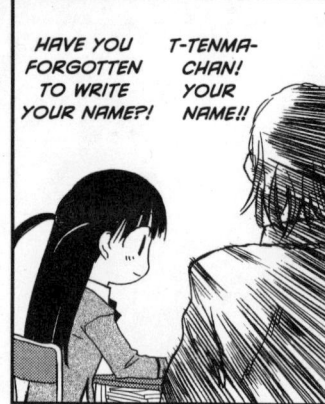

HAVE YOU FORGOTTEN TO WRITE YOUR NAME?!

T-TENMA-CHAN! YOUR NAME!!

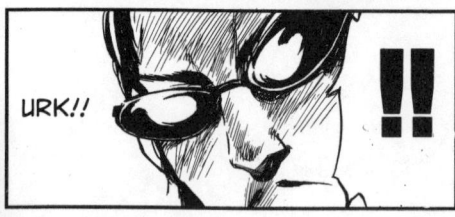

URK!!

!!

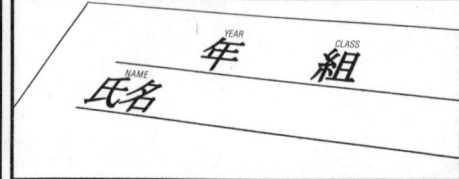

YEAR 年 CLASS 組

NAME 氏名

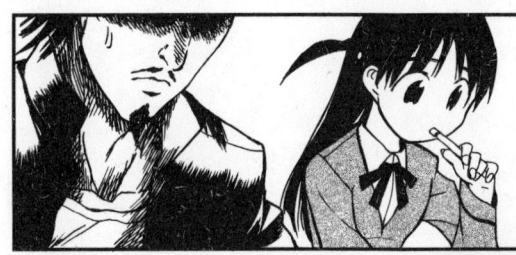

I CAN'T EVEN SPEAK TO WARN HER OF HER DANGER!

MAYBE SHE SIMPLY HASN'T NOTICED.

BUT WE'RE IN THE MIDDLE OF A TEST!

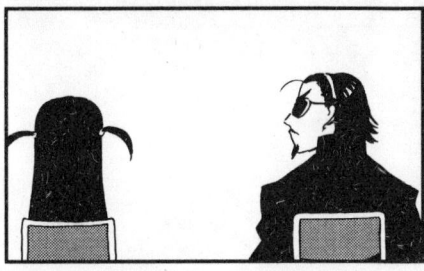

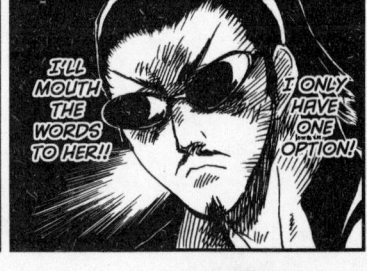

I'LL MOUTH THE WORDS TO HER!!

I ONLY HAVE ONE OPTION!

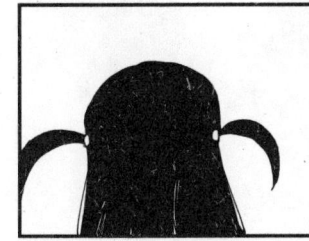

YOU · FOR · GOT · TO · WRITE · YOUR · NAME!

TEN · MA · CHAN!

FLAP FLAP

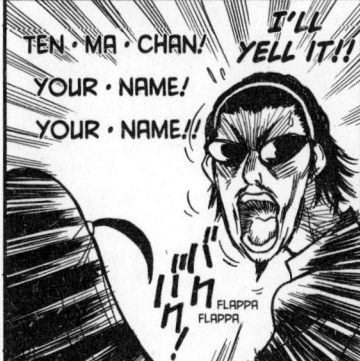

TEN · MA · CHAN!

I'LL YELL IT!!

YOUR · NAME!

YOUR · NAME!!

FLAPPA FLAPPA

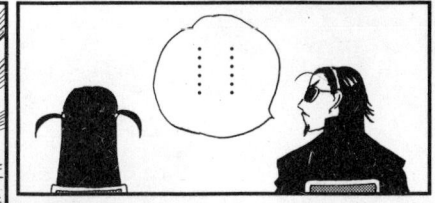

· · ·

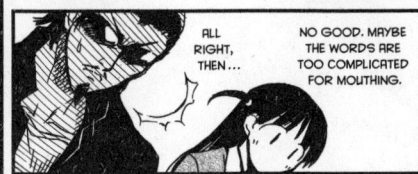

ALL RIGHT, THEN...

NO GOOD. MAYBE THE WORDS ARE TOO COMPLICATED FOR MOUTHING.

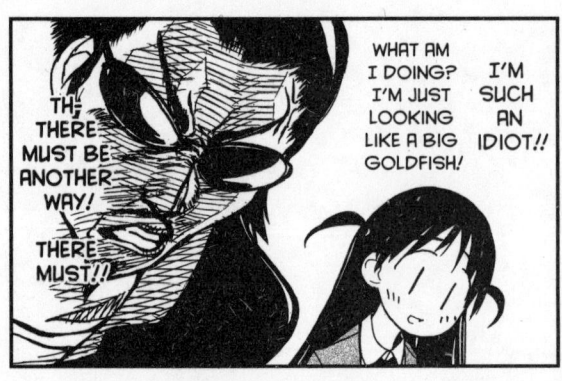

TH- THERE MUST BE ANOTHER WAY! THERE MUST!!

WHAT AM I DOING? I'M JUST LOOKING LIKE A BIG GOLDFISH!

I'M SUCH AN IDIOT!!

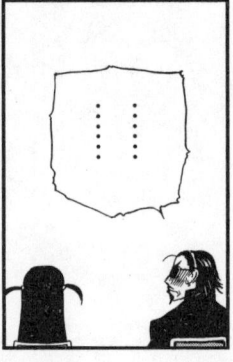

· · · · ·

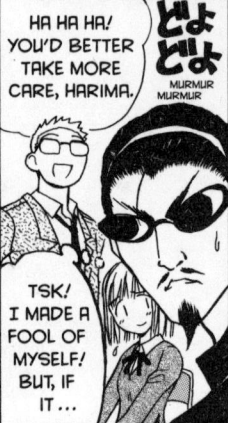

HA HA HA! YOU'D BETTER TAKE MORE CARE, HARIMA.

MURMUR MURMUR

TSK! I MADE A FOOL OF MYSELF! BUT, IF IT ...

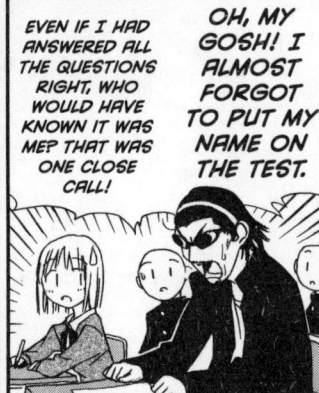

EVEN IF I HAD ANSWERED ALL THE QUESTIONS RIGHT, WHO WOULD HAVE KNOWN IT WAS ME? THAT WAS ONE CLOSE CALL!

OH, MY GOSH! I ALMOST FORGOT TO PUT MY NAME ON THE TEST.

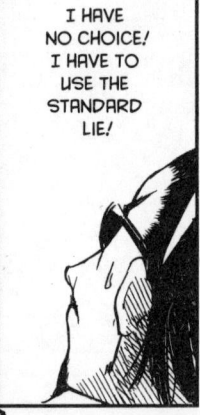

I HAVE NO CHOICE! I HAVE TO USE THE STANDARD LIE!

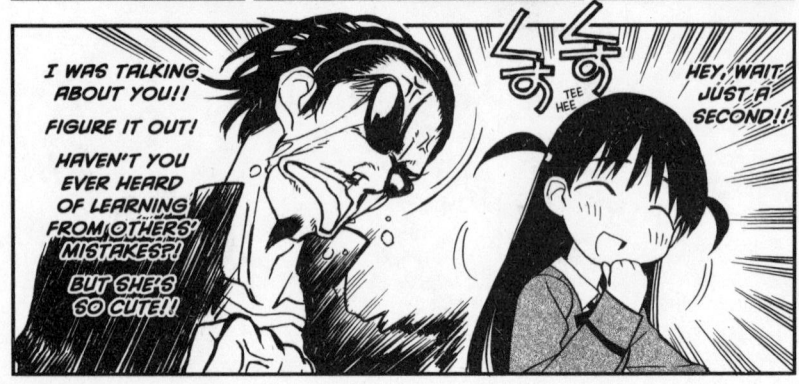

I WAS TALKING ABOUT YOU!! FIGURE IT OUT! HAVEN'T YOU EVER HEARD OF LEARNING FROM OTHERS' MISTAKES?! BUT SHE'S SO CUTE!!

TEE HEE

HEY, WAIT JUST A SECOND!!

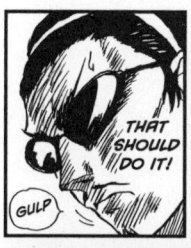

THAT SHOULD DO IT!

GULP

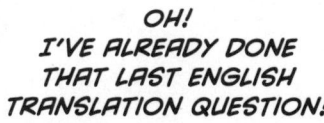

OH! I'VE ALREADY DONE THAT LAST ENGLISH TRANSLATION QUESTION!

WHAT'S GOING ON? IT WAS WAY TOO EASY!

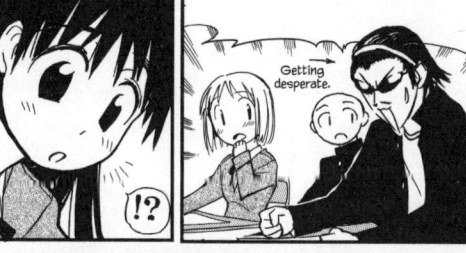

Getting desperate.

!?

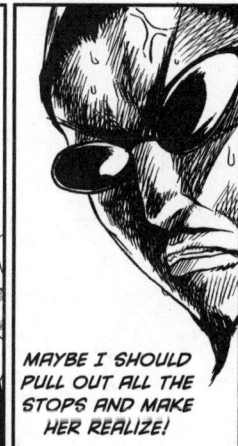

MAYBE I SHOULD PULL OUT ALL THE STOPS AND MAKE HER REALIZE!

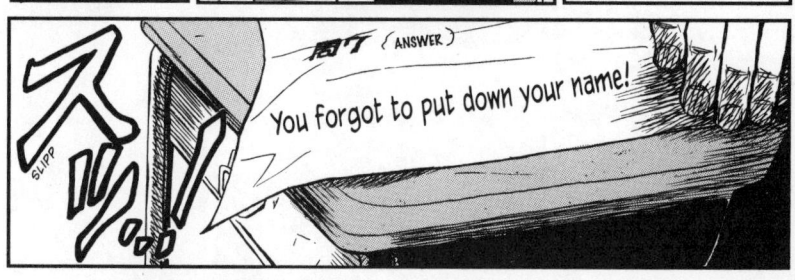

(ANSWER)

You forgot to put down your name!

SLIPP

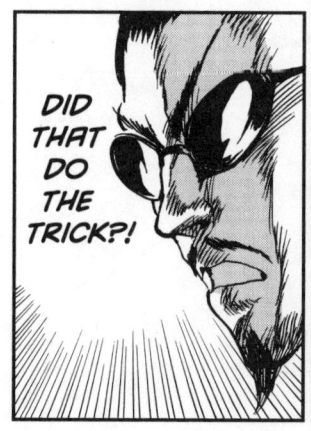

DID THAT DO THE TRICK?!

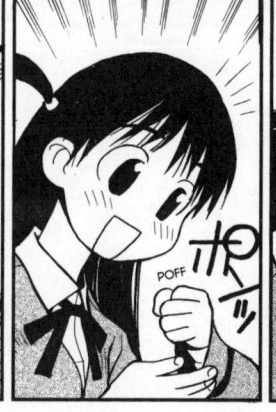

POFF

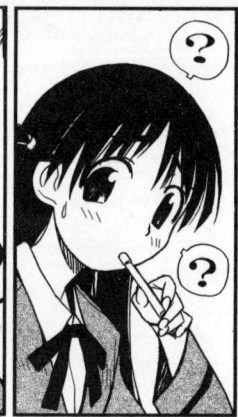

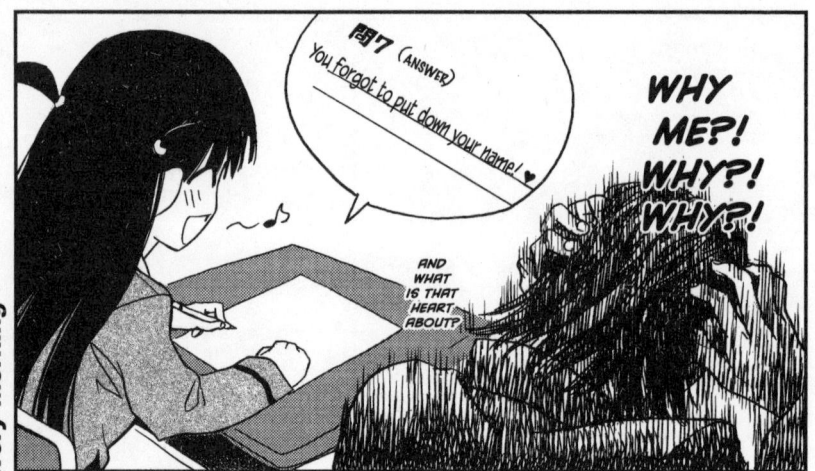

問7 (ANSWER)
You forgot to put down your name! ♥

WHY ME?! WHY?! WHY?!

AND WHAT IS THAT HEART ABOUT?

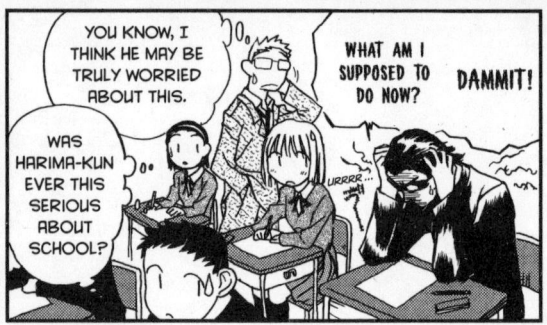

YOU KNOW, I THINK HE MAY BE TRULY WORRIED ABOUT THIS.

WAS HARIMA-KUN EVER THIS SERIOUS ABOUT SCHOOL?

WHAT AM I SUPPOSED TO DO NOW?

DAMMIT!

URRRR...

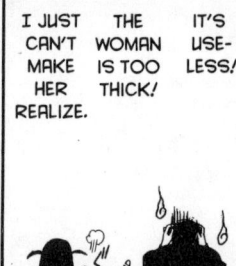

I JUST CAN'T MAKE HER REALIZE.

THE WOMAN IS TOO THICK!

IT'S USE- LESS!

GRIP

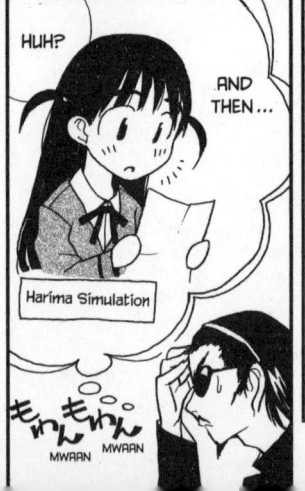

HUH?

...AND THEN...

Harima Simulation

もわんもわん
MWAAN   MWAAN

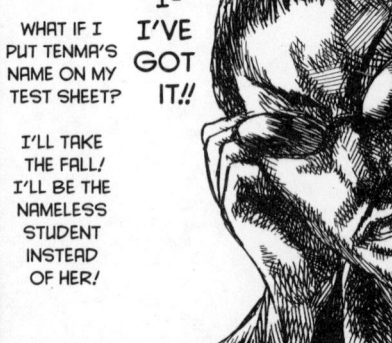

WHAT IF I PUT TENMA'S NAME ON MY TEST SHEET?

I'LL TAKE THE FALL! I'LL BE THE NAMELESS STUDENT INSTEAD OF HER!

I- I'VE GOT IT!!

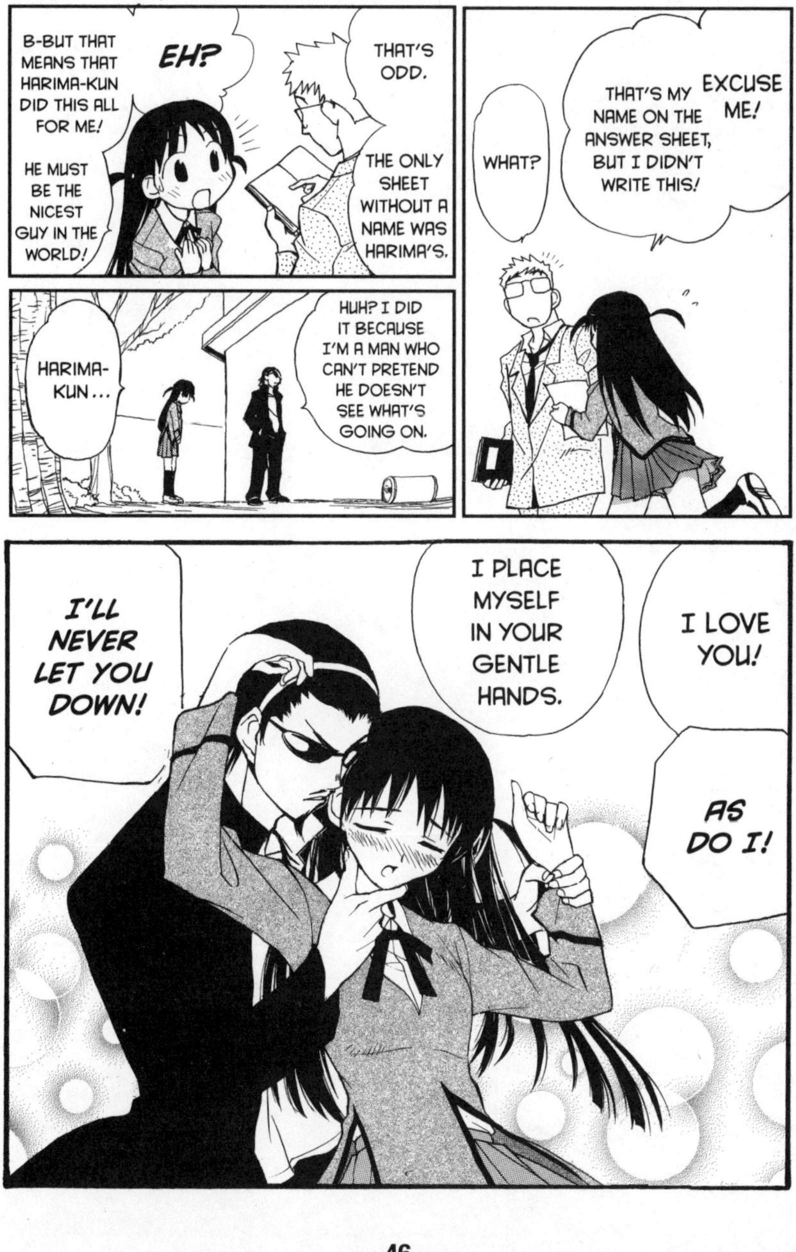

B-BUT THAT MEANS THAT HARIMA-KUN DID THIS ALL FOR ME!

EH?

THAT'S ODD.

HE MUST BE THE NICEST GUY IN THE WORLD!

THE ONLY SHEET WITHOUT A NAME WAS HARIMA'S.

EXCUSE ME!

THAT'S MY NAME ON THE ANSWER SHEET, BUT I DIDN'T WRITE THIS!

WHAT?

HARIMA-KUN...

HUH? I DID IT BECAUSE I'M A MAN WHO CAN'T PRETEND HE DOESN'T SEE WHAT'S GOING ON.

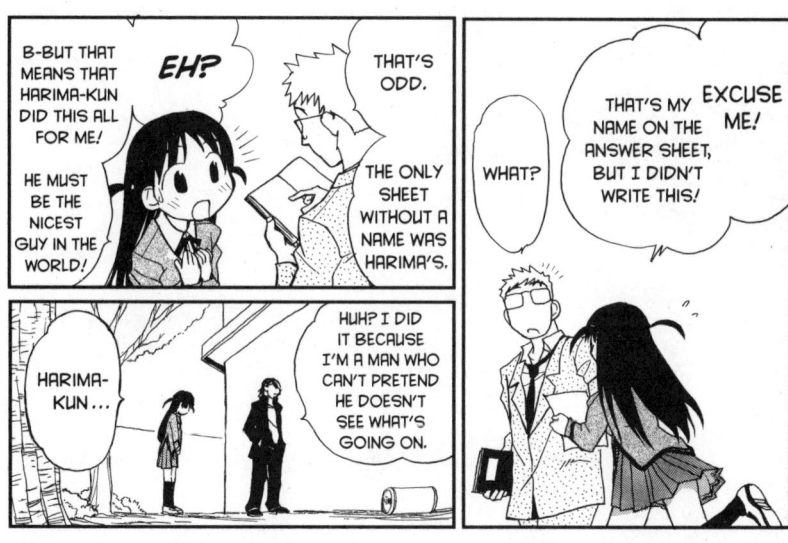

I'LL NEVER LET YOU DOWN!

I PLACE MYSELF IN YOUR GENTLE HANDS.

I LOVE YOU!

AS DO I!

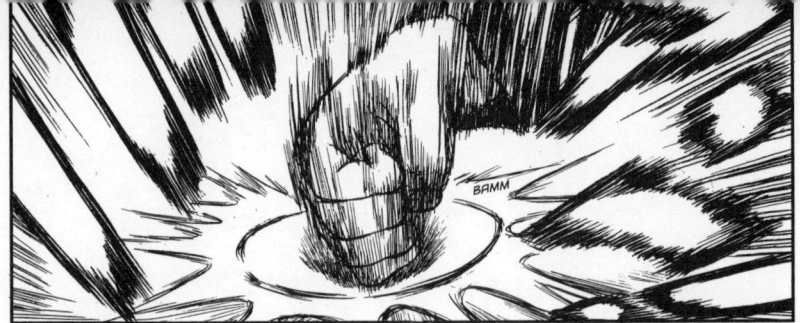

BAMM

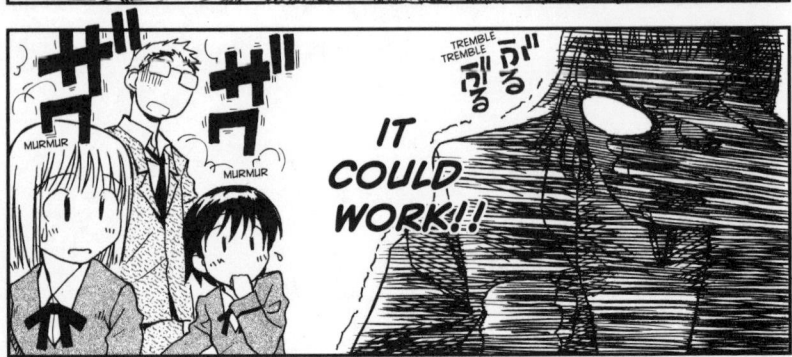

MURMUR

ZZZZ ZZZZ

TREMBLE
TREMBLE

IT COULD WORK!!

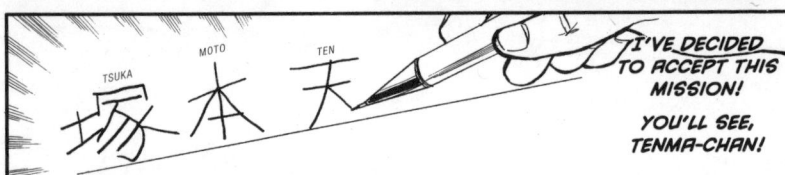

TSUKA　MOTO　TEN

塚 本 天

I'VE DECIDED TO ACCEPT THIS MISSION!

YOU'LL SEE, TENMA-CHAN!

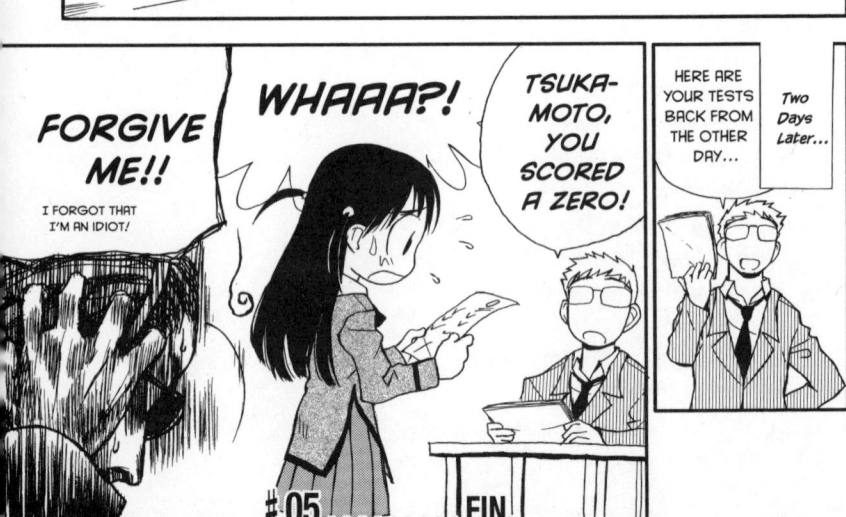

FORGIVE ME!!

I FORGOT THAT I'M AN IDIOT!

WHAAA?!

TSUKA-MOTO, YOU SCORED A ZERO!

HERE ARE YOUR TESTS BACK FROM THE OTHER DAY...

Two Days Later...

#05..........FIN.

DINNER'S ALL READY!!

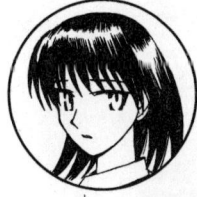

Yakumo introduces...

TSUKA MOTO TEN MA
塚本天満

STATS:

Height: 154 cm (5' 5")

Favorite Thing: Karasuma-san

Least Favorite Thing: She can't eat anything too spicy.

Favorite TV Show: She and I are always watching Edo-period dramas together.

Favorite Book: I see her with manga all the time.

Strong Points: She's an eternal optimist, and she makes friends easily.

One Last Word: She's a big sister that a girl can always rely on.

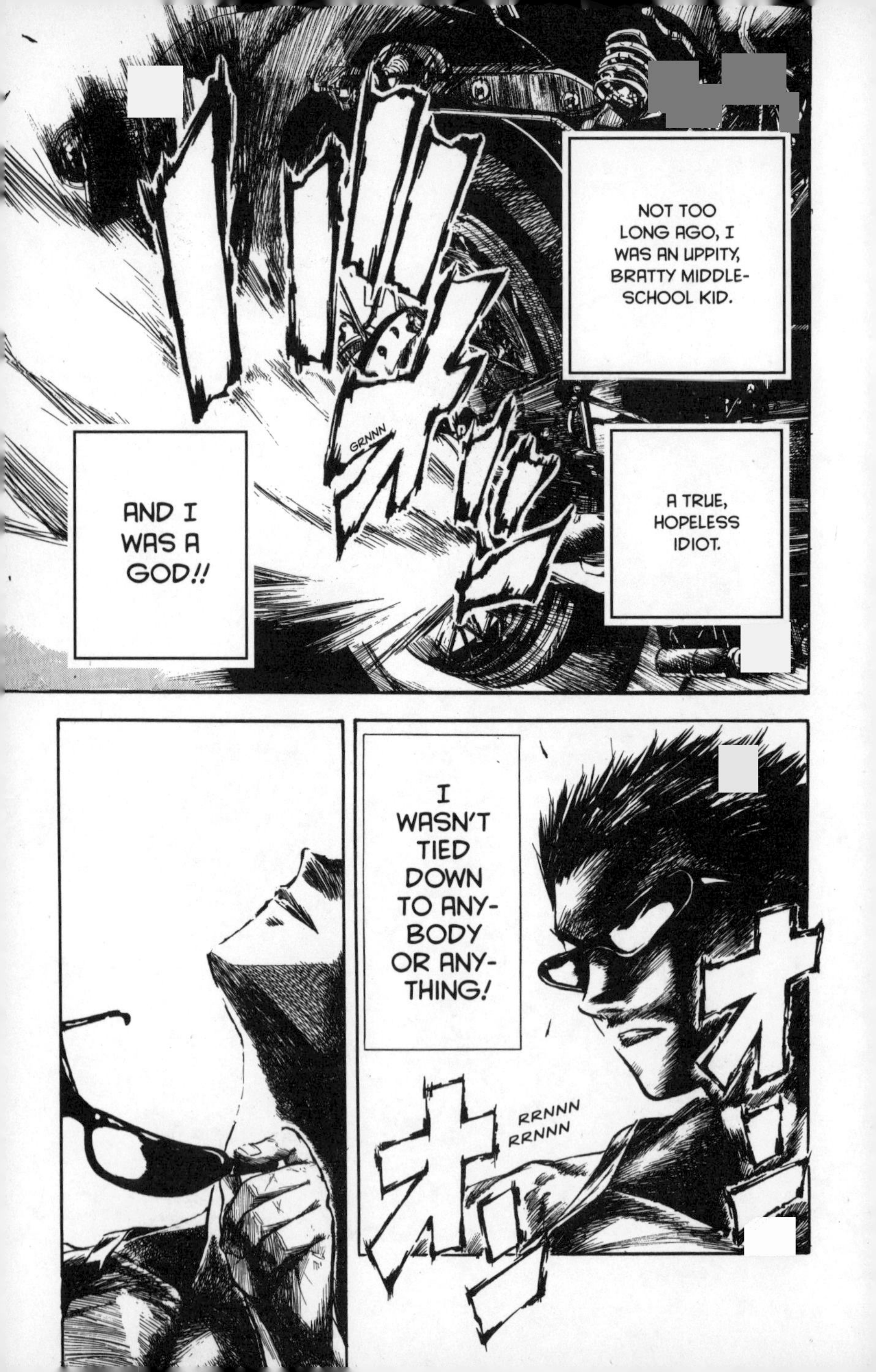
NOT TOO LONG AGO, I WAS AN UPPITY, BRATTY MIDDLE-SCHOOL KID.
A TRUE, HOPELESS IDIOT.
GRNNN
AND I WAS A GOD!!
I WASN'T TIED DOWN TO ANY-BODY OR ANY-THING!
RRNNN RRNNN

#06 YOU'VE GOT MAIL

I...

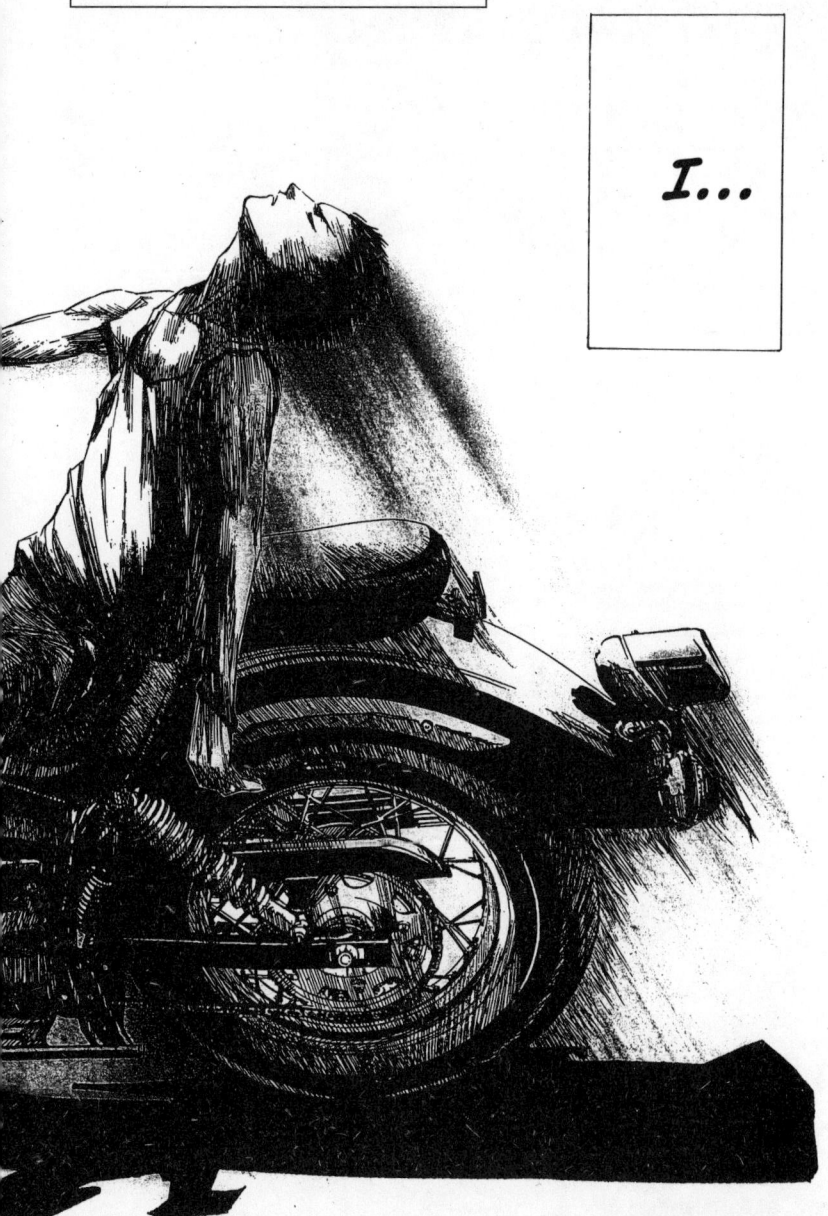

...BELONGED TO NO ONE BUT ME!!

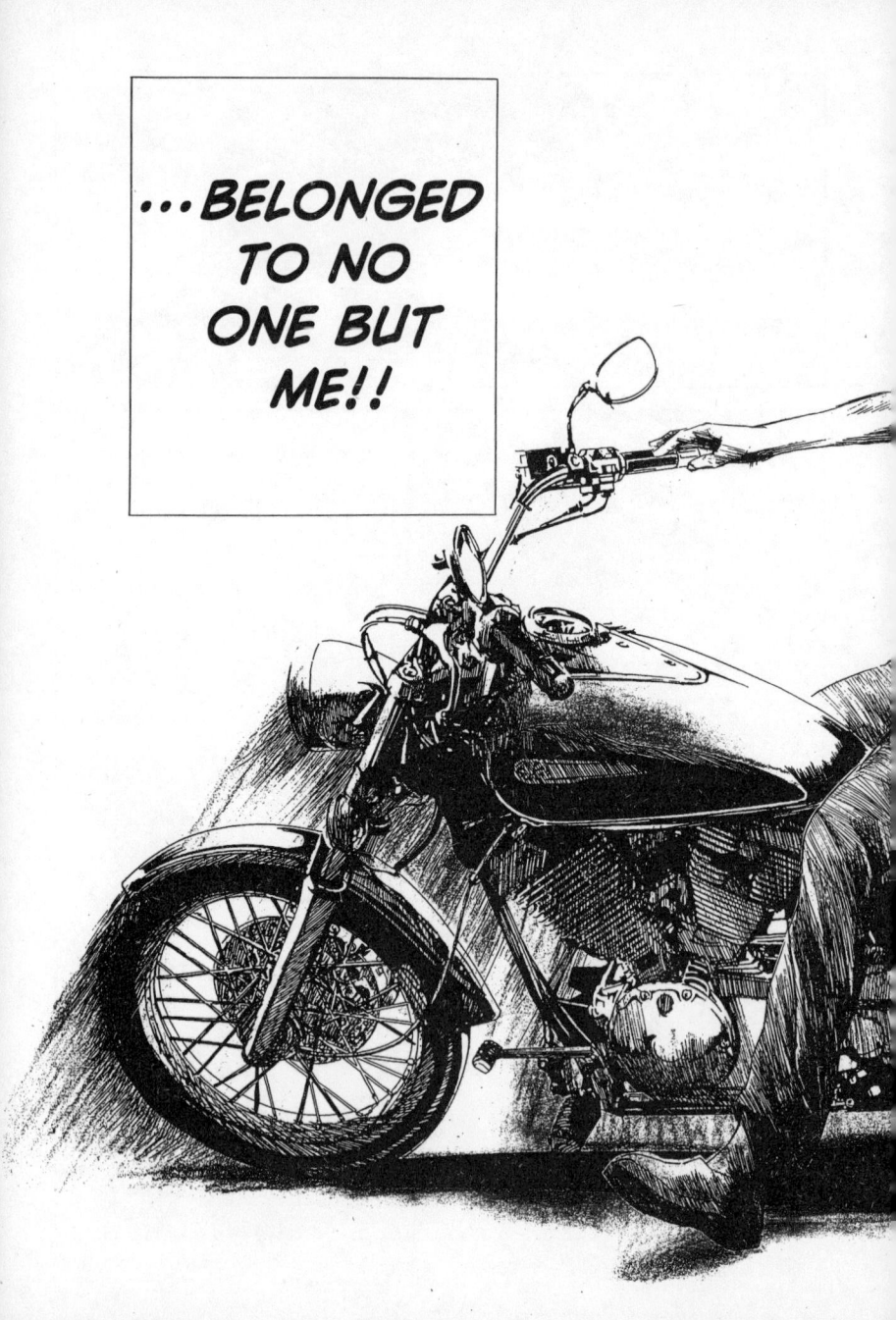

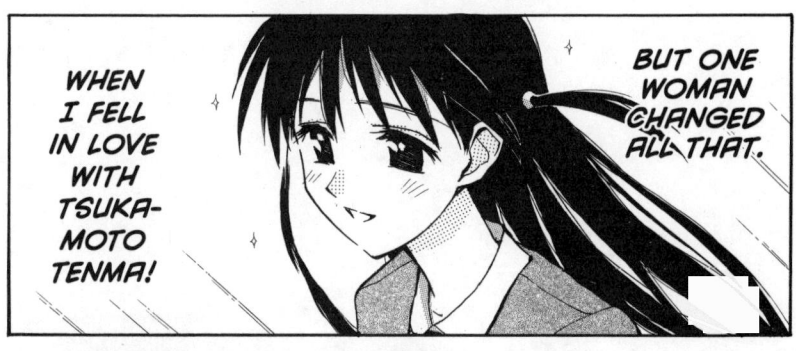

WHEN I FELL IN LOVE WITH TSUKAMOTO TENMA!

BUT ONE WOMAN CHANGED ALL THAT.

Harima Kenji: *Late.*

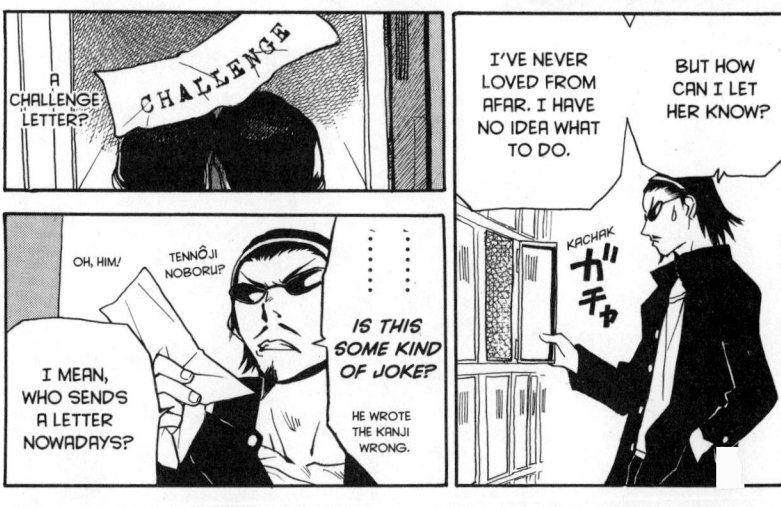

A CHALLENGE LETTER?

CHALLENGE

I'VE NEVER LOVED FROM AFAR. I HAVE NO IDEA WHAT TO DO.

BUT HOW CAN I LET HER KNOW?

KACHAK

OH, HIM!

TENNÔJI NOBORU?

I MEAN, WHO SENDS A LETTER NOWADAYS?

IS THIS SOME KIND OF JOKE?

HE WROTE THE KANJI WRONG.

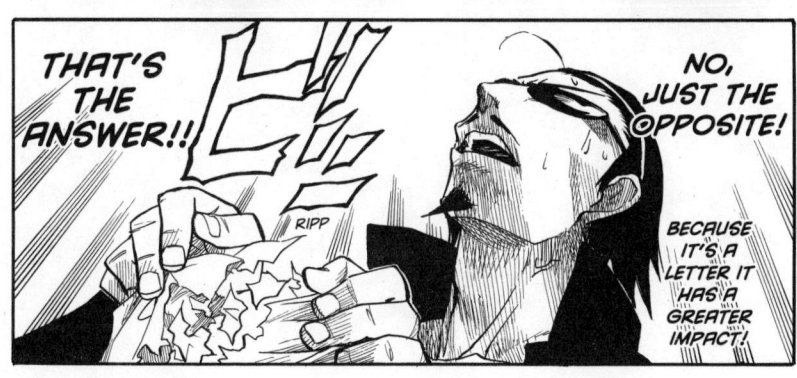

THAT'S THE ANSWER!!

RIPP

NO, JUST THE OPPOSITE!

BECAUSE IT'S A LETTER IT HAS A GREATER IMPACT!

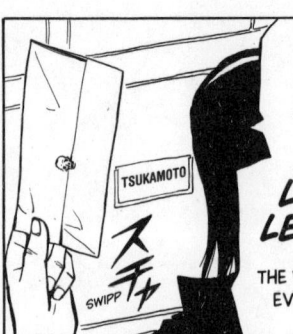

I'LL JUST TAKE A NAP HERE ON THE ROOF.

SHE'LL MEET ME AT 4 P.M. BEHIND THE GYM.

TAKE THIS!

THE MOST PERFECT

LOVE LETTER

THE WORLD HAS EVER SEEN!!

TSUKAMOTO

SWIPP

The Next Day Near the School Entrance...

TSUKAMOTO

THIS IS IT! TENMA-CHAN'S SHOE LOCKER!

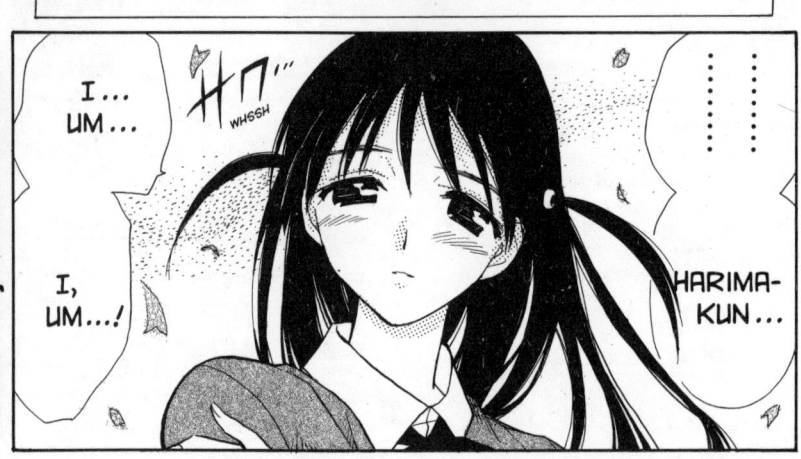

I... UM...

WHSSH

I, UM...!

HARIMA-KUN...

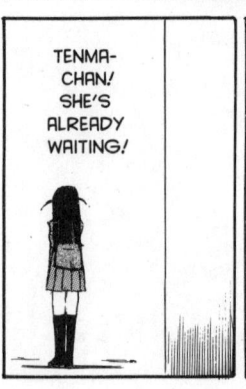

TENMA-CHAN! SHE'S ALREADY WAITING!

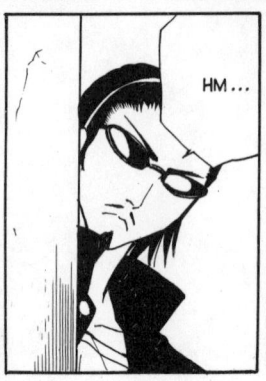

HM...

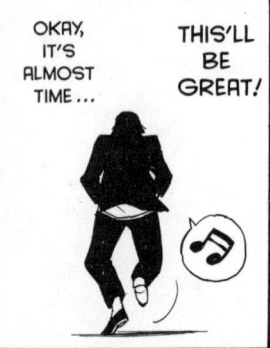

OKAY, IT'S ALMOST TIME...

THIS'LL BE GREAT!

Harima Kenji: Makes His Move.

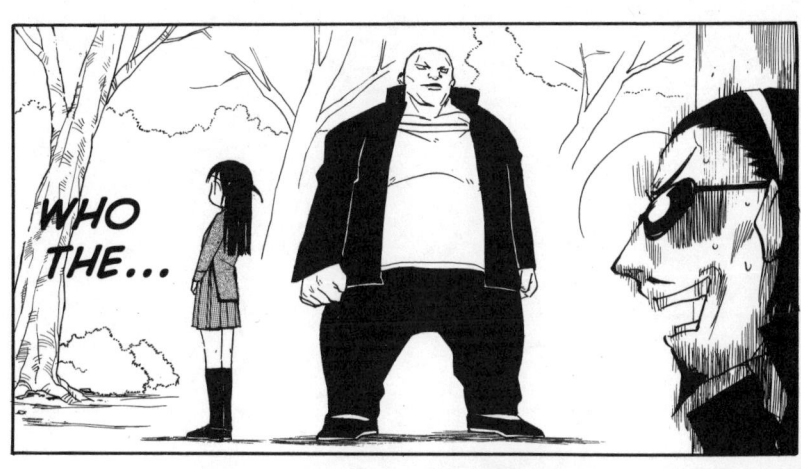

WHO THE...

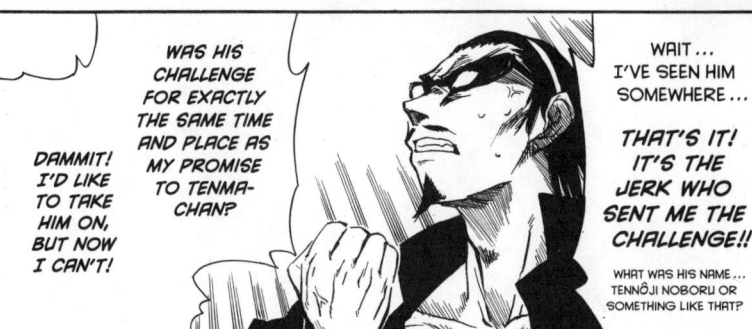

DAMMIT! I'D LIKE TO TAKE HIM ON, BUT NOW I CAN'T!

WAS HIS CHALLENGE FOR EXACTLY THE SAME TIME AND PLACE AS MY PROMISE TO TENMA-CHAN?

WAIT... I'VE SEEN HIM SOMEWHERE...

THAT'S IT! IT'S THE JERK WHO SENT ME THE CHALLENGE!!

WHAT WAS HIS NAME... TENNŌJI NOBORU OR SOMETHING LIKE THAT?

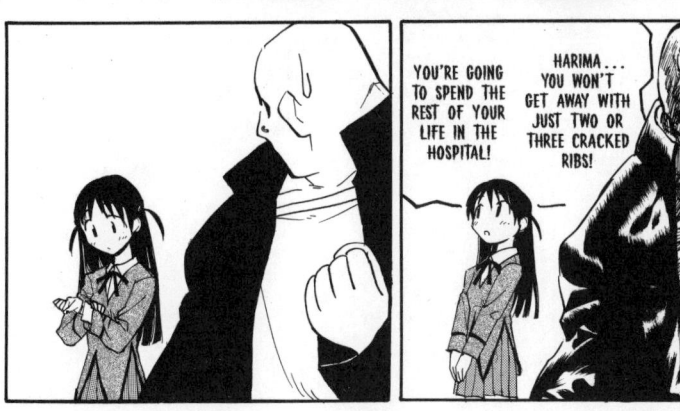

YOU'RE GOING TO SPEND THE REST OF YOUR LIFE IN THE HOSPITAL!

HARIMA... YOU WON'T GET AWAY WITH JUST TWO OR THREE CRACKED RIBS!

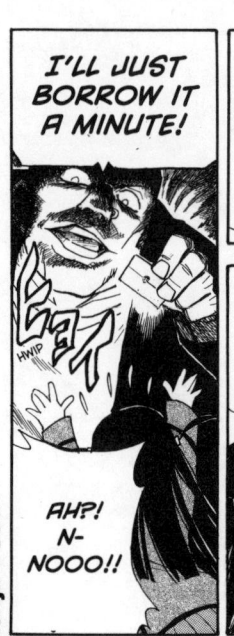

I'LL JUST BORROW IT A MINUTE!

AH?! N-NOOO!!

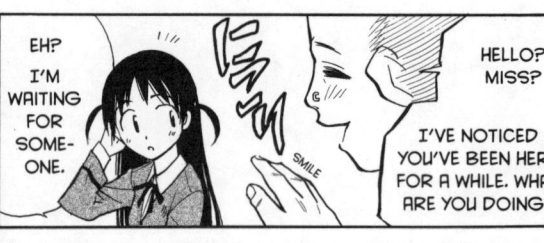

EH? I'M WAITING FOR SOMEONE.

SMILE

HELLO? MISS?

I'VE NOTICED YOU'VE BEEN HERE FOR A WHILE. WHAT ARE YOU DOING?

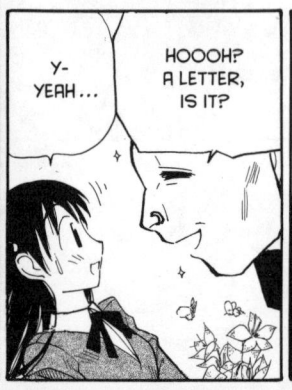

Y-YEAH...

HOOOH? A LETTER, IS IT?

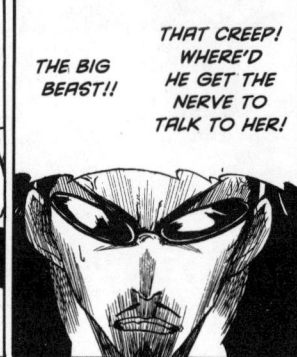

THE BIG BEAST!!

THAT CREEP! WHERE'D HE GET THE NERVE TO TALK TO HER!

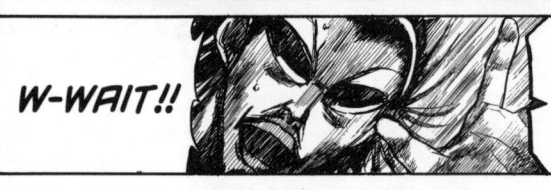

W-WAIT!!

NOW WHAT'S THIS HERE? COULD IT BE A *POEM?!*

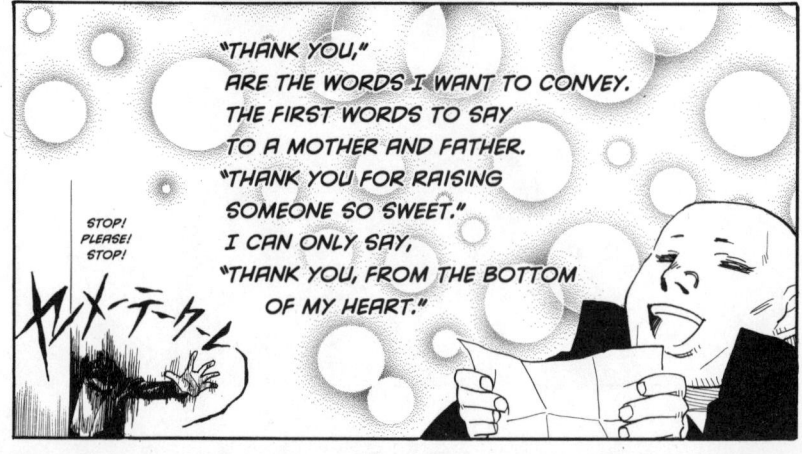

"THANK YOU,"
ARE THE WORDS I WANT TO CONVEY.
THE FIRST WORDS TO SAY
TO A MOTHER AND FATHER.
"THANK YOU FOR RAISING
SOMEONE SO SWEET."
I CAN ONLY SAY,
"THANK YOU, FROM THE BOTTOM
OF MY HEART."

STOP! PLEASE! STOP!

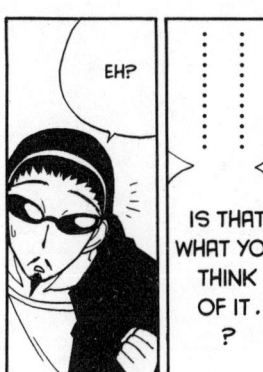

EH?

IS THAT WHAT YOU THINK OF IT...?

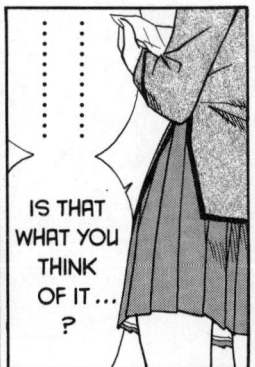

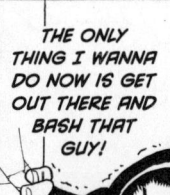

THE ONLY THING I WANNA DO NOW IS GET OUT THERE AND BASH THAT GUY!

GWA HA HA HA!!

WHO COULD FIGURE THAT POEM OUT?! AND WHAT GOOD'S A VERSE THAT MAKES YOU LAUGH?

IT'S TOO BAD HE NEVER SIGNED IT!

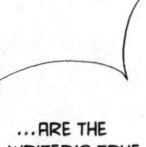

...ARE THE WRITER'S TRUE FEELINGS.

AND... THINK THE FEELING OF LOVE IN THIS LETTER...

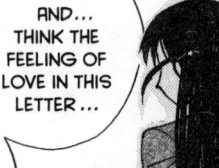

...BUT AT TIMES LIKE THIS, I TRY MY BEST TO FEEL WHAT THE WRITER FEELS.

I KNOW I'M NOT VERY SMART...

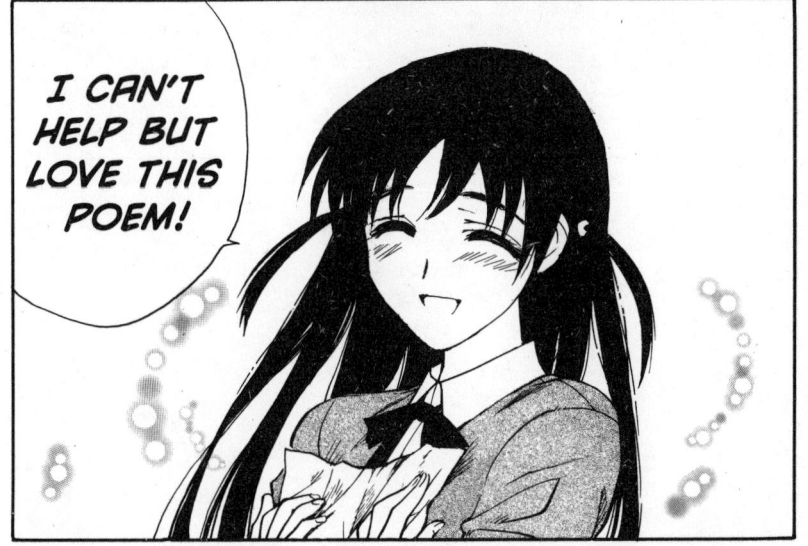

I CAN'T HELP BUT LOVE THIS POEM!

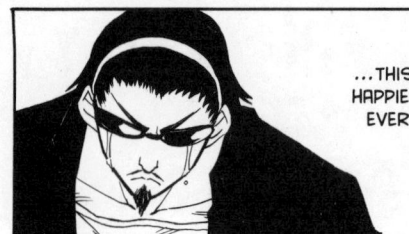

...THIS IS THE HAPPIEST I'VE EVER FELT!

EVER SINCE I FELL FOR TENMA-CHAN...

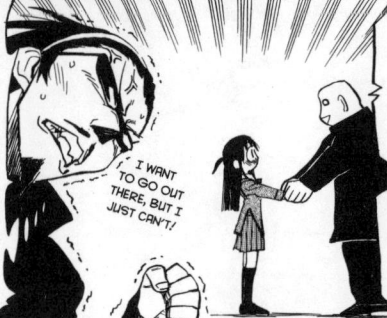

WHAT IS HE TRYING TO PULL?!

YOU'RE THE ONE WHO NOBODY CAN FIGURE OUT!

I WANT TO GO OUT THERE, BUT I JUST CAN'T!

ACTUALLY, *I'M* THE ONE WHO WROTE IT.

I LOVE YOU!!

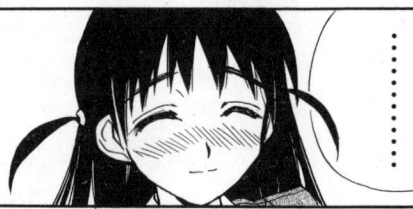

THANK YOU!

BUT...I'M IN LOVE WITH SOMEBODY ELSE.

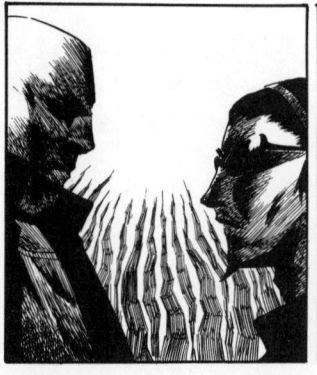

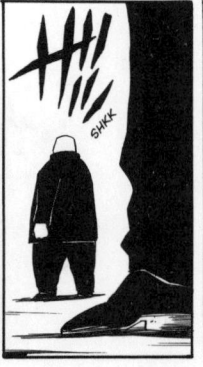

SHKK

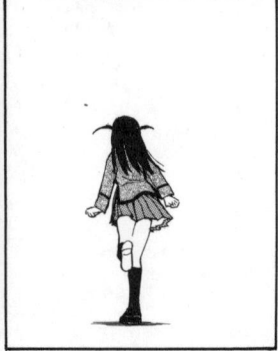

Harima Kenji: *Happy for an Unusual Reason.*

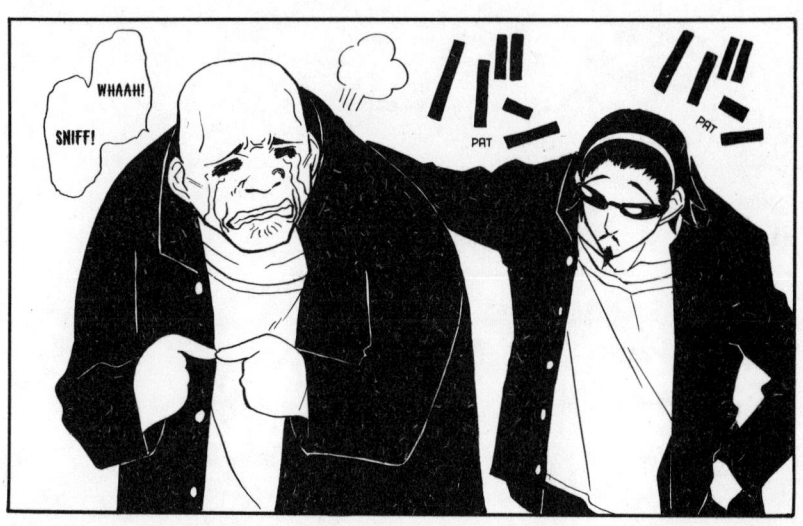

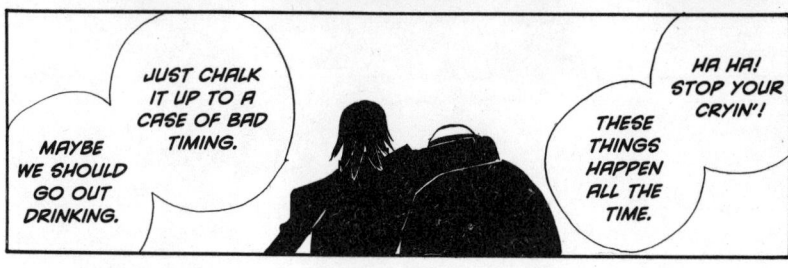

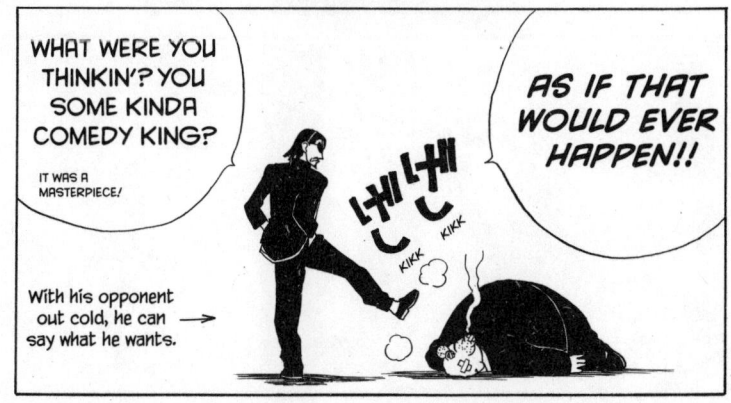

06 . . . . Fin.

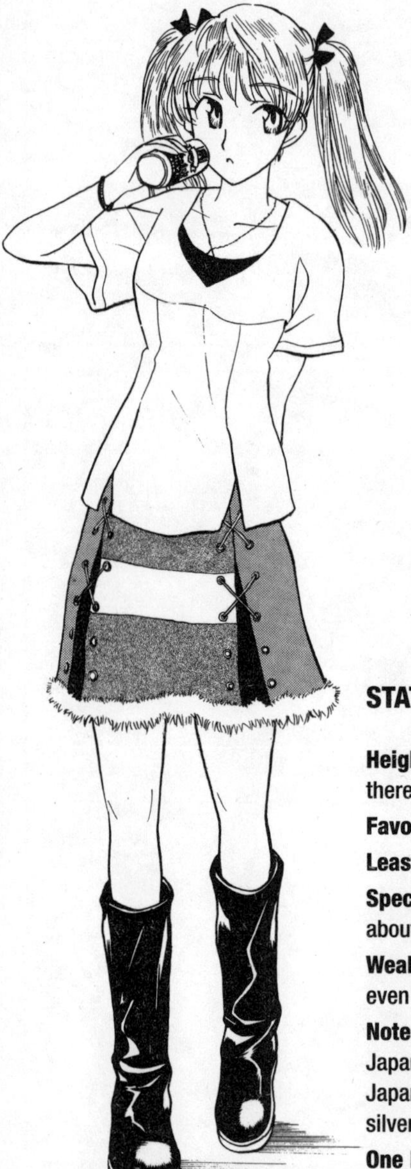
IF IT'S JUST A DATE . . . SURE, I'LL GO.

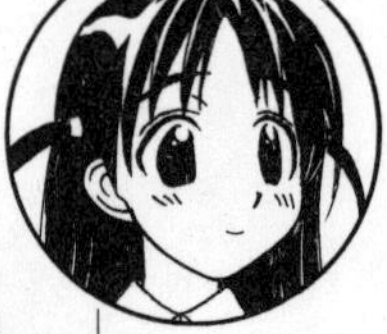

Tsukamoto Tenma introduces . . .

SAWA CHIKA E RI

沢近愛理

STATS:

Height: 165 cm (5' 5") . . . or somewhere around there.

Favorite Thing: She once told me it was the zoo.

Least Favorite Thing: I think it's kanji and cooking.

Special Talent: She's a genius who can master just about anything! I'm sooo jealous!

Weak Points: She may not look it, but she can be even sadder than I get.

Notes: Her father's British and her mother's Japanese, so she's mixed race. She's now back in Japan from living in England. She was raised with a silver spoon in her mouth.

One Last Word: Her language may be a little rough, but really she's a nice girl, I'm sure of it!

#07 DEATH RACE 2003

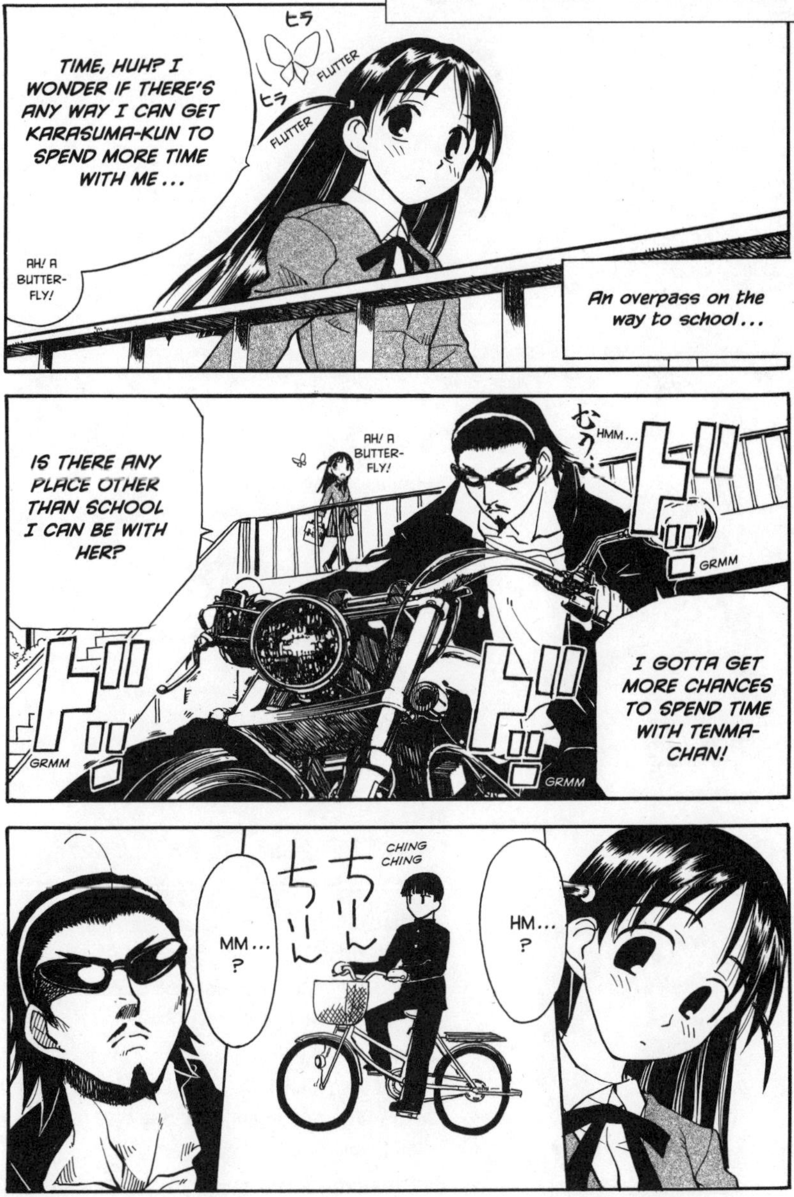
An overpass on the way to school...
ヒラ FLUTTER
ヒラ FLUTTER
AH! A BUTTER-FLY!
TIME, HUH? I WONDER IF THERE'S ANY WAY I CAN GET KARASUMA-KUN TO SPEND MORE TIME WITH ME...
HMM...
GRMM
I GOTTA GET MORE CHANCES TO SPEND TIME WITH TENMA-CHAN!
GRMM
AH! A BUTTER-FLY!
IS THERE ANY PLACE OTHER THAN SCHOOL I CAN BE WITH HER?
GRMM
HM...?
CHING CHING
MM...?

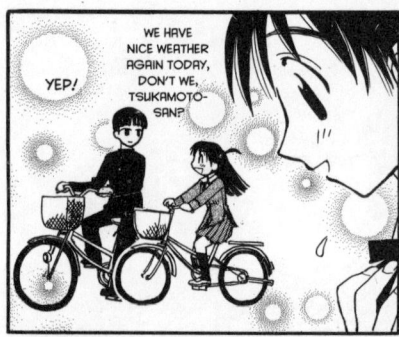

WE HAVE NICE WEATHER AGAIN TODAY, DON'T WE, TSUKAMOTO-SAN?

YEP!

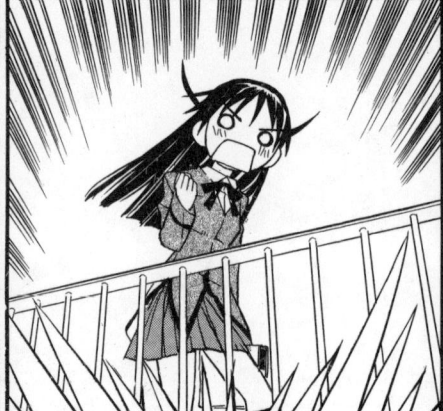

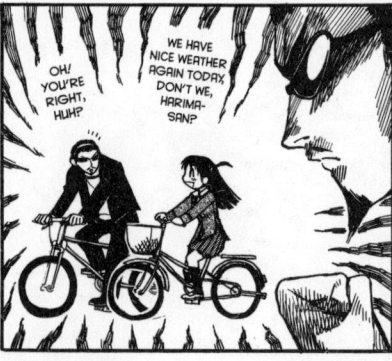

OH! YOU'RE RIGHT, HUH?

WE HAVE NICE WEATHER AGAIN TODAY, DON'T WE, HARIMA-SAN?

THAT'S IT!!!

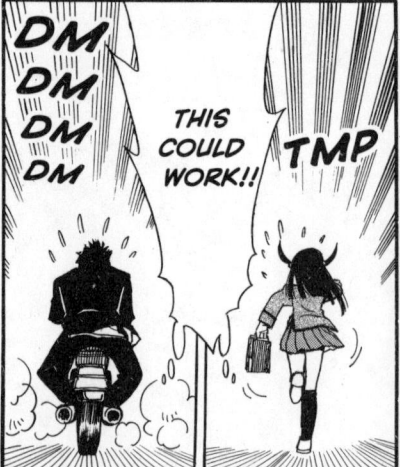

DM DM DM DM

THIS COULD WORK!!

TMP

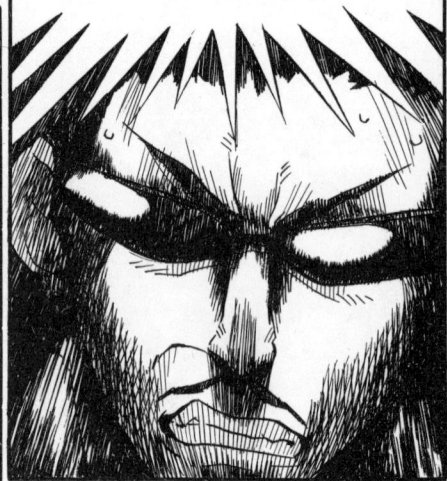

— 61 —

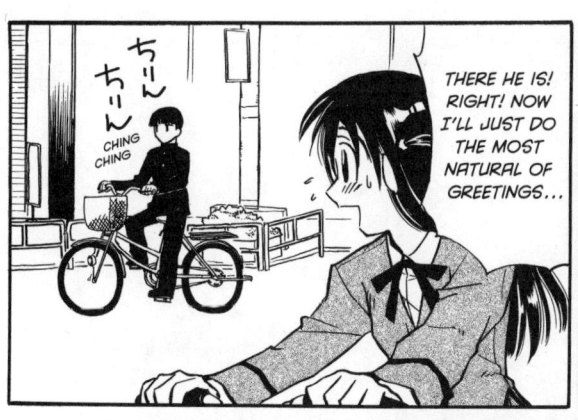

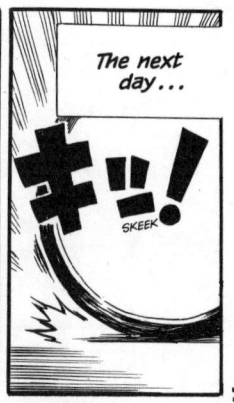

The next day...
キッ!
SKEEK
THERE HE IS! RIGHT! NOW I'LL JUST DO THE MOST NATURAL OF GREETINGS...
ちりん ちりん
CHING CHING
KARASUMA-KUN, GOOD MOR—
SHOOOM
EH?!
CHING CHING
KARASUMA-KUN?! OH, NO! WAIT!
HE'S SO FAST!!
BUT HE'S JUST RIDING A NORMAL MAMA-CHARI, ISN'T HE?!
SHNNK SHNNK SHNNK
WAIT UP, KARASUMA-KUN!!
AH! IT'S TENMA-CHAN! AND SHE HAS A BIKE EVEN BEFORE I ASKED HER TO RIDE WITH ME! THAT MUST BE...
...THE POWER OF LOVE!!
SKEEK

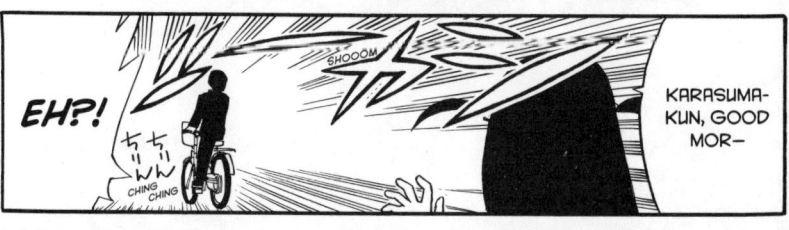

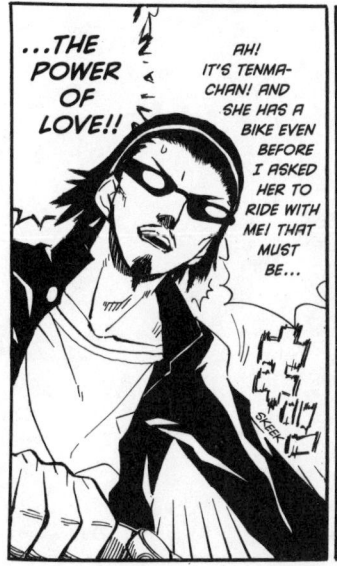

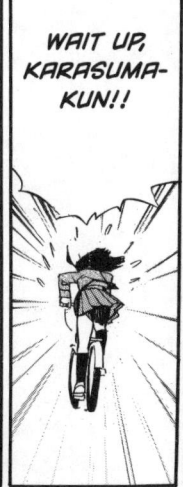

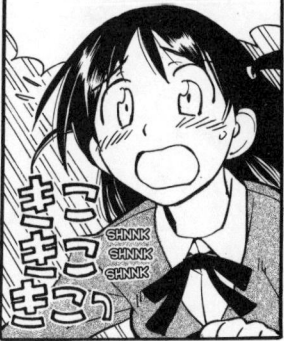

Harima Kenji: *Going All Out Too.*

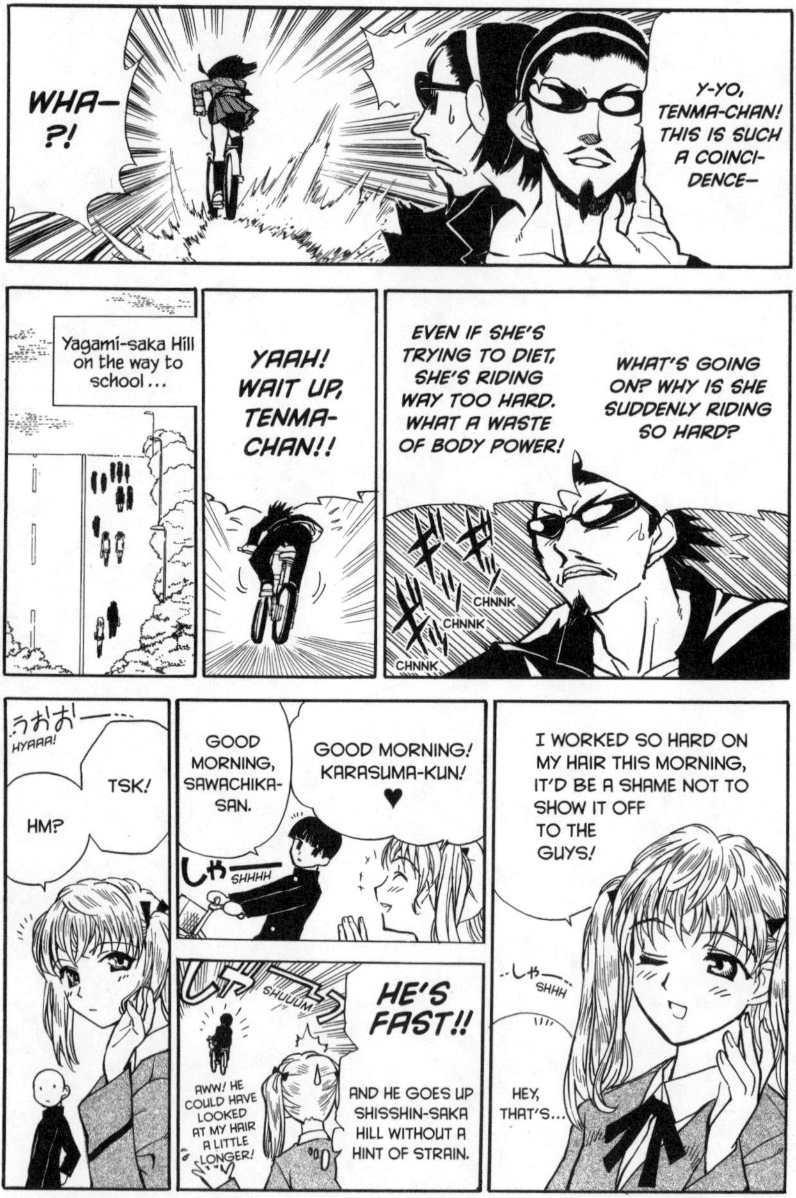
Y-YO, TENMA-CHAN! THIS IS SUCH A COINCIDENCE—
WHA—?!
WHAT'S GOING ON? WHY IS SHE SUDDENLY RIDING SO HARD?
EVEN IF SHE'S TRYING TO DIET, SHE'S RIDING WAY TOO HARD. WHAT A WASTE OF BODY POWER!
CHNNK
CHNNK
CHNNK
YAAH! WAIT UP, TENMA-CHAN!!
Yagami-saka Hill on the way to school…
I WORKED SO HARD ON MY HAIR THIS MORNING, IT'D BE A SHAME NOT TO SHOW IT OFF TO THE GUYS!
しゃー SHHH
HEY, THAT'S…
GOOD MORNING! KARASUMA-KUN! ♥
GOOD MORNING, SAWACHIKA-SAN.
しゃー SHHHH
HE'S FAST!!
AND HE GOES UP SHISSHIN-SAKA HILL WITHOUT A HINT OF STRAIN.
AWW! HE COULD HAVE LOOKED AT MY HAIR A LITTLE LONGER!
しゃー SHUUUM
うおおー HYAAA!
TSK!
HM?

↑ Sawachika misread Yagami-saka Hill as Shisshin-saka Hill.

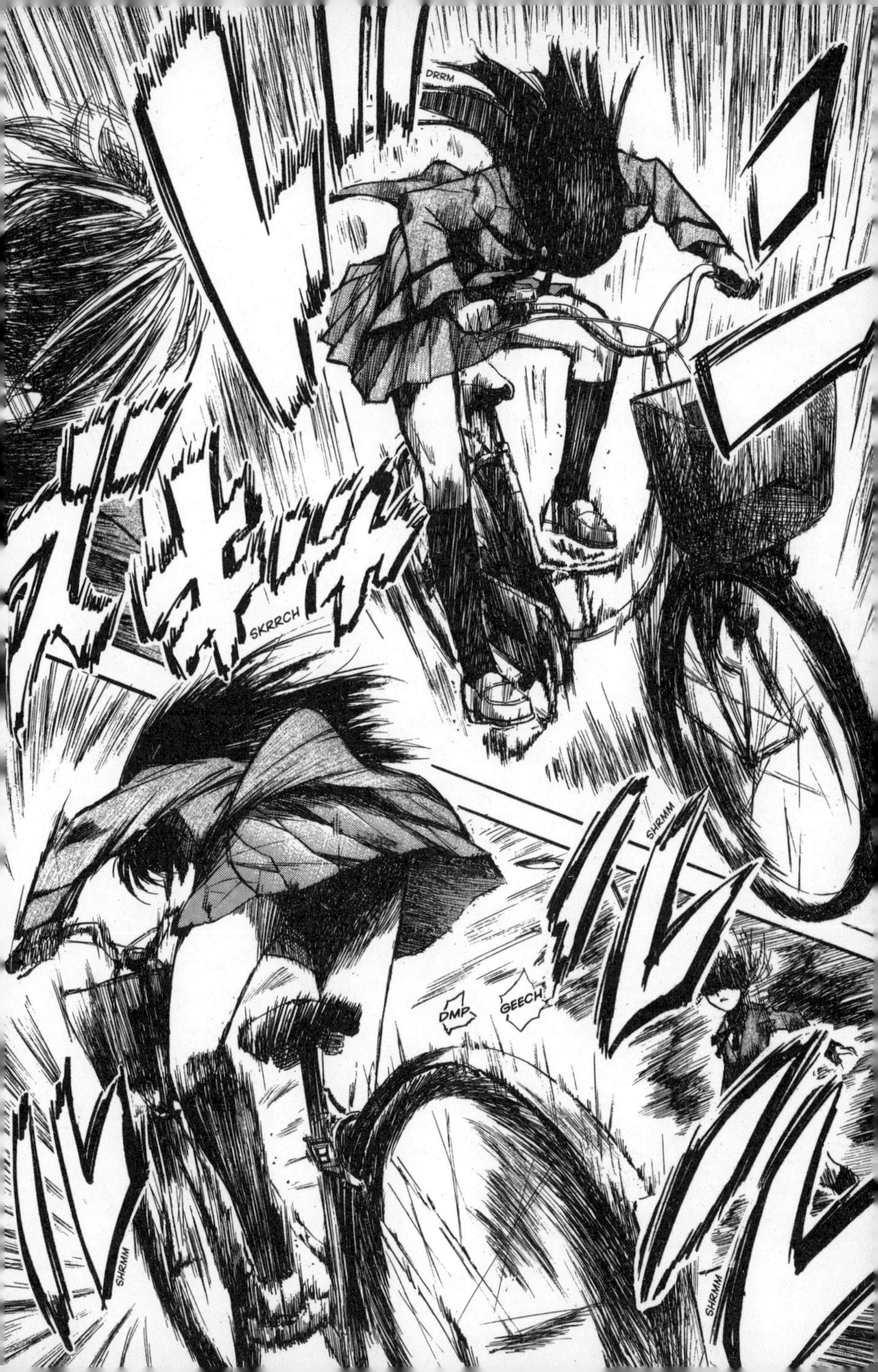
DRRM
SKRRCH
SHRMM
GEECH
DMP
SHRMM
SHRMM

ZHOOOM
SWAAAAAAM
GRRCH

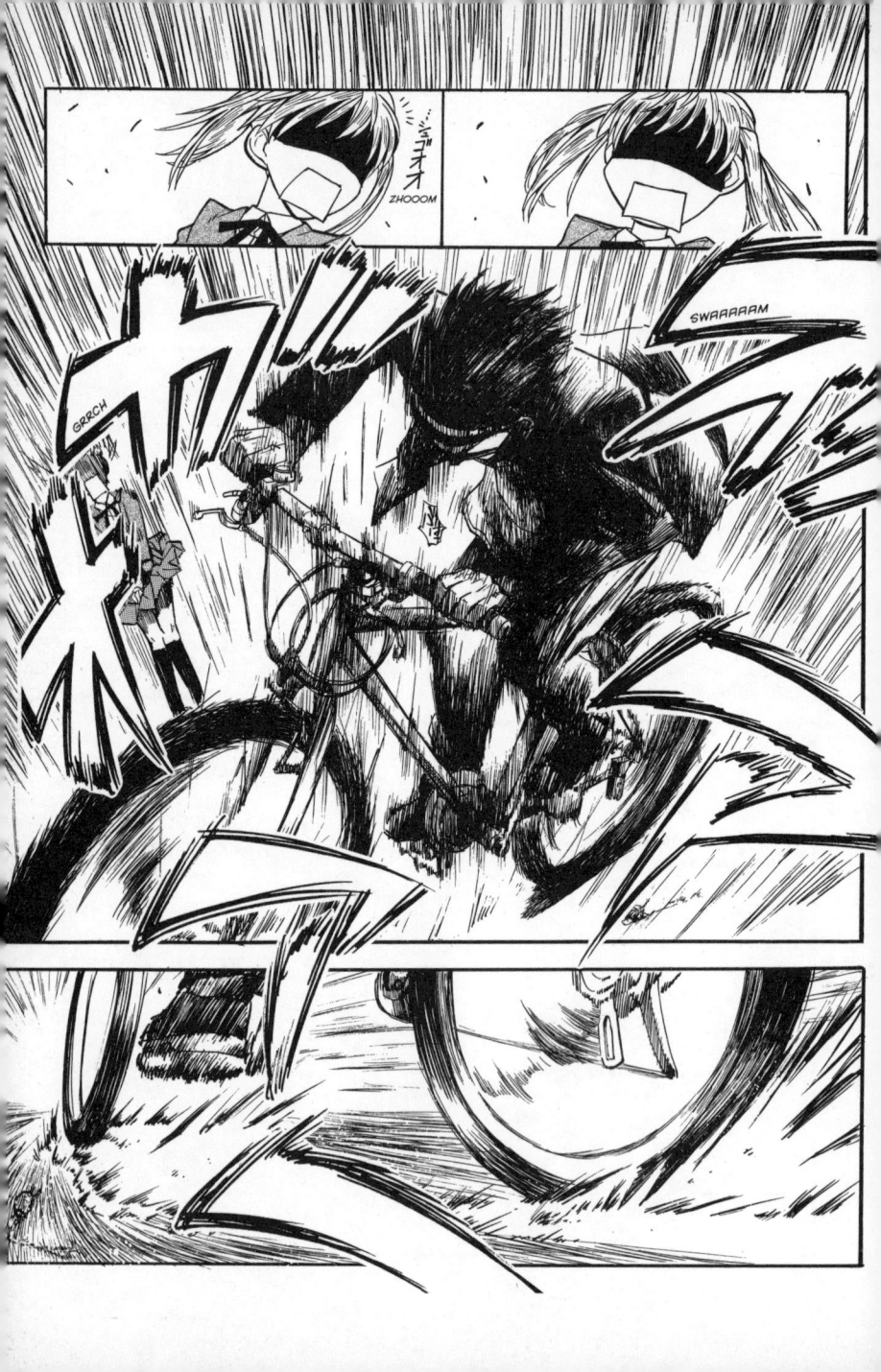

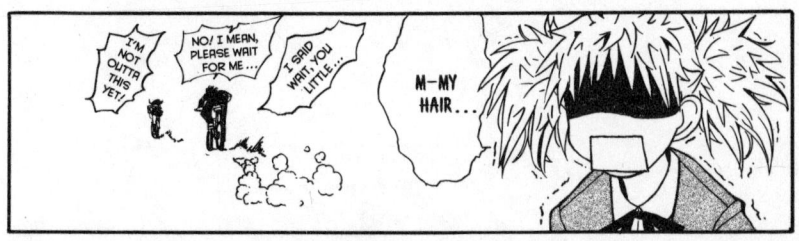

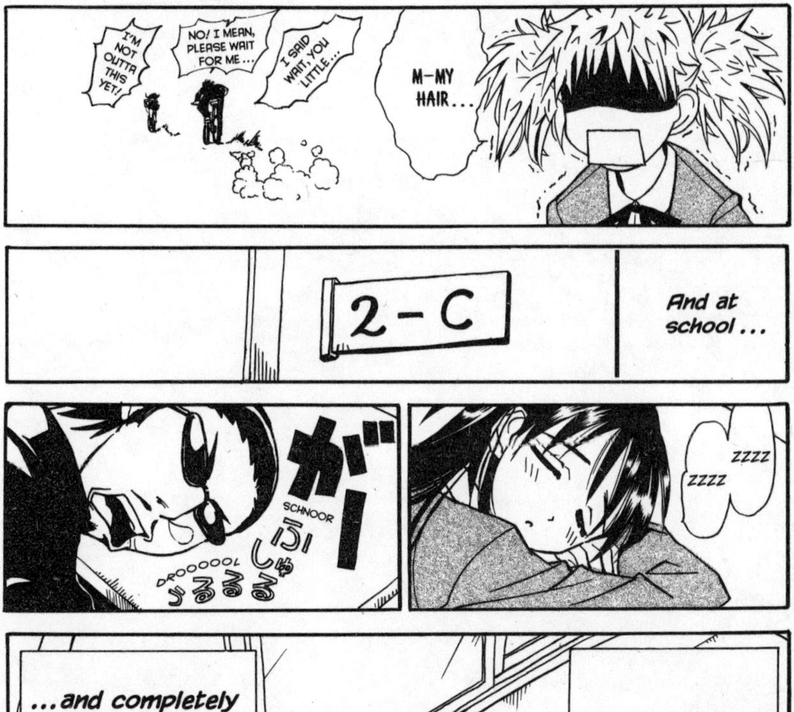

And at school...

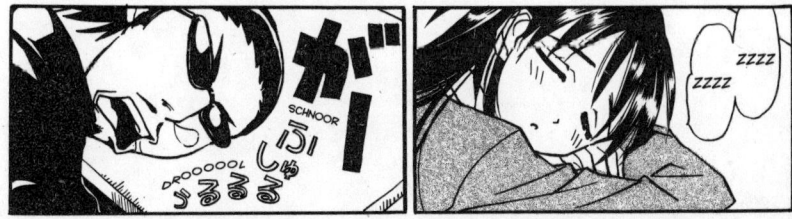

...and completely wasted the time they could have spent with the object of their affections.

The exhausted pair fell quickly asleep...

A completely unfazed Karasuma.

07 .... Fin.

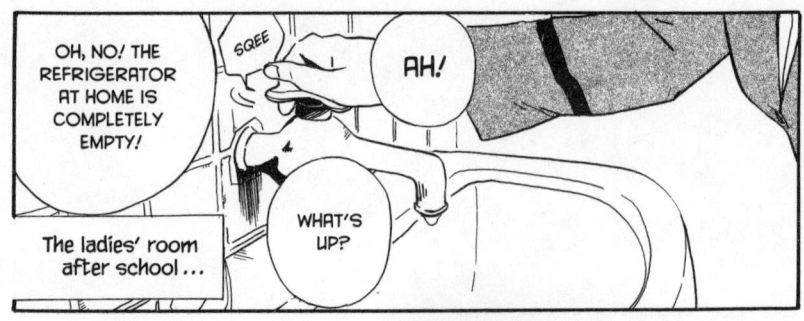

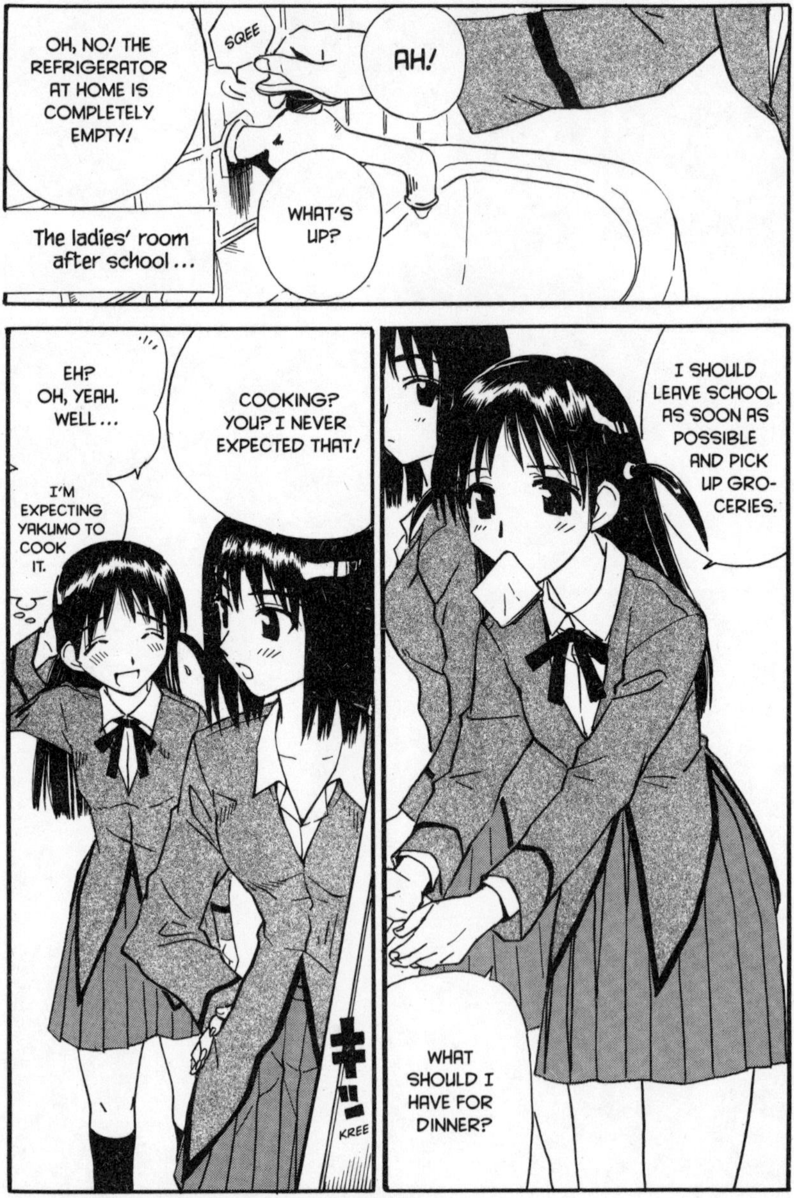

OH, NO! THE REFRIGERATOR AT HOME IS COMPLETELY EMPTY!

SQEE

AH!

WHAT'S UP?

The ladies' room after school ...

EH? OH, YEAH. WELL ...

COOKING? YOU? I NEVER EXPECTED THAT!

I'M EXPECTING YAKUMO TO COOK IT.

KREE

I SHOULD LEAVE SCHOOL AS SOON AS POSSIBLE AND PICK UP GRO-CERIES.

WHAT SHOULD I HAVE FOR DINNER?

#08 THE GREAT ESCAPE

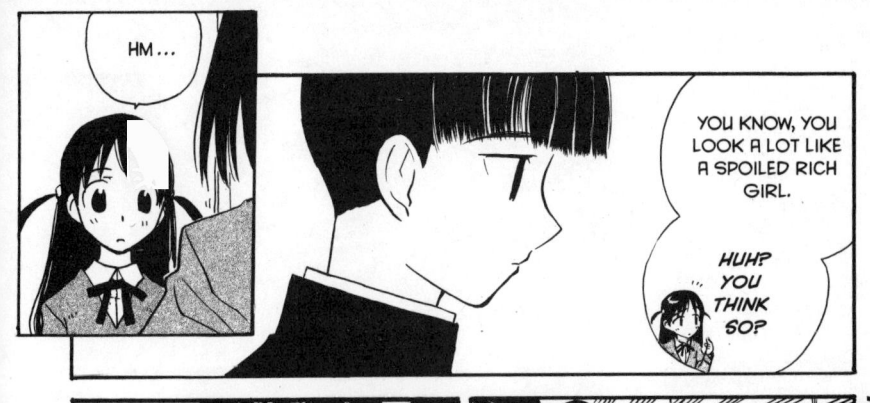

HM...

YOU KNOW, YOU LOOK A LOT LIKE A SPOILED RICH GIRL.

HUH? YOU THINK SO?

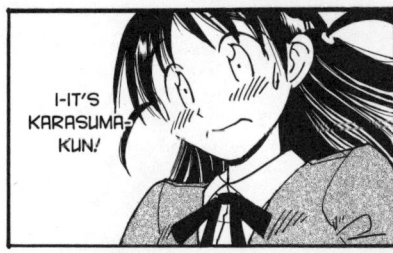

I-IT'S KARASUMA-KUN!

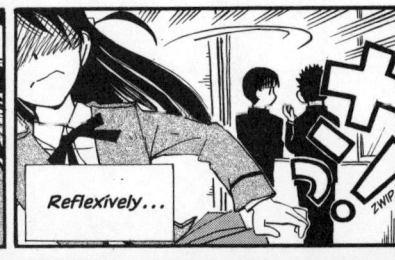

Reflexively...

ZWIP

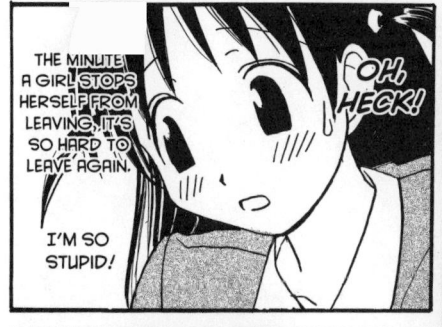

THE MINUTE A GIRL STOPS HERSELF FROM LEAVING, IT'S SO HARD TO LEAVE AGAIN.

I'M SO STUPID!

OH, HECK!

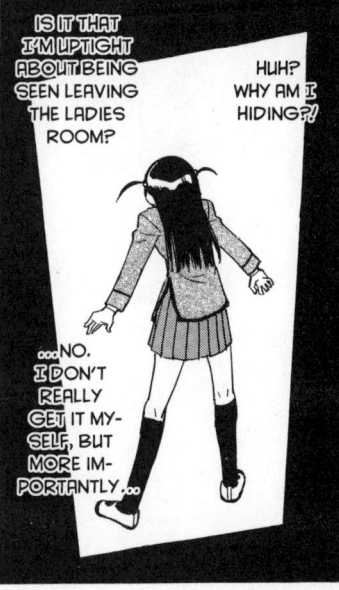

IS IT THAT I'M UPTIGHT ABOUT BEING SEEN LEAVING THE LADIES ROOM?

HUH? WHY AM I HIDING?!

...NO. I DON'T REALLY GET IT MYSELF, BUT MORE IMPORTANTLY...

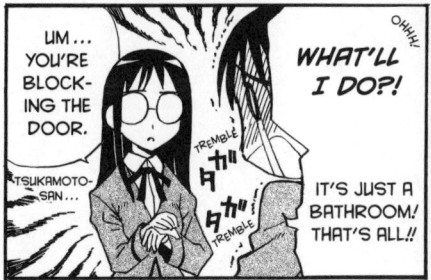

UM... YOU'RE BLOCKING THE DOOR.

OHHH!

WHAT'LL I DO?!

TSUKAMOTO-SAN...

TREMBLE
TREMBLE

IT'S JUST A BATHROOM! THAT'S ALL!!

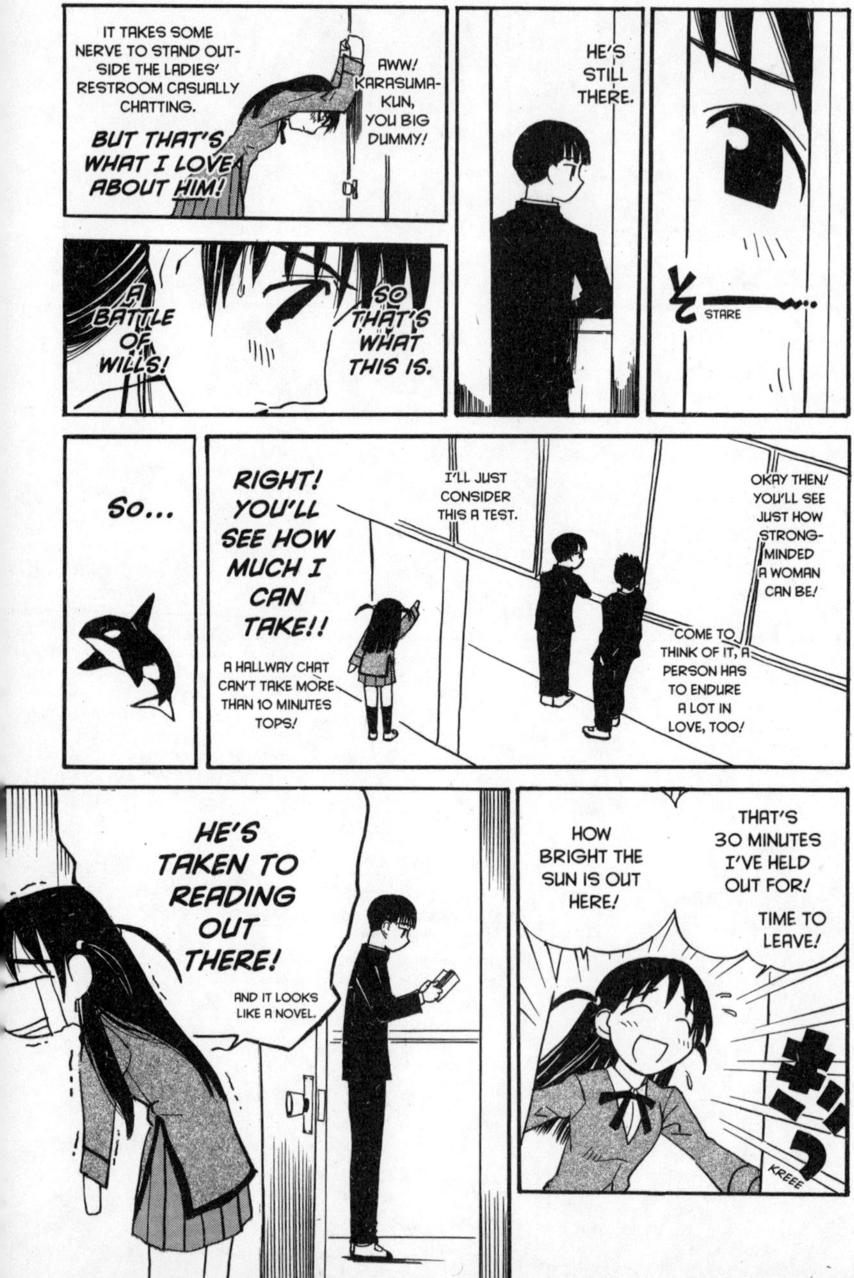
STARE
HE'S STILL THERE.
AWW! KARASUMA-KUN, YOU BIG DUMMY!
IT TAKES SOME NERVE TO STAND OUT-SIDE THE LADIES' RESTROOM CASUALLY CHATTING.
BUT THAT'S WHAT I LOVE ABOUT HIM!
SO THAT'S WHAT THIS IS.
A BATTLE OF WILLS!
OKAY THEN! YOU'LL SEE JUST HOW STRONG-MINDED A WOMAN CAN BE!
COME TO THINK OF IT, A PERSON HAS TO ENDURE A LOT IN LOVE, TOO!
I'LL JUST CONSIDER THIS A TEST.
RIGHT! YOU'LL SEE HOW MUCH I CAN TAKE!!
A HALLWAY CHAT CAN'T TAKE MORE THAN 10 MINUTES TOPS!
So...
THAT'S 30 MINUTES I'VE HELD OUT FOR!
TIME TO LEAVE!
HOW BRIGHT THE SUN IS OUT HERE!
KREEE
HE'S TAKEN TO READING OUT THERE!
AND IT LOOKS LIKE A NOVEL.

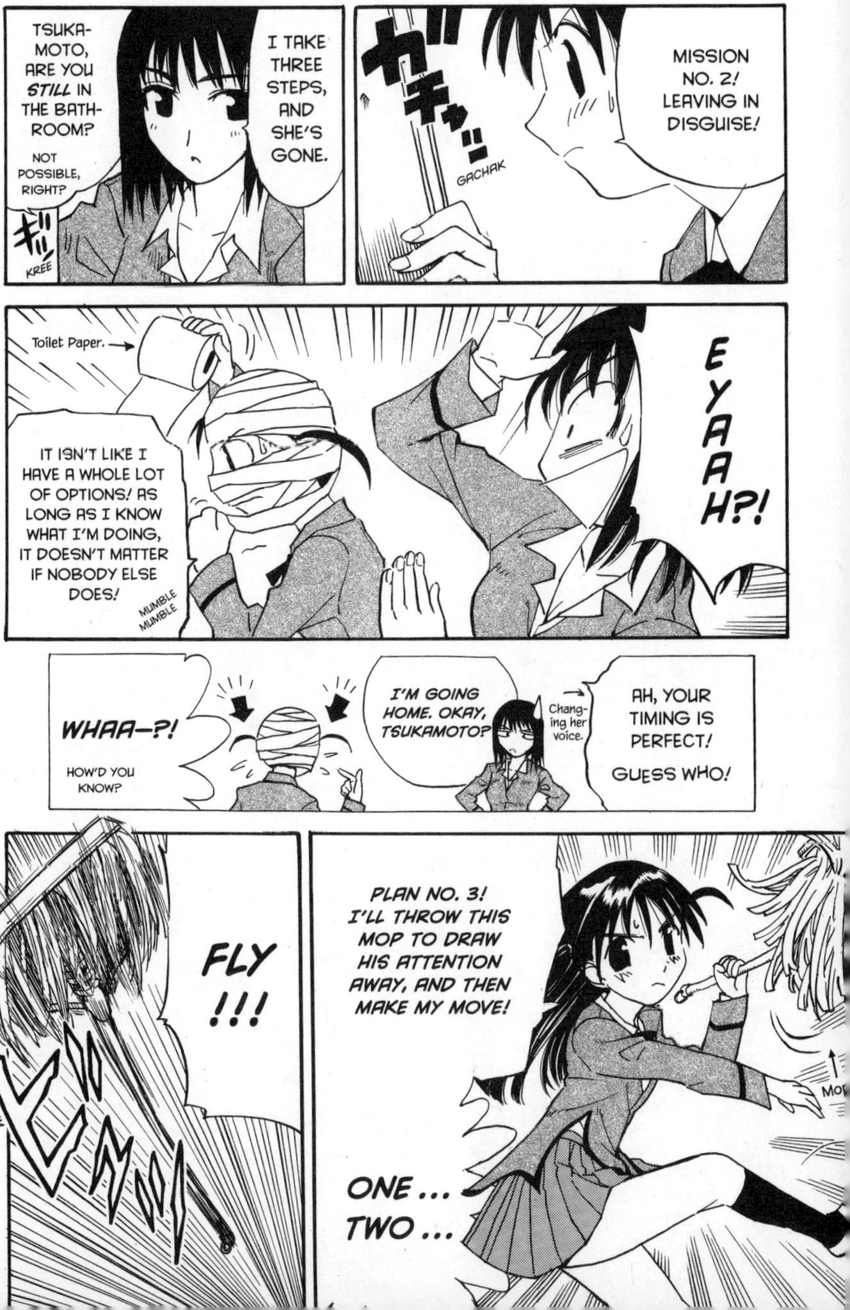
GACHAK
MISSION NO. 2! LEAVING IN DISGUISE!
I TAKE THREE STEPS, AND SHE'S GONE.
TSUKAMOTO, ARE YOU STILL IN THE BATHROOM?
NOT POSSIBLE, RIGHT?
KREE
EYAAAH?!
Toilet Paper.
IT ISN'T LIKE I HAVE A WHOLE LOT OF OPTIONS! AS LONG AS I KNOW WHAT I'M DOING, IT DOESN'T MATTER IF NOBODY ELSE DOES!
MUMBLE MUMBLE
AH, YOUR TIMING IS PERFECT!
GUESS WHO!
Changing her voice.
I'M GOING HOME. OKAY, TSUKAMOTO?
WHAA-?!
HOW'D YOU KNOW?
PLAN NO. 3! I'LL THROW THIS MOP TO DRAW HIS ATTENTION AWAY, AND THEN MAKE MY MOVE!
ONE ... TWO ...
FLY !!!
VYUUUM

Tsukamoto Tenma: *No Self-Control.*

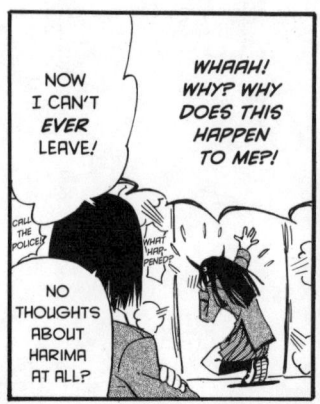

NOW I CAN'T *EVER* LEAVE!

WHAAH! WHY? WHY DOES THIS HAPPEN TO ME?!

CALL THE POLICE?

WHAT HAPPENED?

NO THOUGHTS ABOUT HARIMA AT ALL?

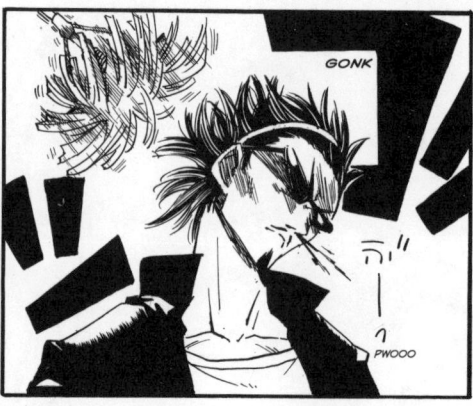

GONK

PWOOO

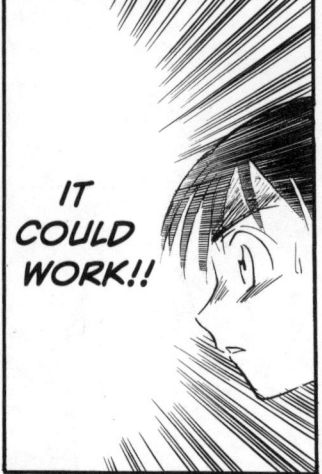

IT COULD WORK!!

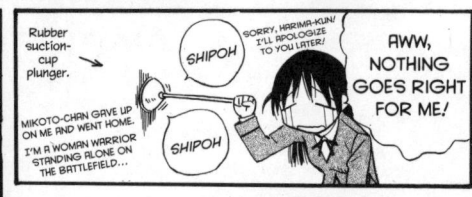

Rubber suction-cup plunger.

SHIPOH

SORRY, HARIMA-KUN! I'LL APOLOGIZE TO YOU LATER!

AWW, NOTHING GOES RIGHT FOR ME!

MIKOTO-CHAN GAVE UP ON ME AND WENT HOME. I'M A WOMAN WARRIOR STANDING ALONE ON THE BATTLEFIELD...

SHIPOH

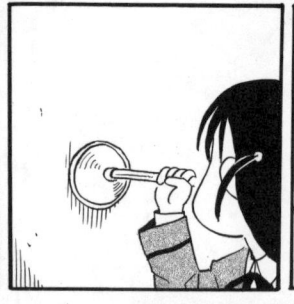

GRNN GRNN

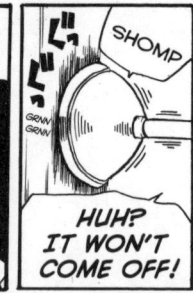

SHOMP

HUH? IT WON'T COME OFF!

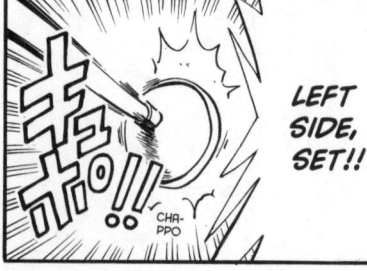

LEFT SIDE, SET!!

CHA-PPO

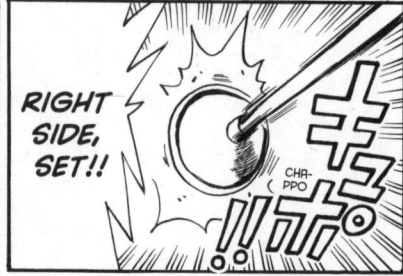

RIGHT SIDE, SET!!

CHA-PPO

HYUUUUUUUU
S-SLOW SPEED DESCENT!
THERE'S NO TURNING BACK NOW!

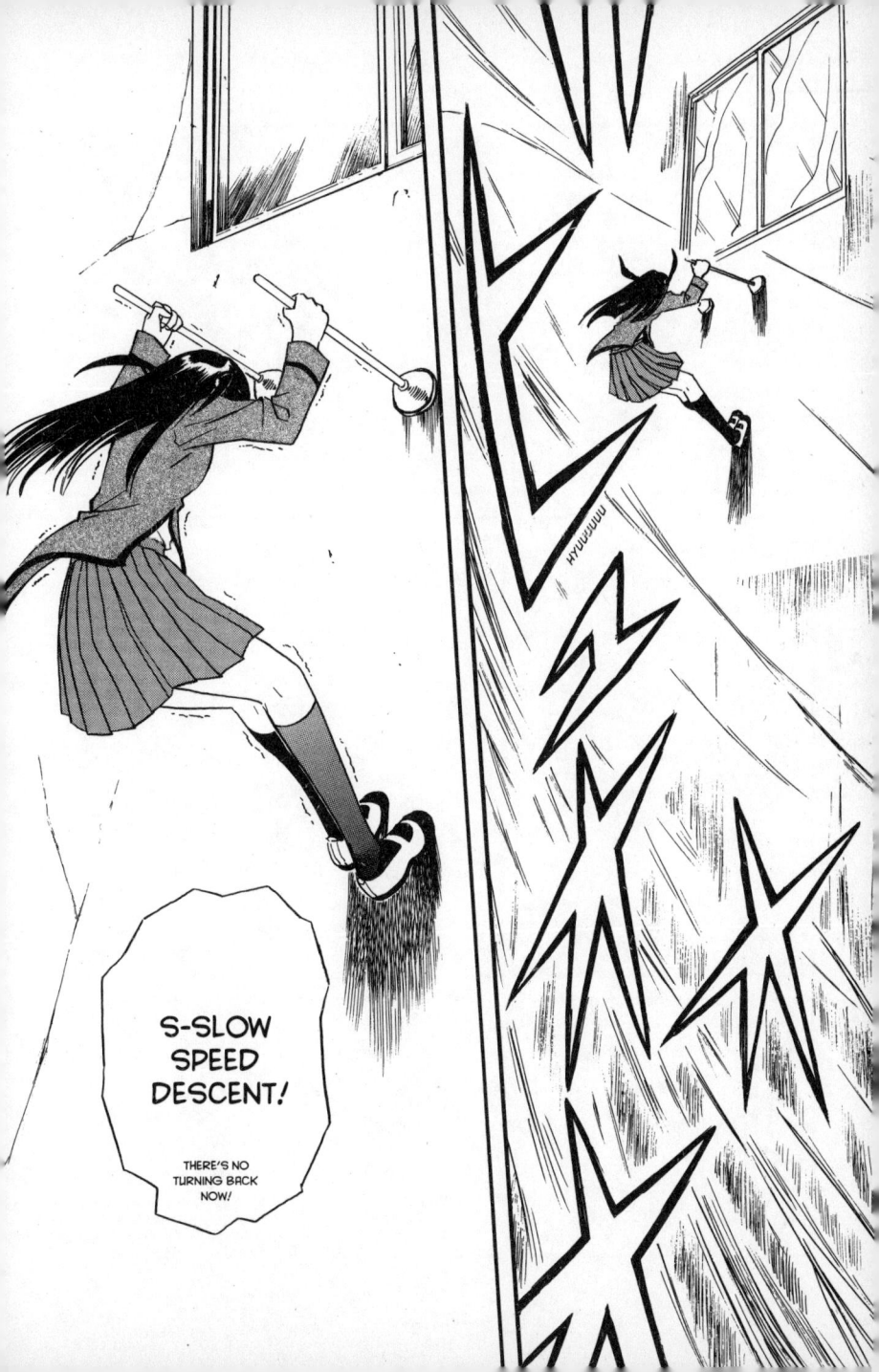

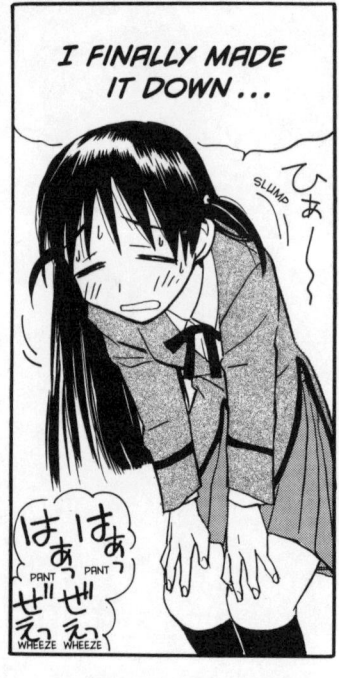

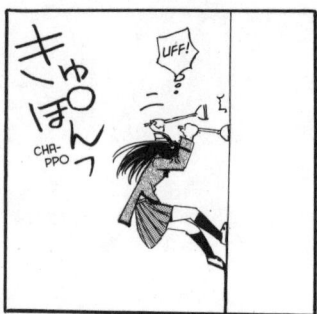

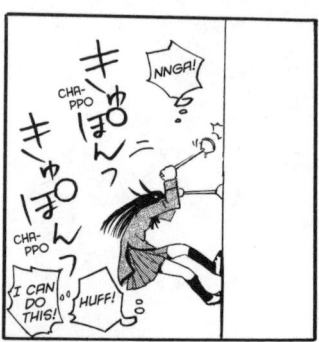

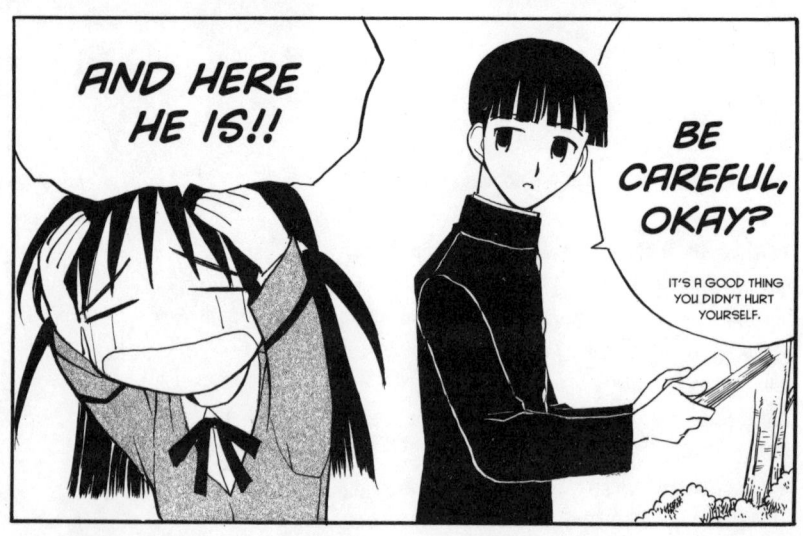

08 . . . . Fin.

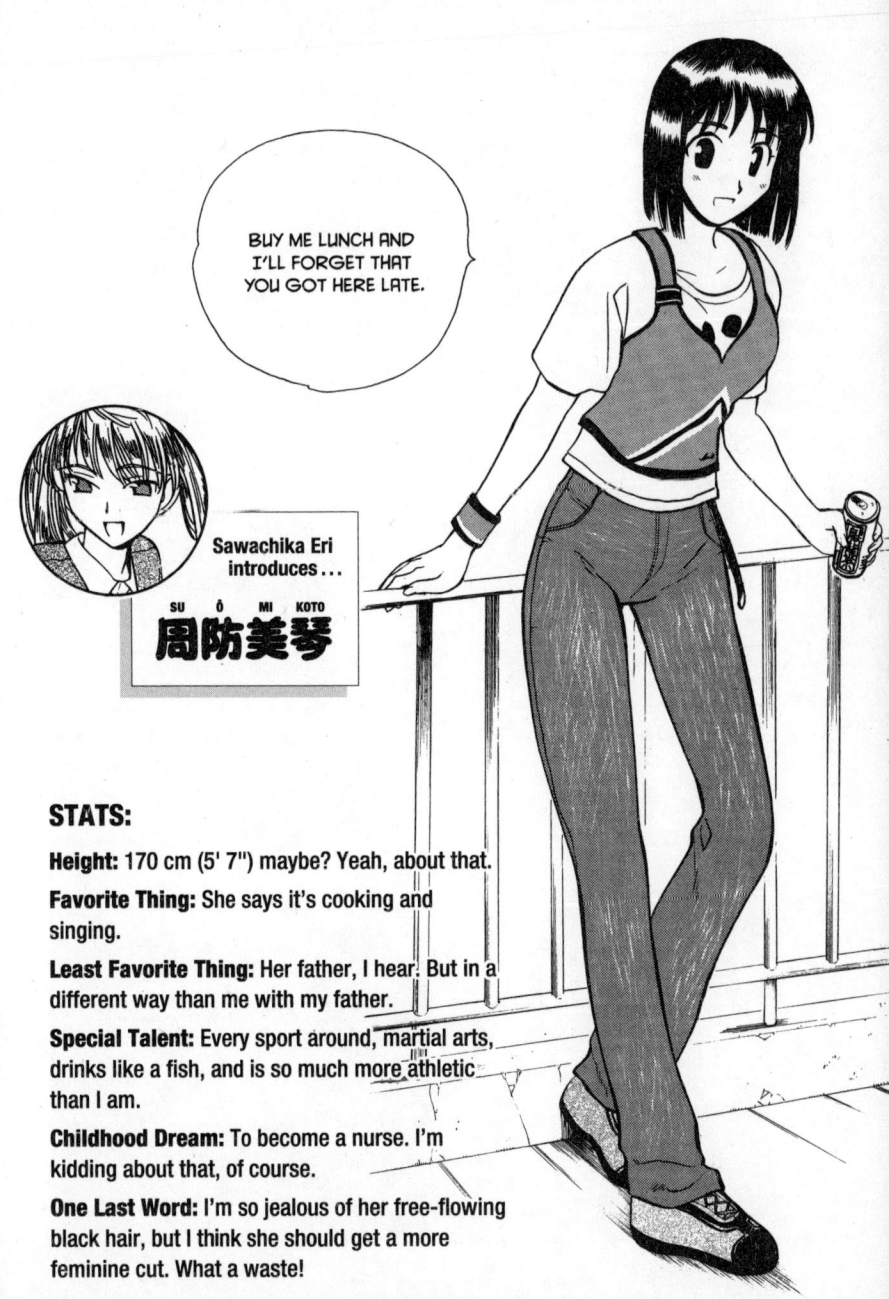

BUY ME LUNCH AND I'LL FORGET THAT YOU GOT HERE LATE.

Sawachika Eri
introduces . . .

SU Ô MI KOTO
周防美琴

STATS:

Height: 170 cm (5' 7") maybe? Yeah, about that.

Favorite Thing: She says it's cooking and singing.

Least Favorite Thing: Her father, I hear. But in a different way than me with my father.

Special Talent: Every sport around, martial arts, drinks like a fish, and is so much more athletic than I am.

Childhood Dream: To become a nurse. I'm kidding about that, of course.

One Last Word: I'm so jealous of her free-flowing black hair, but I think she should get a more feminine cut. What a waste!

#09　THE GIRL WHO KNEW LITTLE

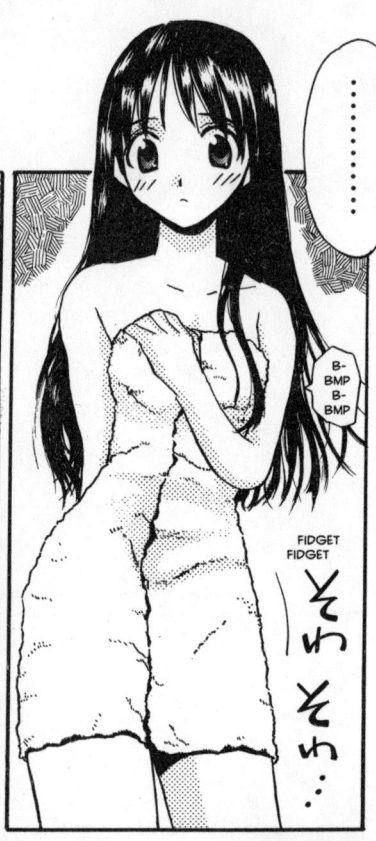

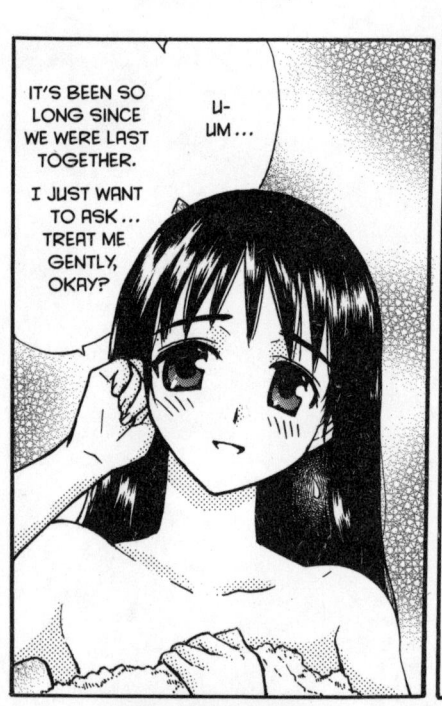

IT'S BEEN SO LONG SINCE WE WERE LAST TOGETHER.

I JUST WANT TO ASK... TREAT ME GENTLY, OKAY?

U-UM...

B-BMP B-BMP

FIDGET FIDGET

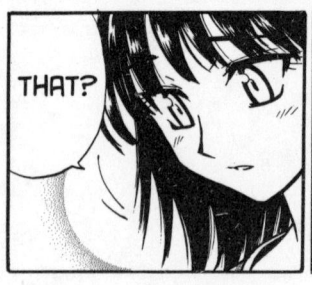

THAT?

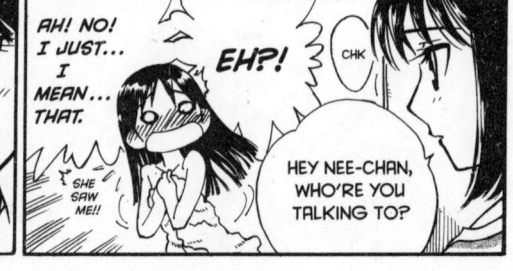

AH! NO! I JUST... I MEAN... THAT.

EH?!

CHK

SHE SAW ME!!

HEY NEE-CHAN, WHO'RE YOU TALKING TO?

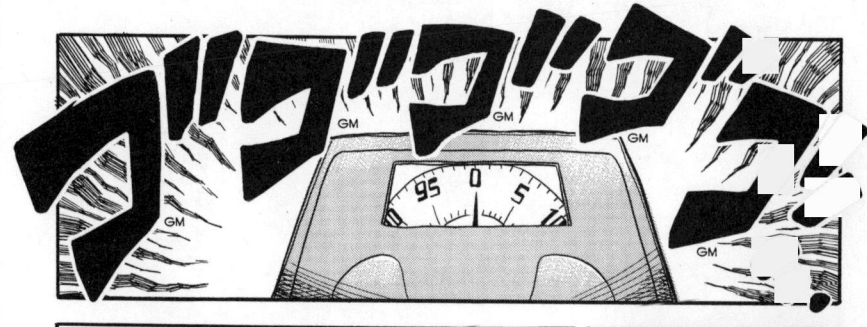

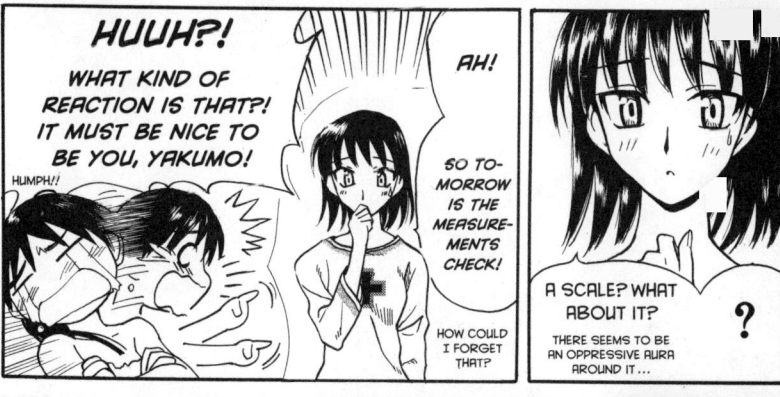

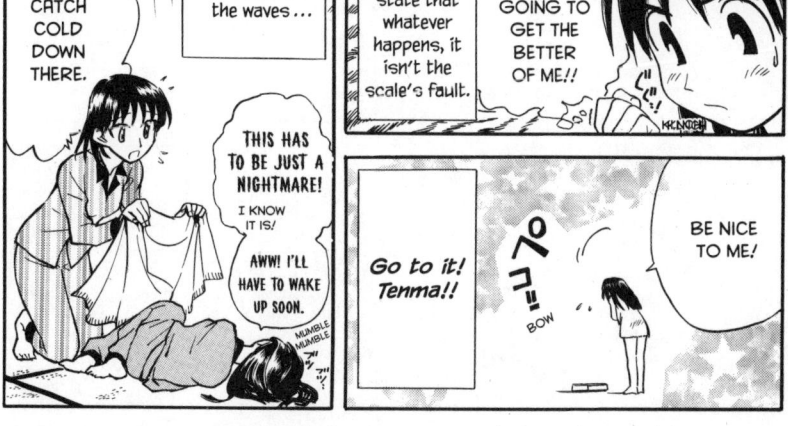

Her Younger Sister's Name: *Tsukamoto Yakumo.*

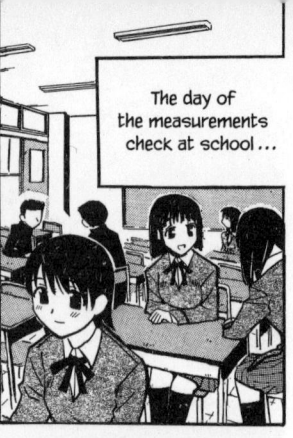

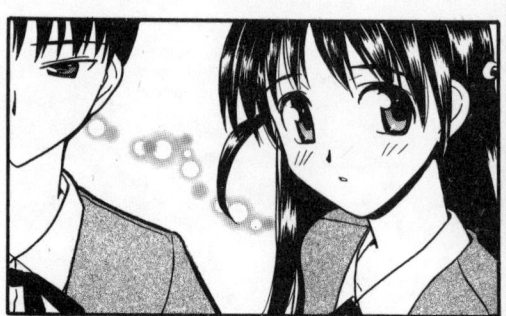

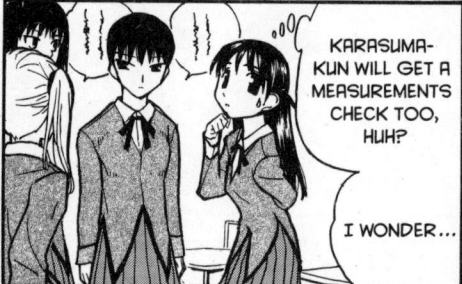

KARASUMA-KUN WILL GET A MEASUREMENTS CHECK TOO, HUH?

I WONDER...

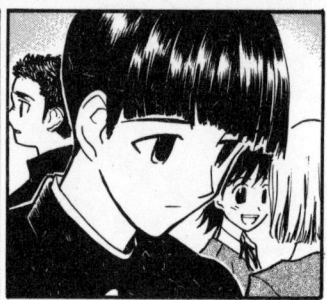

I WANNA KNOW! I WANNA KNOW! IT'S LIKE I'M THE ONLY ONE IN THE WORLD WHO DOESN'T KNOW KARASUMA-KUN'S DATA!

GYAAH!!

WHFF WHFF

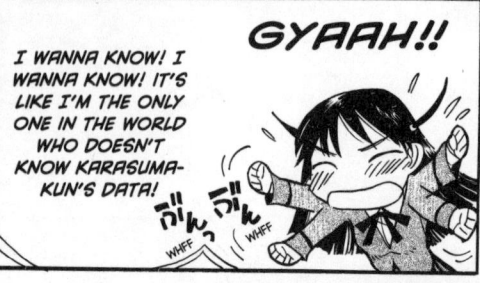

WHAT'S HIS HEIGHT? A HUNDRED SEVENTY... ONE? TWO? (5' 7" OR 5' 8")

HIS WEIGHT SEEMS LIKE IT'D BE PRETTY LIGHT... HE GIVES A LIMBER KIND OF IMPRESSION.

BUT I CAN NEVER REALLY GUESS AT A GUY'S WEIGHT.

HMM...

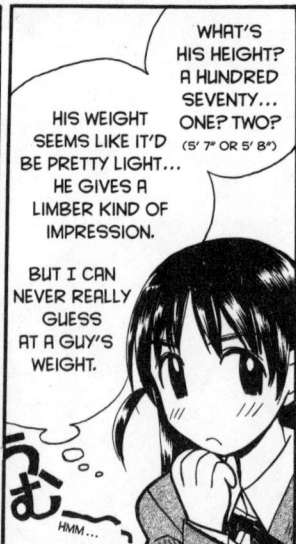

HEY! ABOUT TODAY...

POP

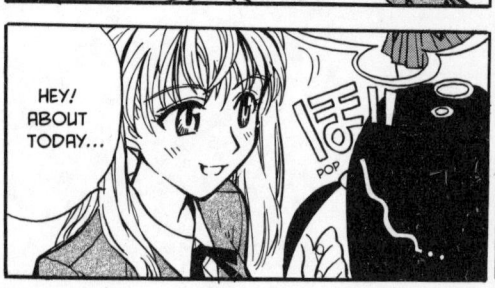

Tsukamoto Tenma: *Skipped Breakfast.*

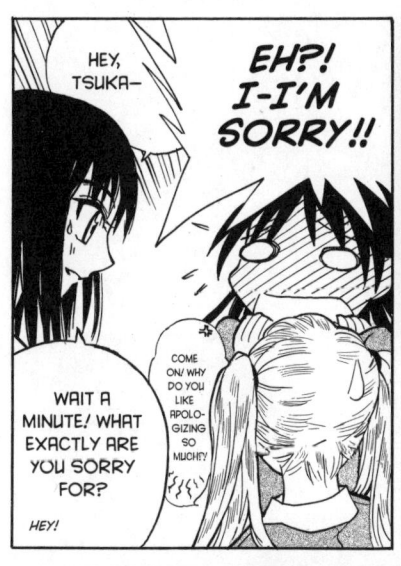

HEY, TSUKA—

EH?! I-I'M SORRY!!

WAIT A MINUTE! WHAT EXACTLY ARE YOU SORRY FOR?

HEY!

COME ON! WHY DO YOU LIKE APOLOGIZING SO MUCH?!

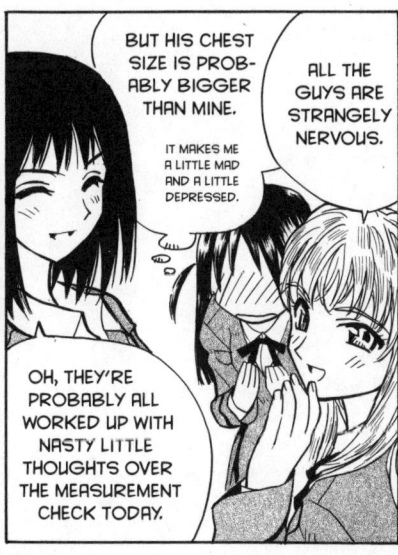

BUT HIS CHEST SIZE IS PROBABLY BIGGER THAN MINE.

IT MAKES ME A LITTLE MAD AND A LITTLE DEPRESSED.

ALL THE GUYS ARE STRANGELY NERVOUS.

OH, THEY'RE PROBABLY ALL WORKED UP WITH NASTY LITTLE THOUGHTS OVER THE MEASUREMENT CHECK TODAY.

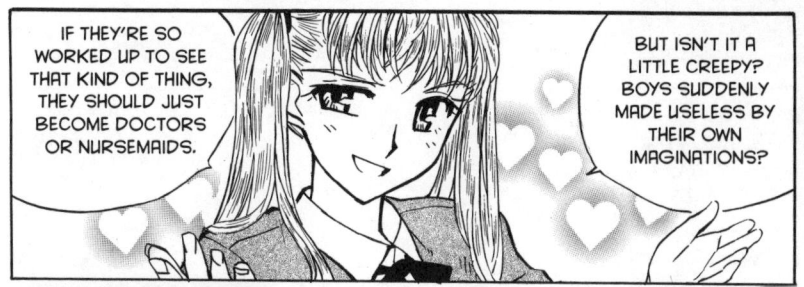

IF THEY'RE SO WORKED UP TO SEE THAT KIND OF THING, THEY SHOULD JUST BECOME DOCTORS OR NURSEMAIDS.

BUT ISN'T IT A LITTLE CREEPY? BOYS SUDDENLY MADE USELESS BY THEIR OWN IMAGINATIONS?

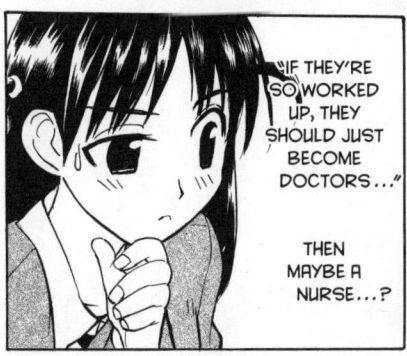

"IF THEY'RE SO WORKED UP, THEY SHOULD JUST BECOME DOCTORS..."

THEN MAYBE A NURSE...?

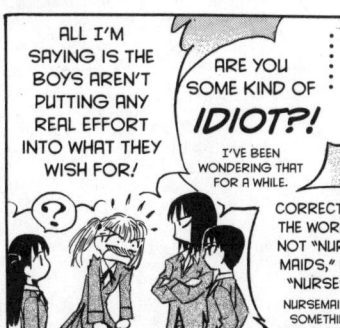

ALL I'M SAYING IS THE BOYS AREN'T PUTTING ANY REAL EFFORT INTO WHAT THEY WISH FOR!

ARE YOU SOME KIND OF IDIOT?!

I'VE BEEN WONDERING THAT FOR A WHILE.

CORRECTION. THE WORD IS NOT "NURSE-MAIDS," BUT "NURSES."

NURSEMAID IS SOMETHING ELSE ENTIRELY.

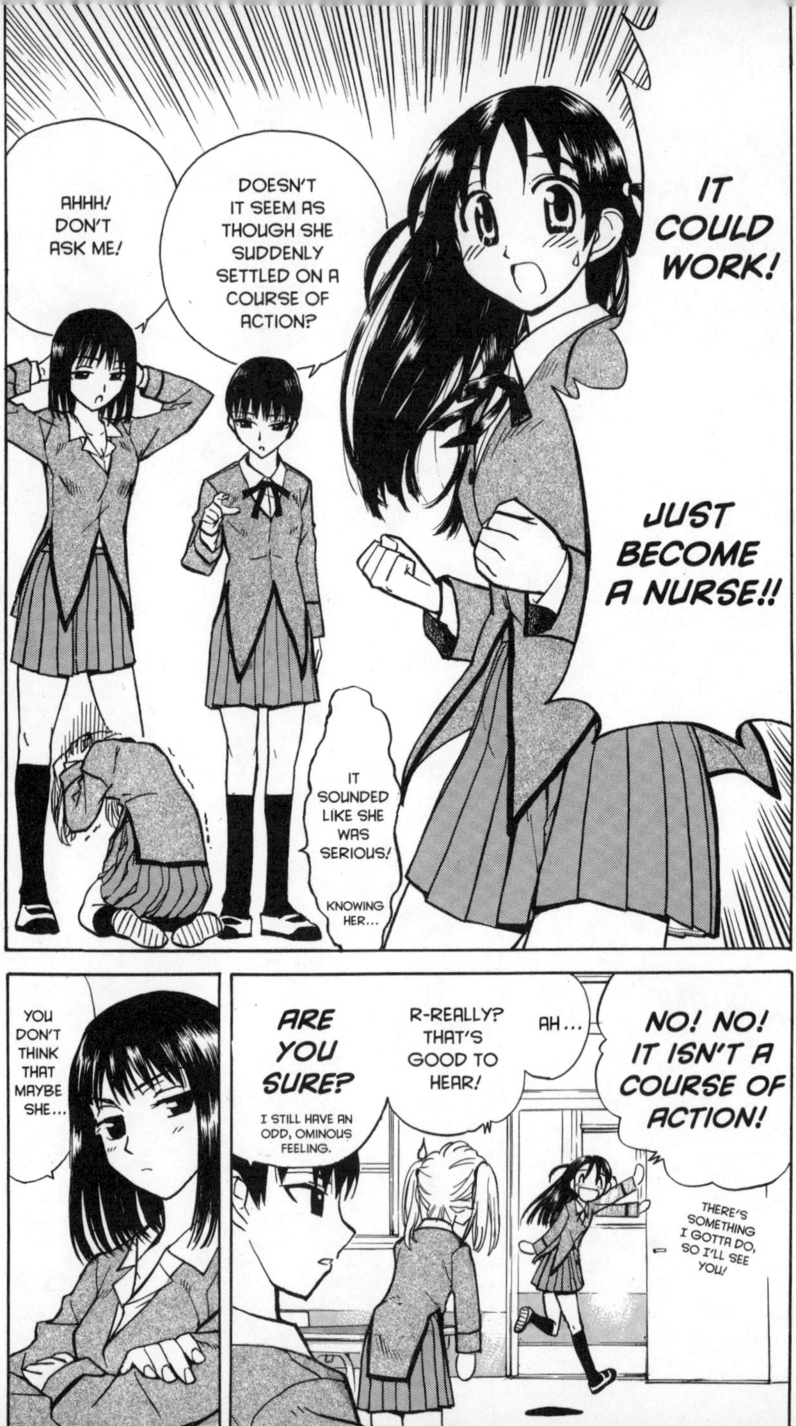

AHHH! DON'T ASK ME!

DOESN'T IT SEEM AS THOUGH SHE SUDDENLY SETTLED ON A COURSE OF ACTION?

IT COULD WORK!

JUST BECOME A NURSE!!

Tsukamoto Tenma: *Completely Illogical.*

IT SOUNDED LIKE SHE WAS SERIOUS!

KNOWING HER...

YOU DON'T THINK THAT MAYBE SHE...

ARE YOU SURE?

I STILL HAVE AN ODD, OMINOUS FEELING.

R-REALLY? THAT'S GOOD TO HEAR!

AH...

NO! NO! IT ISN'T A COURSE OF ACTION!

THERE'S SOMETHING I GOTTA DO, SO I'LL SEE YOU!

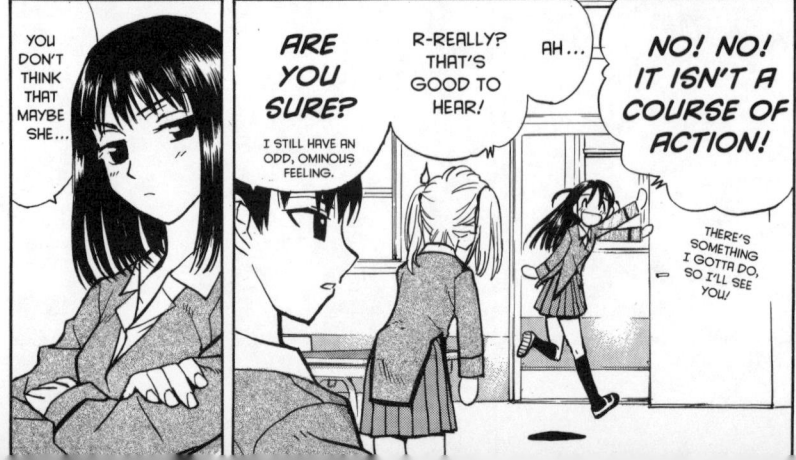

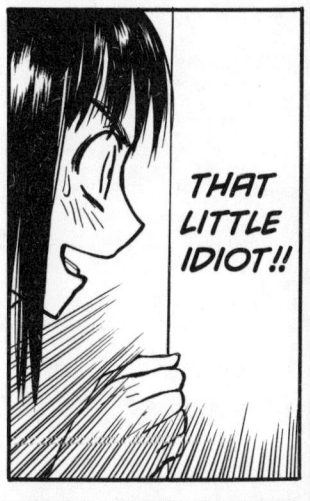

THAT LITTLE IDIOT!!

GREAT!

A COMPLETE TRANSFORMATION!!

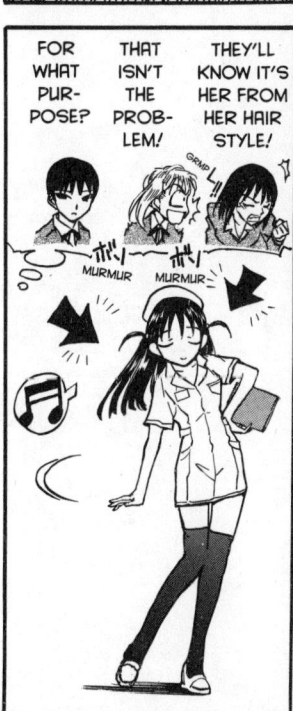

FOR WHAT PURPOSE?

THAT ISN'T THE PROBLEM!

THEY'LL KNOW IT'S HER FROM HER HAIR STYLE!

MURMUR

MURMUR

DOOOM

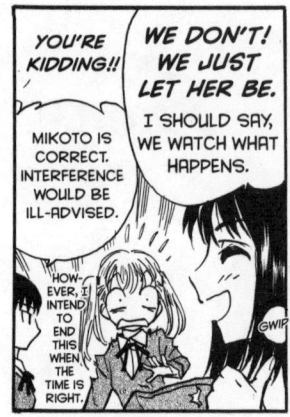

YOU'RE KIDDING!!

WE DON'T! WE JUST LET HER BE.

I SHOULD SAY, WE WATCH WHAT HAPPENS.

MIKOTO IS CORRECT. INTERFERENCE WOULD BE ILL-ADVISED.

HOW-EVER, I INTEND TO END THIS WHEN THE TIME IS RIGHT.

GWIP

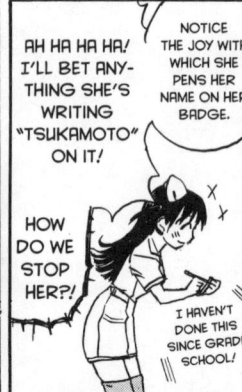

AH HA HA HA! I'LL BET ANY-THING SHE'S WRITING "TSUKAMOTO" ON IT!

HOW DO WE STOP HER?!

NOTICE THE JOY WITH WHICH SHE PENS HER NAME ON HER BADGE.

I HAVEN'T DONE THIS SINCE GRADE SCHOOL!

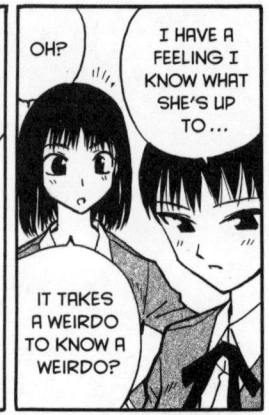

OH?

I HAVE A FEELING I KNOW WHAT SHE'S UP TO...

IT TAKES A WEIRDO TO KNOW A WEIRDO?

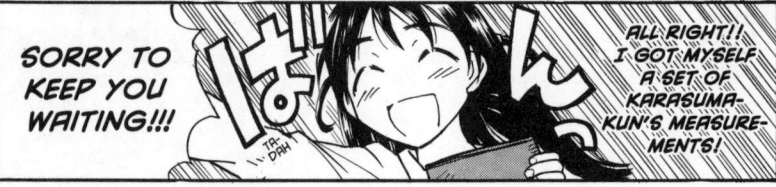

SORRY TO KEEP YOU WAITING!!!

TA-DAH

ALL RIGHT!! I GOT MYSELF A SET OF KARASUMA-KUN'S MEASURE-MENTS!

I'M A SUDDEN TRANSFER. DR. HARIMA. PLEASED TO MEET YOU.

THE SAME GOES FOR ME. SORRY FOR MY LATE ARRIVAL.

IT IS SO NICE TO BE WORKING WITH YOU, DOCTOR!

And not too long afterward, the measurement checks for the day were canceled.

For some reason or other...

#09..........Fin.

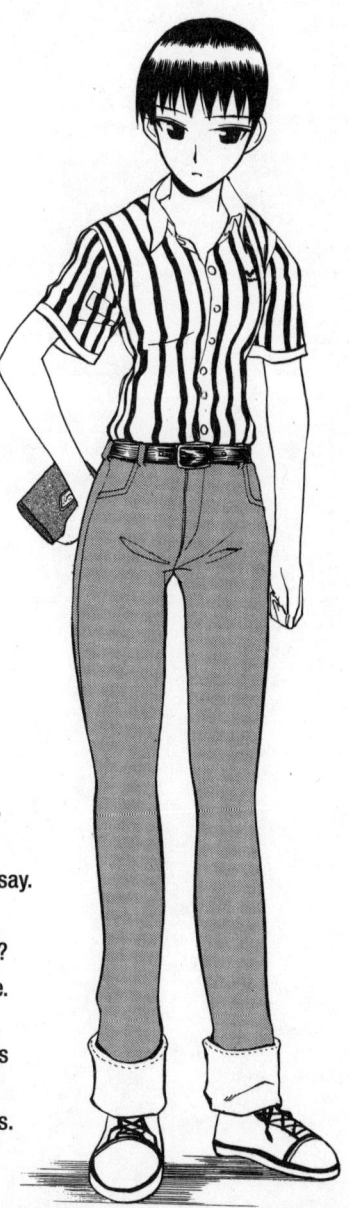

> BE CALM. NOTHING IS IMPOSSIBLE FOR YOU.

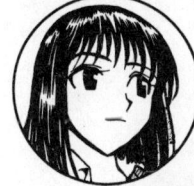

Suô Mikoto
introduces . . .

TAKA   NO   AKIRA
高野　晶

STATS:

Height: 166 cm (5' 5") or thereabouts, I think.

Favorite Thing: Economizing

Least Favorite Thing: Falling into debt, they say.

Favorite Word: Persevere . . . I think.

Hobby: Gunpura . . . what in the world is that?

Special Talent: The koto and Japanese dance. You know that's gotta be a joke, right?

Notes: I don't know the reason for it, but she's loaded down with part-time jobs.

One Last Word: The girl's getting good grades. She's got a lot of stuff going on that we don't have a clue about.

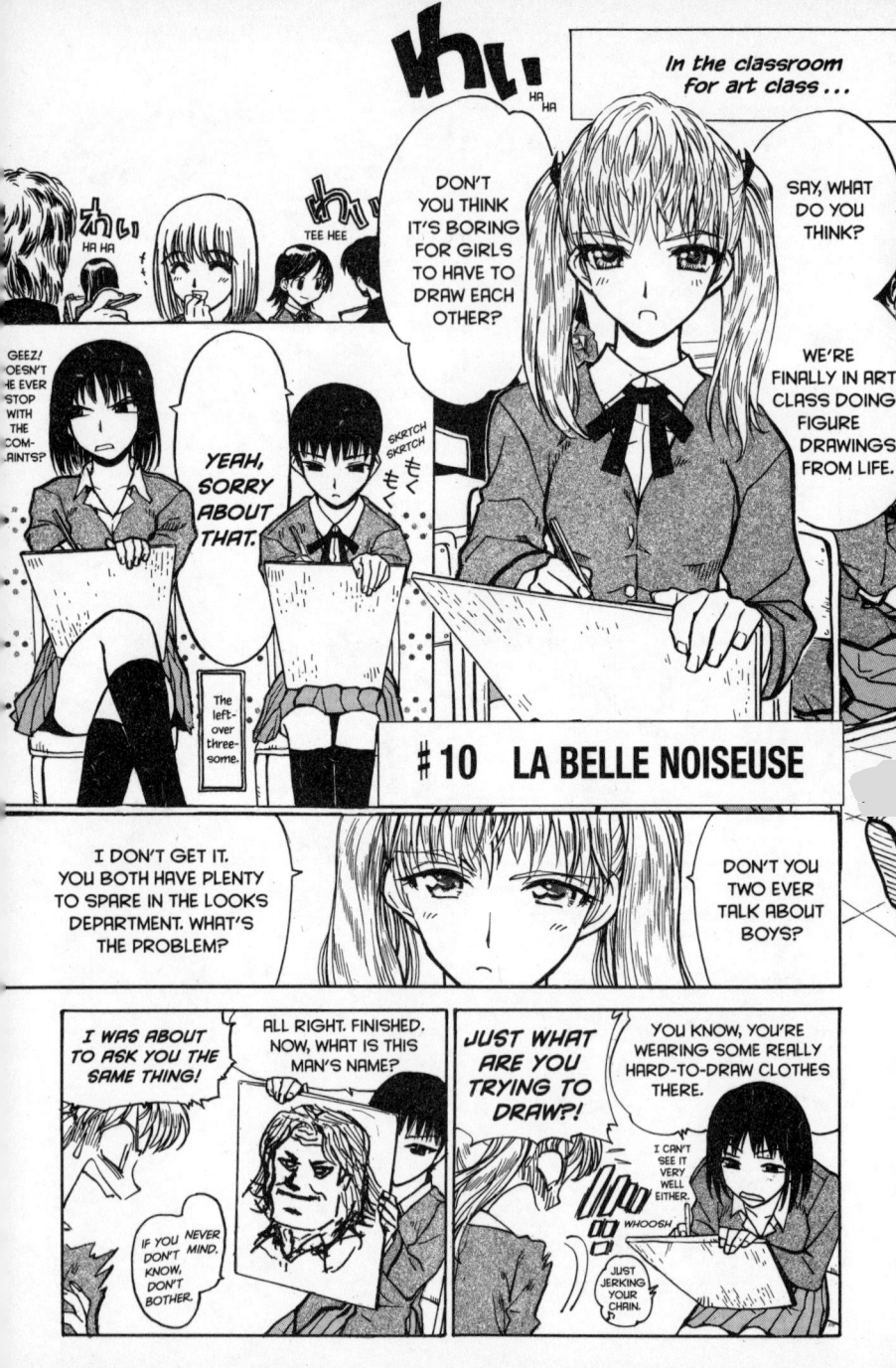

In the classroom for art class...

SAY, WHAT DO YOU THINK?

DON'T YOU THINK IT'S BORING FOR GIRLS TO HAVE TO DRAW EACH OTHER?

WE'RE FINALLY IN ART CLASS DOING FIGURE DRAWINGS FROM LIFE.

HA HA

TEE HEE

HA HA

GEEZ! DOESN'T HE EVER STOP WITH THE COMPLAINTS?

YEAH, SORRY ABOUT THAT.

SKRTCH SKRTCH

The left-over three-some.

#10   LA BELLE NOISEUSE

I DON'T GET IT. YOU BOTH HAVE PLENTY TO SPARE IN THE LOOKS DEPARTMENT. WHAT'S THE PROBLEM?

DON'T YOU TWO EVER TALK ABOUT BOYS?

I WAS ABOUT TO ASK YOU THE SAME THING!

ALL RIGHT. FINISHED. NOW, WHAT IS THIS MAN'S NAME?

IF YOU DON'T KNOW, DON'T BOTHER.

NEVER MIND.

JUST WHAT ARE YOU TRYING TO DRAW?!

YOU KNOW, YOU'RE WEARING SOME REALLY HARD-TO-DRAW CLOTHES THERE.

I CAN'T SEE IT VERY WELL EITHER.

WHOOSH

JUST JERKING YOUR CHAIN.

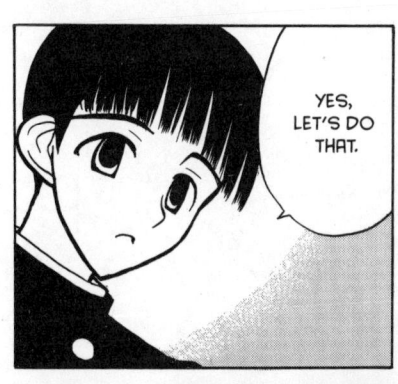

YES, LET'S DO THAT.

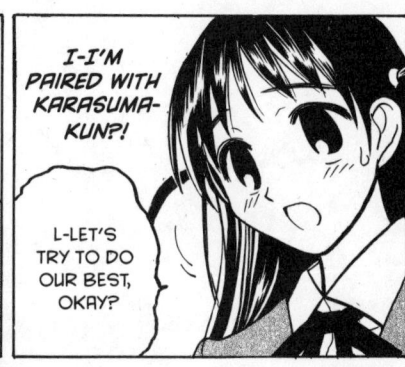

I-I'M PAIRED WITH KARASUMA-KUN?!

L-LET'S TRY TO DO OUR BEST, OKAY?

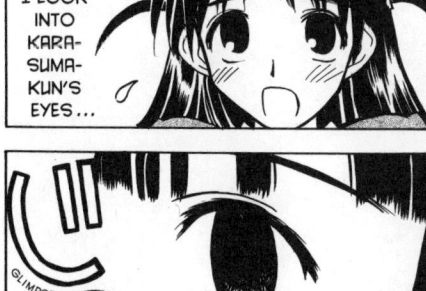

WHEN I LOOK INTO KARASUMA-KUN'S EYES...

GLIMPSE

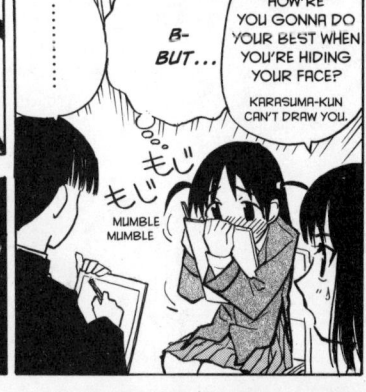

B-BUT...

HOW'RE YOU GONNA DO YOUR BEST WHEN YOU'RE HIDING YOUR FACE? KARASUMA-KUN CAN'T DRAW YOU.

モジモジ

MUMBLE MUMBLE

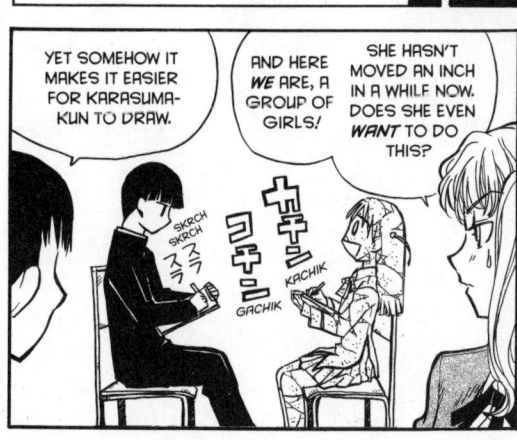

YET SOMEHOW IT MAKES IT EASIER FOR KARASUMA-KUN TO DRAW.

AND HERE *WE* ARE, A GROUP OF GIRLS!

SHE HASN'T MOVED AN INCH IN A WHILE NOW. DOES SHE EVEN *WANT* TO DO THIS?

SKRCH SKRCH

コキン

GACHIK

KACHIK

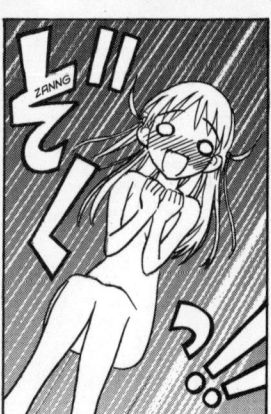

ZANG

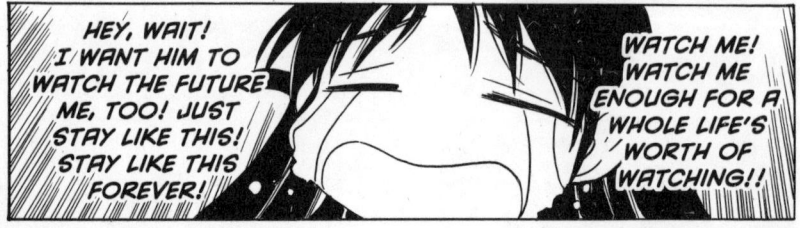

KARASUMA-KUN IS LOOKING AT ME KARASUMA-KUN IS LOOKING AT ME KARASUMA-KUN IS LOOKING AT ME KARASUMA-KUN IS LOOKING AT ME KARASUMA-KUN IS LOOKING AT ME KARASUMA-KUN IS LOOKING AT ME KARASUMA-KUN IS LOOKING AT ME KARASUMA-KUN IS LOOKING AT ME KARASUMA-KUN IS LOOKING AT ME KARASUMA-KUN IS LOOKING AT ME KARASUMA-KUN IS LOOKING AT ME KARASUMA-KUN IS LOOKING AT ME KARASUMA-KUN IS LOOKING AT ME KARASUMA-KUN IS LOOKING AT ME KARASUMA-KUN IS LOOKING AT ME KARASUMA-KUN IS LOOKING AT ME KARASUMA-KUN IS LOOKING AT ME KARASUMA-KUN

HEY, WAIT! I WANT HIM TO WATCH THE FUTURE ME, TOO! JUST STAY LIKE THIS! STAY LIKE THIS FOREVER!

WATCH ME! WATCH ME ENOUGH FOR A WHOLE LIFE'S WORTH OF WATCHING!!

Tsukamoto Tenma: *In Bliss.*

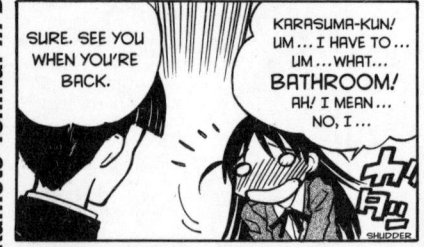

SURE. SEE YOU WHEN YOU'RE BACK.

KARASUMA-KUN! UM... I HAVE TO... UM... WHAT... BATHROOM! AH! I MEAN... NO, I...

SHUDDER

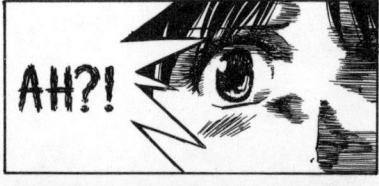

AH?!

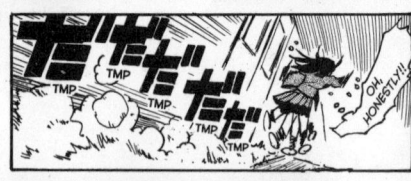

TMP TMP TMP TMP TMP

OH, HONESTLY!!

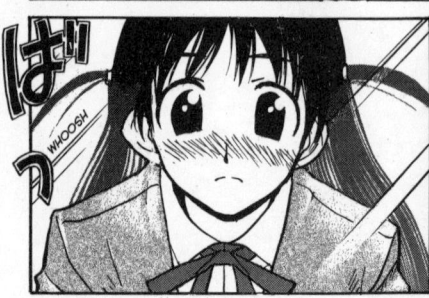

WHOOSH

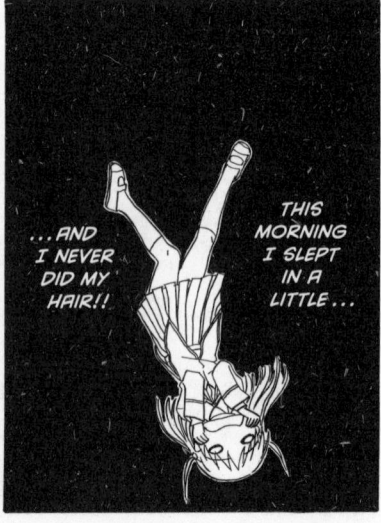

...AND I NEVER DID MY HAIR!!

THIS MORNING I SLEPT IN A LITTLE...

Tsukamoto Tenma: A Victim of Static Electricity.

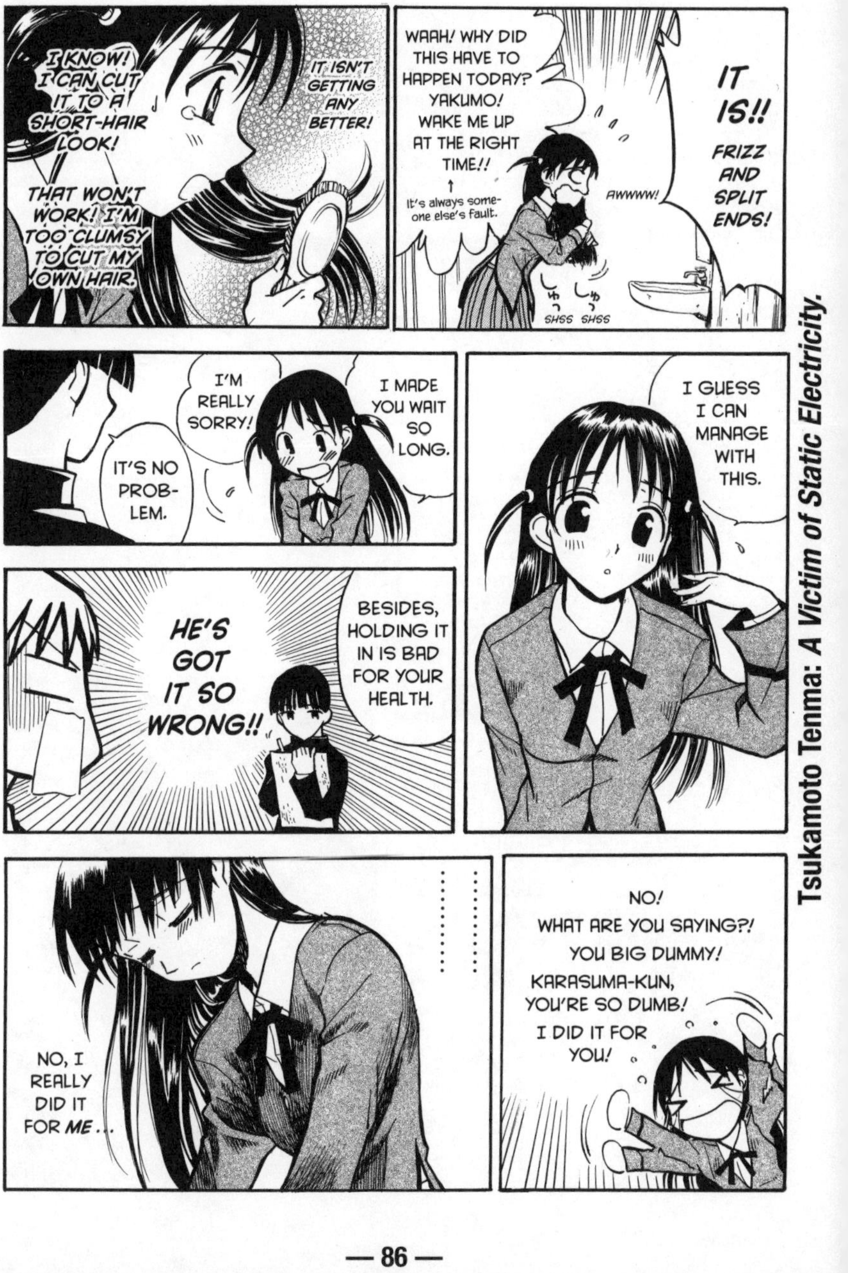
IT IS!!
FRIZZ AND SPLIT ENDS!
WAAH! WHY DID THIS HAVE TO HAPPEN TODAY? YAKUMO! WAKE ME UP AT THE RIGHT TIME!!
It's always someone else's fault.
AWWWW!
SHSS SHSS
IT ISN'T GETTING ANY BETTER!
I KNOW! I CAN CUT IT TO A SHORT-HAIR LOOK!
THAT WON'T WORK! I'M TOO CLUMSY TO CUT MY OWN HAIR.
I GUESS I CAN MANAGE WITH THIS.
I MADE YOU WAIT SO LONG.
I'M REALLY SORRY!
IT'S NO PROBLEM.
BESIDES, HOLDING IT IN IS BAD FOR YOUR HEALTH.
HE'S GOT IT SO WRONG!!
NO!
WHAT ARE YOU SAYING?!
YOU BIG DUMMY!
KARASUMA-KUN, YOU'RE SO DUMB!
I DID IT FOR YOU!
......
......
NO, I REALLY DID IT FOR *ME*...

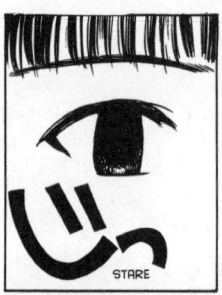

I'D BETTER STOP THINKING LIKE THIS.
I'LL JUST DO A NORMAL DRAWING.
ちらっ
GLIMPSE
じっ
STARE
W-WHAT'LL I DO?
IF I WANT TO PLACE KARASUMA-KUN'S IMAGE ON PAPER, OUR GAZES MUST NATURALLY MEET AND INTERTWINE.
Gross overstatement.
I'M SO NERVOUS, I HAVEN'T BEEN ABLE TO LOOK AT HIM.
Y-YES, THAT'S IT.
しゃっ
SHFF
しゃっ
SHFF
HMMM
むー
IF I DRAW HIM WITH MY EYES SLIGHTLY OUT OF FOCUS ...
THERE! ♥ I DID IT!

Tsukamoto Tenma: *Dimwit.*

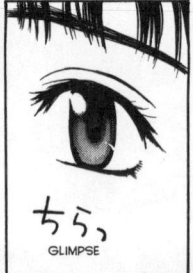

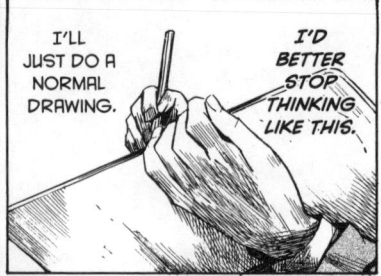

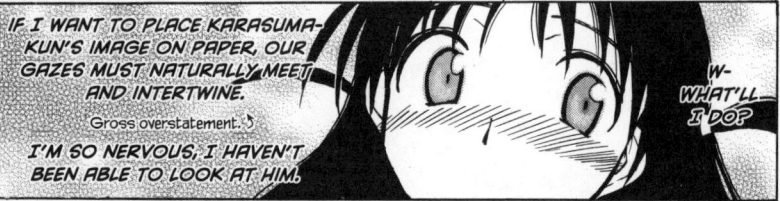

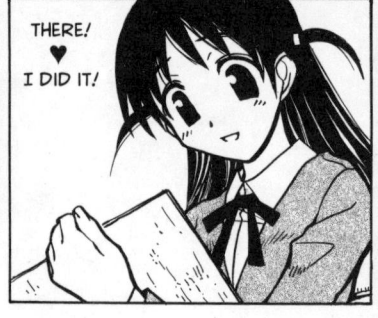

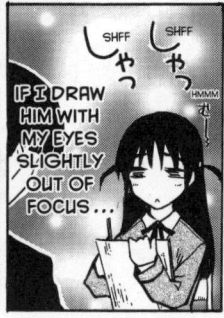

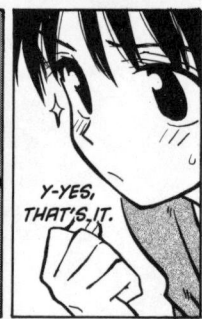

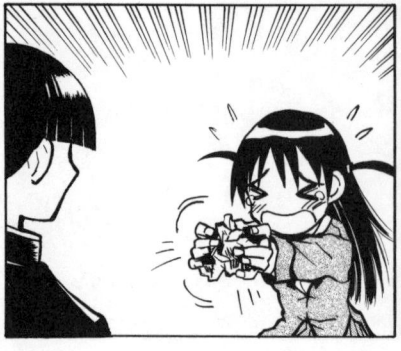

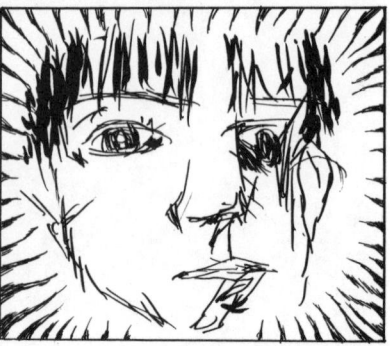

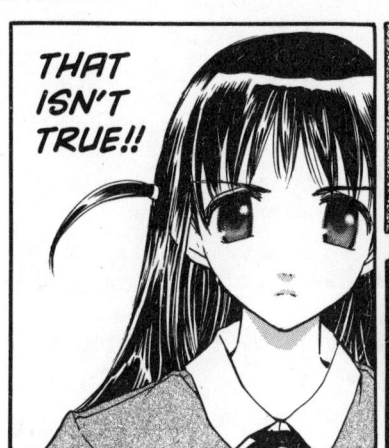

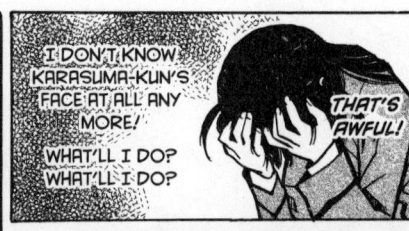

I DON'T KNOW KARASUMA-KUN'S FACE AT ALL ANY MORE!
WHAT'LL I DO? WHAT'LL I DO?
THAT'S AWFUL!
WAIT JUST ONE SECOND! AM I REALLY SAYING THAT I DON'T KNOW KARASUMA-KUN'S FACE?
"DON'T KNOW"?
THAT ISN'T TRUE!!
I KNOW IT!
HIS IMAGE BURNED INTO MY RETINAS!
I CAN JUST CLOSE MY EYES, AND...
I WILL NEVER...
...LOSE SIGHT OF HIM!!
ZZT
GLANCE
LOOK AT TSUKA-MOTO-SAN. SHE'S ON TOP OF THE WORLD!
AT LEAST DRAW LIKE A NORMAL PERSON, OKAY?
SNAPP

Tsukamoto Tenma: *Mind's Eye.*

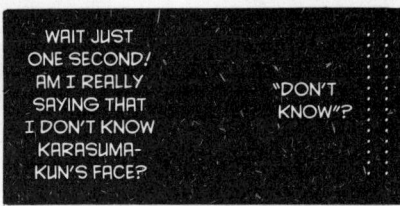

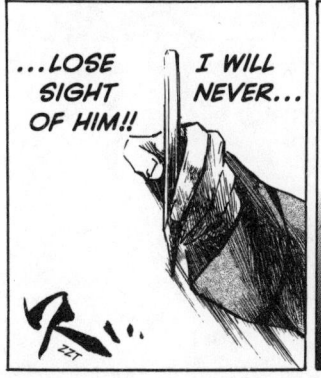

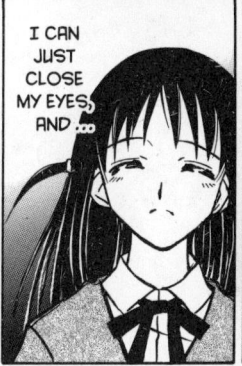

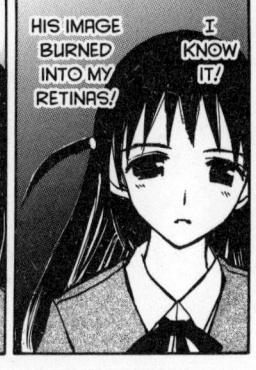

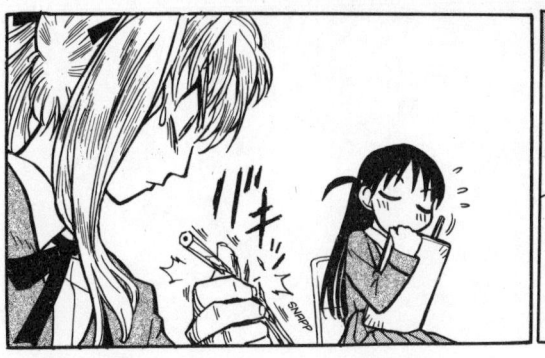

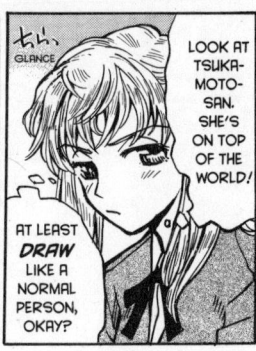

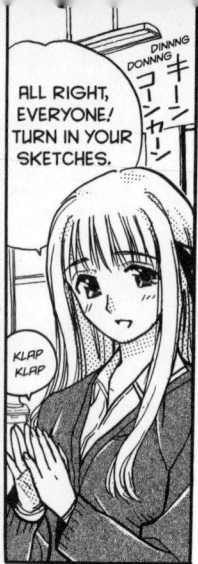

DINNNG DONNNG
キーンコーンカーン
ALL RIGHT, EVERYONE! TURN IN YOUR SKETCHES.
KLAP KLAP
HEY, THAT'S A SURPRISE! YOU'RE NOT A BAD ARTIST, TSUKAMOTO. YOU BEEN PRACTICING?
NOPE! IT'S JUST THAT EVERY SO OFTEN I COME UP WITH A GOOD PICTURE.
WHAT'S THAT SUPPOSED TO MEAN?
SHE WAS DRAWING WITH HER EYES CLOSED! WHAT'S WITH THIS GIRL?
BUT HOW'D YOU DRAW HIM AT AN ANGLE WITH HIM LOOKING AT YOU?
AAH! I'VE BEEN CAUGHT!

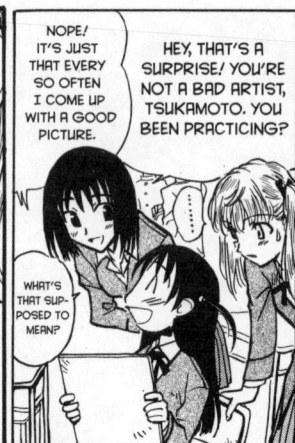

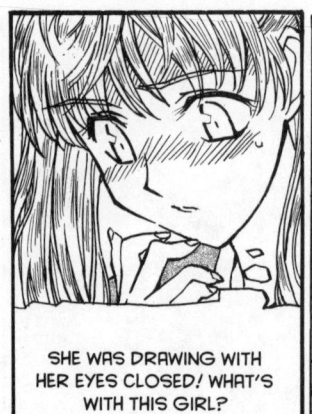

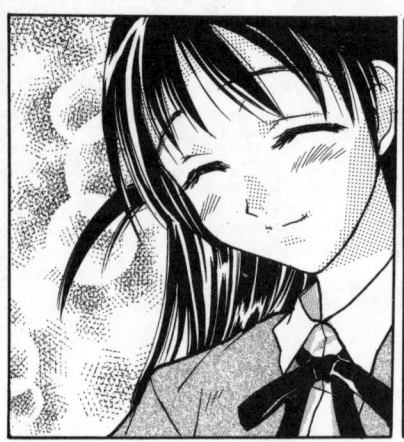

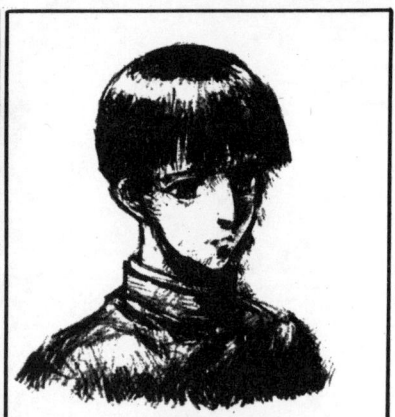

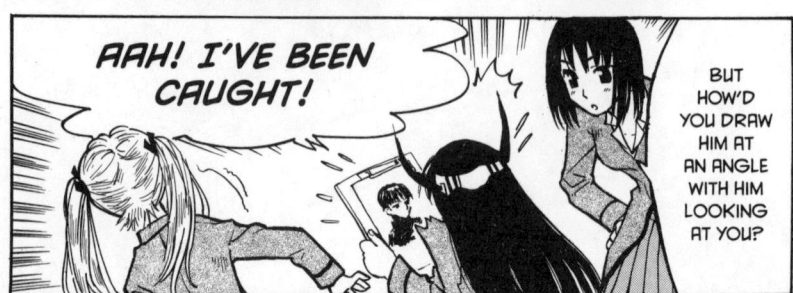

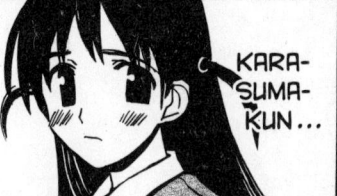

WHAT STYLE DID YOU DRAW ME IN?

KARA-SUMA-KUN...

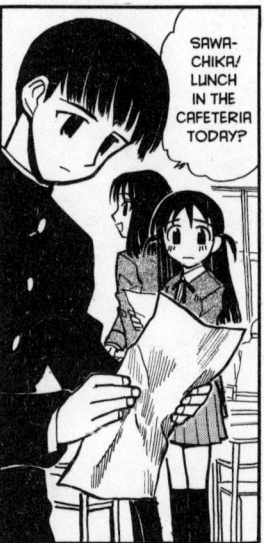

SAWA-CHIKA! LUNCH IN THE CAFETERIA TODAY?

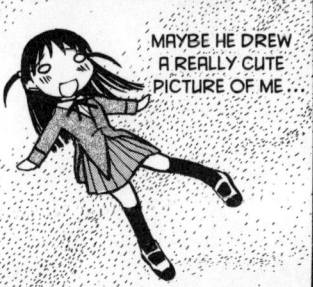

MAYBE HE DREW A REALLY CUTE PICTURE OF ME...

WOULD THAT MEAN THAT HE THOUGHT THE REAL ME WAS CUTE? WELL, IT *MAY* NOT MEAN THAT...

BUT THAT'S HOW I'D TAKE IT!

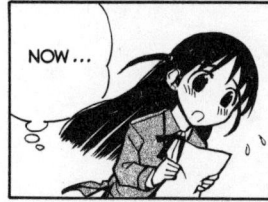

NOW...

OKAY, THEN I'LL SUBMIT MINE RIGHT AFTER KARASUMA-KUN SUBMITS HIS.

THEN I'LL TAKE JUST A QUICK GLANCE.

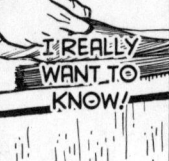

I REALLY WANT TO KNOW!

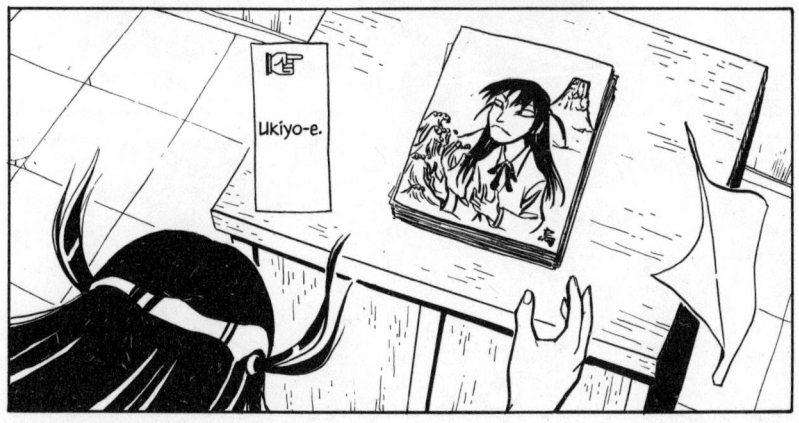

Ukiyo-e.

10 .... Fin.

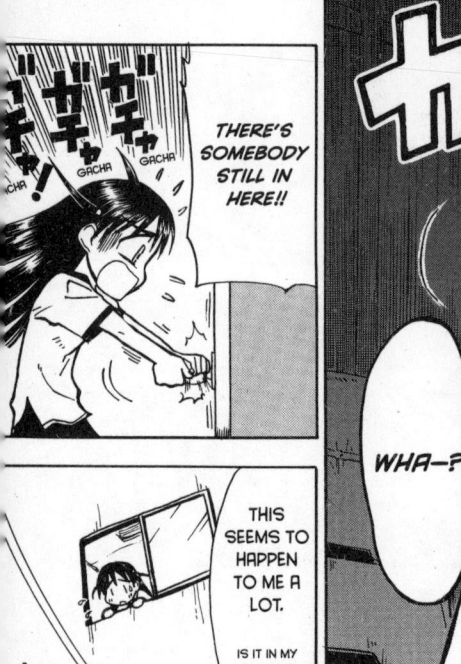

ガチャ!!
GACHANK

GACHA GACHA GACHA

THERE'S SOMEBODY STILL IN HERE!!

WHA-?

THIS SEEMS TO HAPPEN TO ME A LOT.

IS IT IN MY BLOOD?

ヒュウ ウウ...
HYUUUU

IT'S NO GOOD. I DON'T THINK I CAN GET DOWN FROM HERE.

Gym Storeroom, 2nd Floor...

#11   THE TOWERING INFERNO

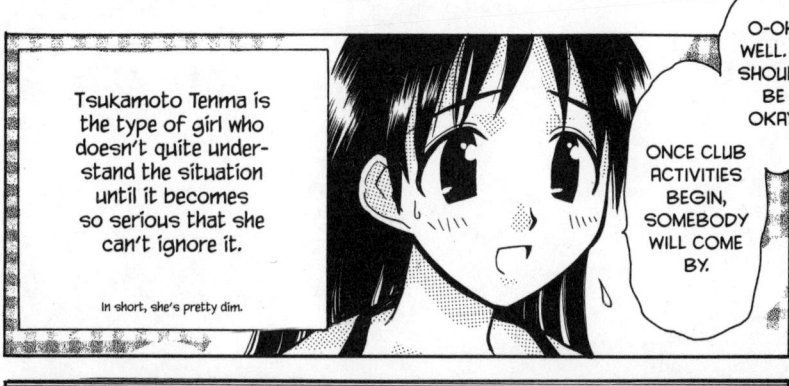

Tsukamoto Tenma: *Gym During Sixth Period.*

O-OH, WELL. IT SHOULD BE OKAY.
ONCE CLUB ACTIVITIES BEGIN, SOMEBODY WILL COME BY.
Tsukamoto Tenma is the type of girl who doesn't quite understand the situation until it becomes so serious that she can't ignore it.
In short, she's pretty dim.
とっぷり
AFTER A LONG TIME
うわーんっ
WAAAH!
ALL OF THE CLUBS HAVE THE DAY OFF!!
ごろんっ
ROLLL
AWWW! THERE'S A TV PROGRAM I REALLY WANTED TO SEE!
I WONDER IF YAKUMO IS RECORDING IT FOR ME.
I CAN'T EVEN DO HOMEWORK. I'LL HAVE TO EXPLAIN WHY TOMORROW.
"I WAS LOCKED UP, AND I WASN'T ABLE TO DO IT." MAYBE THAT'LL WORK.
I HAVE TO STOP THIS!
I HAVE TO BE OPTIMISTIC! I CAN PUT THIS SITUATION TO USE TO HELP ME SOMEHOW!
がばっ
GAMPH
RIGHT! IT'S AN EXPERIENCE! IT ISN'T LIKE MY LIFE IS IN DANGER. YEAH, THAT'S HOW TO SEE IT!

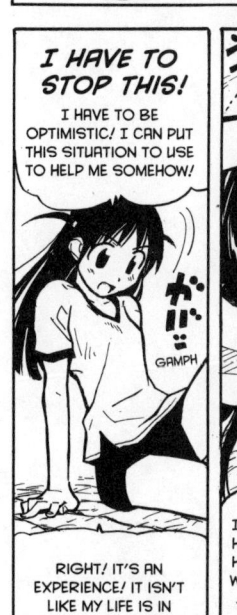

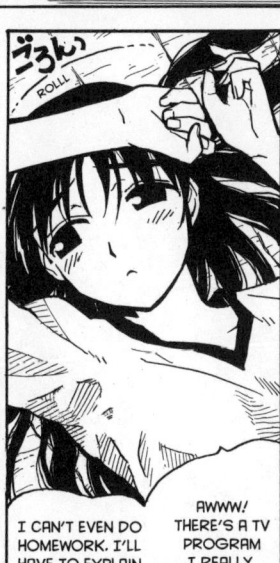

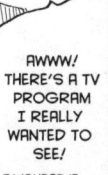

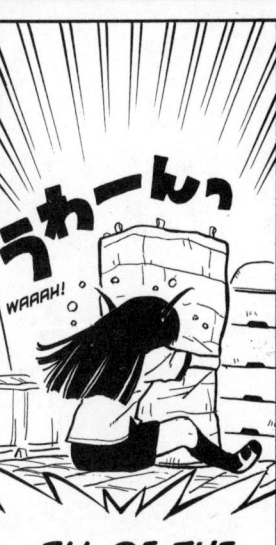

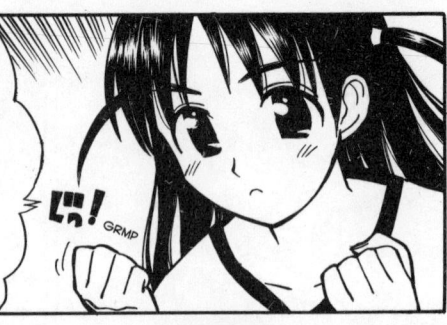

I'LL THINK OF THIS AS HAVING JUST ARRIVED ASHORE ON A DESERT ISLAND. IMAGINE THIS AS AN EXTREME SITUATION. RIGHT! THIS IS A TEST FOR ME! THIS IS A CHANCE TO PROVE MY PRESENCE OF MIND!

GRMP

Tsukamoto Tenma: *Uselessly Optimistic.*

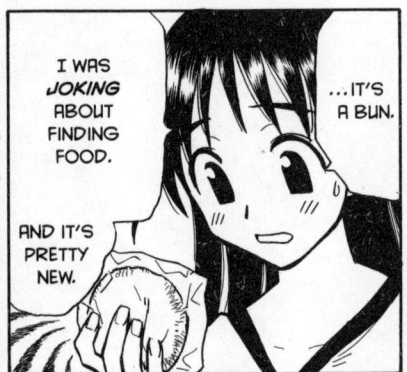

I WAS *JOKING* ABOUT FINDING FOOD.

...IT'S A BUN.

AND IT'S PRETTY NEW.

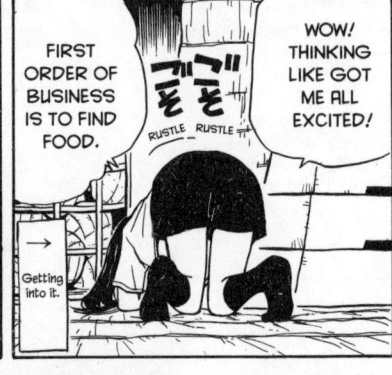

FIRST ORDER OF BUSINESS IS TO FIND FOOD.

RUSTLE RUSTLE

WOW! THINKING LIKE GOT ME ALL EXCITED!

→ Getting into it.

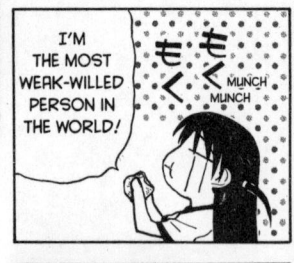

I'M THE MOST WEAK-WILLED PERSON IN THE WORLD!

MUNCH MUNCH

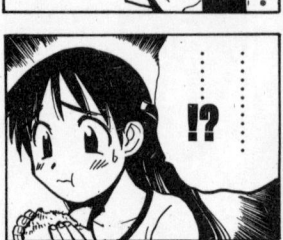

⁝ ⁝ ⁝
!?

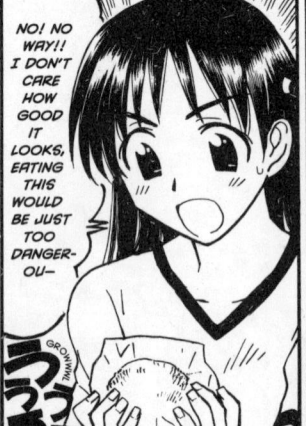

NO! NO WAY!! I DON'T CARE HOW GOOD IT LOOKS, EATING THIS WOULD BE JUST TOO DANGEROU—

GROWWW

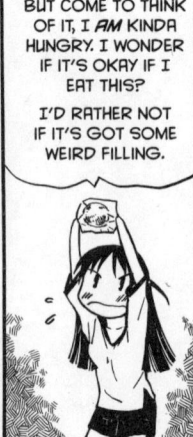

BUT COME TO THINK OF IT, I *AM* KINDA HUNGRY. I WONDER IF IT'S OKAY IF I EAT THIS?

I'D RATHER NOT IF IT'S GOT SOME WEIRD FILLING.

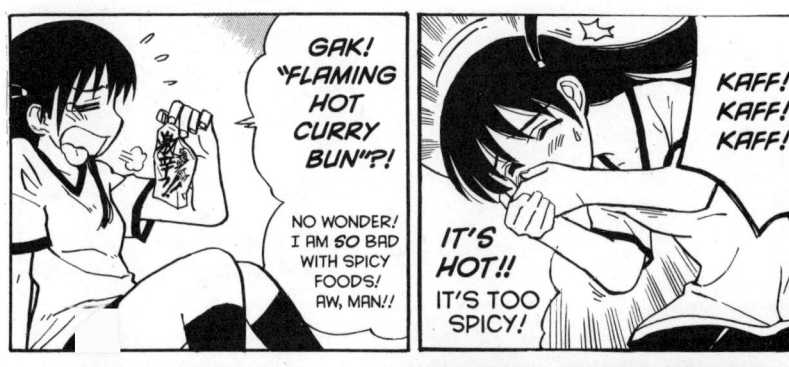
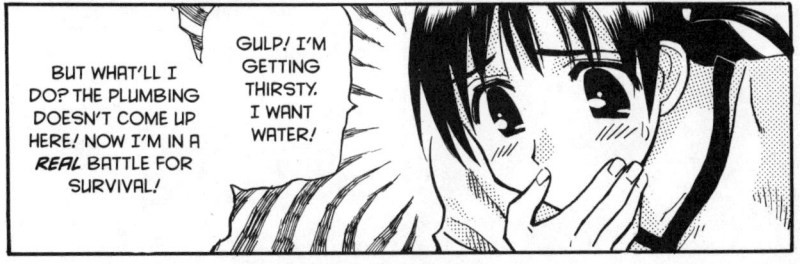

Tsukamoto Tenma: *Candy Is Her Style.*

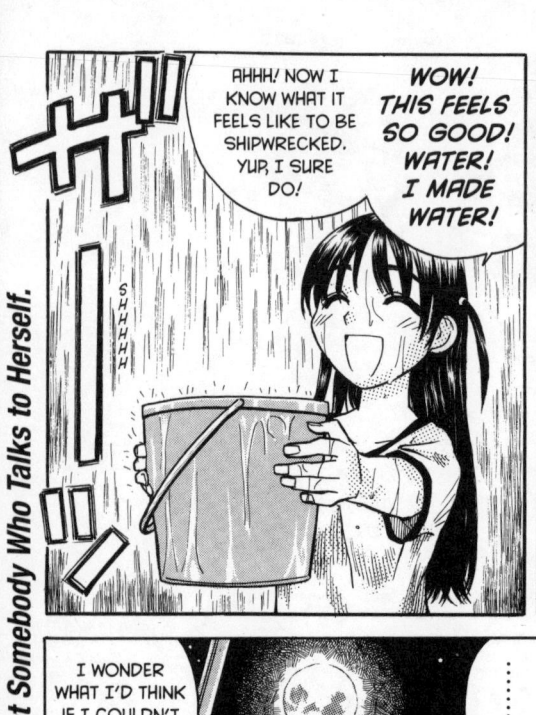

AHHH! NOW I KNOW WHAT IT FEELS LIKE TO BE SHIPWRECKED. YUP, I SURE DO!

WOW! THIS FEELS SO GOOD! WATER! I MADE WATER!

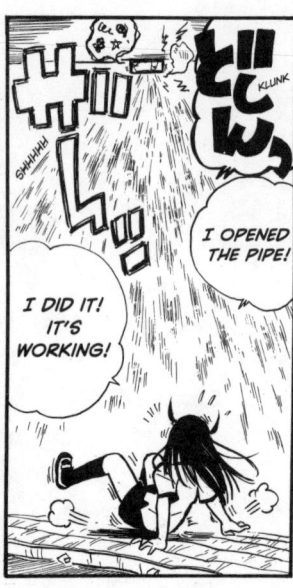

I OPENED THE PIPE!

I DID IT! IT'S WORKING!

KLUNK

I WONDER WHAT I'D THINK IF I COULDN'T EVER GET OUT OF HERE.

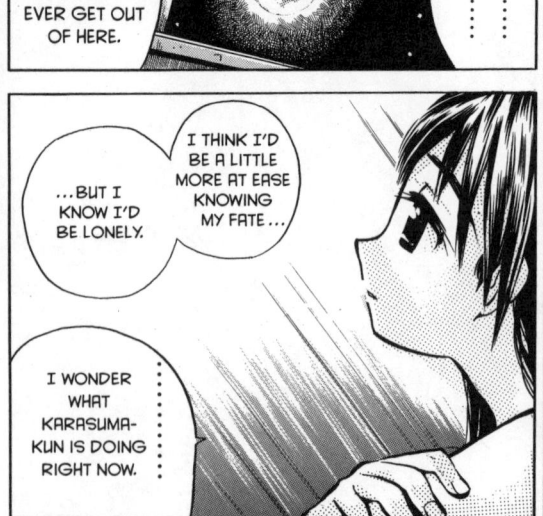

I THINK I'D BE A LITTLE MORE AT EASE KNOWING MY FATE...

...BUT I KNOW I'D BE LONELY.

I WONDER WHAT KARASUMA-KUN IS DOING RIGHT NOW.

WHY DON'T I EVER REALIZE THE OBVIOUS THINGS LIKE THAT? IT'S A MYSTERY.

I DON'T HAVE A CHANGE OF CLOTHES OR A TOWEL.

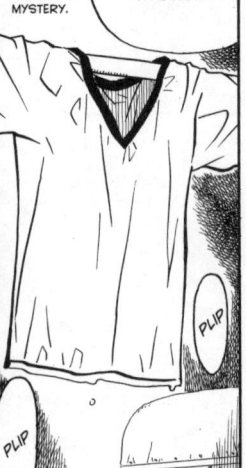

PLIP

PLIP

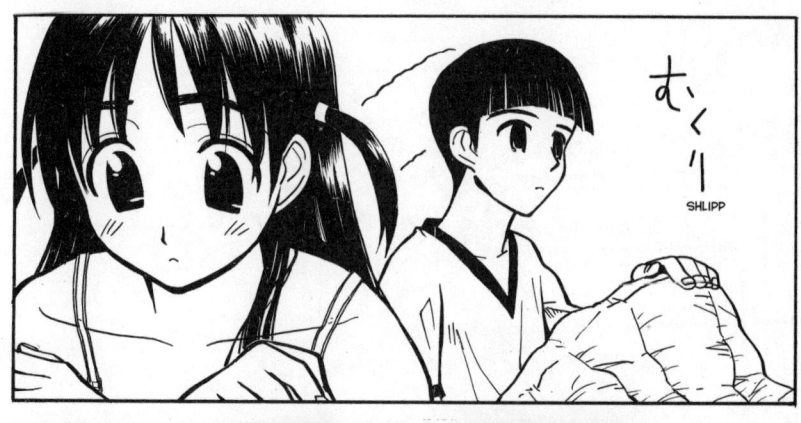

むくり
SHLIPP

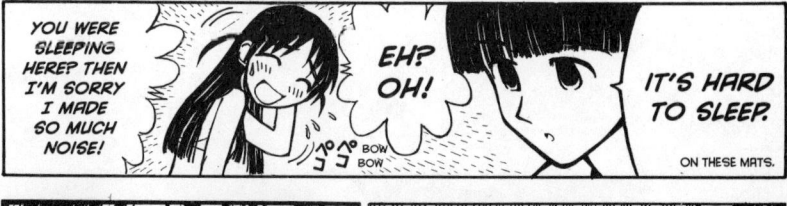

YOU WERE SLEEPING HERE? THEN I'M SORRY I MADE SO MUCH NOISE!

BOW BOW

EH? OH!

IT'S HARD TO SLEEP.

ON THESE MATS.

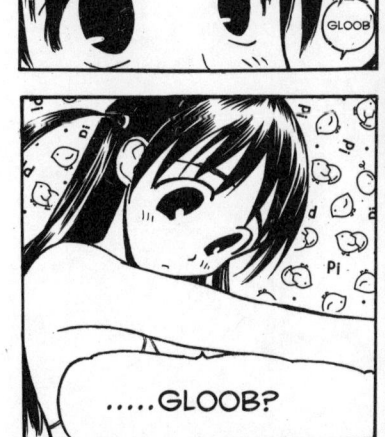

GLOOB

.....GLOOB?

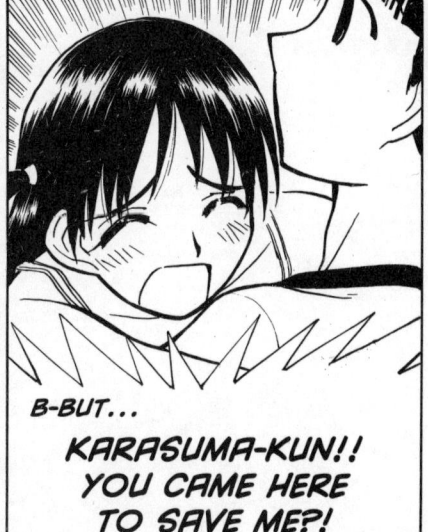

B-BUT...

KARASUMA-KUN!! YOU CAME HERE TO SAVE ME?!

— 96 —

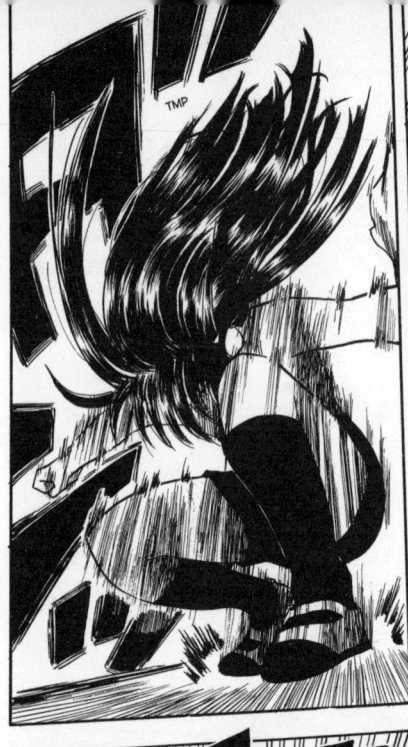

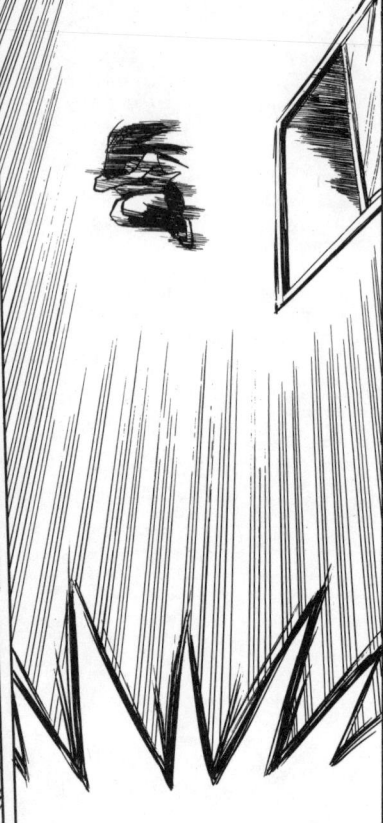

TSUKAMOTO-SAN IS PRETTY AMAZING.

Actually, that was Karasuma-kun's bun.

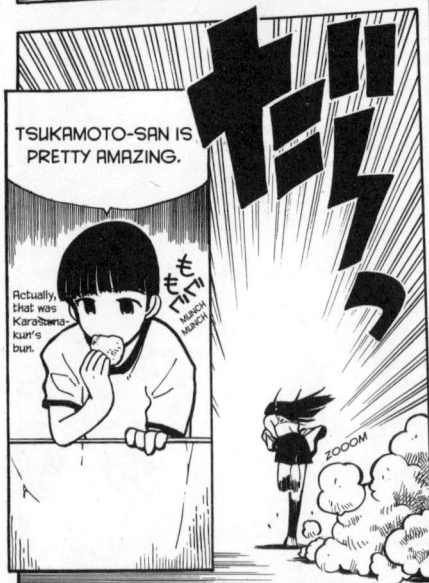

I AM SO EMBARRASSED!!!

11 . . . . Fin.

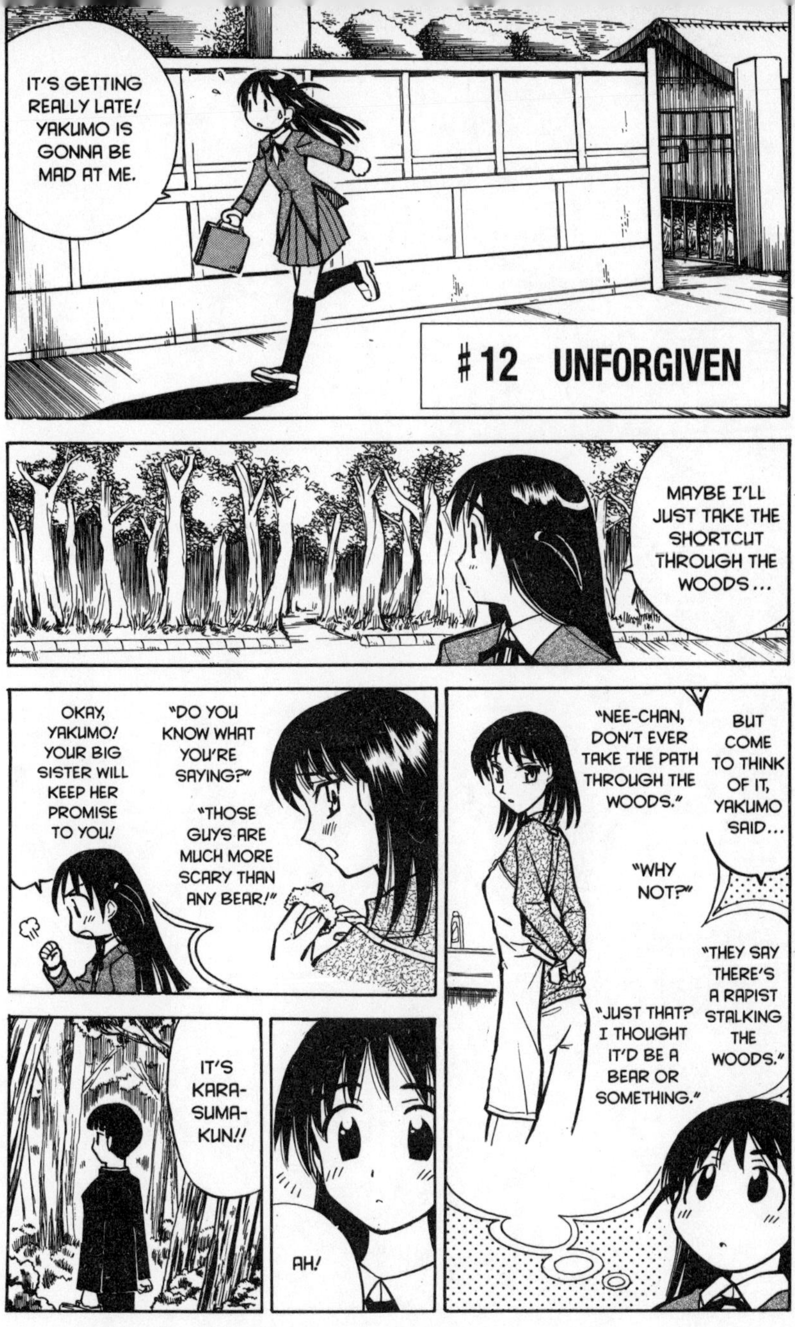
IT'S GETTING REALLY LATE! YAKUMO IS GONNA BE MAD AT ME.
12 UNFORGIVEN
MAYBE I'LL JUST TAKE THE SHORTCUT THROUGH THE WOODS...
BUT COME TO THINK OF IT, YAKUMO SAID...
"NEE-CHAN, DON'T EVER TAKE THE PATH THROUGH THE WOODS."
"WHY NOT?"
"THEY SAY THERE'S A RAPIST STALKING THE WOODS."
"JUST THAT? I THOUGHT IT'D BE A BEAR OR SOMETHING."
"DO YOU KNOW WHAT YOU'RE SAYING?"
"THOSE GUYS ARE MUCH MORE SCARY THAN ANY BEAR!"
OKAY, YAKUMO! YOUR BIG SISTER WILL KEEP HER PROMISE TO YOU!
AH!
IT'S KARA-SUMA-KUN!!

TH-THAT'S IT!!
I COULD USE THIS OPPORTUNITY TO DEEPEN OUR LOVE!
Rapist.
TSUKAMOTO-SAN! I'LL PROTECT YOU!
KARASUMA-KUN! ♡ → STANDING UP TO THE BEAST WITH HIS BARE HANDS!
KARASUMA-KUN!
YOU'D DO THAT FOR ME?
Me.
NOW TO THE PATH!
SWITCH ON!
TMP
SHKK
AWW, TENMA-CHAN! THIS PATH THROUGH THE WOODS IS SUCH A DANGEROUS PLACE FOR YOUNG GIRLS TO WALK. I CAN'T SIMPLY STAND BY!
I'M GLAD I FOLLOWED YOU HERE.
TSK!
THIS IS MY CHANCE! FIRST, I MUST FOLLOW HER. THEN TENMA-CHAN WILL SOON BE THREATENED BY THE RAPIST!
THAT IS WHEN I WILL STEP IN AND SAVE HER! THEN WILL SPROUT THE SEEDS OF LOVE!!
KLNCH
IT'S PERFECT! THIS IS THE START OF A LOVE STORY SO WONDERFUL, IT SCARES EVEN ME!
HOWEVER... HUMPH! ANYONE CAN SEE WHAT'S COMING. JUST AS MY PLAN IS COMING TO FRUITION...
GLEEM
I'M SURE THAT SOMEBODY WILL MISTAKE ME FOR THE RAPIST AND I'LL BE ARRESTED.
THAT'S WHAT'LL REALLY HAPPEN.
THAT'S PROBABLY JUST WHAT HE IS HOPING FOR, BUT...

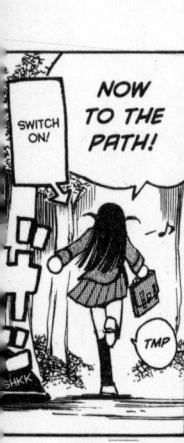

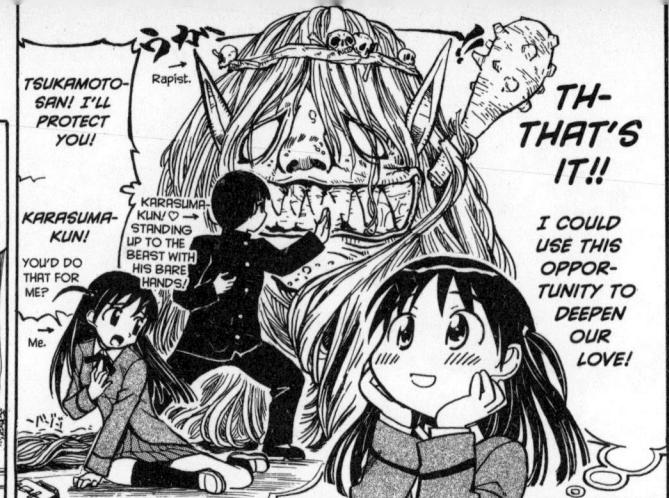

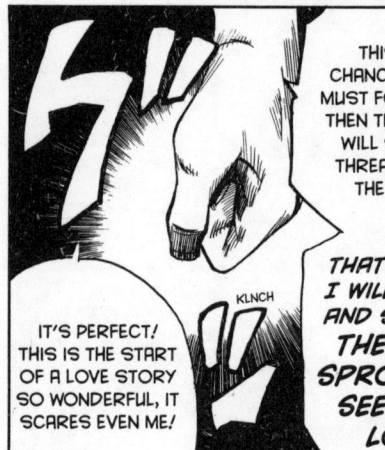

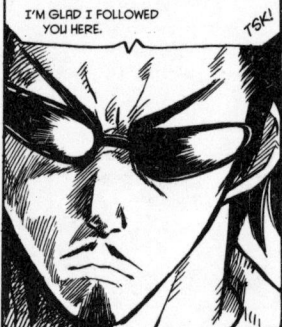

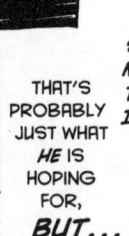

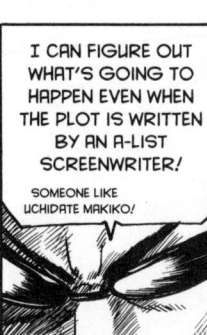

I CAN FIGURE OUT WHAT'S GOING TO HAPPEN EVEN WHEN THE PLOT IS WRITTEN BY AN A-LIST SCREENWRITER!

SOMEONE LIKE UCHIDATE MAKIKO!

TODAY, YOU'LL FIND THAT SOMETHING IS DIFFERENT ABOUT ME!

YES...

HE UNDER-ESTIMATES ME!

MY POLICE OFFICER DISGUISE IS PERFECT!

スチャ！

SKTCH!

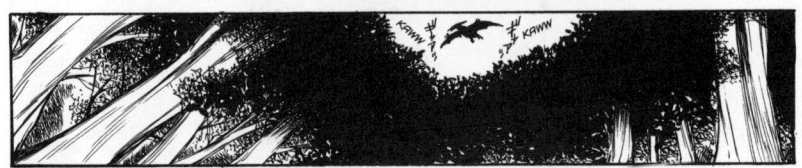

KAWW KAWW KAWW

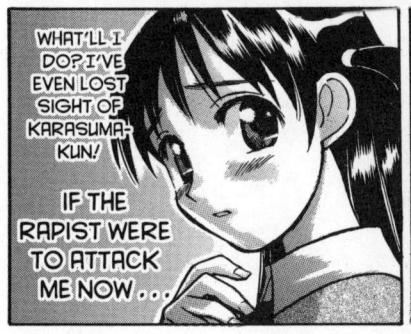

WHAT'LL I DO? I'VE EVEN LOST SIGHT OF KARASUMA-KUN!

IF THE RAPIST WERE TO ATTACK ME NOW...

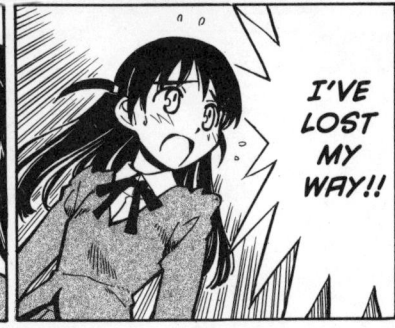

I'VE LOST MY WAY!!

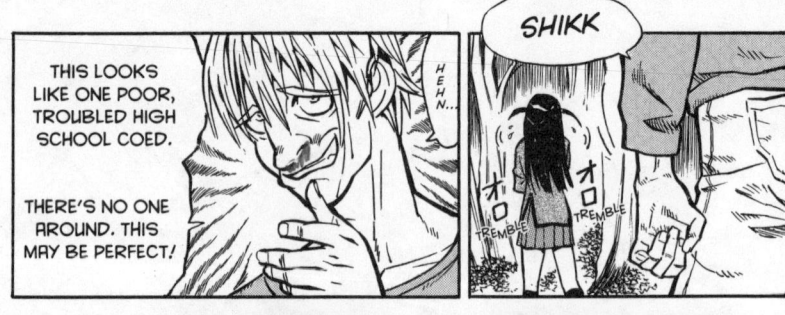

SHIKK

THIS LOOKS LIKE ONE POOR, TROUBLED HIGH SCHOOL COED.

THERE'S NO ONE AROUND. THIS MAY BE PERFECT!

HEH...

オロ
オロ

TREMBLE   TREMBLE

Tsukamoto Tenma: *Purity in Danger.*

EH?!

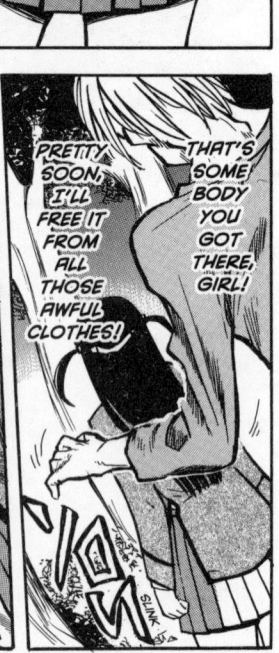

PRETTY SOON, I'LL FREE IT FROM ALL THOSE AWFUL CLOTHES!

THAT'S SOME BODY YOU GOT THERE, GIRL!

SLINK

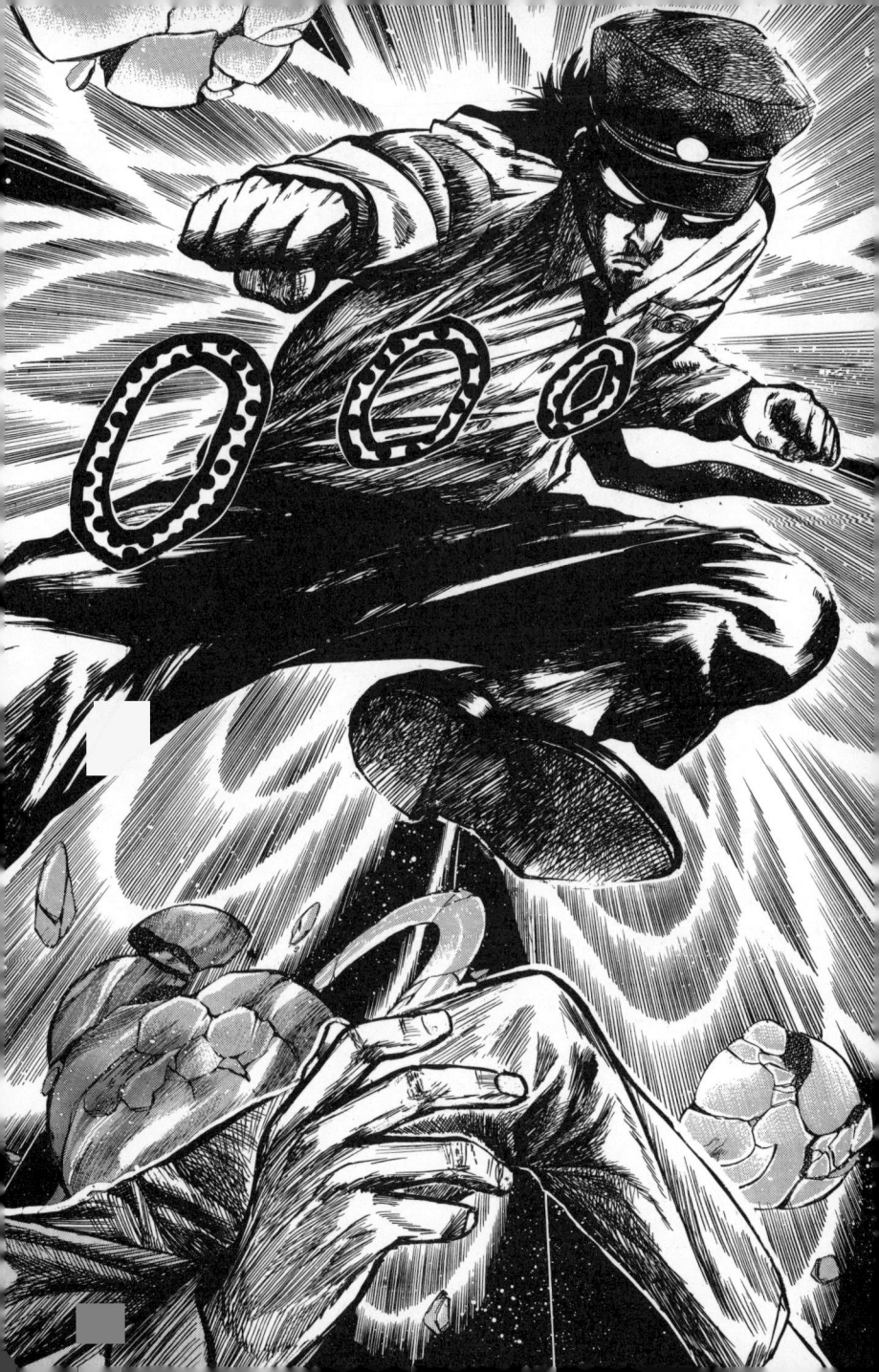

HURRICANE KICK!!!

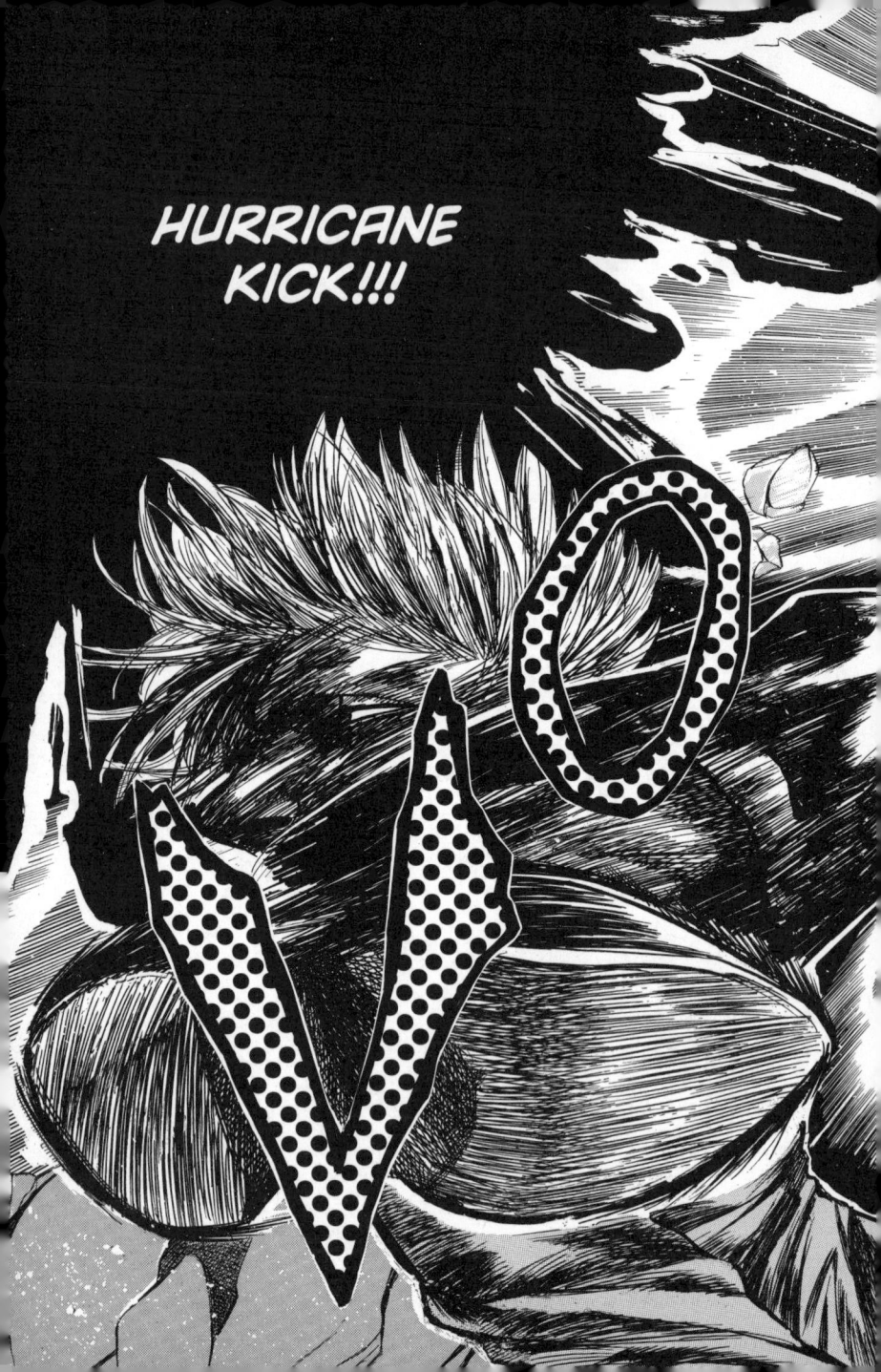

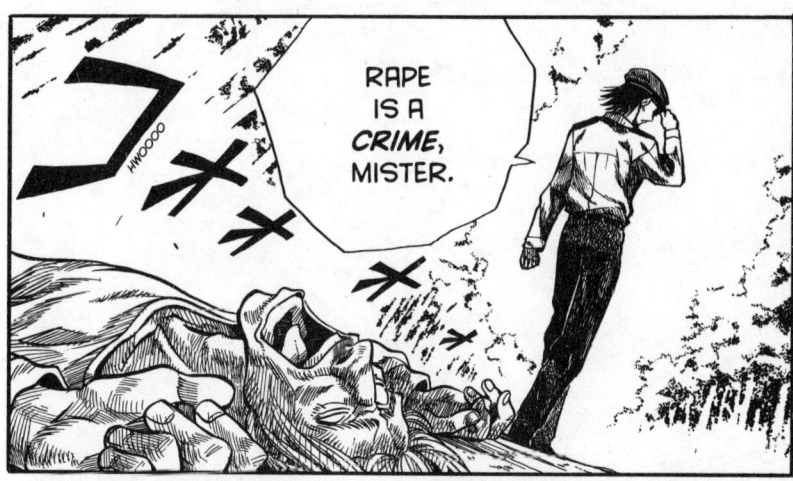

RAPE IS A *CRIME,* MISTER.

HWOOOO

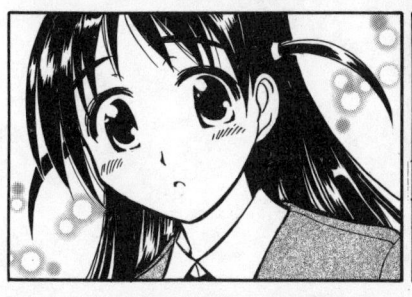

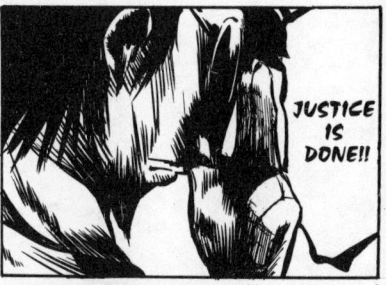

JUSTICE IS DONE!!

Harima Kenji: *The Winner.*

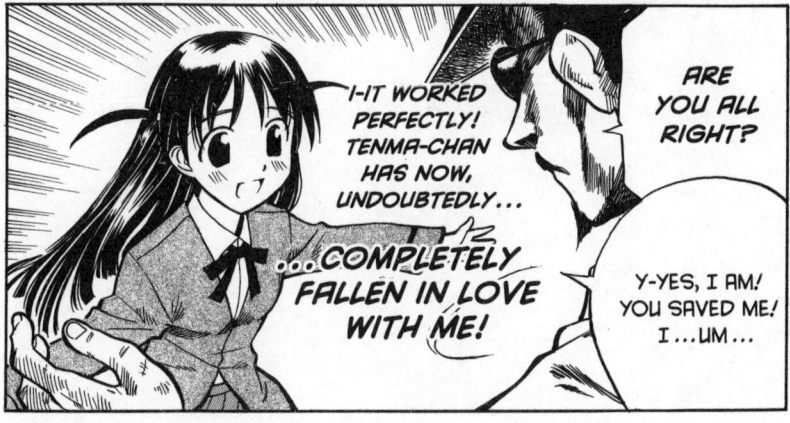

ARE YOU ALL RIGHT?

I-IT WORKED PERFECTLY! TENMA-CHAN HAS NOW, UNDOUBTEDLY...

...COMPLETELY FALLEN IN LOVE WITH ME!

Y-YES, I AM! YOU SAVED ME! I...UM...

OHHHH,

NOOOO!!!

THANK YOU SO MUCH, MR. POLICEMAN!!

BOW

Like she trusts him absolutely.

WHAT WONDER-FUL WORK YOU DO.

H-HOW THICK CAN A GIRL GET?! YES, I AM A POLICEMAN AT THIS MOMENT, BUT IF I SIMPLY TAKE OFF THE HAT, SHE CAN'T HELP BUT REALIZE THAT I'M HARIMA!

BUT EVEN SO, I THINK IT'S SO GREAT THAT YOU'D GO OUT OF YOUR WAY TO HELP ME, A COMPLETE STRANGER!

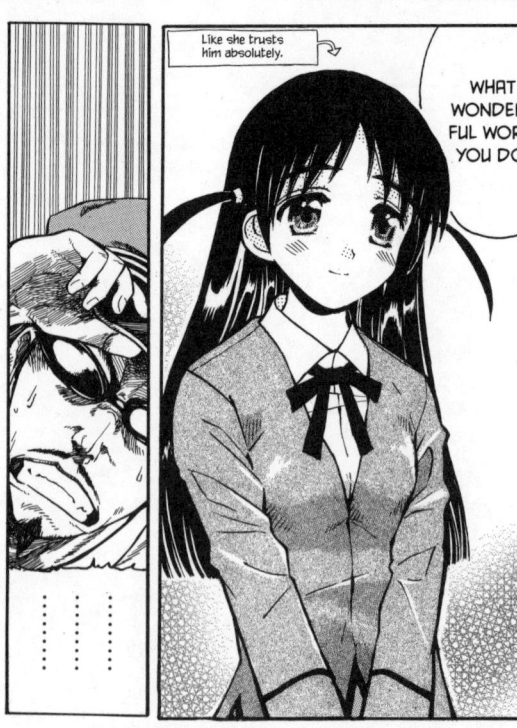

YEAH...

— 105 —

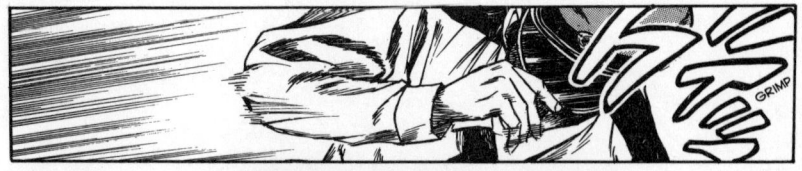

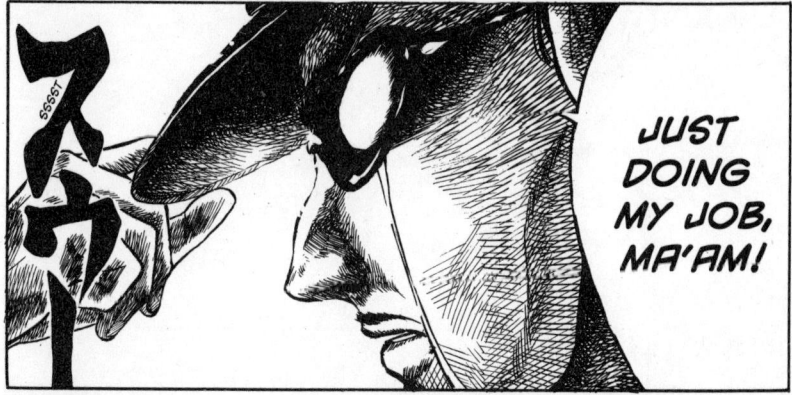

JUST DOING MY JOB, MA'AM!

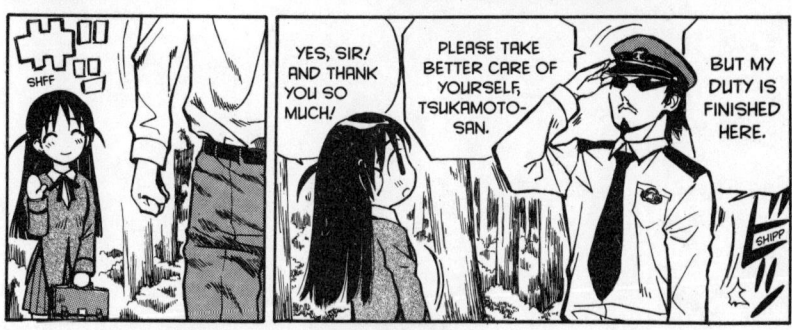

YES, SIR! AND THANK YOU SO MUCH!

PLEASE TAKE BETTER CARE OF YOURSELF, TSUKAMOTO-SAN.

BUT MY DUTY IS FINISHED HERE.

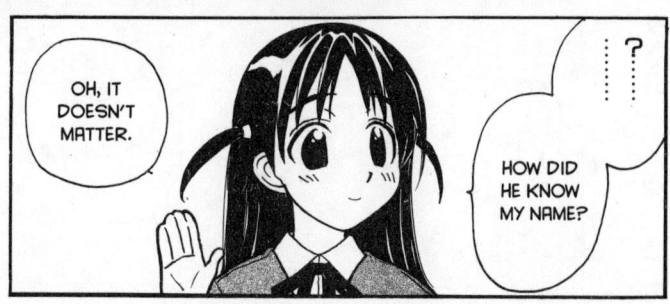

OH, IT DOESN'T MATTER.

HOW DID HE KNOW MY NAME?

12 . . . . Fin.

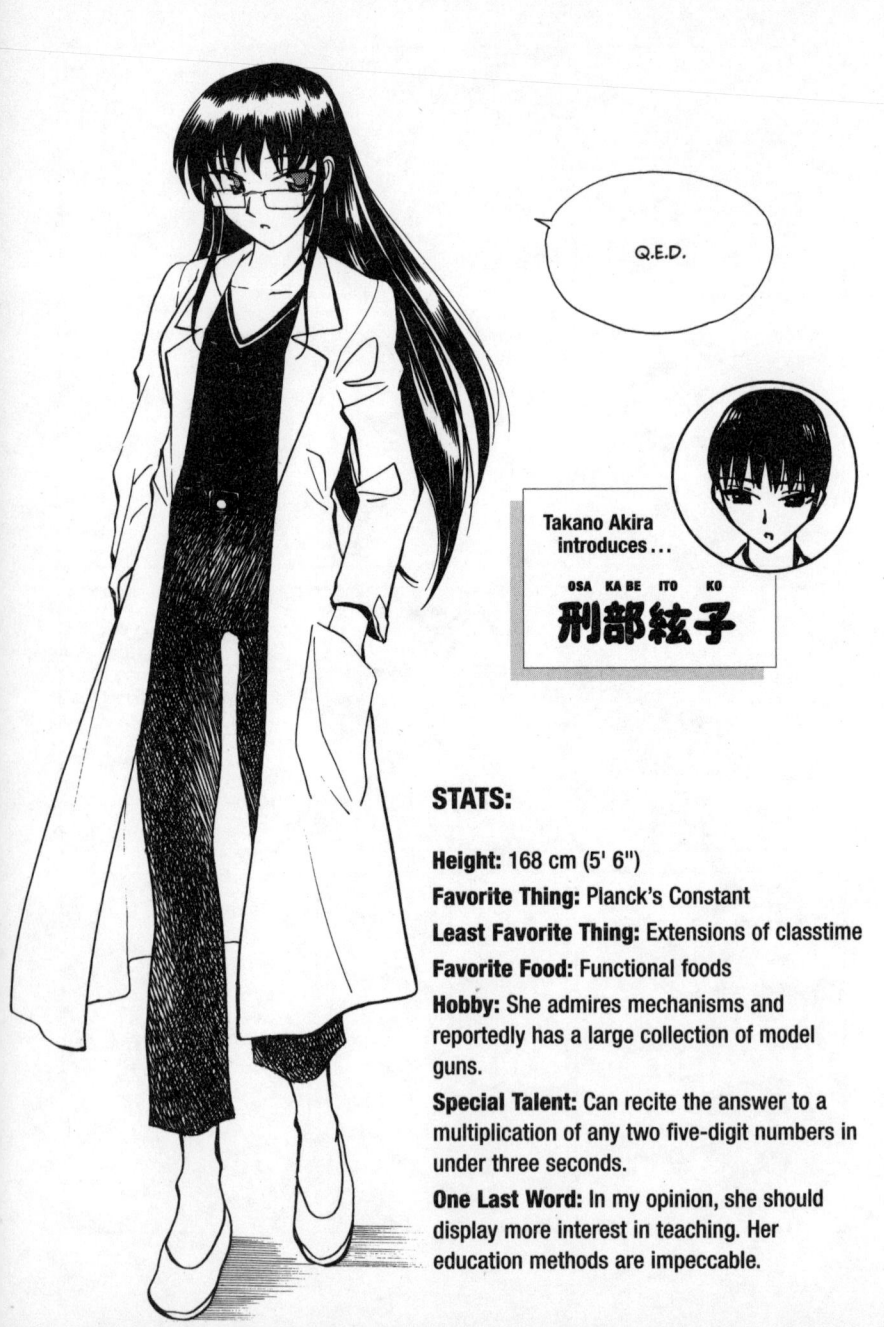

Q.E.D.

Takano Akira introduces...

OSA KA BE ITO KO

刑部絃子

STATS:

Height: 168 cm (5' 6")

Favorite Thing: Planck's Constant

Least Favorite Thing: Extensions of classtime

Favorite Food: Functional foods

Hobby: She admires mechanisms and reportedly has a large collection of model guns.

Special Talent: Can recite the answer to a multiplication of any two five-digit numbers in under three seconds.

One Last Word: In my opinion, she should display more interest in teaching. Her education methods are impeccable.

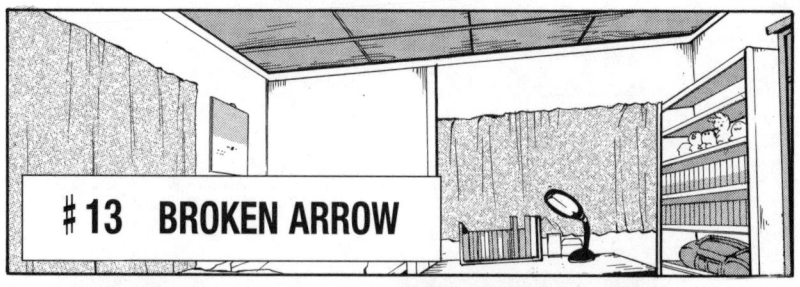

#13 BROKEN ARROW

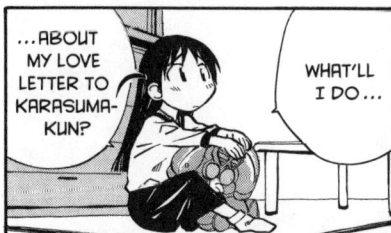

...ABOUT MY LOVE LETTER TO KARASUMA-KUN?

WHAT'LL I DO...

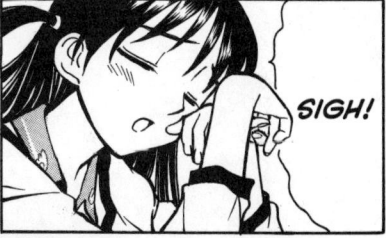

SIGH!

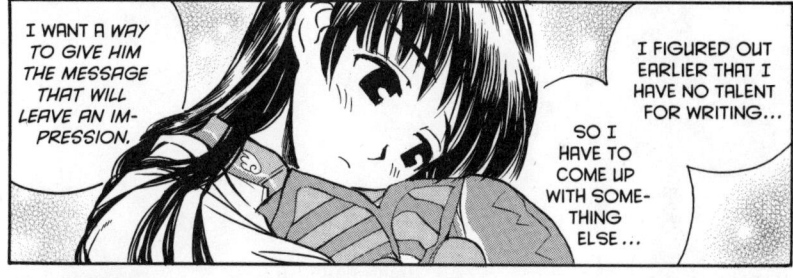

I WANT A *WAY TO GIVE HIM THE MESSAGE THAT WILL LEAVE AN IMPRESSION.*

I FIGURED OUT EARLIER THAT I HAVE NO TALENT FOR WRITING...

SO I HAVE TO COME UP WITH SOMETHING ELSE...

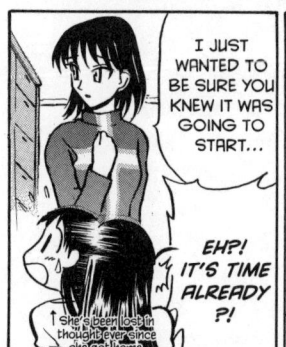

I JUST WANTED TO BE SURE YOU KNEW IT WAS GOING TO START...

EH?! IT'S TIME ALREADY?!

† She's been lost in thought ever since she got home.

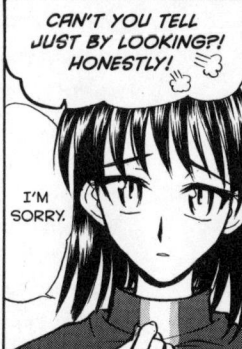

CAN'T YOU TELL JUST BY LOOKING?! HONESTLY!

I'M SORRY.

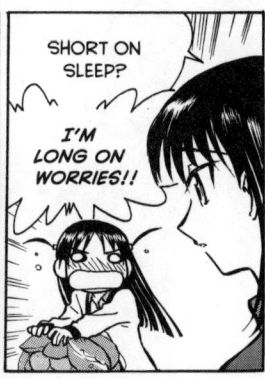

SHORT ON SLEEP?

I'M LONG ON WORRIES!!

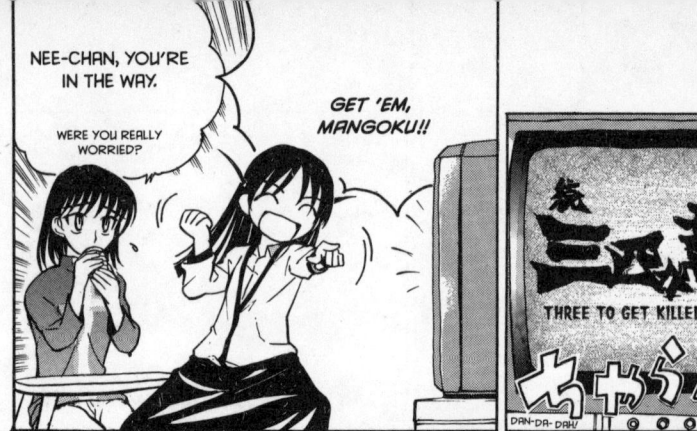

NEE-CHAN, YOU'RE IN THE WAY.

WERE YOU REALLY WORRIED?

GET 'EM, MANGOKU!!

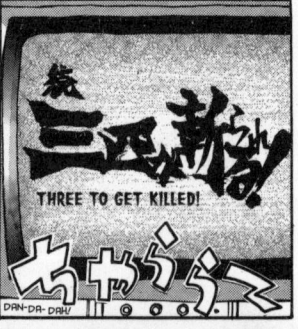

THREE TO GET KILLED!

DAN-DA-DAH!

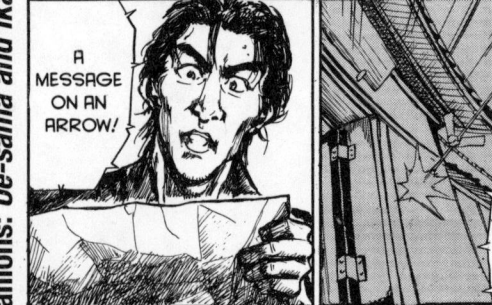

A MESSAGE ON AN ARROW!

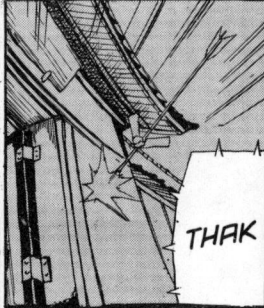

THAK

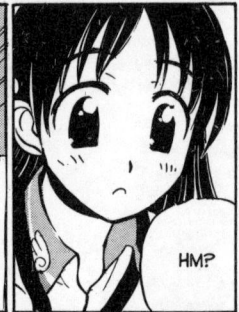

HM?

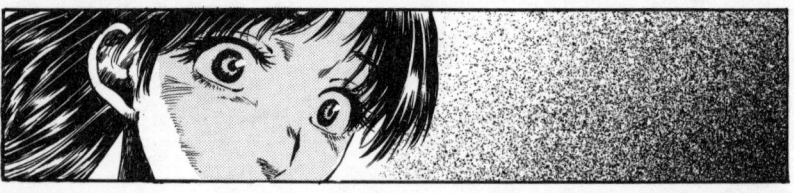

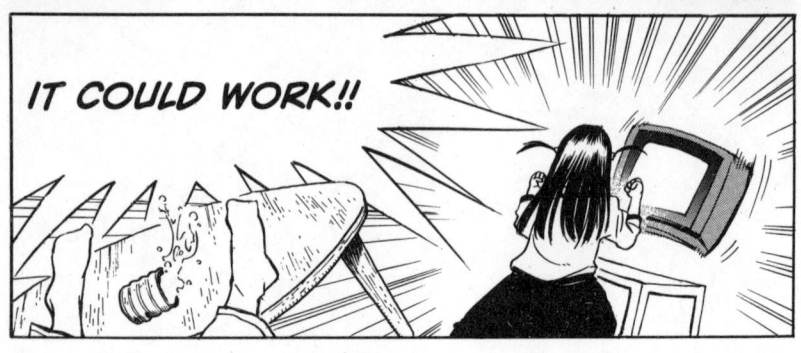

IT COULD WORK!!

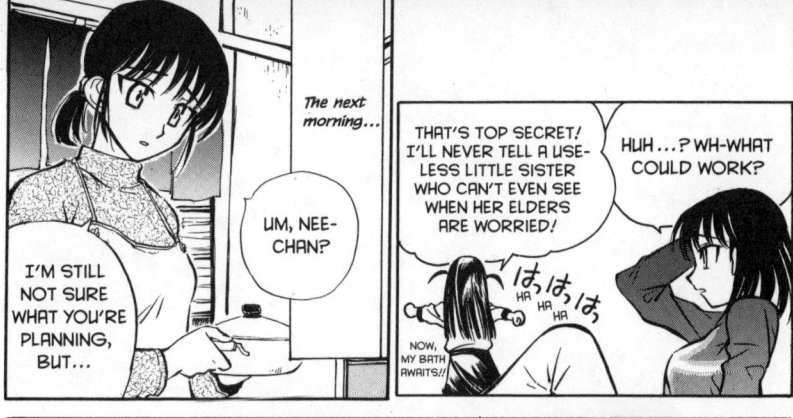

The next morning...

UM, NEE-CHAN?

I'M STILL NOT SURE WHAT YOU'RE PLANNING, BUT...

THAT'S TOP SECRET! I'LL NEVER TELL A USE-LESS LITTLE SISTER WHO CAN'T EVEN SEE WHEN HER ELDERS ARE WORRIED!

HUH...? WH-WHAT COULD WORK?

は、は、は、
HA HA HA

NOW, MY BATH AWAITS!!

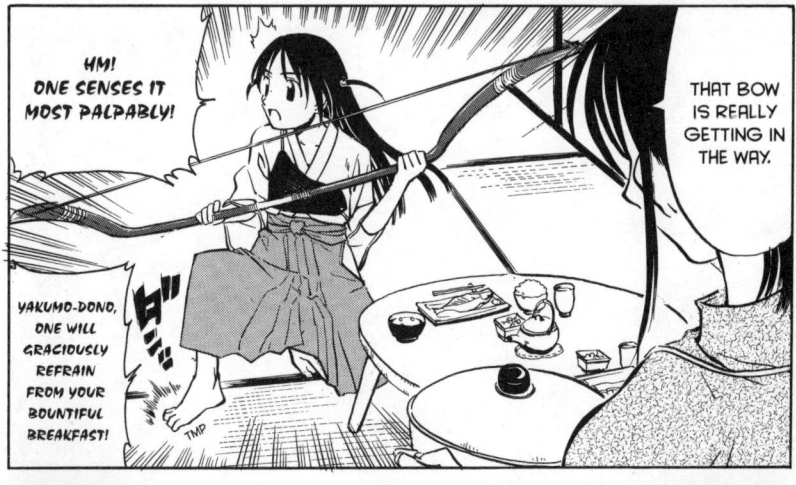

HM! ONE SENSES IT MOST PALPABLY!

THAT BOW IS REALLY GETTING IN THE WAY.

YAKUMO-DONO, ONE WILL GRACIOUSLY REFRAIN FROM YOUR BOUNTIFUL BREAKFAST!

TMP

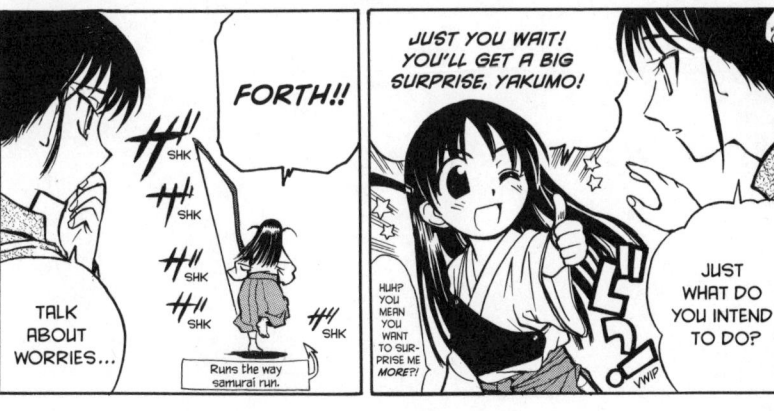

FORTH!!

SHK SHK SHK SHK SHK

TALK ABOUT WORRIES...

Runs the way samurai run.

JUST YOU WAIT! YOU'LL GET A BIG SURPRISE, YAKUMO!

HUH? YOU MEAN YOU WANT TO SURPRISE ME MORE?!

JUST WHAT DO YOU INTEND TO DO?

VWIP

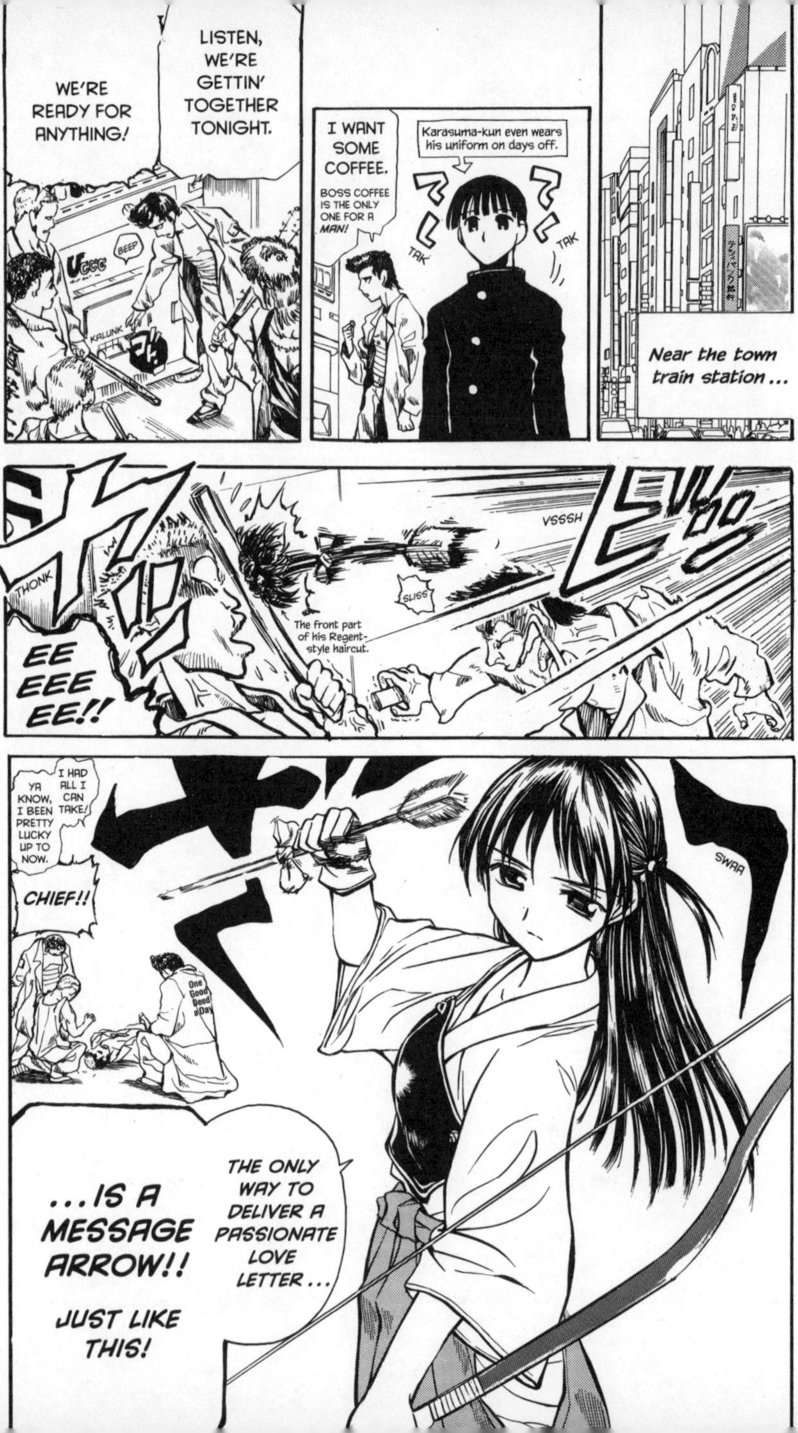
Near the town train station...
I WANT SOME COFFEE.
BOSS COFFEE IS THE ONLY ONE FOR A MAN!
Karasuma-kun even wears his uniform on days off.
TAK
TAK
LISTEN, WE'RE GETTIN' TOGETHER TONIGHT.
WE'RE READY FOR ANYTHING!
BEEP
KALUNK
VSSSH
SLISS
The front part of his Regent-style haircut.
THONK
EE EEE EE!!
SWAA
I HAD ALL I CAN TAKE!
YA KNOW, I BEEN PRETTY LUCKY UP TO NOW.
CHIEF!!
One Good Deed a Day
THE ONLY WAY TO DELIVER A PASSIONATE LOVE LETTER...
...IS A MESSAGE ARROW!!
JUST LIKE THIS!

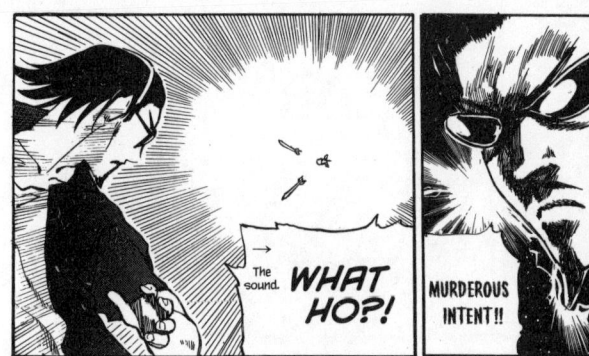

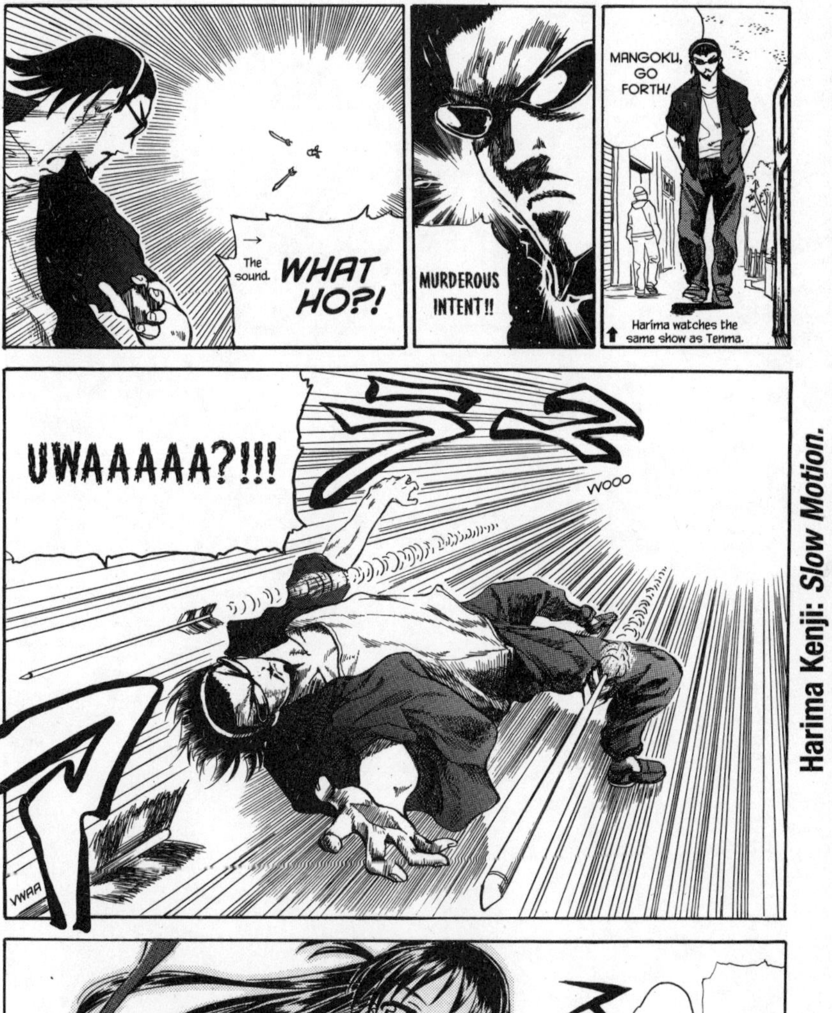

The sound. → **WHAT HO?!**

MURDEROUS INTENT!!

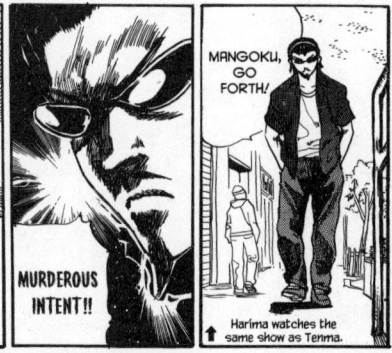

MANGOKU, GO FORTH!

↑ Harima watches the same show as Tenma.

UWAAAAAA?!!!

WOOO

VWAR

Harima Kenji: *Slow Motion.*

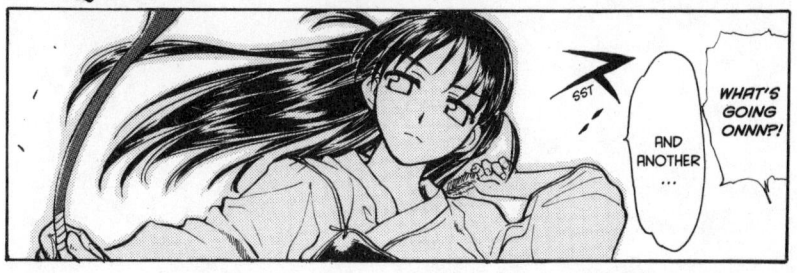

SST

AND ANOTHER ...

WHAT'S GOING ONNN?!

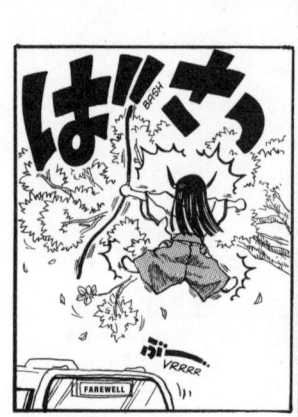

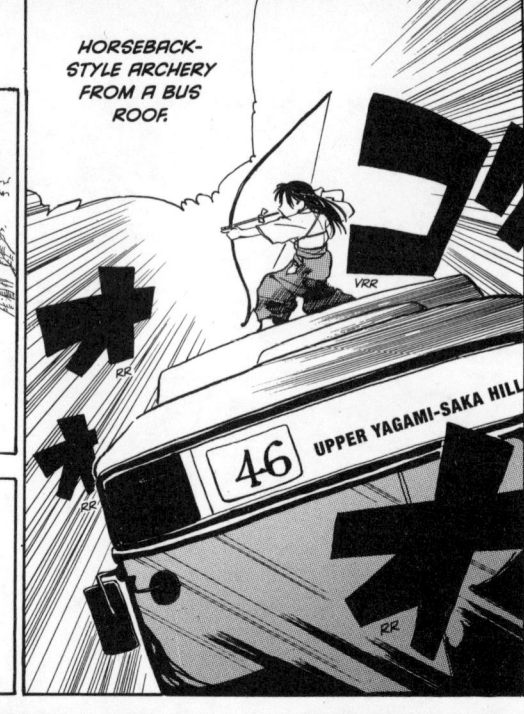

HORSEBACK-STYLE ARCHERY FROM A BUS ROOF.

46 UPPER YAGAMI-SAKA HILL

FAREWELL

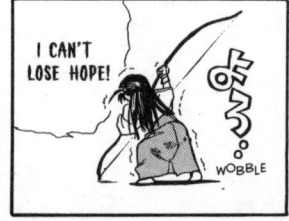

I CAN'T LOSE HOPE!

WOBBLE

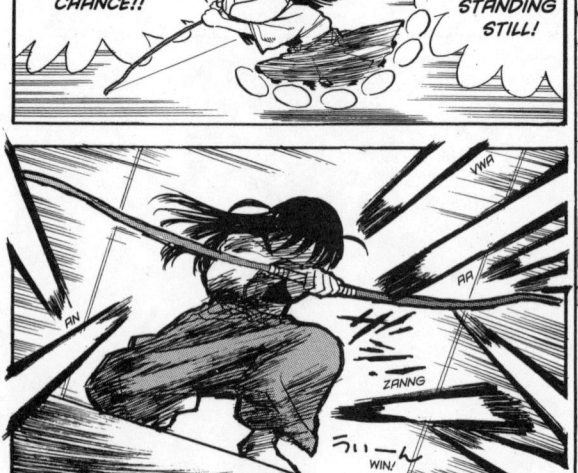

NOW'S MY CHANCE!!

MY TARGET'S STANDING STILL!

ZANNG

WIN!

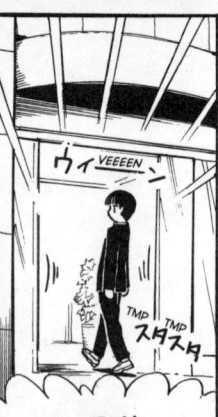

VEEEEN

TMP TMP

AH! KARASUMA-KUN'S GOING INTO A BANK!

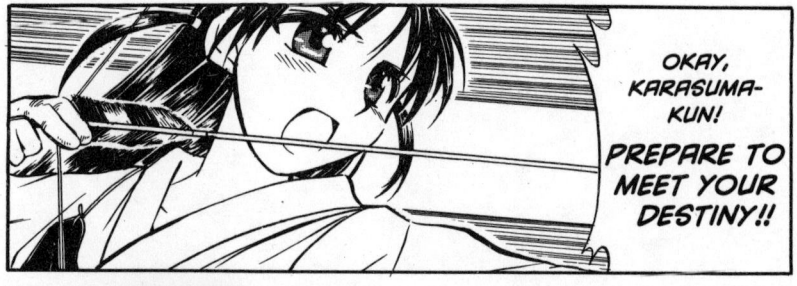

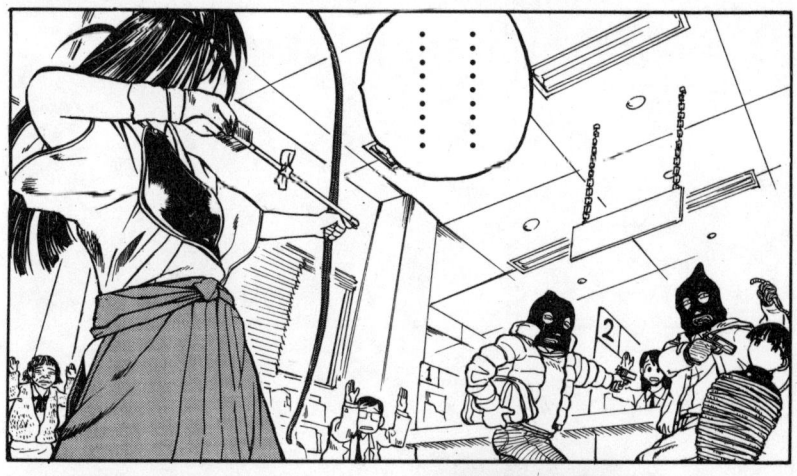

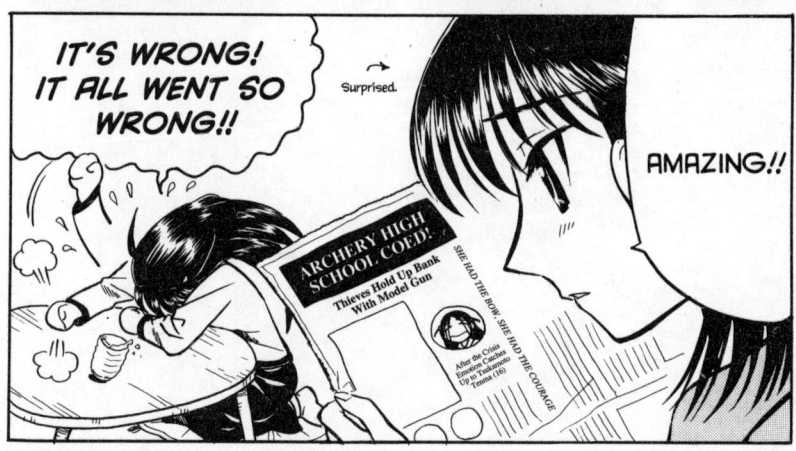

13 . . . . Fin.

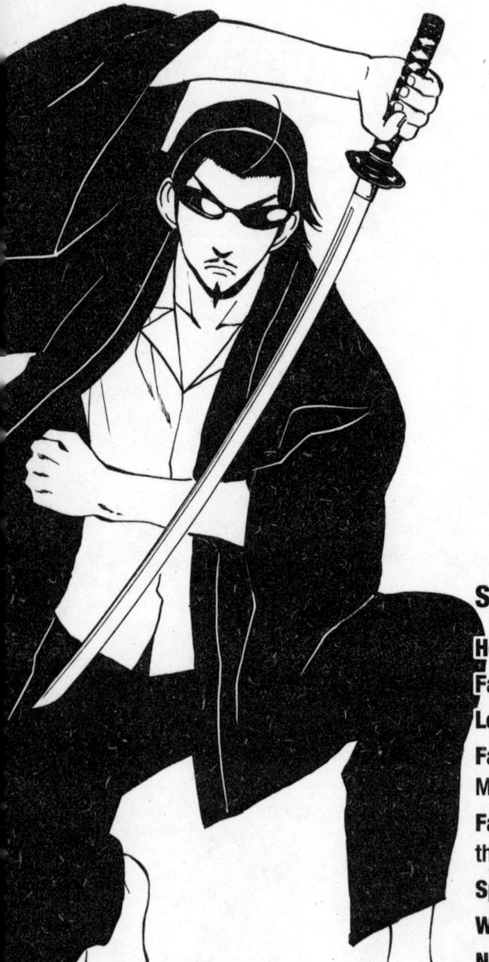
THE WORLD'S BIGGEST FOOL FOR TENMA!

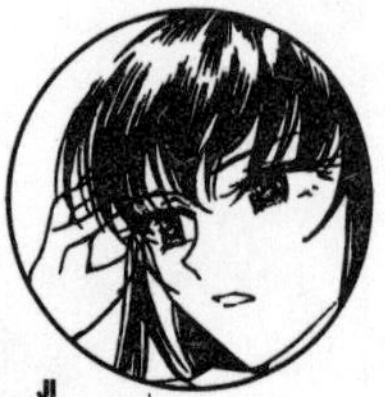

Osakabe Itoko introduces . . .

HARI MA KEN JI

播磨拳児

STATS:

Height: 180 cm (5' 11")
Favorite Thing: Curry
Least Favorite Thing: Shellfish, study
Favorite Actor: Yakushamaru Kôji (plays Mangoku)
Favorite Song: I'm always hearing the theme song from "Project A."
Special Talent: Fighting
Weak Point: Dim-witted
Notes: During his middle-school years, he was so much trouble nobody could do a thing with him, but nowadays he's a lot quieter.
One Last Word: He needs to pay his rent by the end of each month!

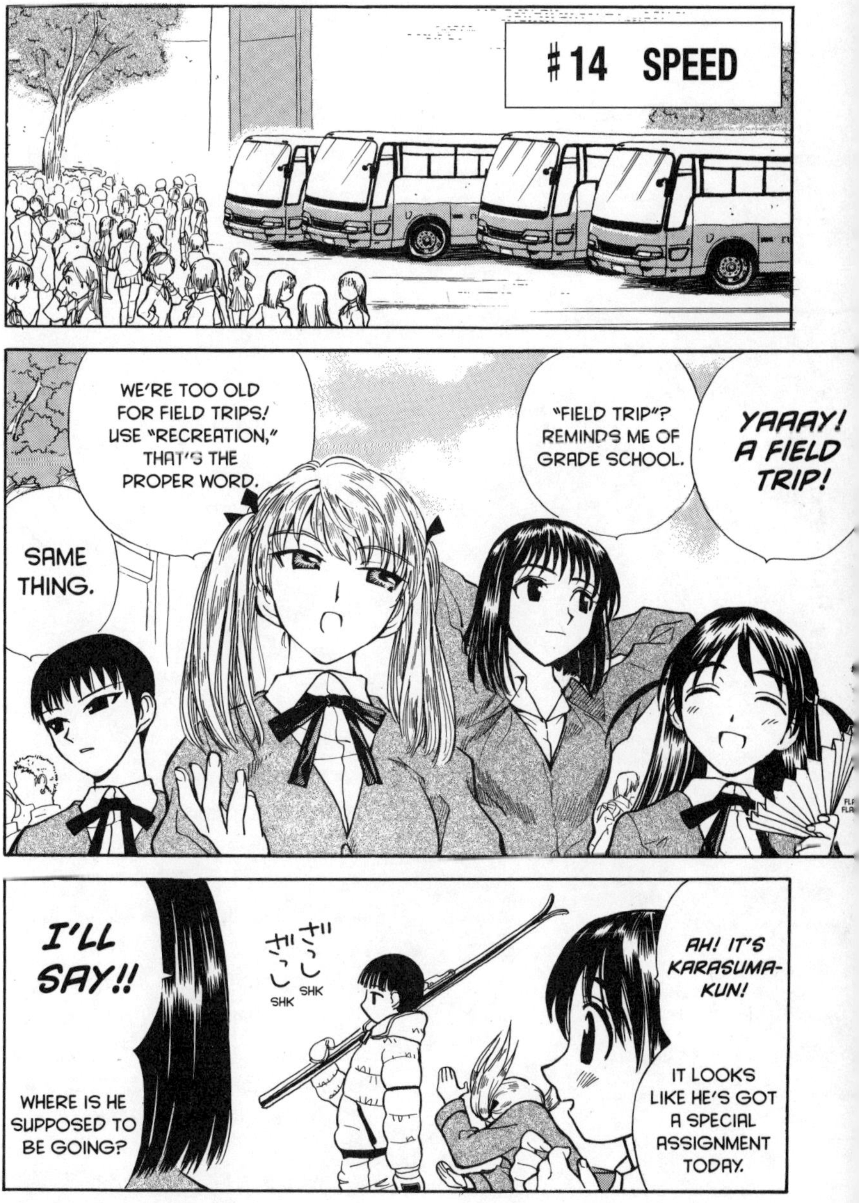
#14 SPEED
YAAAY! A FIELD TRIP!
"FIELD TRIP"? REMINDS ME OF GRADE SCHOOL.
WE'RE TOO OLD FOR FIELD TRIPS! USE "RECREATION," THAT'S THE PROPER WORD.
SAME THING.
AH! IT'S KARASUMA-KUN!
IT LOOKS LIKE HE'S GOT A SPECIAL ASSIGNMENT TODAY.
ざっし ざっし
SHK SHK
I'LL SAY!!
WHERE IS HE SUPPOSED TO BE GOING?

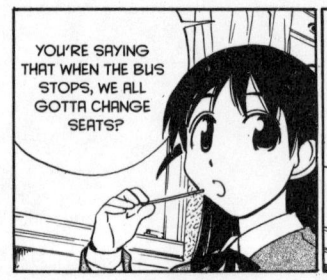

YOU'RE SAYING THAT WHEN THE BUS STOPS, WE ALL GOTTA CHANGE SEATS?

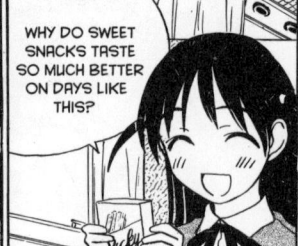

WHY DO SWEET SNACKS TASTE SO MUCH BETTER ON DAYS LIKE THIS?

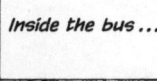

Inside the bus...

Tsukamoto Tenma: *Snack Food Bill, ¥500.*

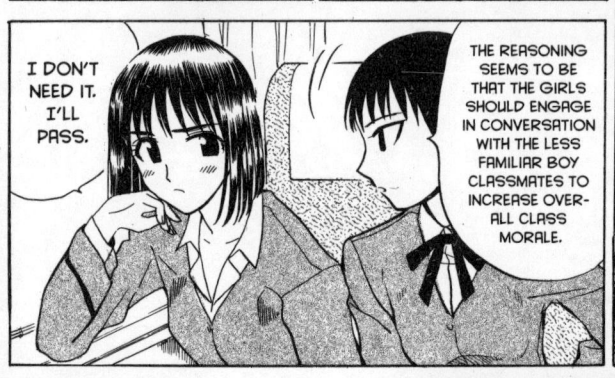

I DON'T NEED IT. I'LL PASS.

THE REASONING SEEMS TO BE THAT THE GIRLS SHOULD ENGAGE IN CONVERSATION WITH THE LESS FAMILIAR BOY CLASSMATES TO INCREASE OVERALL CLASS MORALE.

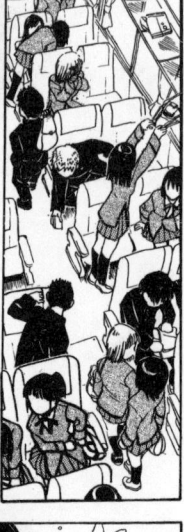

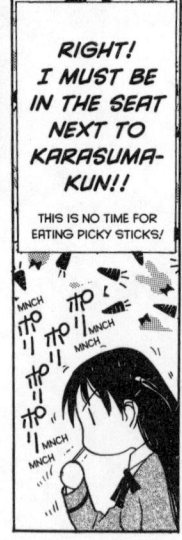

RIGHT! I MUST BE IN THE SEAT NEXT TO KARASUMA-KUN!!

THIS IS NO TIME FOR EATING PICKY STICKS!

MNCH MNCH MNCH MNCH

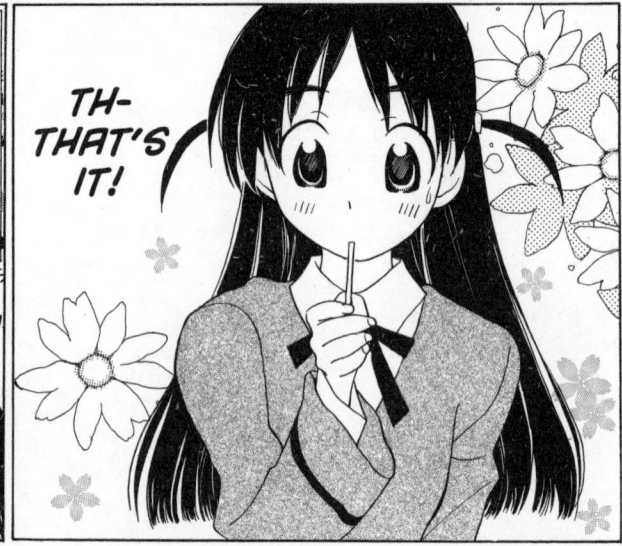

TH-THAT'S IT!

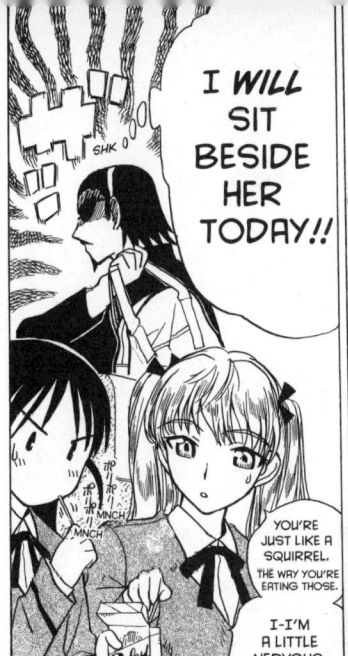

I **WILL** SIT BESIDE HER TODAY!!

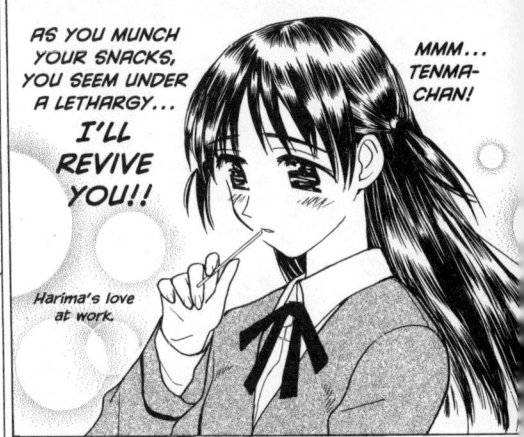

AS YOU MUNCH YOUR SNACKS, YOU SEEM UNDER A LETHARGY... *I'LL REVIVE YOU!!*

Harima's love at work.

MMM... TENMA-CHAN!

YOU'RE JUST LIKE A SQUIRREL. THE WAY YOU'RE EATING THOSE.

I-I'M A LITTLE NERVOUS.

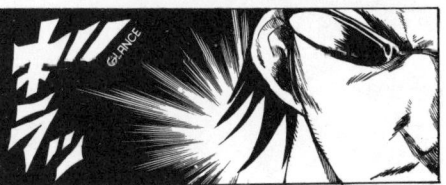

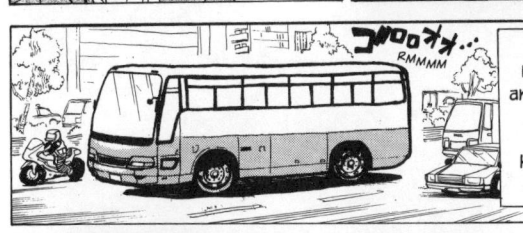

As a wide variety of thoughts and intentions intermingle within the bus, the journey begins.

However...

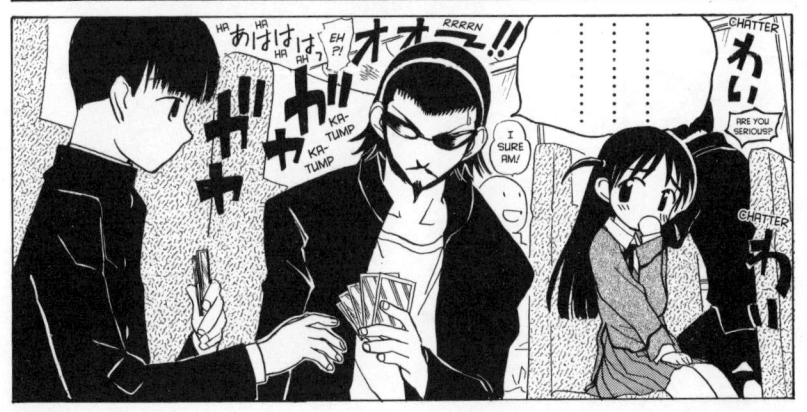

EH P!

I SURE AM!

ARE YOU SERIOUS?

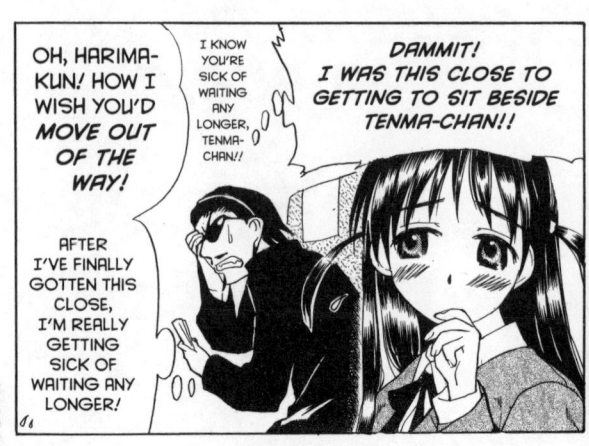

OH, HARIMA-KUN! HOW I WISH YOU'D **MOVE OUT OF THE WAY!**

AFTER I'VE FINALLY GOTTEN THIS CLOSE, I'M REALLY GETTING SICK OF WAITING ANY LONGER!

I KNOW YOU'RE SICK OF WAITING ANY LONGER, TENMA-CHAN!!

DAMMIT! I WAS THIS CLOSE TO GETTING TO SIT BESIDE TENMA-CHAN!!

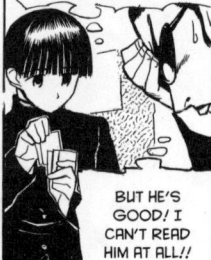

HEY!! WHY AM I SITTING HERE QUIETLY PLAYING OLD MAID?!

BUT HE'S GOOD! I CAN'T READ HIM AT ALL!!

AFTER I READ A MOUNTAIN OF MAGAZINES JUST TO HAVE TOPICS OF CONVERSATION READY TO USE TODAY, I'M NOT GOING TO LET HER GET AWAY!

I WONDER IF TENMA LIKES MANGOKU?

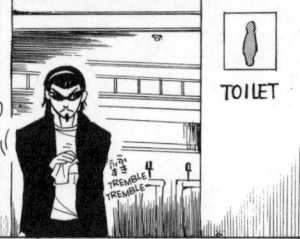

TOILET

TREMBLE TREMBLE

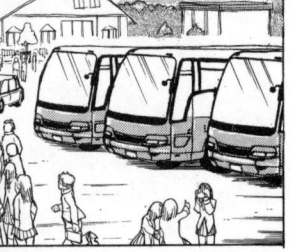

AND THAT'S THE WAY IT WAS ALL THE WAY TO THE PARKING AREA.

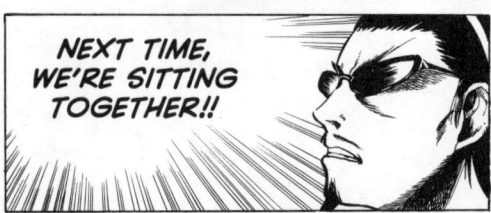

NEXT TIME, WE'RE SITTING TOGETHER!!

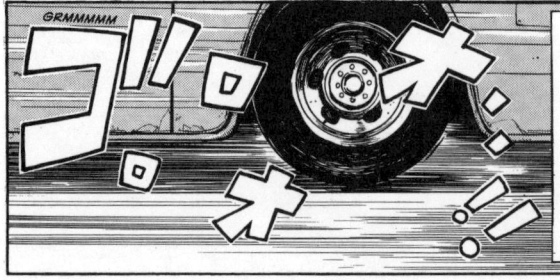

GRMMMMM

ゴ!! ロ ボ !! !!

NOW, IT'S TIME TO GO!!

I CAUGHT THE WRONG BUS!!
YEAH, THANKS.
WHAT A SPLENDID YOUNG MAN YOU ARE!
AND SUCH A CUTE CHILD.
HEY, YOUNGSTER! IF YOU CAUGHT THE EYE OF TSURU-SAN, THEN YOU MUST BE ONE IMPRESSIVE KIDDO!
MAKES ME WANT TO ADOPT YOU!
Flower Playing Cards
NOOO!!
AND THIS OLD GUY'S PRETTY GOOD AT CARDS, TOO!
GRRRMM
Meanwhile, Tenma-chan is ...
FINALLY! THE SEAT NEXT TO KARASUMA-KUN IS EMPTY!
NOW'S MY CHANCE!
TMP
BAMP
WHY DON'T I SIT NEXT TO HIM?
OWWW!

Harima Kenji: Joins an Old Folks' Community

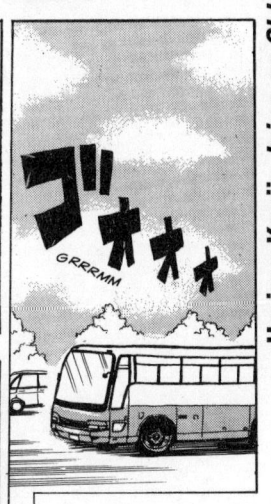

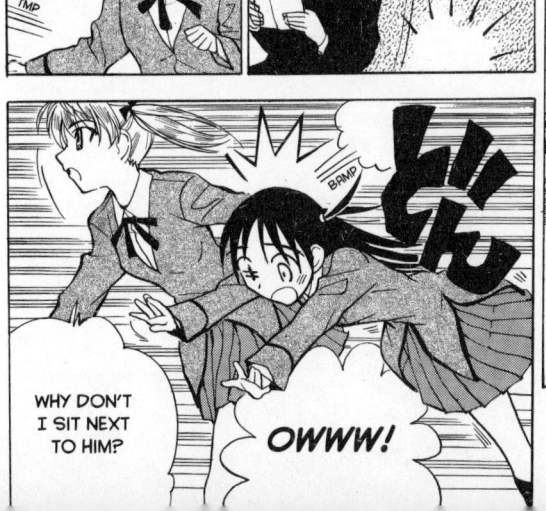

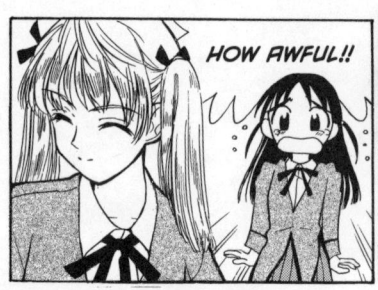

HOW AWFUL!!

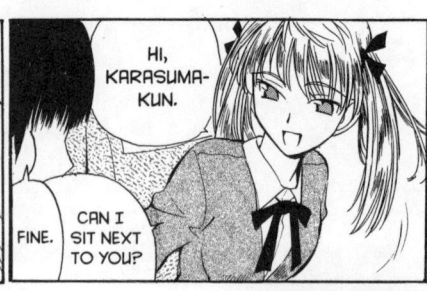

HI, KARASUMA-KUN.

FINE.

CAN I SIT NEXT TO YOU?

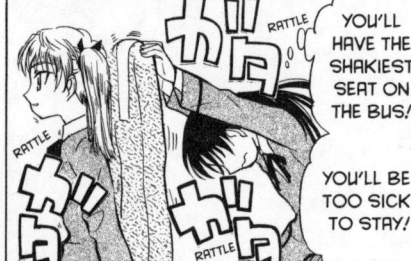

RATTLE

RATTLE

RATTLE

YOU'LL HAVE THE SHAKIEST SEAT ON THE BUS!

YOU'LL BE TOO SICK TO STAY!

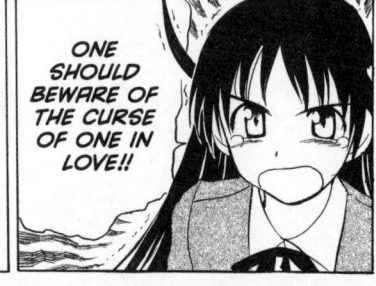

ONE SHOULD BEWARE OF THE CURSE OF ONE IN LOVE!!

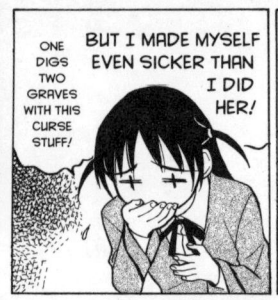

ONE DIGS TWO GRAVES WITH THIS CURSE STUFF!

BUT I MADE MYSELF EVEN SICKER THAN I DID HER!

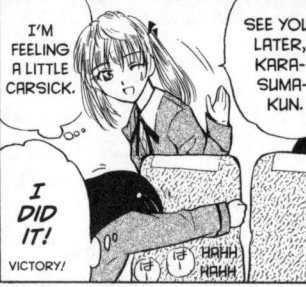

I'M FEELING A LITTLE CARSICK.

I DID IT!

VICTORY!

SEE YOU LATER, KARA-SUMA-KUN.

HAHH HAHH

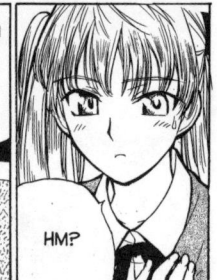

HM?

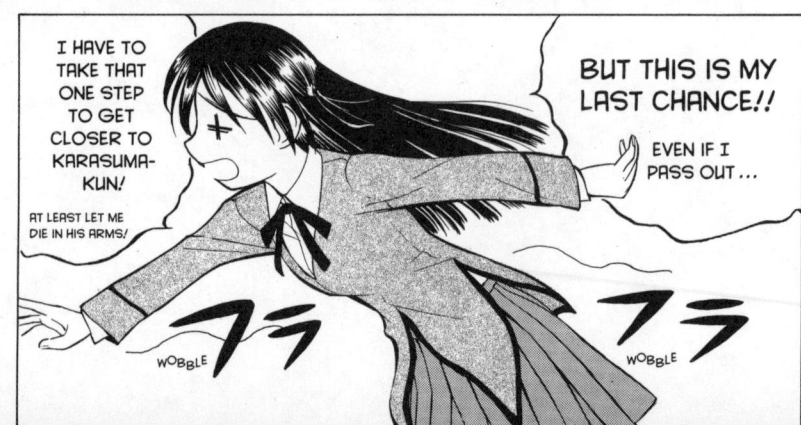

I HAVE TO TAKE THAT ONE STEP TO GET CLOSER TO KARASUMA-KUN!

AT LEAST LET ME DIE IN HIS ARMS!

BUT THIS IS MY LAST CHANCE!!

EVEN IF I PASS OUT...

WOBBLE

WOBBLE

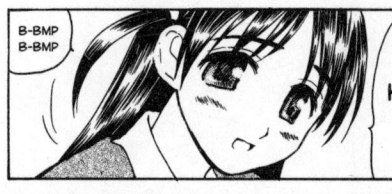

B-BMP
B-BMP

U-UM... KARASUMA-KUN?

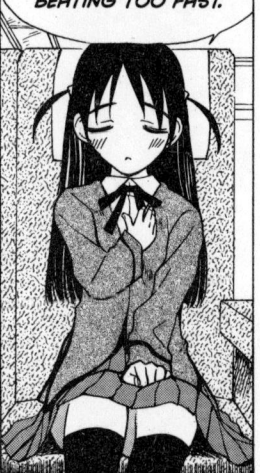

UFF!
I'M FINALLY SITTING NEXT TO HIM! I WANT TO SAY SOMETHING, BUT MY HEART'S BEATING TOO FAST.

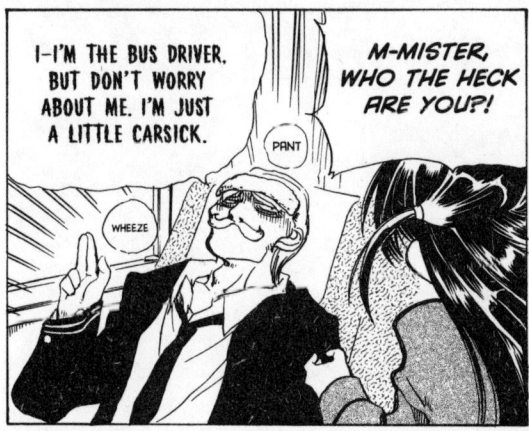

I-I'M THE BUS DRIVER, BUT DON'T WORRY ABOUT ME. I'M JUST A LITTLE CARSICK.

PANT

WHEEZE

M-MISTER, WHO THE HECK ARE YOU?!

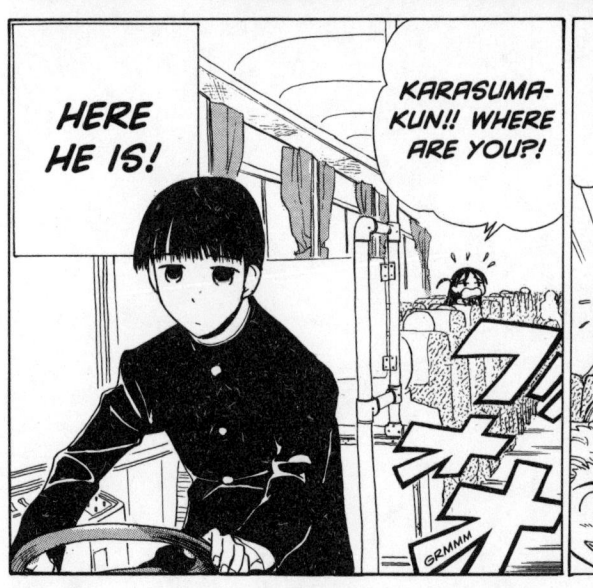

HERE HE IS!

KARASUMA-KUN!! WHERE ARE YOU?!

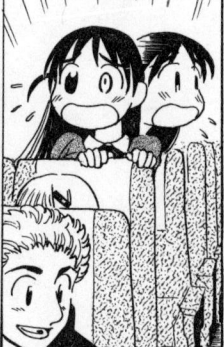

HUH?! THEN WHERE DID KARASUMA-KUN GO OFF TO?!

ブ
ォ
ォ

GRMMM

14 . . . . Fin.

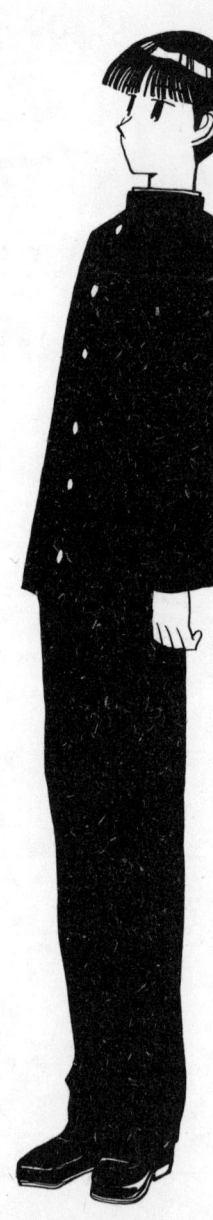

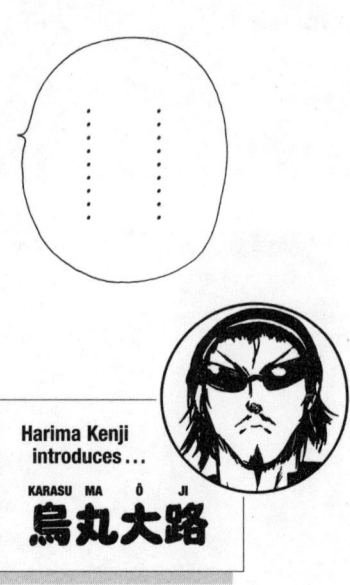

Harima Kenji
introduces...

KARASU MA Ô JI
烏丸大路

STATS:

Height: Dunno. A little shorter than me. 175 cm (5' 9") maybe?

Favorite Thing: Dunno

Least Favorite Thing: Dunno

Special Talent: Probably being judgmental. Aside from that, I hear he's good at school.

Hair Style: Really weird, huh?

Name: I always thought it was Torimaru.

Distinguishing Feature: He's always sitting alone spacing out.

Notes: He'll be transferring away in a year. For me, that's perfect timing!

One Last Word: I got no idea what he's thinking, but I don't think he's all that annoying.

At the exit...

SHHHHHH

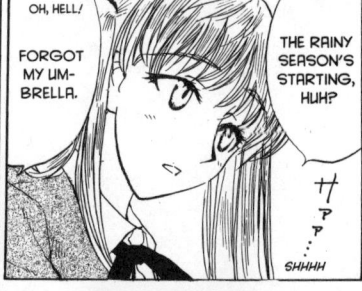

OH, HELL!

FORGOT MY UM-BRELLA.

THE RAINY SEASON'S STARTING, HUH?

H
P
P
...
SHHHH

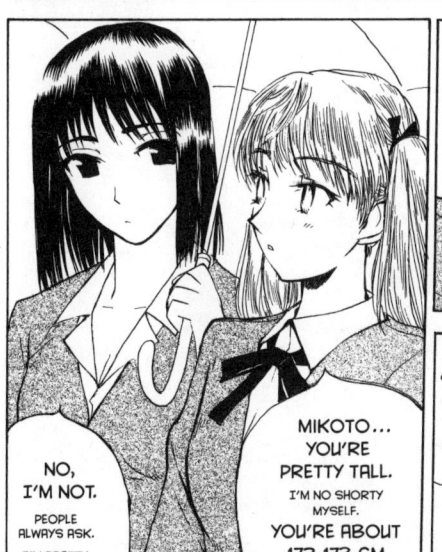

MIKOTO... YOU'RE PRETTY TALL.

I'M NO SHORTY MYSELF.

YOU'RE ABOUT 172-173 CM (5' 8")?

NO, I'M NOT.

PEOPLE ALWAYS ASK.

I'M PRETTY CLOSE TO THAT, THOUGH.

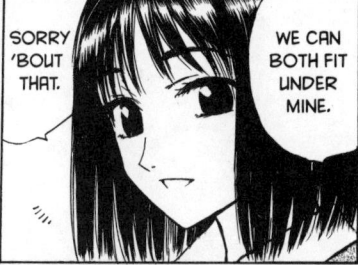

SORRY 'BOUT THAT.

WE CAN BOTH FIT UNDER MINE.

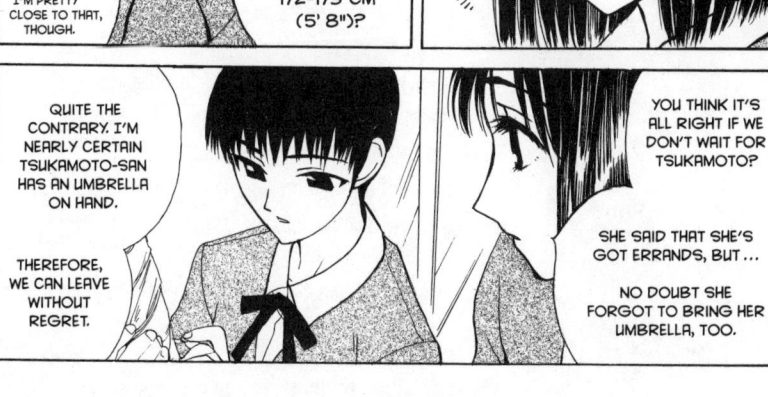

QUITE THE CONTRARY. I'M NEARLY CERTAIN TSUKAMOTO-SAN HAS AN UMBRELLA ON HAND.

THEREFORE, WE CAN LEAVE WITHOUT REGRET.

YOU THINK IT'S ALL RIGHT IF WE DON'T WAIT FOR TSUKAMOTO?

SHE SAID THAT SHE'S GOT ERRANDS, BUT ...

NO DOUBT SHE FORGOT TO BRING HER UMBRELLA, TOO.

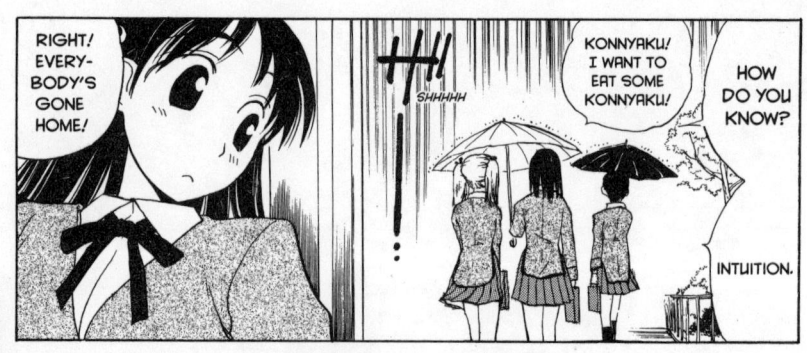

RIGHT! EVERYBODY'S GONE HOME!

SHHHHH

KONNYAKU! I WANT TO EAT SOME KONNYAKU!

HOW DO YOU KNOW?

INTUITION.

Tsukamoto Tenma: Always Depending on Her Sister.

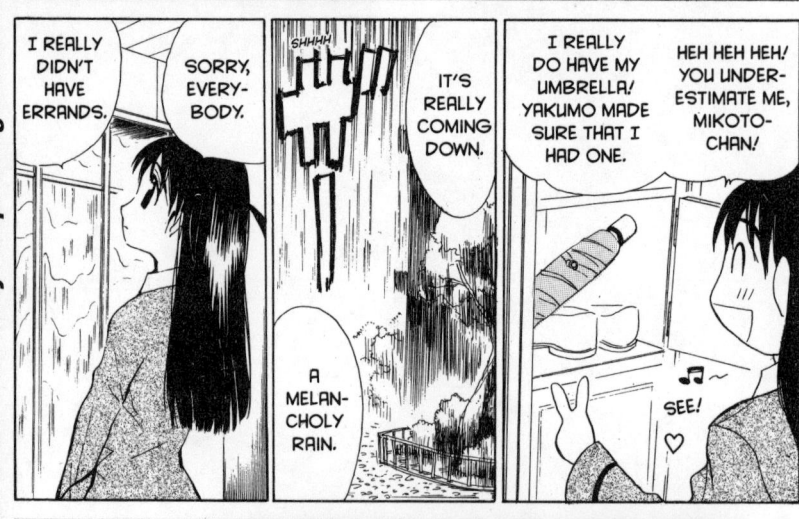

I REALLY DIDN'T HAVE ERRANDS.

SORRY, EVERYBODY.

SHHHH

IT'S REALLY COMING DOWN.

A MELANCHOLY RAIN.

I REALLY DO HAVE MY UMBRELLA! YAKUMO MADE SURE THAT I HAD ONE.

HEH HEH HEH! YOU UNDERESTIMATE ME, MIKOTO-CHAN!

SEE! ♥

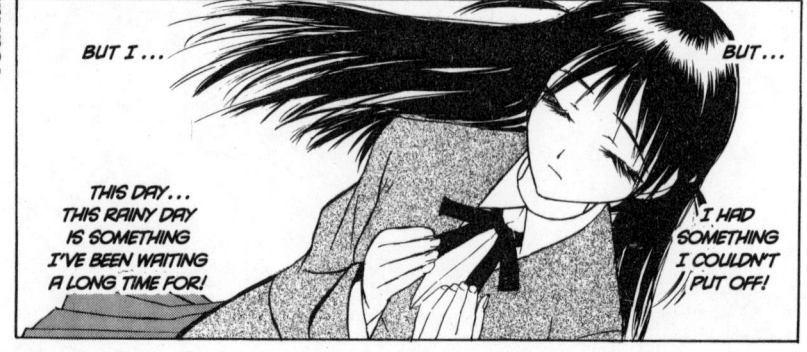

BUT I...

BUT...

THIS DAY... THIS RAINY DAY IS SOMETHING I'VE BEEN WAITING A LONG TIME FOR!

I HAD SOMETHING I COULDN'T PUT OFF!

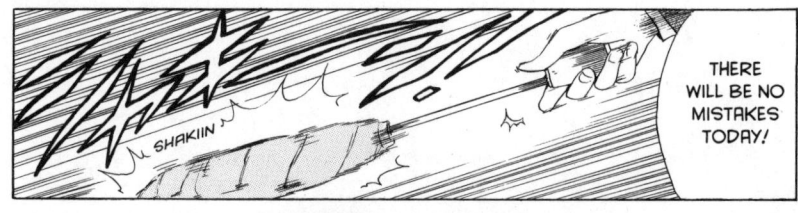

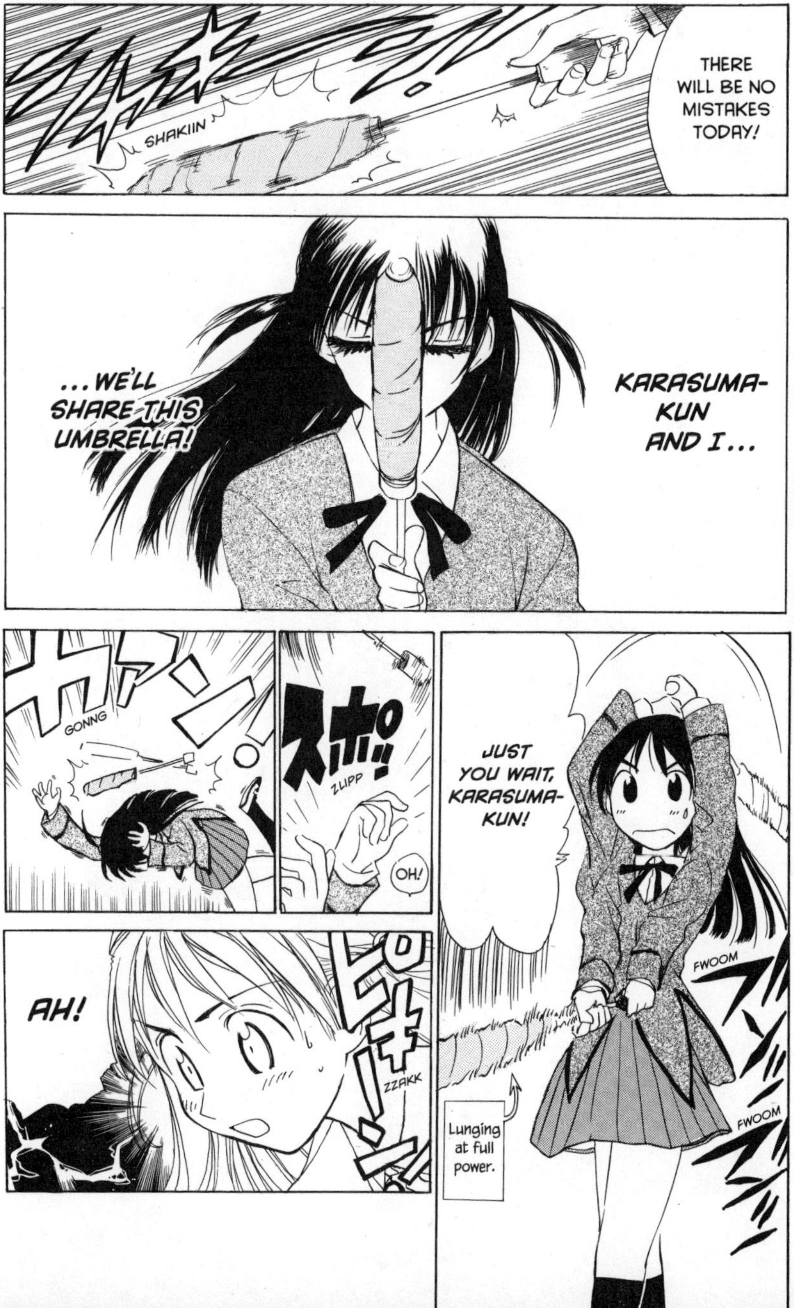

SHAKIIN

THERE WILL BE NO MISTAKES TODAY!

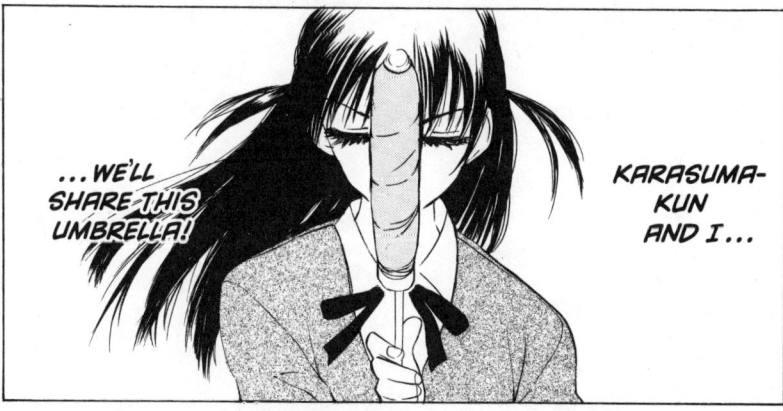

KARASUMA-KUN AND I...

...WE'LL SHARE THIS UMBRELLA!

GONNG

ZUPP

OH!

JUST YOU WAIT, KARASUMA-KUN!

FWOOM

FWOOM

Lunging at full power.

AH!

ZZAKK

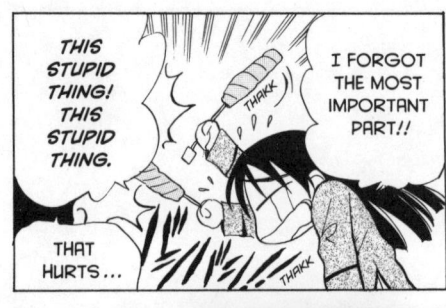

THIS STUPID THING! THIS STUPID THING.

THAK

THAT HURTS...

I FORGOT THE MOST IMPORTANT PART!!

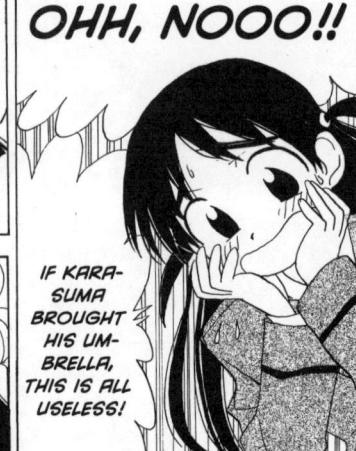

OHH, NOOO!!

IF KARASUMA BROUGHT HIS UMBRELLA, THIS IS ALL USELESS!

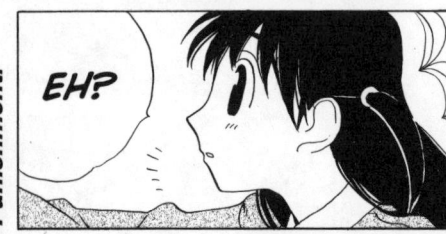

EH?

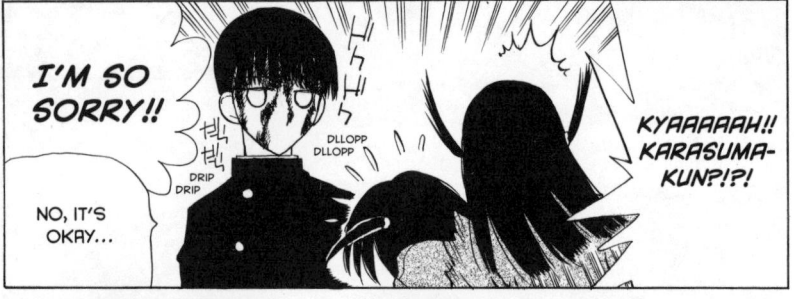

I'M SO SORRY!!

NO, IT'S OKAY...

DRIP DRIP

DLLOPP DLLOPP

KYAAAAAH!! KARASUMA-KUN?!?!

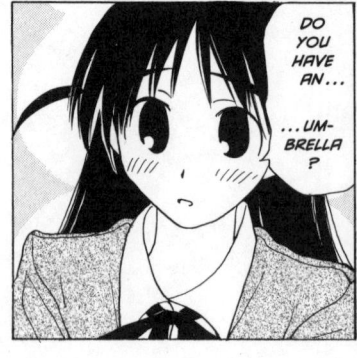

DO YOU HAVE AN...

...UM-BRELLA?

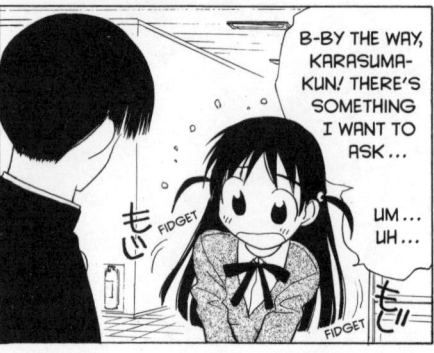

B-BY THE WAY, KARASUMA-KUN! THERE'S SOMETHING I WANT TO ASK...

UM... UH...

FIDGET

FIDGET

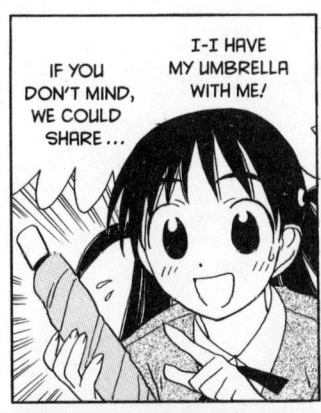

IF YOU DON'T MIND, WE COULD SHARE...

I-I HAVE MY UMBRELLA WITH ME!

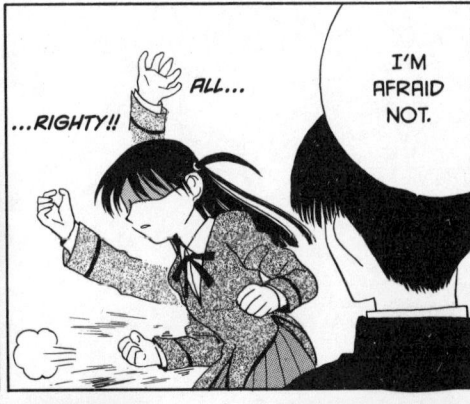

...RIGHTY!!

ALL...

I'M AFRAID NOT.

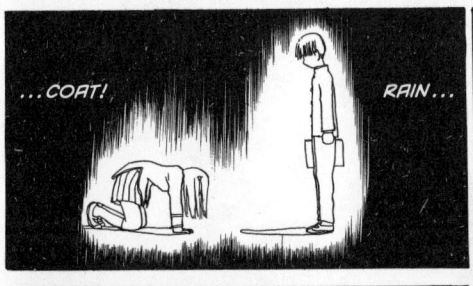

...COAT!

RAIN...

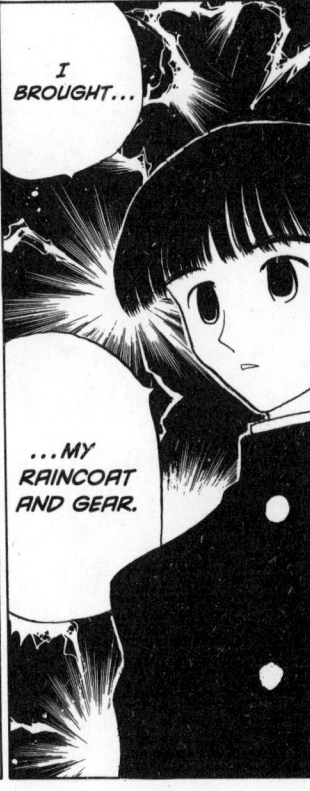

I BROUGHT...

...MY RAINCOAT AND GEAR.

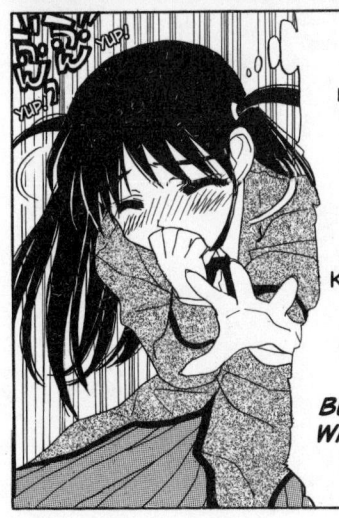

YUP! YUP! YUP!

S-SURE! MODERN HIGH-SCHOOL STUDENTS BRING RAIN-COATS THESE DAYS!

THAT'S KARASUMA-KUN FOR YOU! TWO STEPS AHEAD OF THE NORMAL STUDENT!

BUT THAT'S WHY I LOVE HIM!

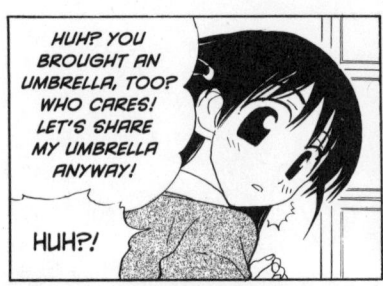

HUH? YOU BROUGHT AN UMBRELLA, TOO? WHO CARES! LET'S SHARE MY UMBRELLA ANYWAY!

HUH?!

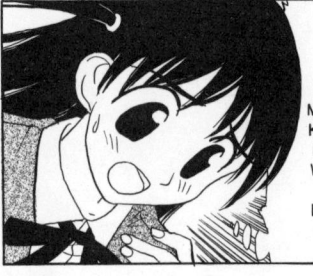

B-BUT WHAT'LL I DO? THAT MEANS THAT KARASUMA-KUN AND I WILL NEVER SHARE AN UMBRELLA!

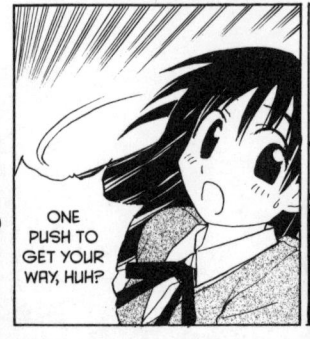

ONE PUSH TO GET YOUR WAY, HUH?

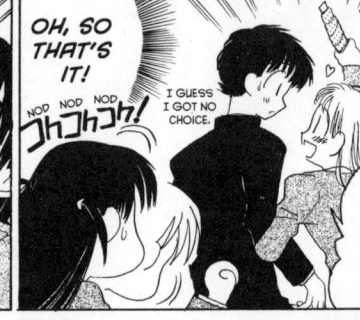

OH, SO THAT'S IT!

NOD NOD NOD

I GUESS I GOT NO CHOICE.

YOU MEAN USE ONLY ONE UMBRELLA ON PURPOSE?!

I'VE *ALWAYS* WANTED TO DO THAT! YOU'LL LIKE IT! I PROMISE! ♥

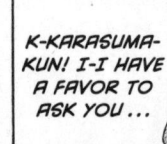

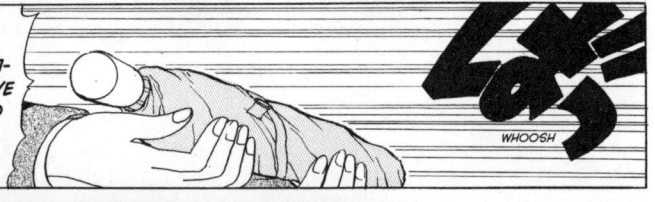

K-KARASUMA-KUN! I-I HAVE A FAVOR TO ASK YOU ...

WHOOSH

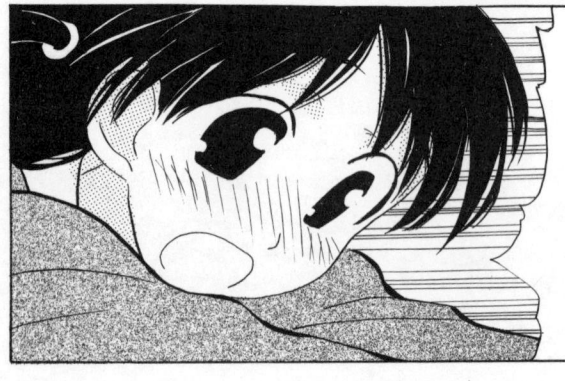

C-COULD YOU PLEASE GO WITH ME UNDER MY UMBRELLA?

I P-PROMISE I'LL LIKE IT! I-I MEAN, YOU'LL LIKE IT!

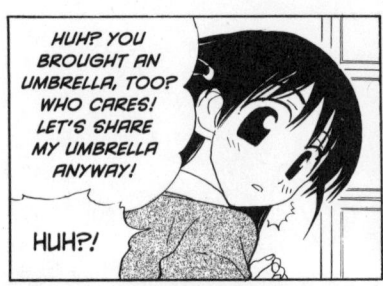

Tsukamoto Tenma: *Hang in There*

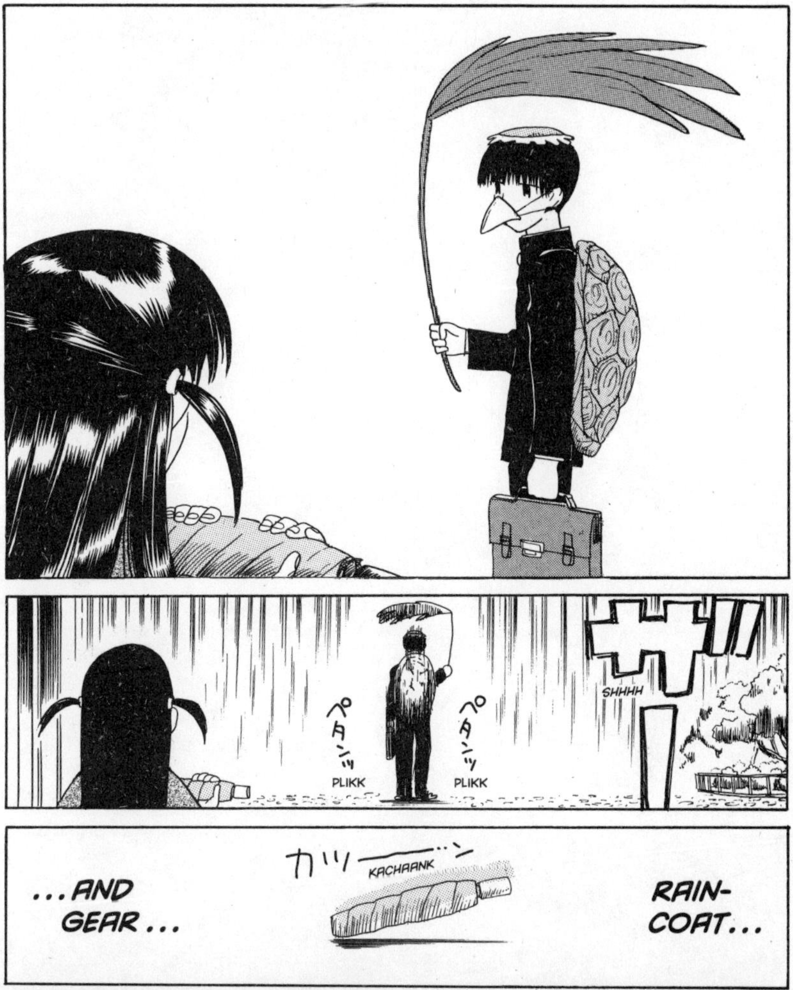

...AND
GEAR...

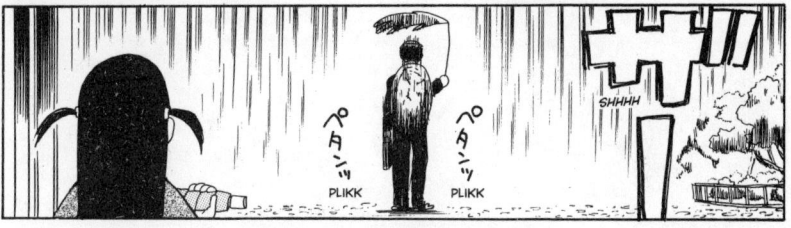
KACHAANK

RAIN-
COAT...

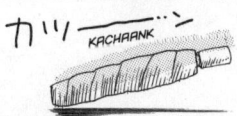

I've completely forgotten the countdown, but Karasuma-kun has only 302 days left before the transfer!!

15 . . . . Fin.

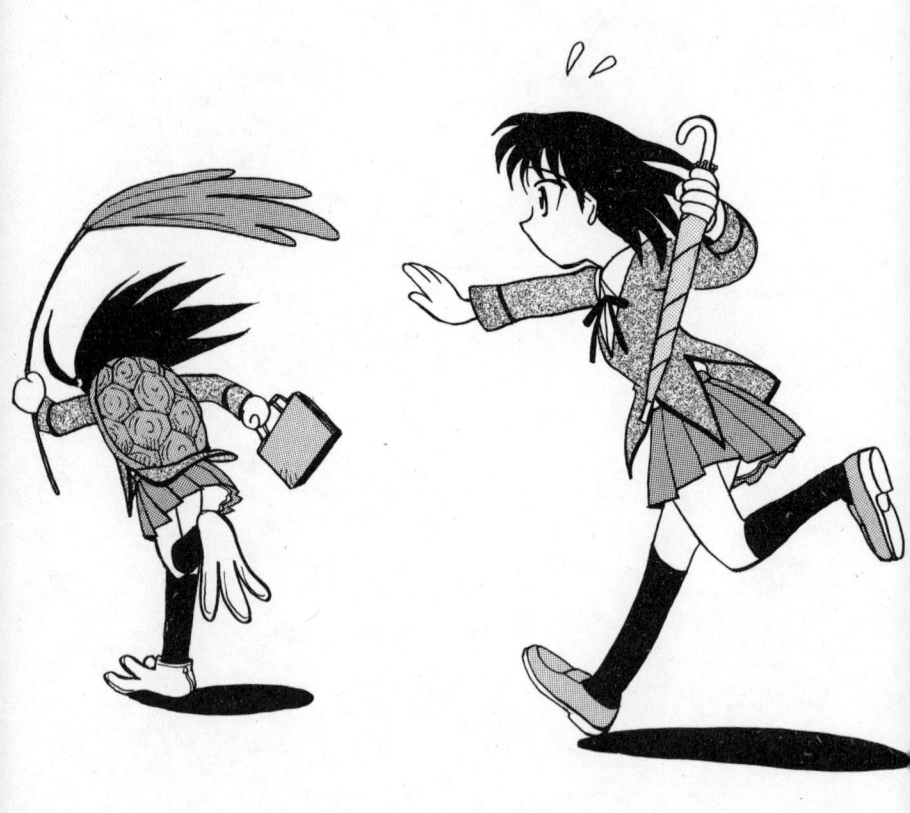

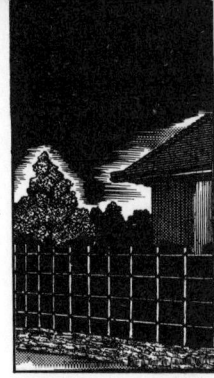

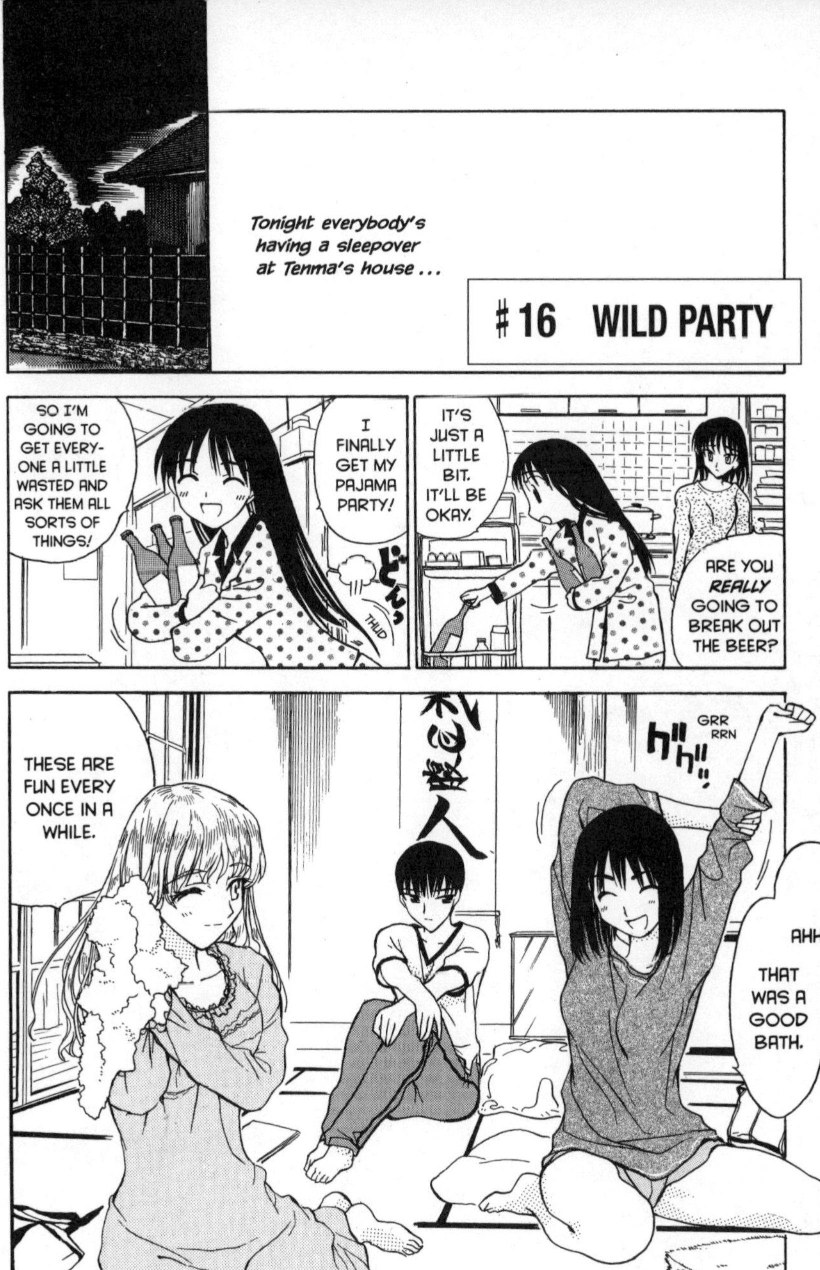

Tonight everybody's having a sleepover at Tenma's house ...

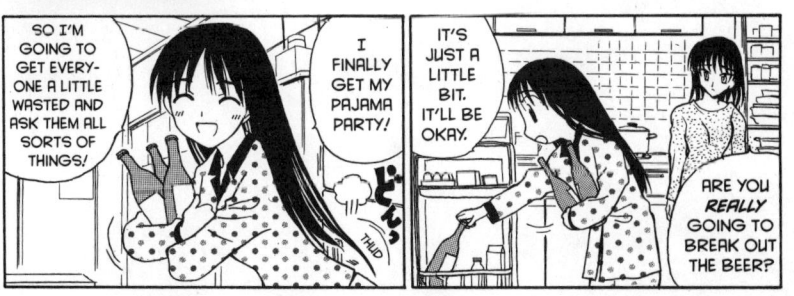

#16 WILD PARTY

SO I'M GOING TO GET EVERY-ONE A LITTLE WASTED AND ASK THEM ALL SORTS OF THINGS!

I FINALLY GET MY PAJAMA PARTY!

THUD

IT'S JUST A LITTLE BIT. IT'LL BE OKAY.

ARE YOU *REALLY* GOING TO BREAK OUT THE BEER?

THESE ARE FUN EVERY ONCE IN A WHILE.

GRR RRN

AHHH! THAT WAS A GOOD BATH.

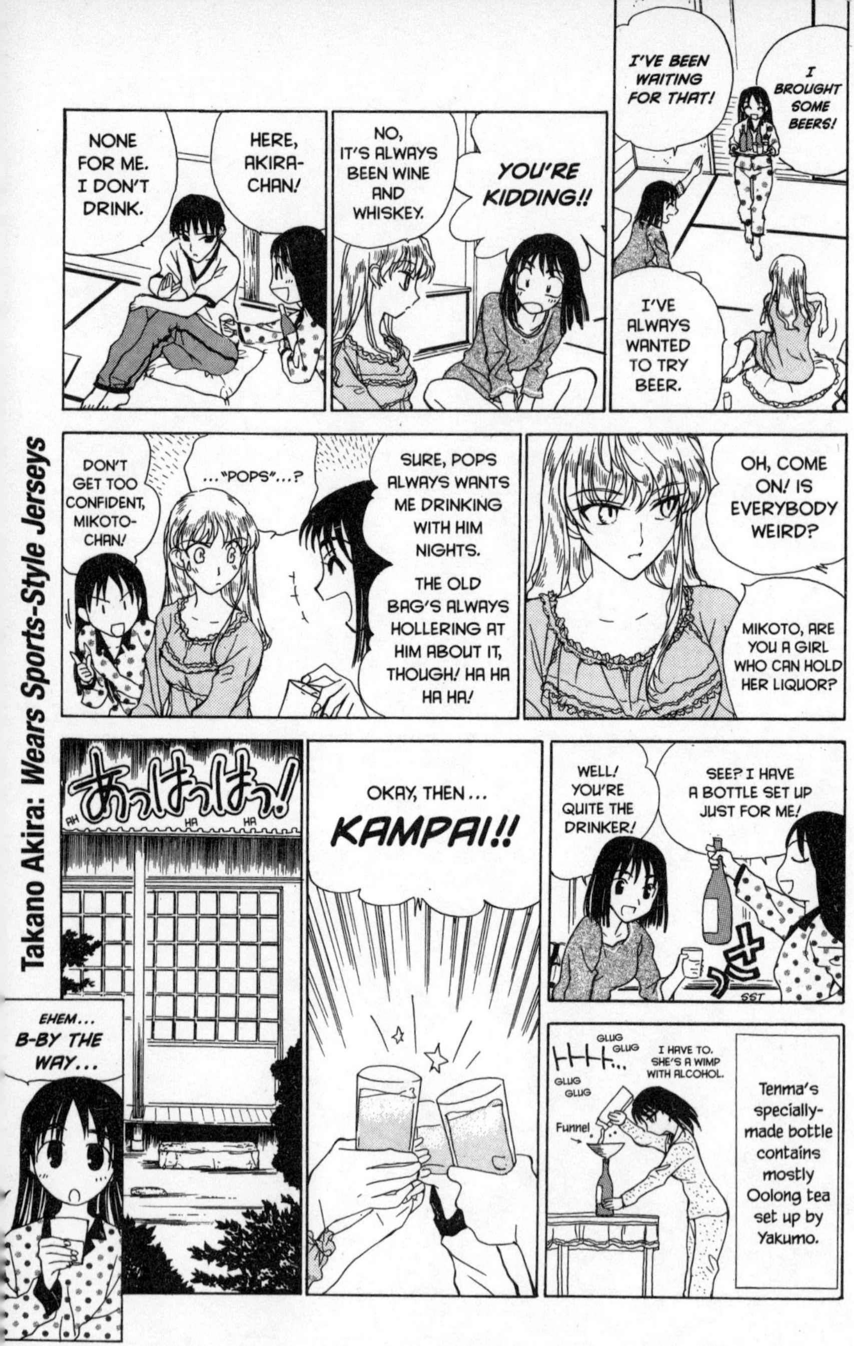

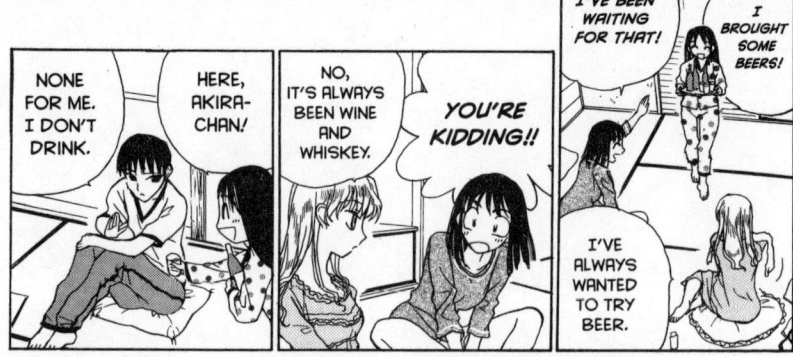

NONE FOR ME. I DON'T DRINK.

HERE, AKIRA-CHAN!

NO, IT'S ALWAYS BEEN WINE AND WHISKEY.

YOU'RE KIDDING!!

I'VE BEEN WAITING FOR THAT!

I BROUGHT SOME BEERS!

I'VE ALWAYS WANTED TO TRY BEER.

DON'T GET TOO CONFIDENT, MIKOTO-CHAN!

..."POPS"...?

SURE, POPS ALWAYS WANTS ME DRINKING WITH HIM NIGHTS.

THE OLD BAG'S ALWAYS HOLLERING AT HIM ABOUT IT, THOUGH! HA HA HA HA!

OH, COME ON! IS EVERYBODY WEIRD?

MIKOTO, ARE YOU A GIRL WHO CAN HOLD HER LIQUOR?

あっはっはっ！

OKAY, THEN...

KAMPAI!!

WELL! YOU'RE QUITE THE DRINKER!

SEE? I HAVE A BOTTLE SET UP JUST FOR ME!

EHEM... B-BY THE WAY...

GLUG GLUG
GLUG GLUG
Funnel!

I HAVE TO. SHE'S A WIMP WITH ALCOHOL.

Tenma's specially-made bottle contains mostly Oolong tea set up by Yakumo.

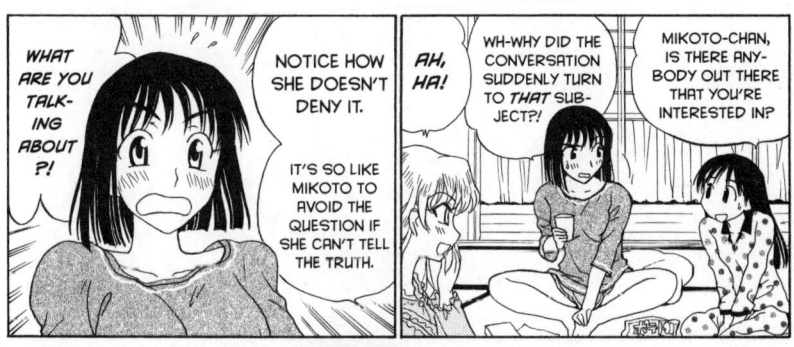

WHAT ARE YOU TALKING ABOUT?!

NOTICE HOW SHE DOESN'T DENY IT.

IT'S SO LIKE MIKOTO TO AVOID THE QUESTION IF SHE CAN'T TELL THE TRUTH.

AH, HA!

WH-WHY DID THE CONVERSATION SUDDENLY TURN TO *THAT* SUBJECT?!

MIKOTO-CHAN, IS THERE ANYBODY OUT THERE THAT YOU'RE INTERESTED IN?

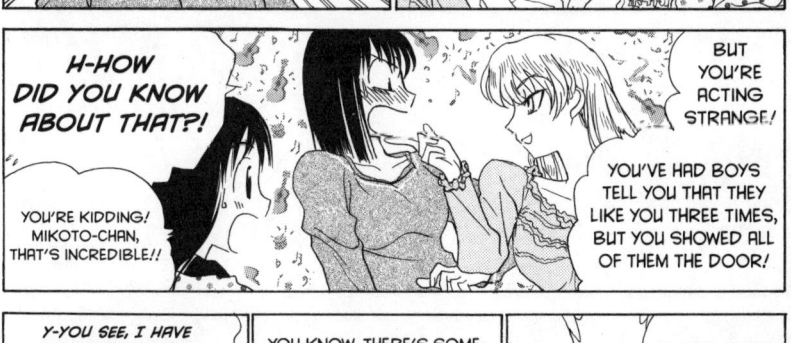

H-HOW DID YOU KNOW ABOUT THAT?!

YOU'RE KIDDING! MIKOTO-CHAN, THAT'S INCREDIBLE!!

BUT YOU'RE ACTING STRANGE!

YOU'VE HAD BOYS TELL YOU THAT THEY LIKE YOU THREE TIMES, BUT YOU SHOWED ALL OF THEM THE DOOR!

Tsukamoto Yakumo: *Loves the Period Pieces.*

Y-YOU SEE, I HAVE THIS FRIEND WHO IS WORRIED ABOUT IT... MUMBLE, MUMBLE...

YOU KNOW, THERE'S SOMETHING I'VE BEEN MEANING TO ASK ABOUT THAT... H-HOW DOES A PERSON GO ABOUT SAYING THEY LIKE SOMEBODY?

YOU'VE FOOLED THEM ALL, HUH?

FIVE TIMES?!

NOT TO BRAG, BUT I'VE HAD IT FIVE TIMES.

AH-HAAAAH!

I GET IT.

IS *THAT* HOW IT IS?

NO IMAGINATION, HUH?

I'LL GET YOU! HYAAH! HYAAH!

SIP SIP

Eight times.

Yakumo at the ready, just in case.

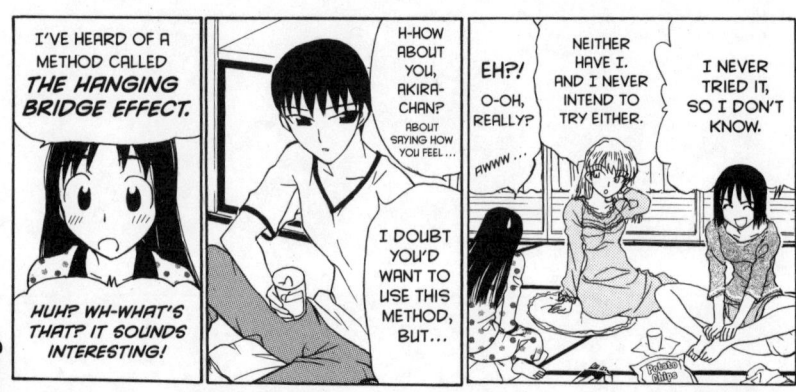

I'VE HEARD OF A METHOD CALLED *THE HANGING BRIDGE EFFECT.*

HUH? WH-WHAT'S THAT? IT SOUNDS INTERESTING!

H-HOW ABOUT YOU, AKIRA-CHAN? ABOUT SAYING HOW YOU FEEL...

I DOUBT YOU'D WANT TO USE THIS METHOD, BUT...

EH?! O-OH, REALLY?

AWWW...

NEITHER HAVE I. AND I NEVER INTEND TO TRY EITHER.

I NEVER TRIED IT, SO I DON'T KNOW.

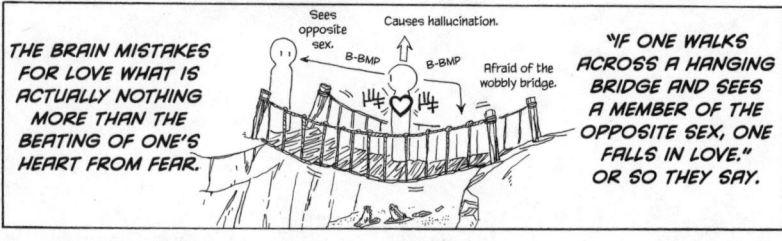

Sees opposite sex.
Causes hallucination.
B-BMP
B-BMP
Afraid of the wobbly bridge.

THE BRAIN MISTAKES FOR LOVE WHAT IS ACTUALLY NOTHING MORE THAN THE BEATING OF ONE'S HEART FROM FEAR.

"IF ONE WALKS ACROSS A HANGING BRIDGE AND SEES A MEMBER OF THE OPPOSITE SEX, ONE FALLS IN LOVE." OR SO THEY SAY.

IN SIMPLE TERMS, THAT'S ABOUT IT.

HMM... SO WHAT YOU'RE SAYING IS IF A GUY IS REALLY SCARED AT THE MOMENT HE LOOKS AT YOU, HE'LL FALL IN LOVE WITH YOU? DID I GET THAT RIGHT?

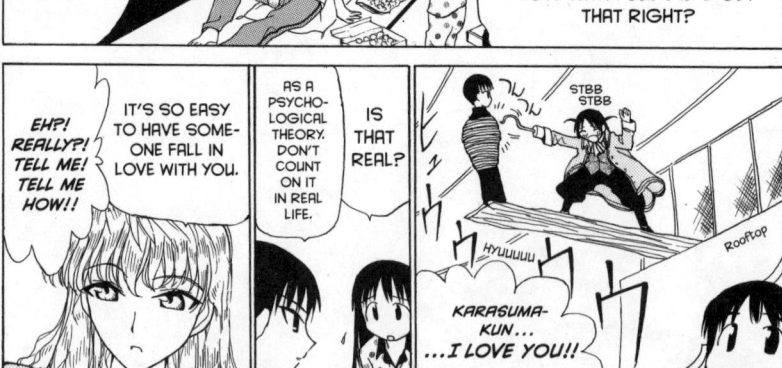

EH?! REALLY?! TELL ME! TELL ME HOW!!

IT'S SO EASY TO HAVE SOMEONE FALL IN LOVE WITH YOU.

AS A PSYCHOLOGICAL THEORY. DON'T COUNT ON IT IN REAL LIFE.

IS THAT REAL?

STBB STBB

HYUUUUU

Rooftop

KARASUMA-KUN... ...I LOVE YOU!!

LOOK, YOU'RE ABOUT TO FALL! YOU'RE GONNA FALL!

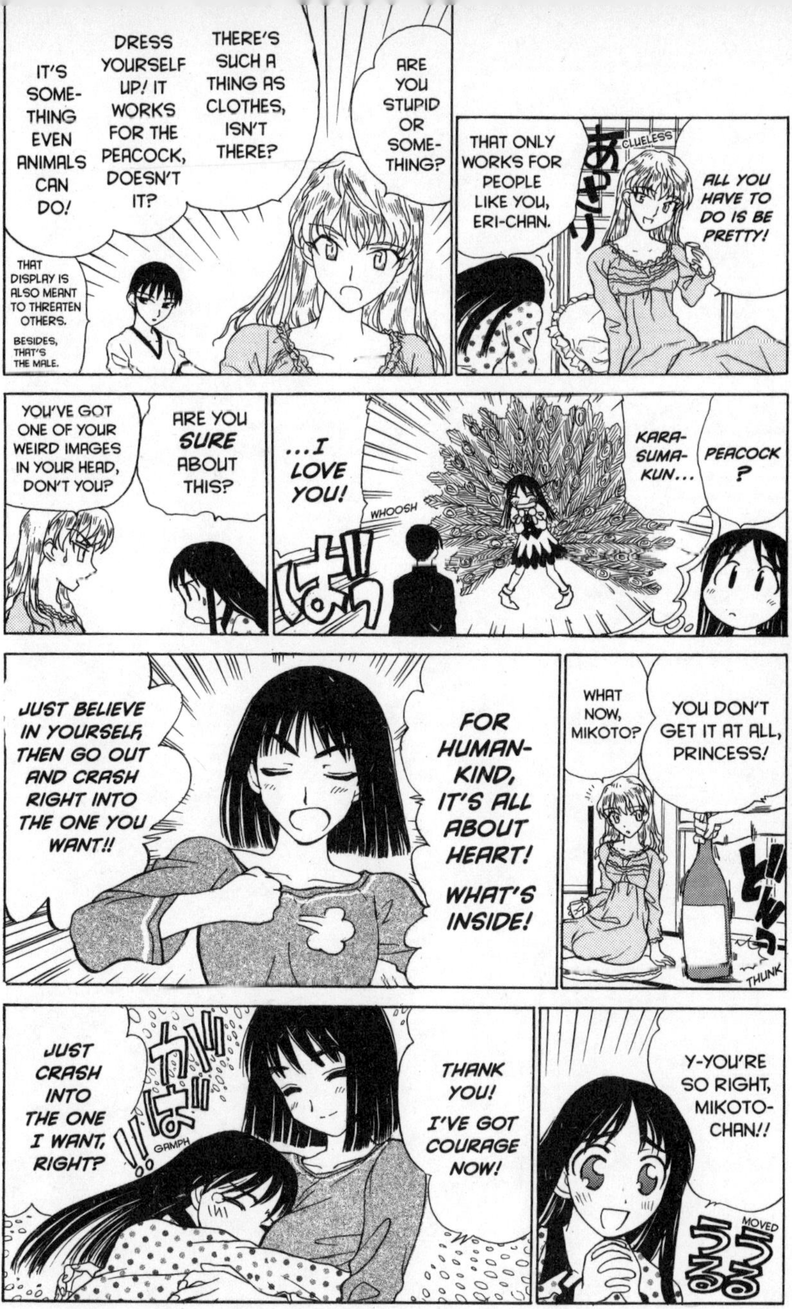
ALL YOU HAVE TO DO IS BE PRETTY!
CLUELESS
THAT ONLY WORKS FOR PEOPLE LIKE YOU, ERI-CHAN.
ARE YOU STUPID OR SOME-THING?
THERE'S SUCH A THING AS CLOTHES, ISN'T THERE?
DRESS YOURSELF UP! IT WORKS FOR THE PEACOCK, DOESN'T IT?
IT'S SOME-THING EVEN ANIMALS CAN DO!
THAT DISPLAY IS ALSO MEANT TO THREATEN OTHERS.
BESIDES, THAT'S THE MALE.
PEACOCK?
KARA-SUMA-KUN...
...I LOVE YOU!
WHOOSH
ARE YOU SURE ABOUT THIS?
YOU'VE GOT ONE OF YOUR WEIRD IMAGES IN YOUR HEAD, DON'T YOU?
YOU DON'T GET IT AT ALL, PRINCESS!
WHAT NOW, MIKOTO?
THUNK
FOR HUMAN-KIND, IT'S ALL ABOUT HEART!
WHAT'S INSIDE!
JUST BELIEVE IN YOURSELF, THEN GO OUT AND CRASH RIGHT INTO THE ONE YOU WANT!!
Y-YOU'RE SO RIGHT, MIKOTO-CHAN!!
MOVED
THANK YOU! I'VE GOT COURAGE NOW!
JUST CRASH INTO THE ONE I WANT, RIGHT?
GAMPH

Suô Mikoto: ***Drinks Like a Fish.***

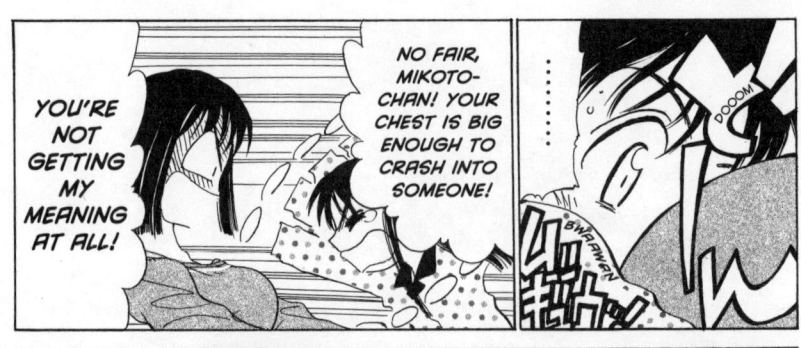

Tsukamoto Tenma: Looking Miserable.

YOU'RE NOT GETTING MY MEANING AT ALL!

NO FAIR, MIKOTO-CHAN! YOUR CHEST IS BIG ENOUGH TO CRASH INTO SOMEONE!

DOOOM

SWARWEN

IF I TAKE EVERYTHING THEY JUST SAID AND PUT IT TO-GETHER...

BEFORE I FORGET, I'LL PUT THESE DOWN IN MY NOTES.

NOW MY COURAGE IS ALL MELTING AWAY... AND I'VE GOTTA GO TO THE BATHROOM.

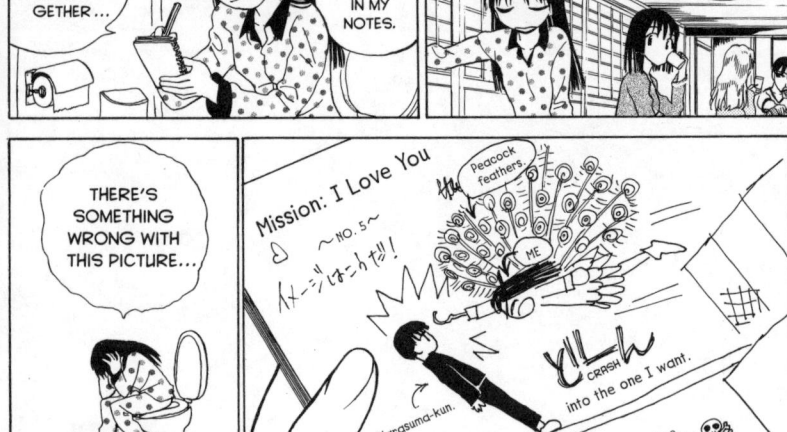

THERE'S SOMETHING WRONG WITH THIS PICTURE...

Mission: I Love You

~NO. 5~

Peacock feathers.

ME

CRASH

into the one I want.

Karasuma-kun.

Dangerous place.

The school roof?

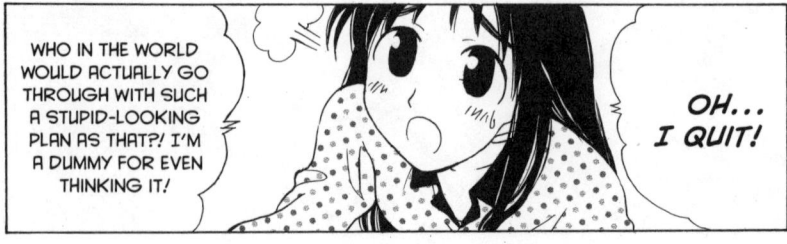

WHO IN THE WORLD WOULD ACTUALLY GO THROUGH WITH SUCH A STUPID-LOOKING PLAN AS THAT?! I'M A DUMMY FOR EVEN THINKING IT!

OH... I QUIT!

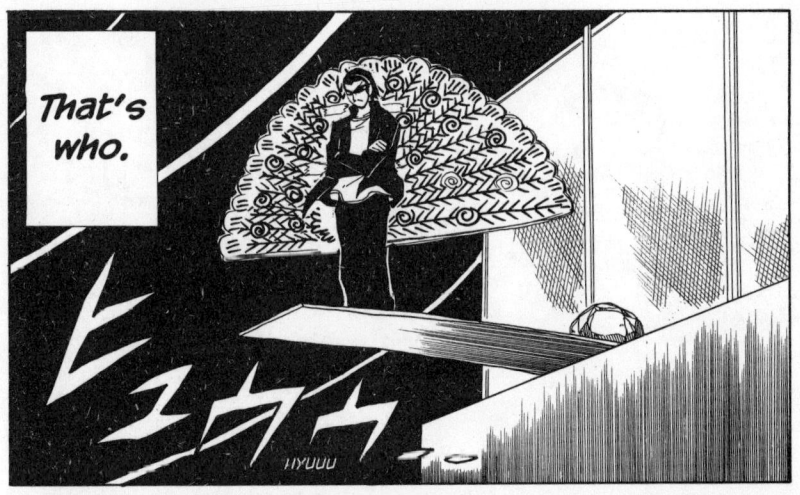

That's who.

HYUUU

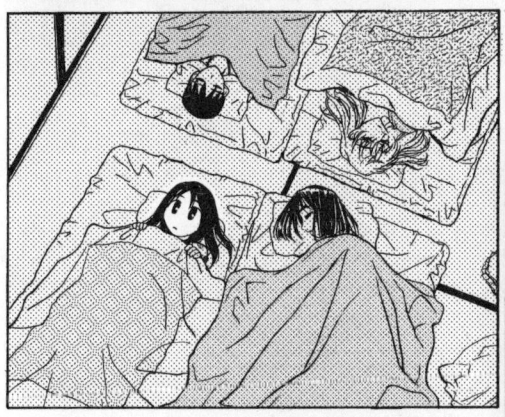

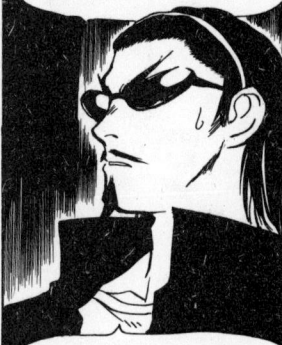

IT'S A MAN'S DUTY TO ACCEPT ANY CHALLENGE, AS LONG AS THERE IS EVEN A 1 % CHANCE OF SUCCESS!

MAYBE I'M WRONG. I'LL BET IT ISN'T JUST A MAN'S DUTY, BUT A HUMAN BEING'S DUTY!

IF I WAIT LONG ENOUGH, MAYBE THEY'LL HOLD A "BIRDMAN" CONTEST.

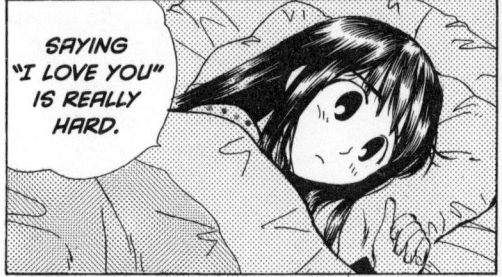

SAYING "I LOVE YOU" IS REALLY HARD.

16 . . . . Fin.

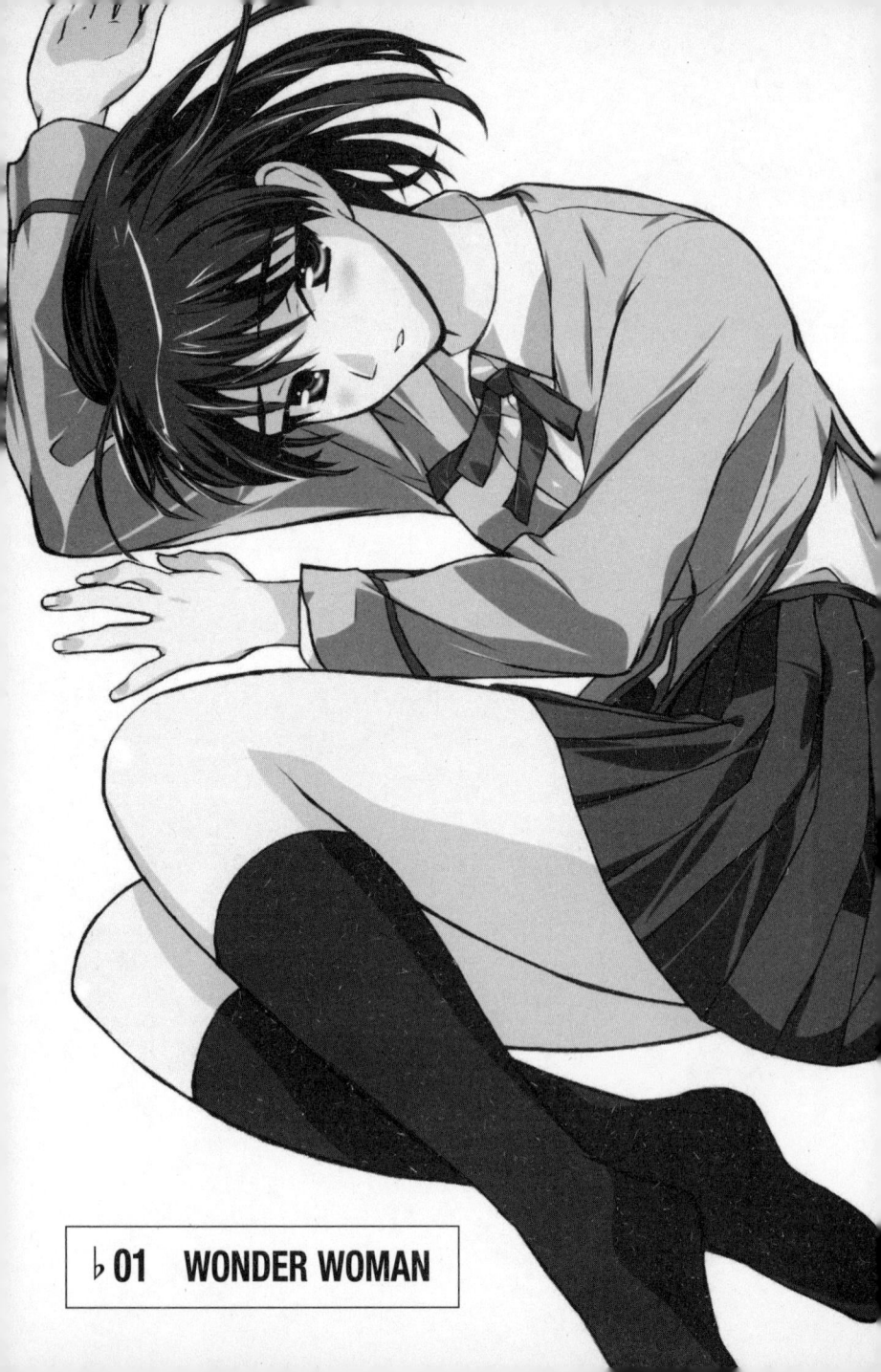

♭01 WONDER WOMAN

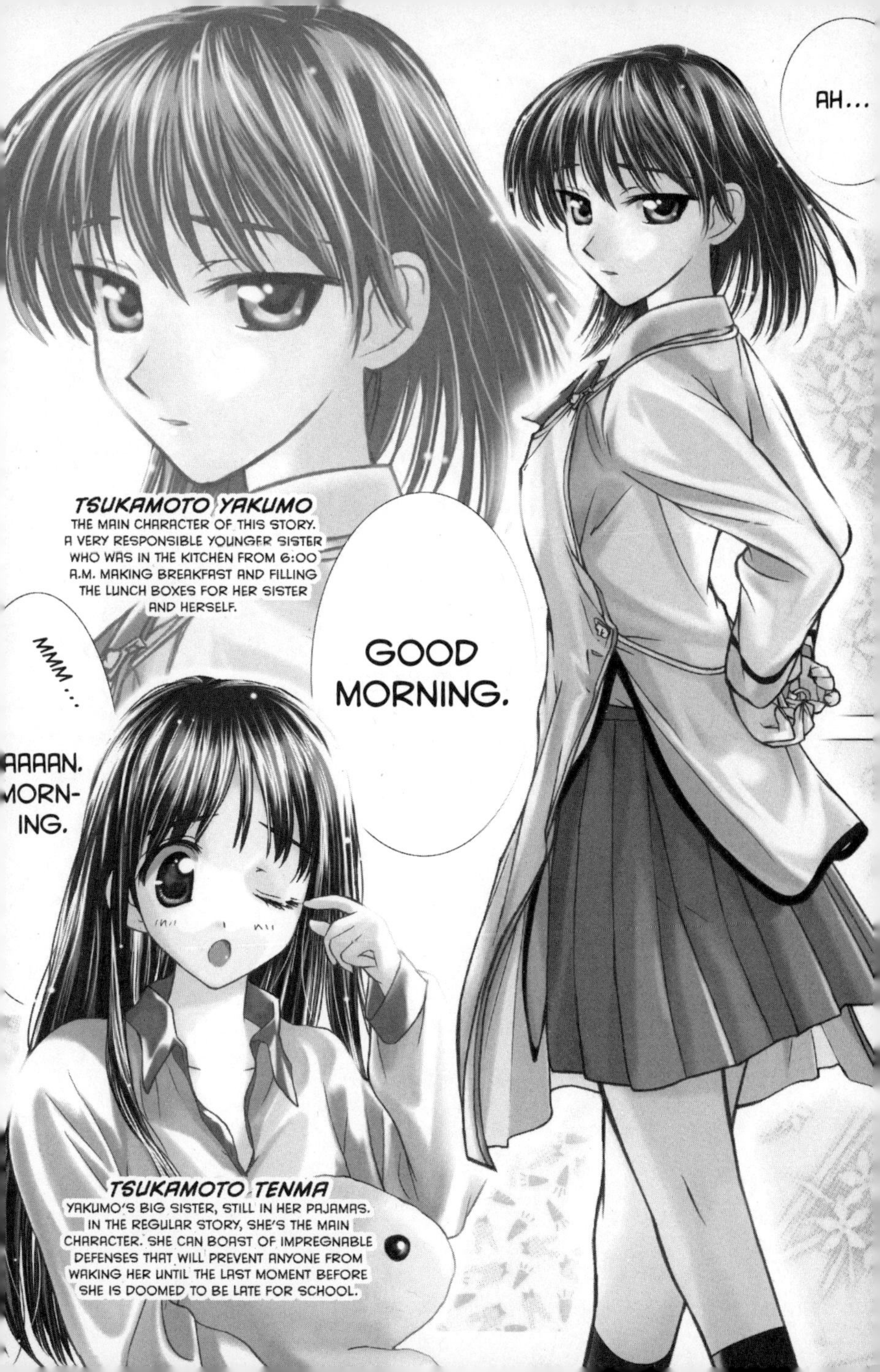
AH...
GOOD MORNING.
TSUKAMOTO YAKUMO
THE MAIN CHARACTER OF THIS STORY. A VERY RESPONSIBLE YOUNGER SISTER WHO WAS IN THE KITCHEN FROM 6:00 A.M. MAKING BREAKFAST AND FILLING THE LUNCH BOXES FOR HER SISTER AND HERSELF.
MMM...
AAAAN. MORN-ING.
TSUKAMOTO TENMA
YAKUMO'S BIG SISTER, STILL IN HER PAJAMAS. IN THE REGULAR STORY, SHE'S THE MAIN CHARACTER. SHE CAN BOAST OF IMPREGNABLE DEFENSES THAT WILL PREVENT ANYONE FROM WAKING HER UNTIL THE LAST MOMENT BEFORE SHE IS DOOMED TO BE LATE FOR SCHOOL.

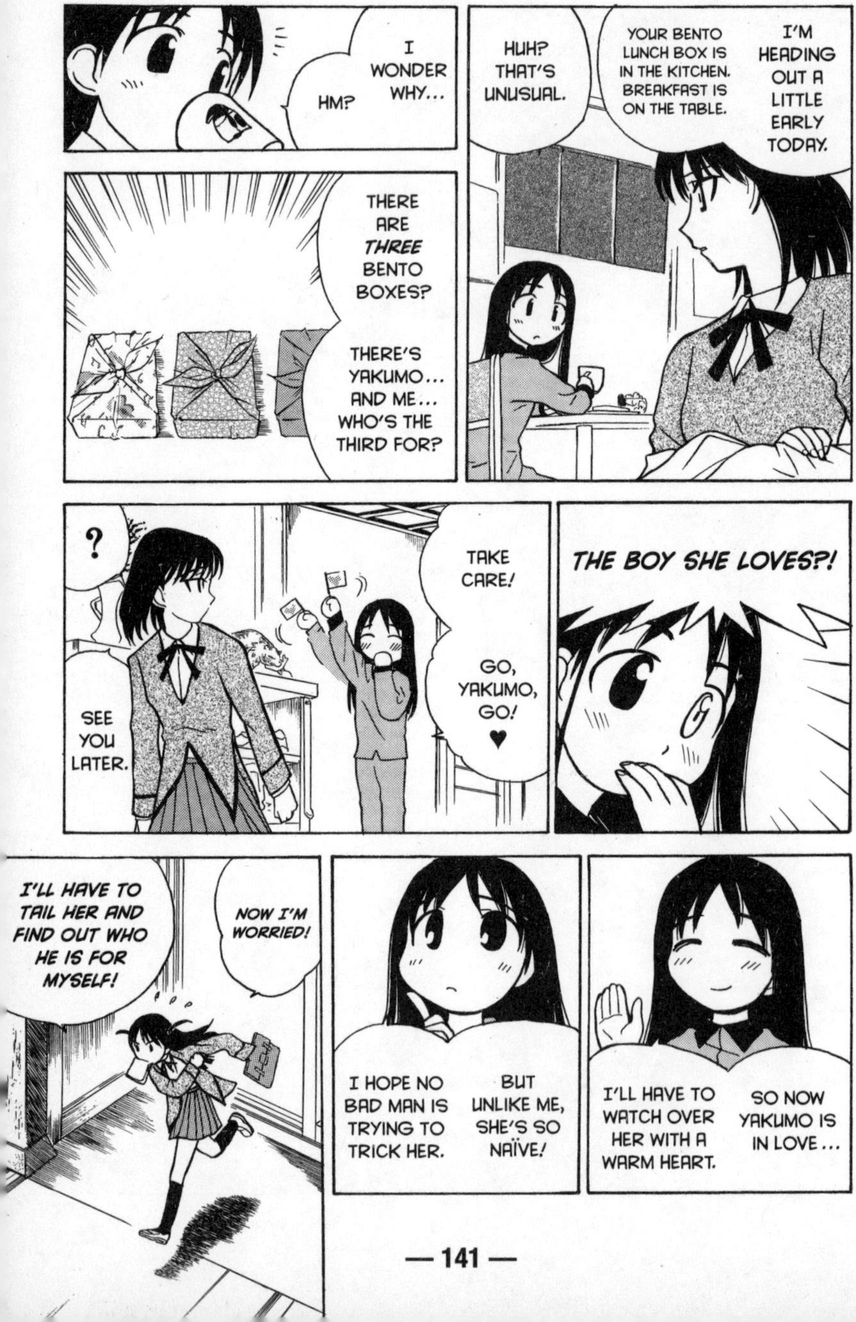
I'M HEADING OUT A LITTLE EARLY TODAY.
YOUR BENTO LUNCH BOX IS IN THE KITCHEN. BREAKFAST IS ON THE TABLE.
HUH? THAT'S UNUSUAL.
I WONDER WHY...
HM?
THERE ARE *THREE* BENTO BOXES?
THERE'S YAKUMO... AND ME... WHO'S THE THIRD FOR?
THE BOY SHE LOVES?!
TAKE CARE!
GO, YAKUMO, GO! ♥
?
SEE YOU LATER.
SO NOW YAKUMO IS IN LOVE...
I'LL HAVE TO WATCH OVER HER WITH A WARM HEART.
BUT UNLIKE ME, SHE'S SO NAÏVE!
I HOPE NO BAD MAN IS TRYING TO TRICK HER.
NOW I'M WORRIED!
I'LL HAVE TO TAIL HER AND FIND OUT WHO HE IS FOR MYSELF!

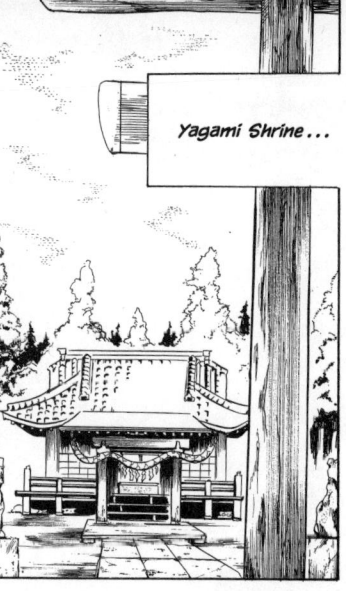

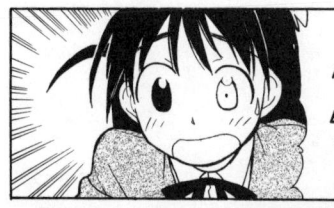

Yagami Shrine...
A BENTO LUNCH BOX FOR A CAT?!
NEE-CHAN...
YOU KNOW, YOU REALLY DIS-APPOINT ME!
I THOUGHT FOR SURE YOU HAD CAUGHT THE BUG!
BUG?
NO, A CAT.
SO... A STRAY CAT, HUH?
HAVE YOU BEEN LOOKING AFTER IT LONG?
YEAH, BUT...
AH!
VWIP

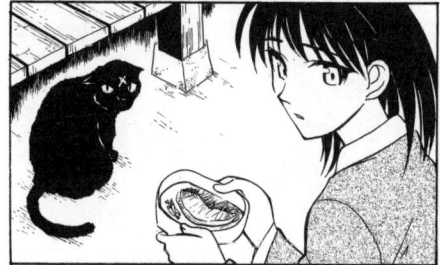

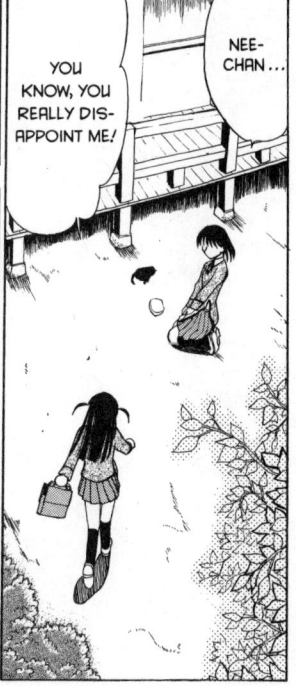

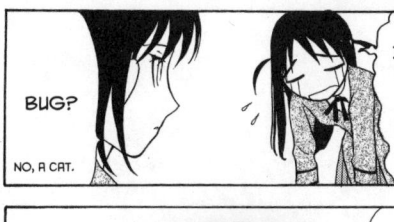

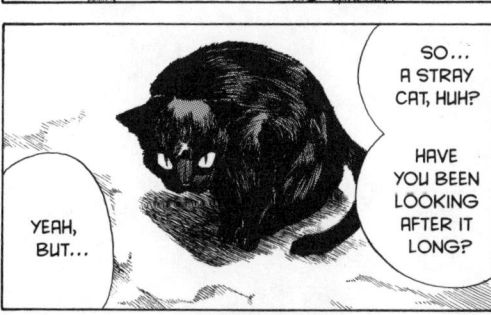

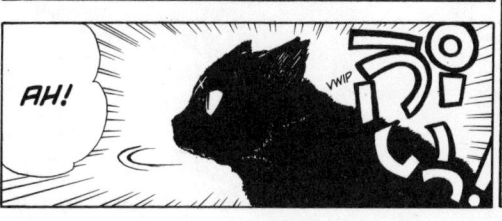

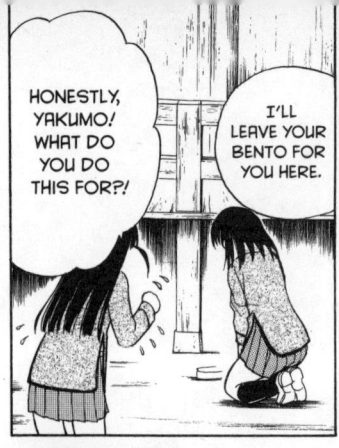

HONESTLY, YAKUMO! WHAT DO YOU DO THIS FOR?!

I'LL LEAVE YOUR BENTO FOR YOU HERE.

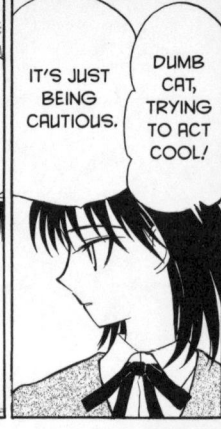

IT'S JUST BEING CAUTIOUS.

DUMB CAT, TRYING TO ACT COOL!

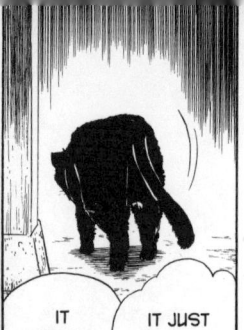

IT WASN'T NICE TO YOU AT ALL!

IT JUST IGNORED YOU AND WENT AWAY!

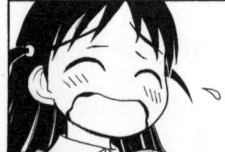

FORGET THE CAT! TRY OUT LOVE AT LEAST ONCE!

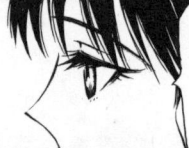

IT'S JUST SOMETHING I WANT TO TRY OUT.

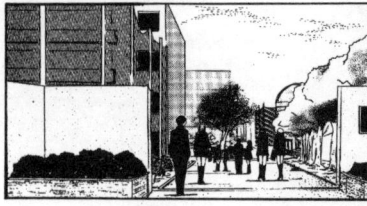

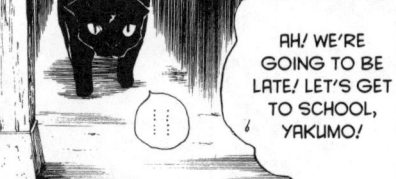

AH! WE'RE GOING TO BE LATE! LET'S GET TO SCHOOL, YAKUMO!

STUDENT C
SHE'S REALLY GOT STYLE!

STUDENT D
IS SHE REALLY THE MOST POPULAR OF ALL THE NEW STUDENTS?

STUDENT A
ISN'T THAT TSUKAMOTO, THE FIRST-YEAR STUDENT?

STUDENT B
MAN, IS SHE CUTE!

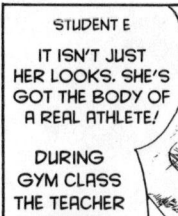

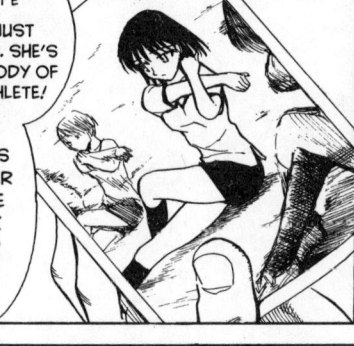

STUDENT E
IT ISN'T JUST HER LOOKS. SHE'S GOT THE BODY OF A REAL ATHLETE!
DURING GYM CLASS THE TEACHER IN CHARGE OF TRACK AND FIELD SCOUTED HER OUT.
7 Minami Shingo
8 Tsukamoto Yak
9 Yoshino Aya
STUDENTS E & F
IT TURNS OUT SHE'S REALLY SMART, TOO. SHE PLACED 8TH IN THE MID-TERMS.
SO THEY DO EXIST! THE "PERFECT WOMAN" THAT WE'RE ALWAYS HEARING ABOUT.
ALL THE BOYS ARE AFTER HER, HUH?
WHAT? IS SHE JUST TOO PICKY?
MAYBE, BUT IF SO...
...SHE WON'T HAVE ANYTHING TO DO WITH THEM.
IT'S ALMOST LIKE SHE'S NOT AWARE OF ALL THE ATTENTION.
AW! WHATTA WASTE!
THE ONE UGLY POINT ABOUT TSUKAMOTO YAKUMO.
?
THAT CAT. OR DID I JUST IMAGINE IT?
YOU'RE SURE YOU FELT SOME-ONE'S EYES ON YOU?
THEN I'D BE REALLY CAREFUL IF I WERE YOU.

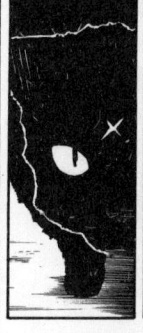

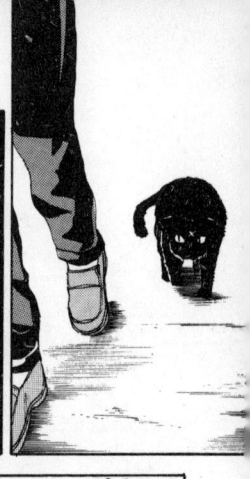

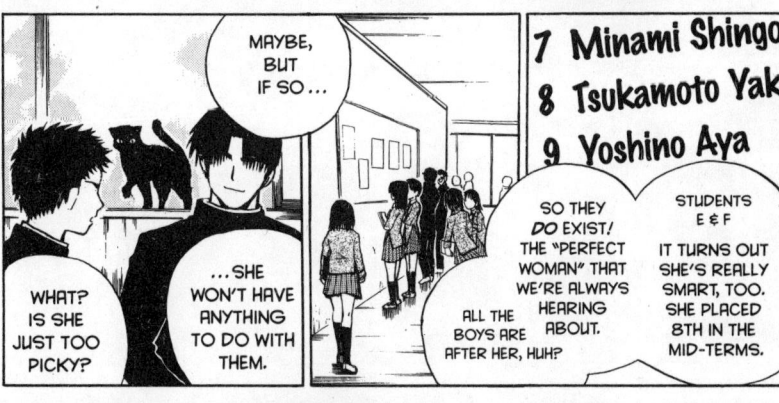

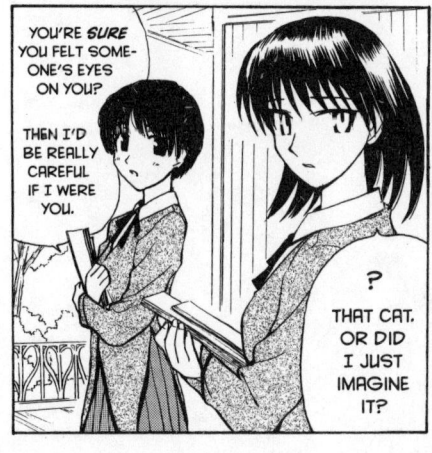

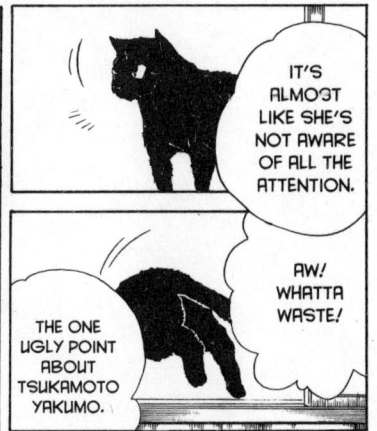

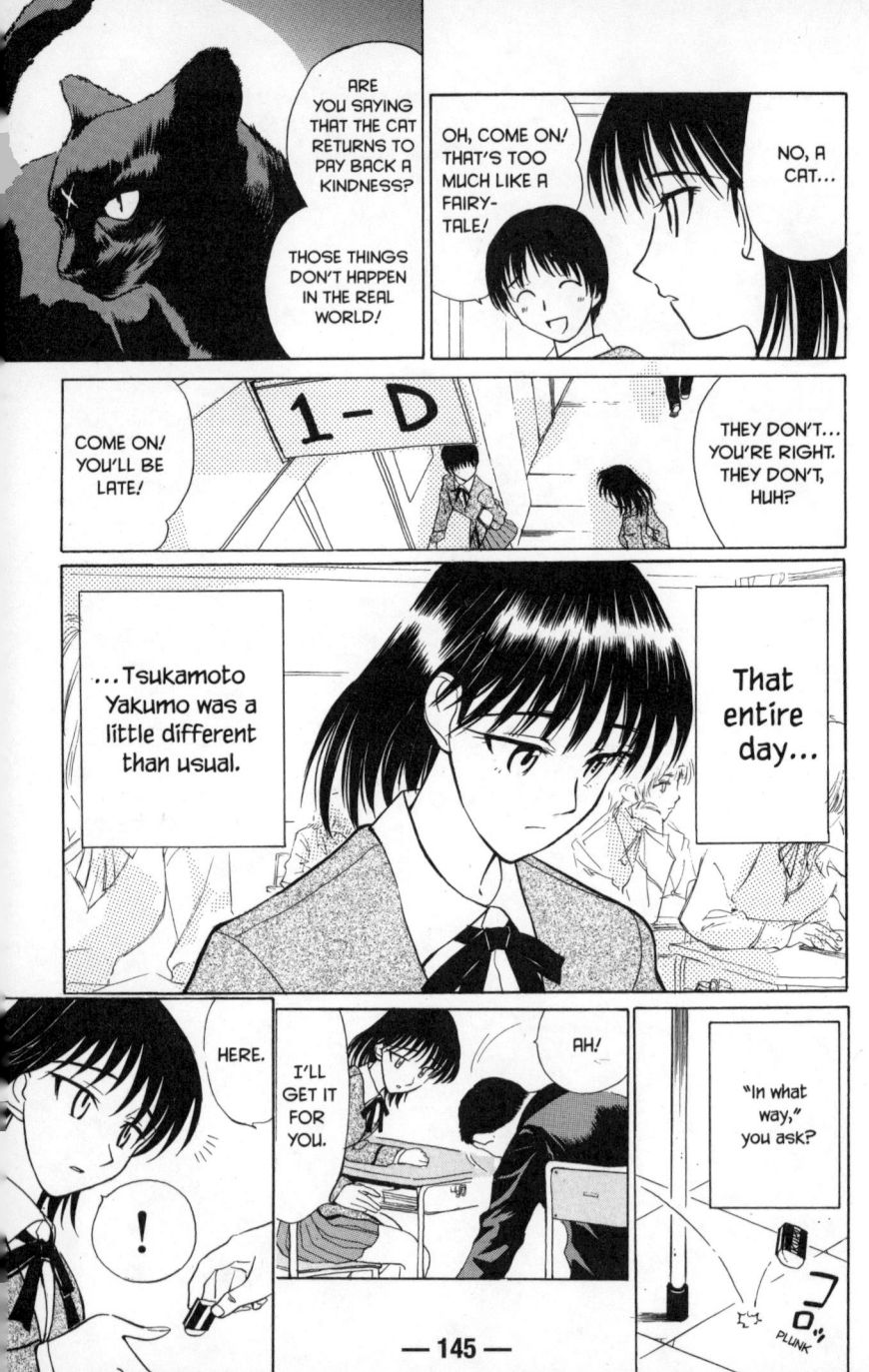

ARE YOU SAYING THAT THE CAT RETURNS TO PAY BACK A KINDNESS?

THOSE THINGS DON'T HAPPEN IN THE REAL WORLD!

OH, COME ON! THAT'S TOO MUCH LIKE A FAIRY-TALE!

NO, A CAT...

COME ON! YOU'LL BE LATE!

THEY DON'T... YOU'RE RIGHT. THEY DON'T, HUH?

1-D

...Tsukamoto Yakumo was a little different than usual.

That entire day...

HERE.

I'LL GET IT FOR YOU.

AH!

"In what way," you ask?

!

PLUNK

— 145 —

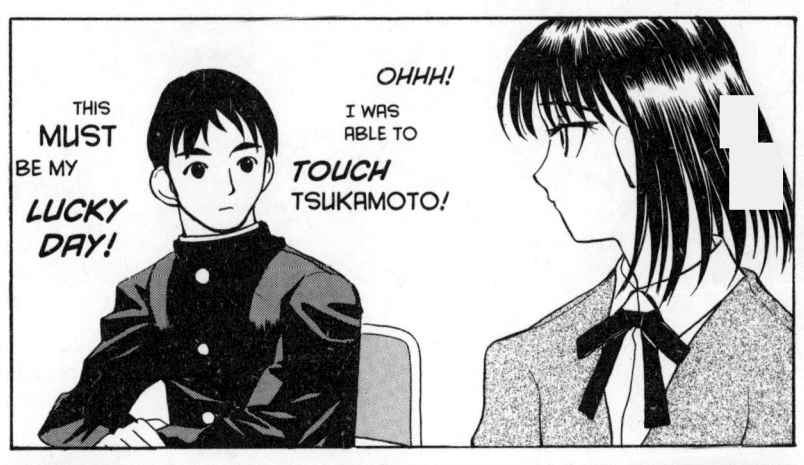

OHHH! I WAS ABLE TO **TOUCH** TSUKAMOTO!

THIS **MUST** BE MY *LUCKY DAY!*

If anyone likes Yakumo, she can hear the whisper of his heart.

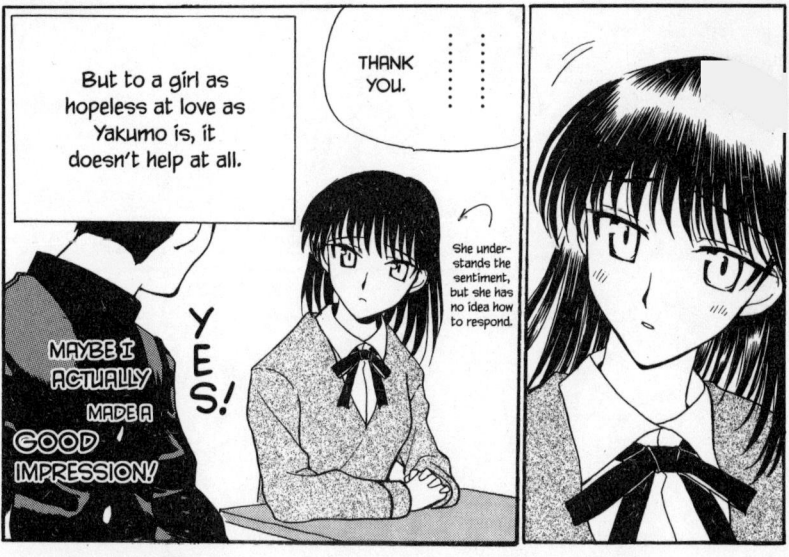

But to a girl as hopeless at love as Yakumo is, it doesn't help at all.

THANK YOU. : : :

MAYBE I **ACTUALLY** MADE A **GOOD IMPRESSION!**

YES!

She understands the sentiment, but she has no idea how to respond.

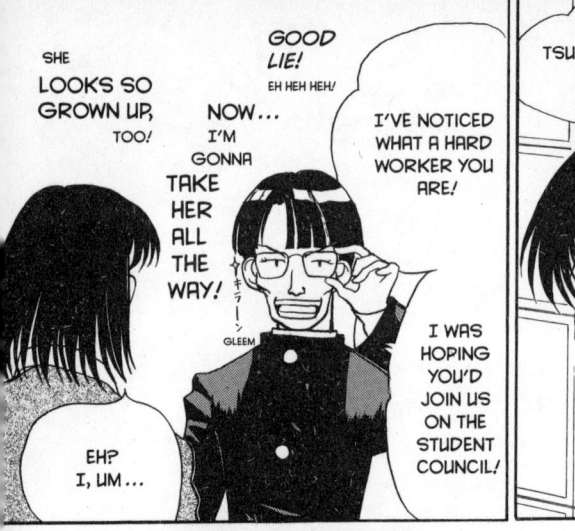
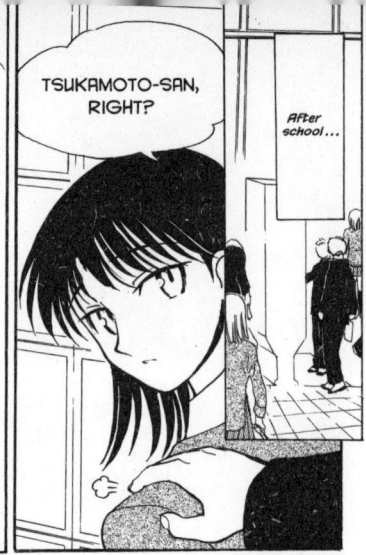

SHE LOOKS SO GROWN UP, TOO!

NOW... I'M GONNA TAKE HER ALL THE WAY!

GLEEM

EH? I, UM...

GOOD LIE! EH HEH HEH!

I'VE NOTICED WHAT A HARD WORKER YOU ARE!

I WAS HOPING YOU'D JOIN US ON THE STUDENT COUNCIL!

TSUKAMOTO-SAN, RIGHT?

After school...

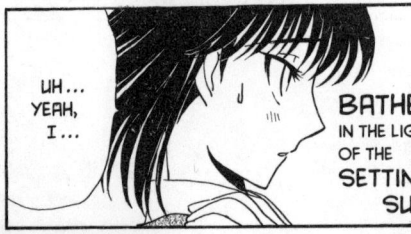

UH... YEAH, I...

WE'LL BE **ALONE** IN THE STUDENT COUNCIL ROOM, **BATHED** IN THE LIGHT OF THE **SETTING SUN!**

IT'S FOR THE SAKE OF THE SCHOOL!

I JUST KNOW YOU WANT TO MAKE A DIFFERENCE, DON'T YOU?!

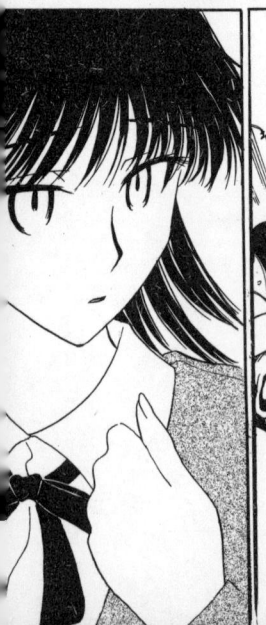
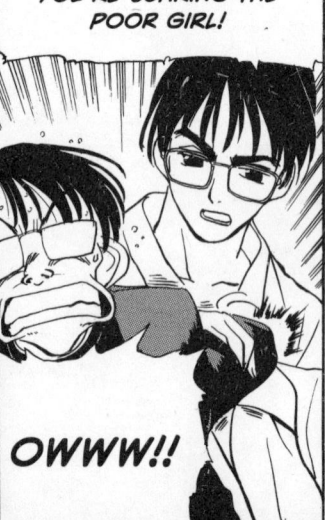
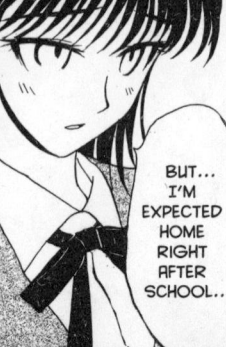

STOP THAT RIGHT NOW! YOU'RE SCARING THE POOR GIRL!

OWWW!!

THE FIRST STEP IS TO COME TO THE STUDENT COUNCIL ROOM AND HAVE A QUICK LOOK AROUND. LET'S GO!

BUT... I'M EXPECTED HOME RIGHT AFTER SCHOOL...

I'LL GET RIGHT TO THE POINT!

MY NAME IS HANAI HARUKI.

SHUMP

OH, IT'S HANAI-KUN. AGAIN

I'M THE AIKIDO CLUB PRESIDENT!

SHFF SHFF

TSUKAMOTO-KUN, WOULD YOU LIKE TO LEARN *AIKIDO*?

AND I'M IN THE SAME GRADE AS YOUR SISTER, TSUKAMOTO TENMA.

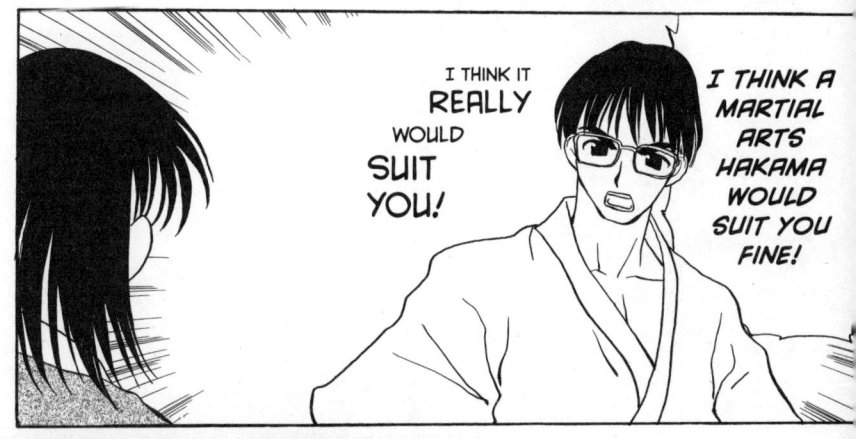

I THINK IT **REALLY** WOULD **SUIT YOU!**

I THINK A MARTIAL ARTS HAKAMA WOULD SUIT YOU FINE!

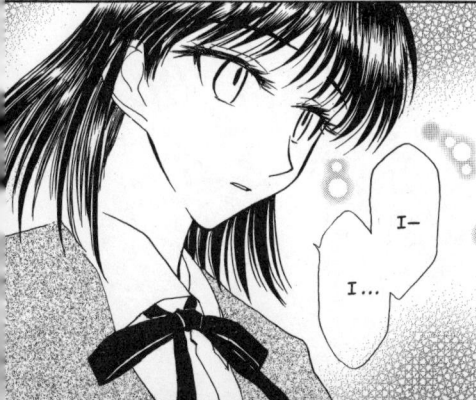

I—

I...

This is a man whose words and thoughts match nearly perfectly. Yakumo has never met such a man before.

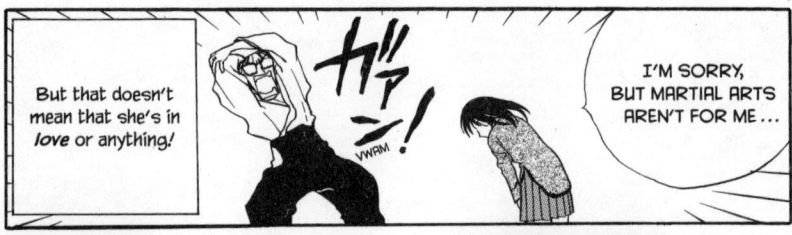

But that doesn't mean that she's in *love* or anything!

I'M SORRY, BUT MARTIAL ARTS AREN'T FOR ME...

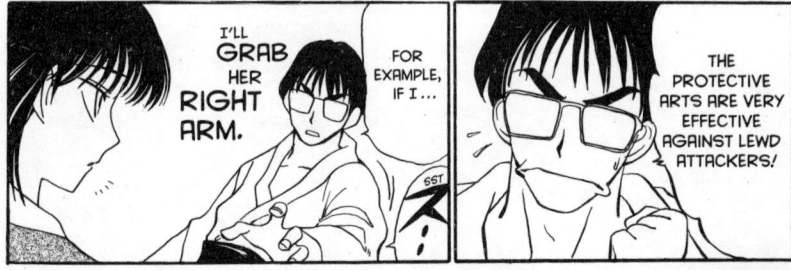

I'LL GRAB HER RIGHT ARM.

FOR EXAMPLE, IF I...

THE PROTECTIVE ARTS ARE VERY EFFECTIVE AGAINST LEWD ATTACKERS!

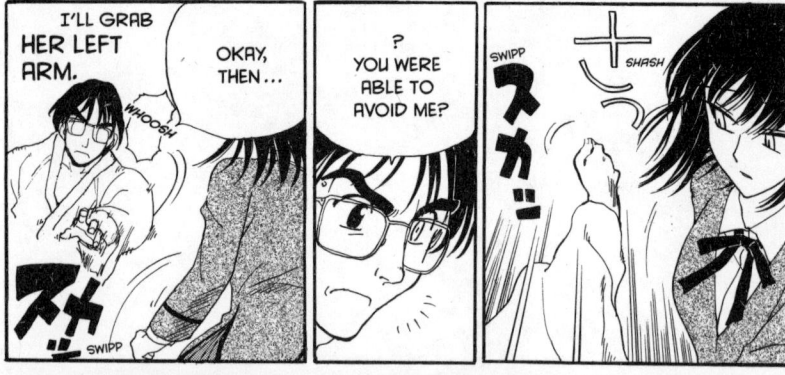

I'LL GRAB HER LEFT ARM.

OKAY, THEN...

? YOU WERE ABLE TO AVOID ME?

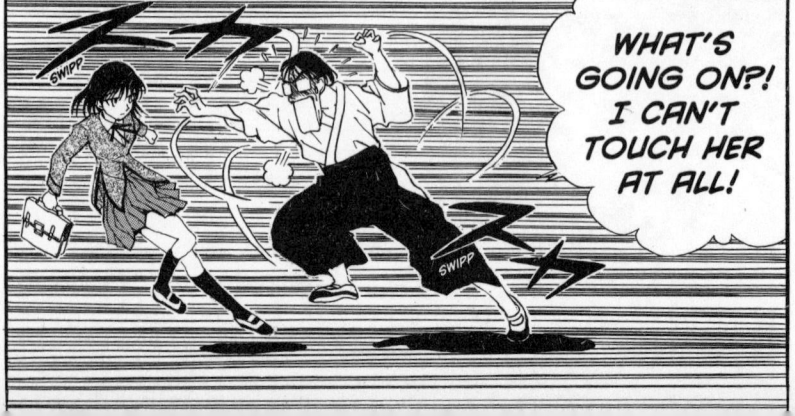

WHAT'S GOING ON?! I CAN'T TOUCH HER AT ALL!

It's easy for her to avoid him, since she can read his mind.
HOW CAN YOU BE SO FAST WHEN YOUR SISTER IS SUCH A FRIGGIN' DOLT?!
!
ZWAAA
AH!
WHAMM
I- I'M SORRY...
When she hears her sister being bad-mouthed, Yakumo finally gets serious.

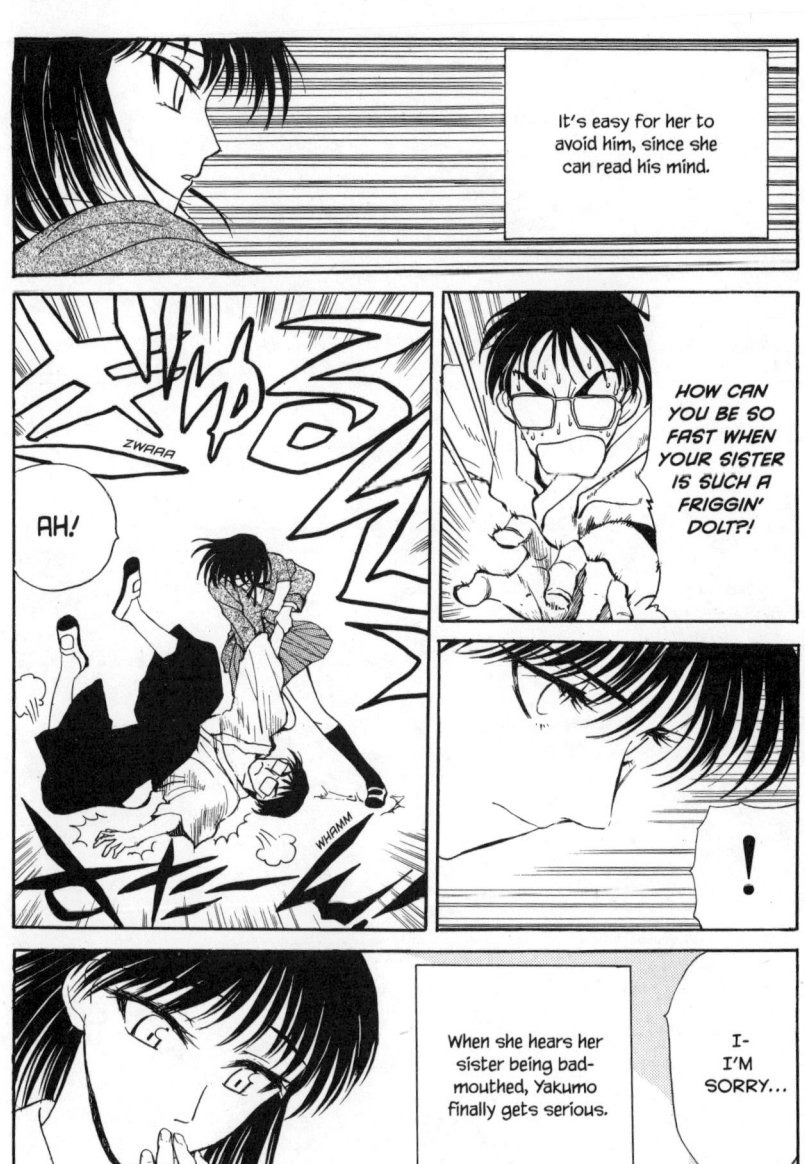

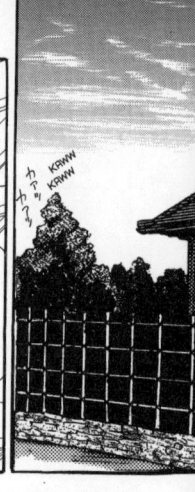

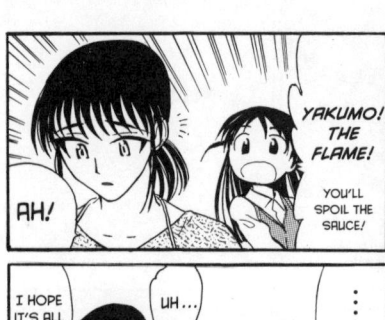

AH!

YAKUMO! THE FLAME!

YOU'LL SPOIL THE SAUCE!

I HOPE IT'S ALL RIGHT.

UH...

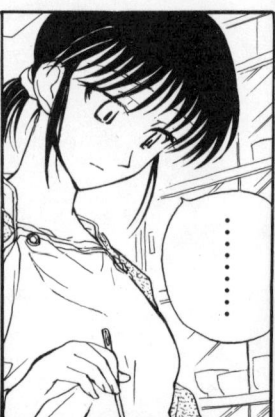

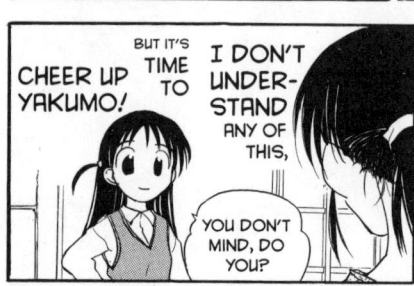

CHEER UP YAKUMO!

BUT IT'S TIME TO

I DON'T UNDERSTAND ANY OF THIS,

YOU DON'T MIND, DO YOU?

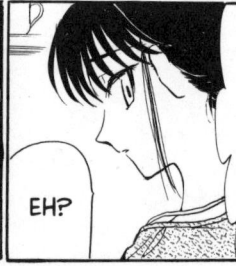

EH?

YAKUMO, LET'S HAVE SOMETHING UNUSUAL ON THE MENU TODAY!

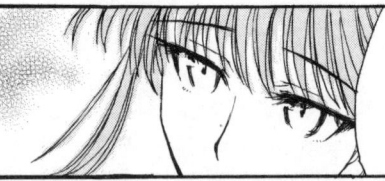

It looks like Yakumo can hear the whispers of Tenma's heart, too.

NEE-CHAN...

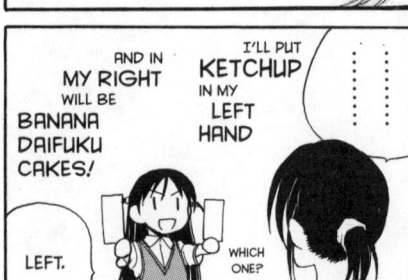

AND IN MY RIGHT WILL BE BANANA DAIFUKU CAKES!

I'LL PUT KETCHUP IN MY LEFT HAND

LEFT.

WHICH ONE?

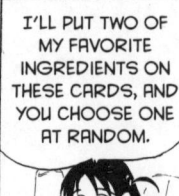

I'LL PUT TWO OF MY FAVORITE INGREDIENTS ON THESE CARDS, AND YOU CHOOSE ONE AT RANDOM.

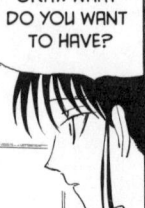

OKAY. WHAT DO YOU WANT TO HAVE?

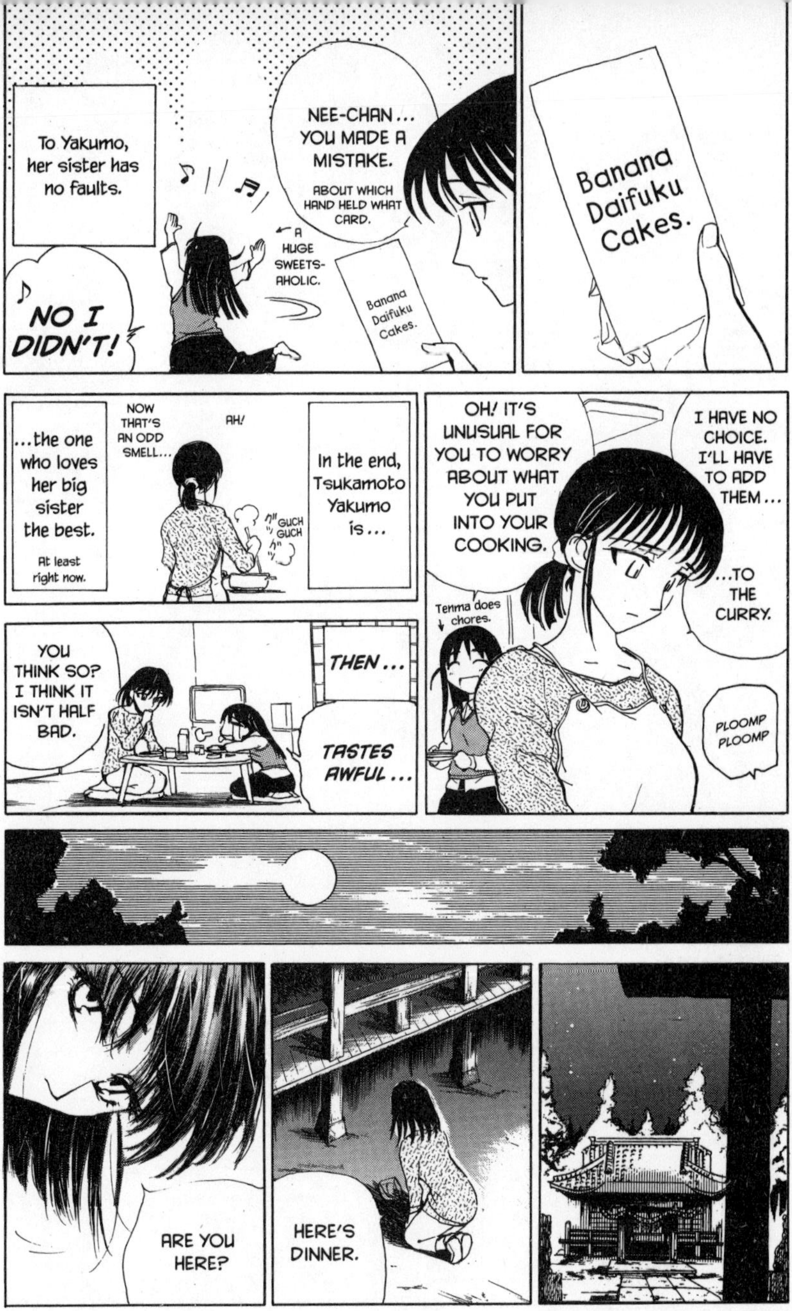
Banana Daifuku Cakes.
NEE-CHAN... YOU MADE A MISTAKE.
ABOUT WHICH HAND HELD WHAT CARD.
Banana Daifuku Cakes.
A HUGE SWEETS-AHOLIC.
To Yakumo, her sister has no faults.
NO I DIDN'T!
I HAVE NO CHOICE. I'LL HAVE TO ADD THEM...
...TO THE CURRY.
OH! IT'S UNUSUAL FOR YOU TO WORRY ABOUT WHAT YOU PUT INTO YOUR COOKING.
PLOOMP PLOOMP
Tenma does chores.
In the end, Tsukamoto Yakumo is...
AH!
GUCH GUCH
NOW THAT'S AN ODD SMELL...
...the one who loves her big sister the best.
At least right now.
THEN...
TASTES AWFUL...
YOU THINK SO? I THINK IT ISN'T HALF BAD.
HERE'S DINNER.
ARE YOU HERE?

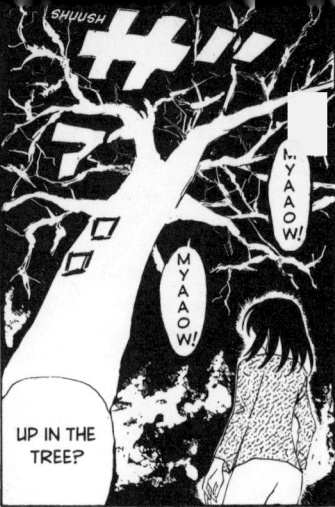

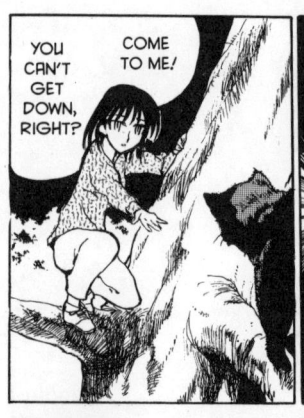

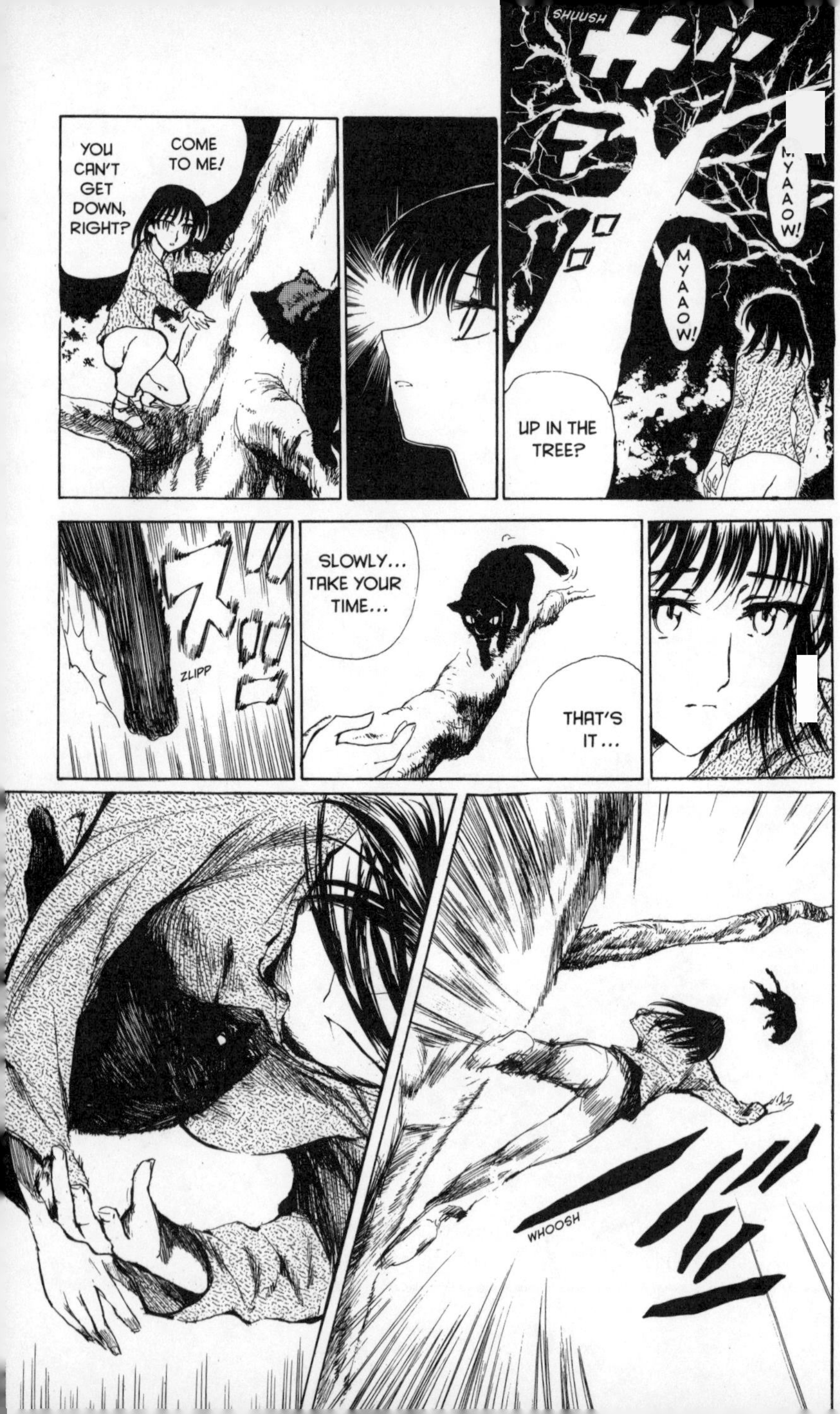
SHUUSH
MYAAOW!
MYAAOW!
UP IN THE TREE?
COME TO ME!
YOU CAN'T GET DOWN, RIGHT?
SLOWLY... TAKE YOUR TIME...
THAT'S IT...
ZLIPP
WHOOSH

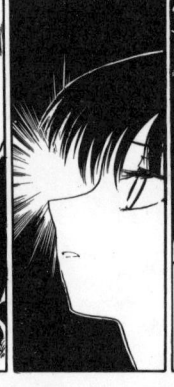

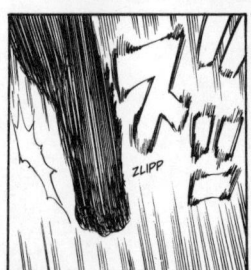

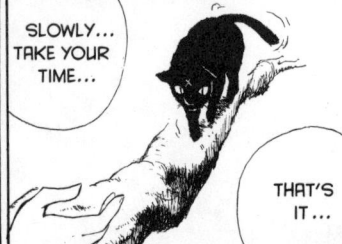

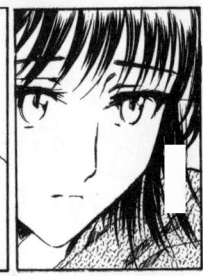

SHUMP
OWW...
......
ARE YOU ALL RIGHT?
AH!
MYAOW!
MEOWW.
LICK LICK
I HEARD!
YOU KNOW, I CAN READ PEOPLE'S THOUGHTS SOMETIMES.
I WAS WONDERING WHAT YOU'D SAY IN YOUR HEART, SO I WAS HOPING I'D HEAR YOU TOO.
BUT I GUESS IN A CAT'S HEART, YOU GUYS JUST SAY MEOW, MEOW, HUH?
TOO BAD.

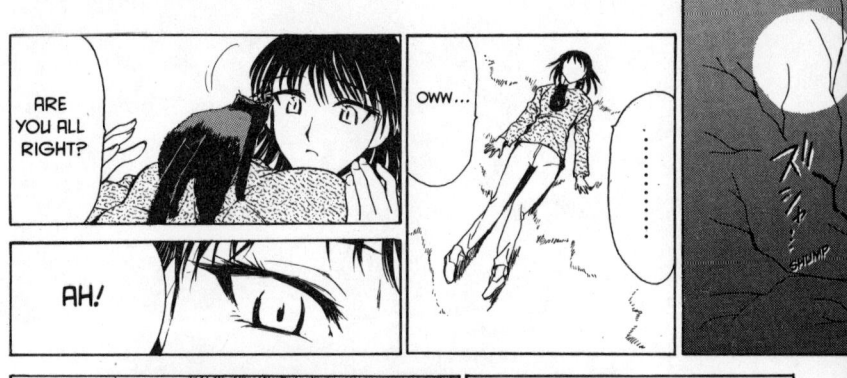

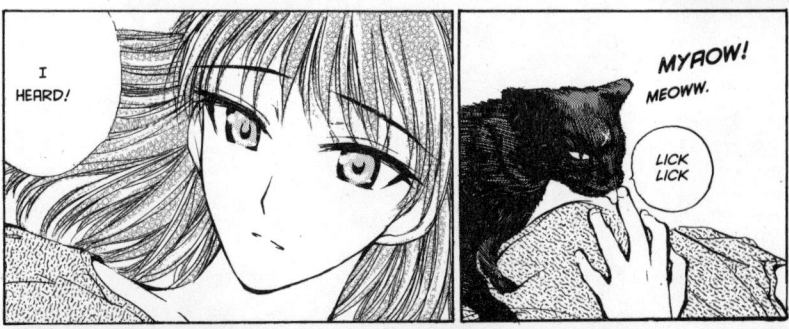

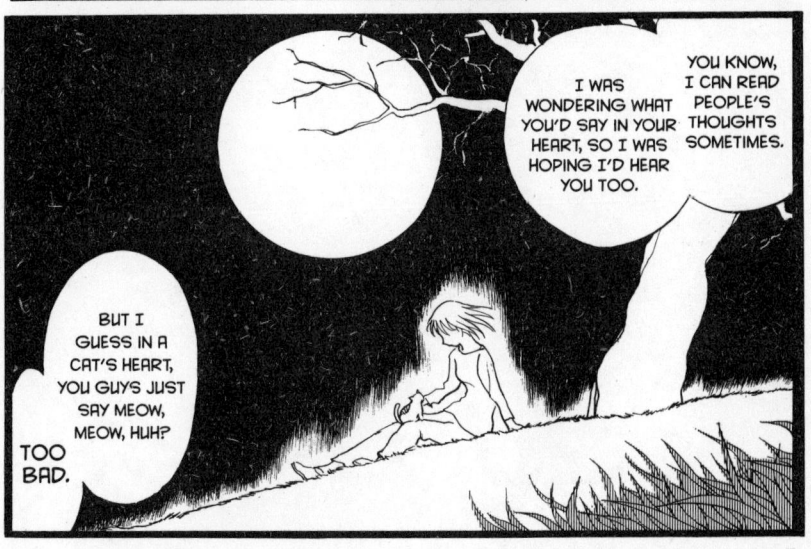

♭01 ....Fin.

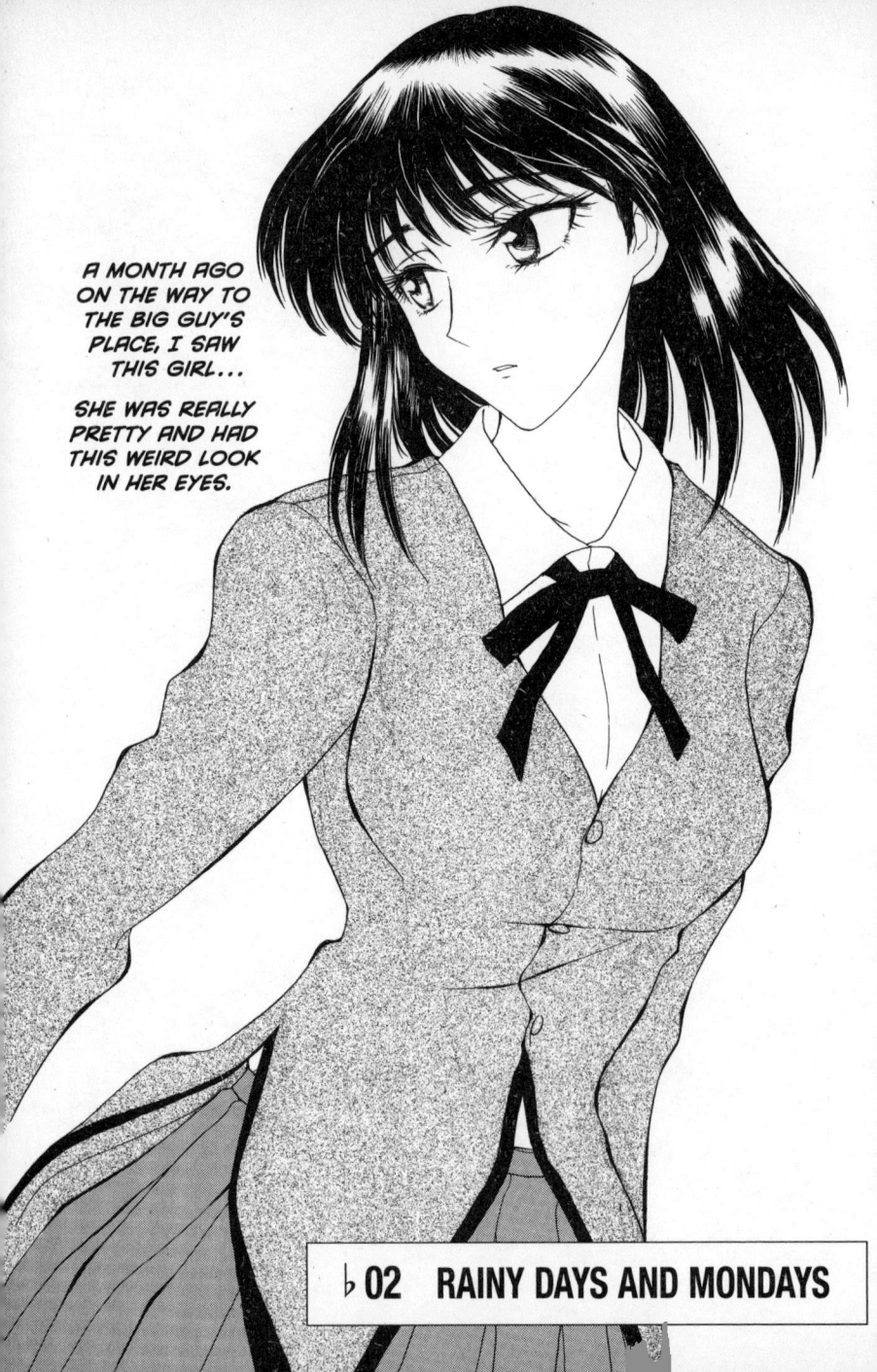

A MONTH AGO ON THE WAY TO THE BIG GUY'S PLACE, I SAW THIS GIRL...

SHE WAS REALLY PRETTY AND HAD THIS WEIRD LOOK IN HER EYES.

♭02   RAINY DAYS AND MONDAYS

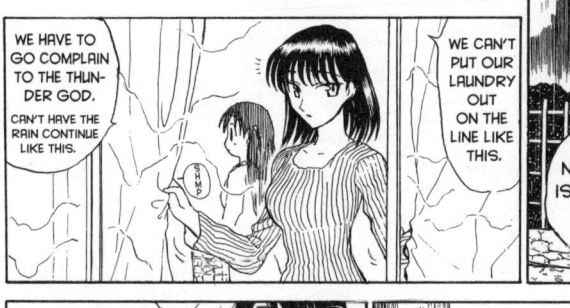

SHHHH
WELL?
NO LUCK. IT ISN'T GOING TO STOP.
WE CAN'T PUT OUR LAUNDRY OUT ON THE LINE LIKE THIS.
SHMP
WE HAVE TO GO COMPLAIN TO THE THUNDER GOD.
CAN'T HAVE THE RAIN CONTINUE LIKE THIS.
HUH?
AT OUR GATE...
TREMBLE TREMBLE
SHHH
HM? WHAT IS IT, YAKUMO?
I SEE A THUNDER KID.
WHAT ARE YOU DOING HERE?
THE RAIN GOT YOU PRETTY GOOD, HUH?
SST
TWITCH
EH?! AH! NO!
I'M NOT DOING ANYTHING WRONG! I JUST GOT HERE BY ACCIDENT!
YOU'LL ...
... CATCH COLD.
UH ...

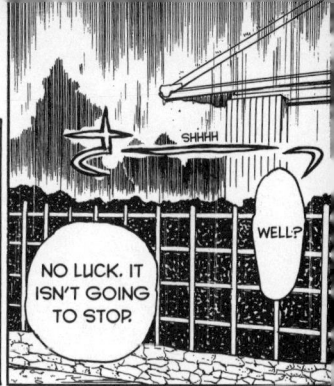

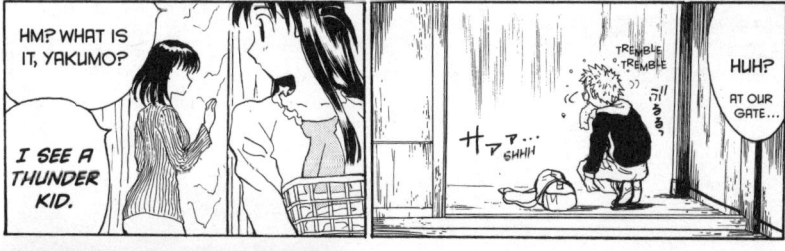

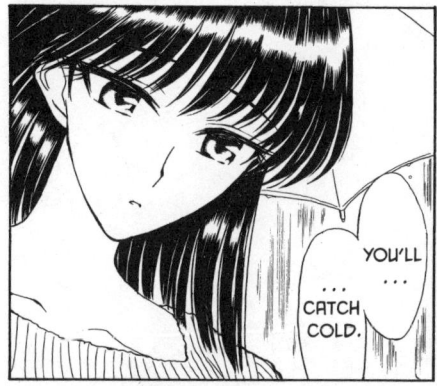

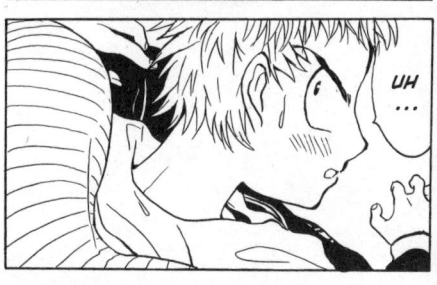

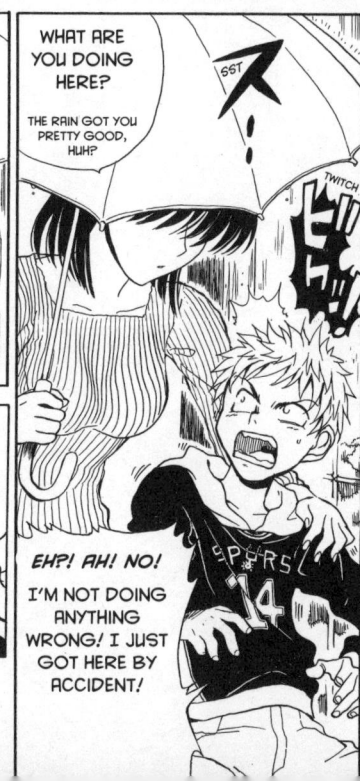

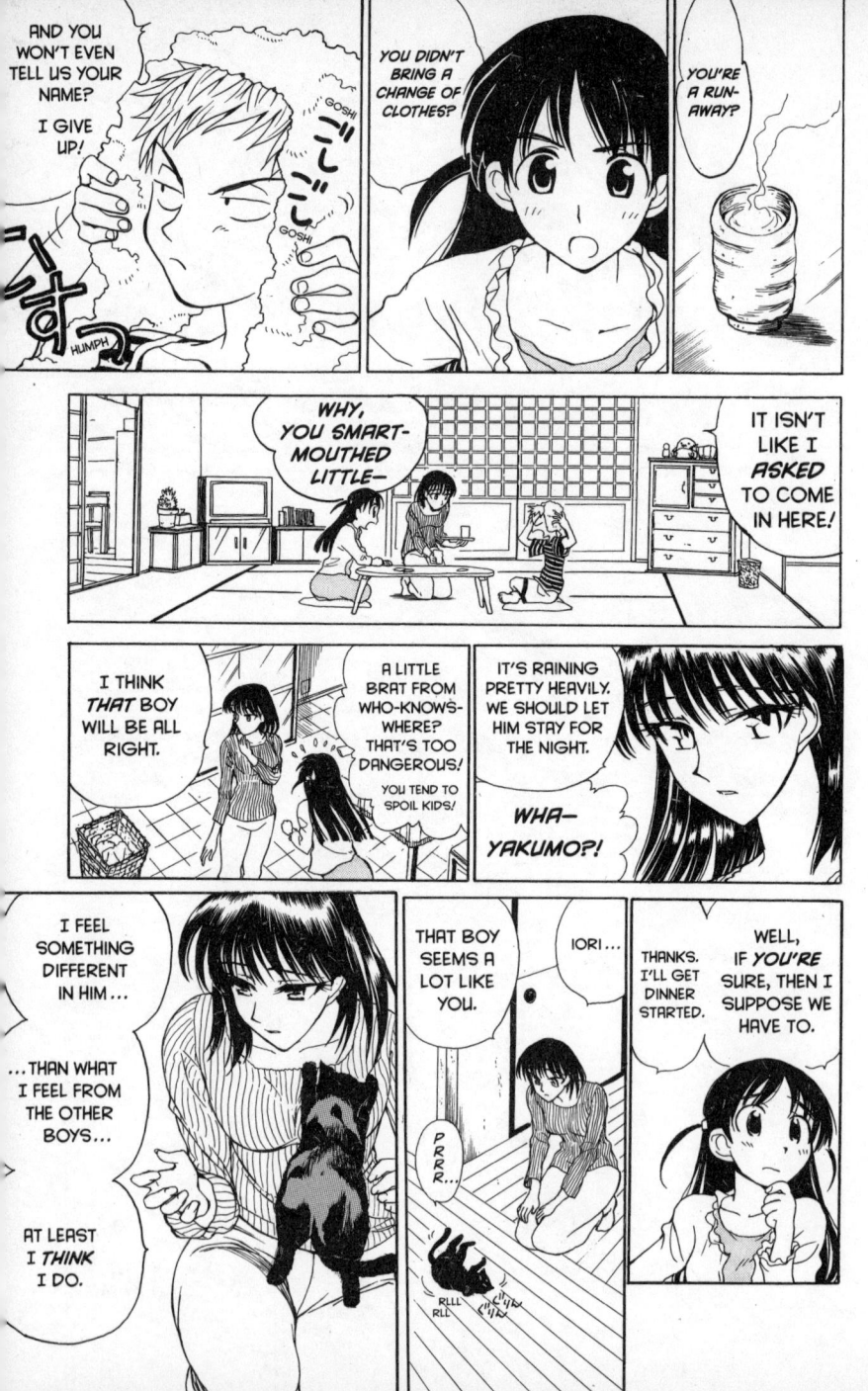

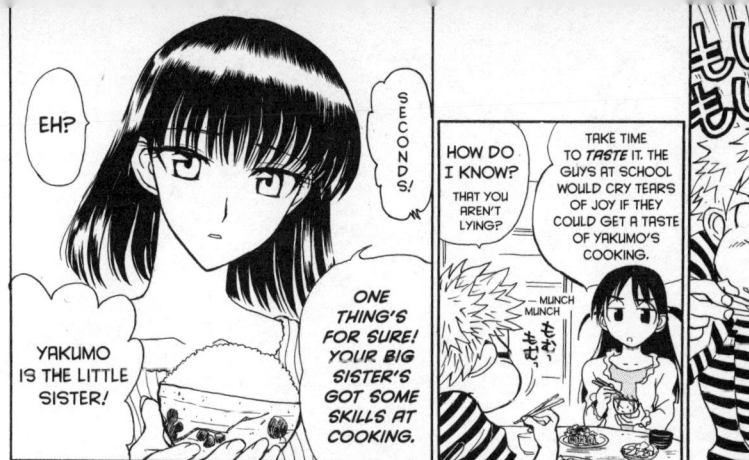

もしゃ
MUNCH
もしゃ
MUNCH
GOBBLE GOBBLE
TAKE TIME TO TASTE IT. THE GUYS AT SCHOOL WOULD CRY TEARS OF JOY IF THEY COULD GET A TASTE OF YAKUMO'S COOKING.
HOW DO I KNOW?
THAT YOU AREN'T LYING?
— MUNCH MUNCH
もむっ もむっ
SECONDS!
ONE THING'S FOR SURE! YOUR BIG SISTER'S GOT SOME SKILLS AT COOKING.
EH?
YAKUMO IS THE LITTLE SISTER!
HUH?! YOU MEAN MISS FLAT-CHESTED HERE IS THE OLDER SISTER?!
YOU'RE LYIN'! YOU'RE STILL IN MIDDLE SCHOOL, RIGHT?
WHA—?!
THAT'S WHY I DON'T WANT BRATS IN THE HOUSE! THEY DON'T UNDERSTAND THE DELICACY OF WOMEN!
MAYBE YAKUMO HAS A BIGGER BUST SIZE. BUT MY FRIEND'S BUST SIZE IS BIGGER STILL!
AND IF SHE HEARD YOU, SHE'D BE SHOCKED!
UM ... NEE-CHAN ...
WHEN A PERVERTED BRAT SHOWS AN INTEREST IN YAKUMO'S CHEST, I BRING THE PUNISHMENT!
WHAT?!
I CHALLENGE YOU TO A GAME!
GREAT! I ACCEPT!
I MAY NOT LOOK IT, BUT I GET GOOD GRADES!
OLD MAID!!
OTHELLO!!
SHOGI!
YOU'RE REALLY BAD!?
THAT THING ABOUT YOU BEING A HIGH-SCHOOL STUDENT WAS A LIE, RIGHT?
I WON EVERY GAME.
IT ISN'T OVER YET! I STILL HAVE MY FINAL MOVE!!
MASTER, IF YOU PLEASE...
Getting into it a little.
......
すいっ
ZLIP

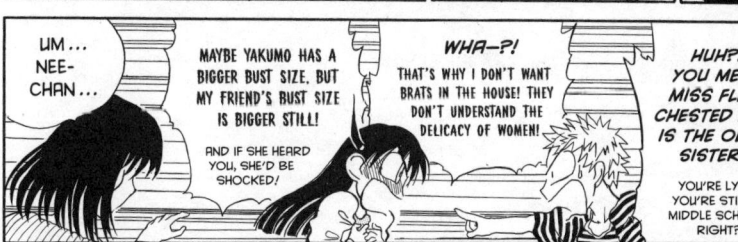

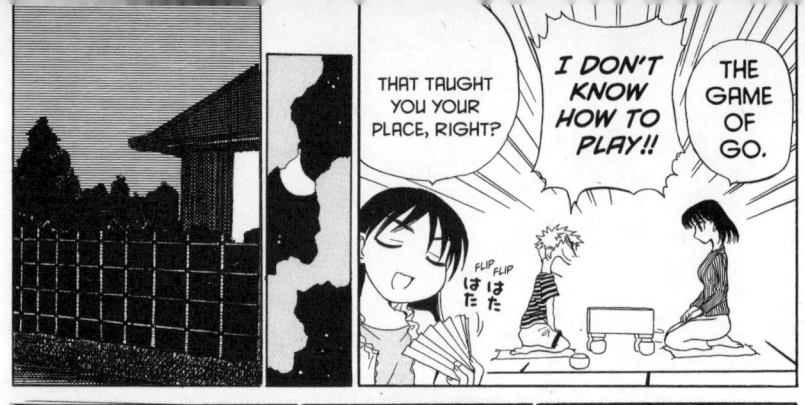

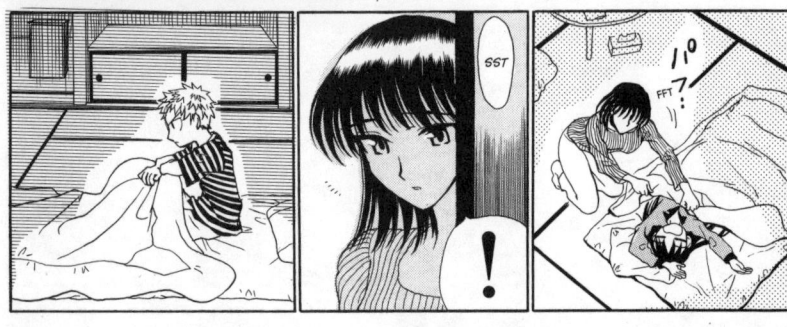

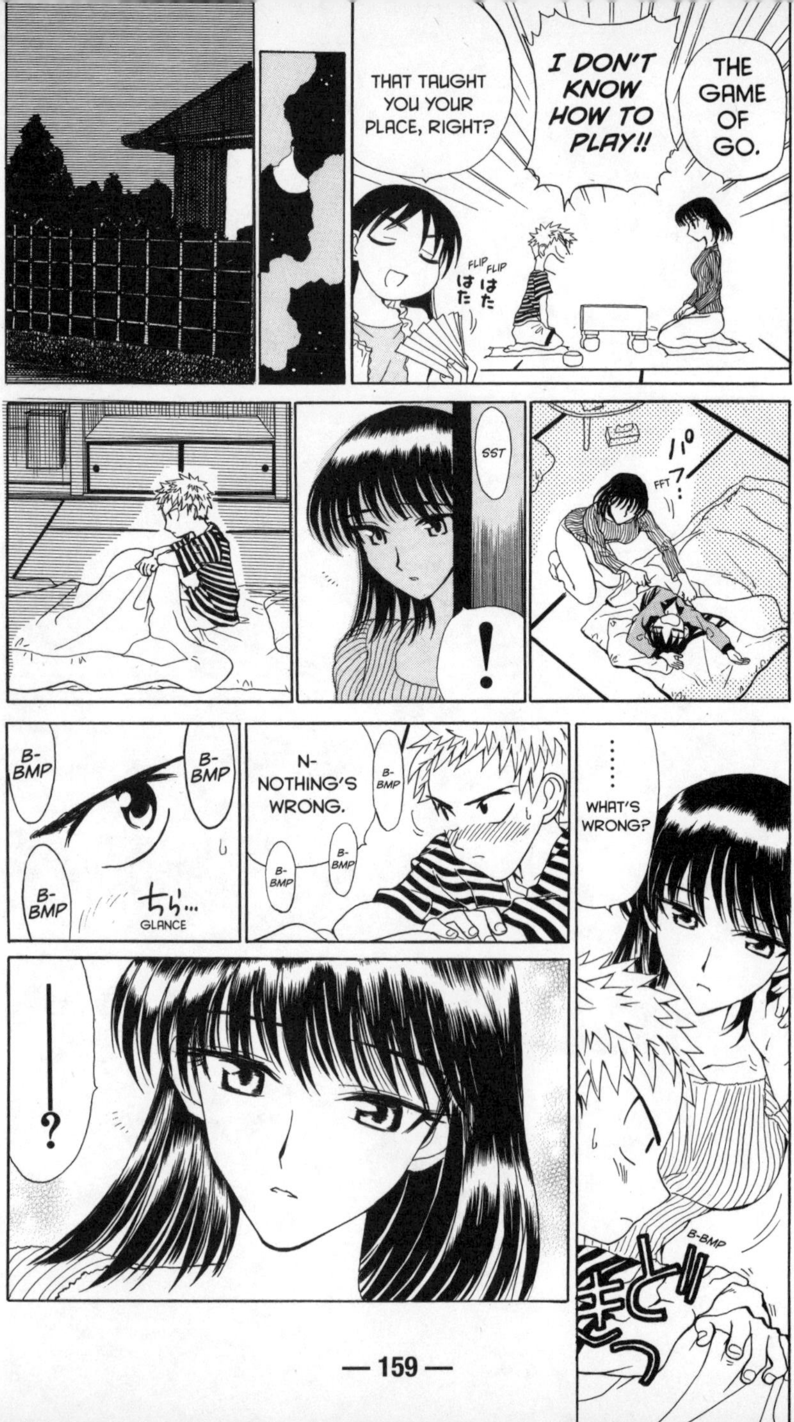

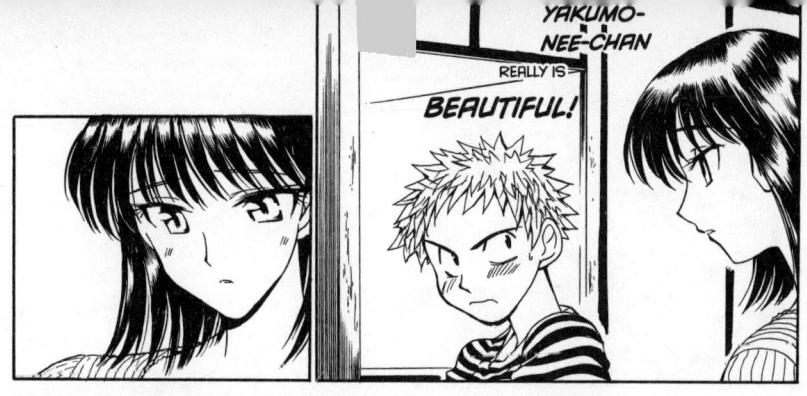

YAKUMO-NEE-CHAN REALLY IS **BEAUTIFUL!**

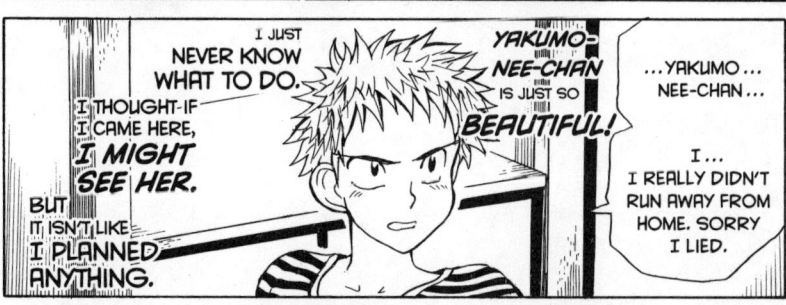

I JUST NEVER KNOW WHAT TO DO.

I THOUGHT—IF I CAME HERE, **I MIGHT SEE HER.**

BUT IT ISN'T LIKE I PLANNED ANYTHING.

YAKUMO-NEE-CHAN IS JUST SO **BEAUTIFUL!**

...YAKUMO... NEE-CHAN...

I... I REALLY DIDN'T RUN AWAY FROM HOME. SORRY I LIED.

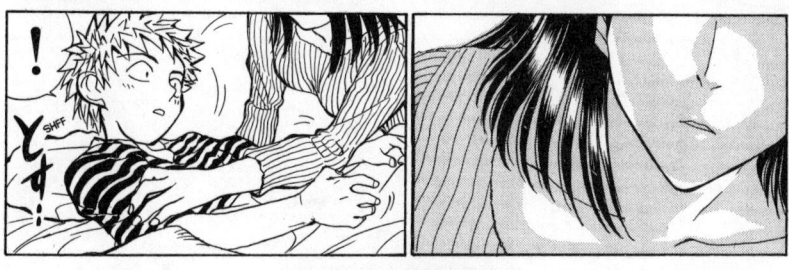

!

Y

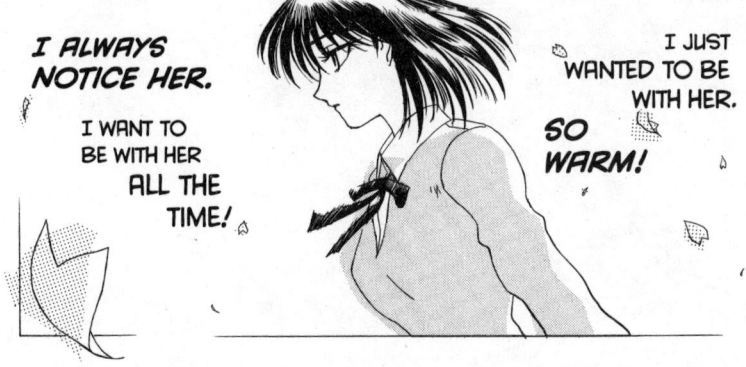

I ALWAYS NOTICE HER.

I WANT TO BE WITH HER **ALL THE TIME!**

I JUST WANTED TO BE WITH HER.

SO WARM!

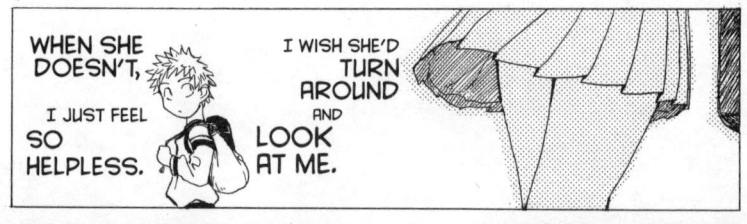

WHEN SHE DOESN'T, I WISH SHE'D TURN AROUND AND LOOK AT ME.

I JUST FEEL SO HELPLESS.

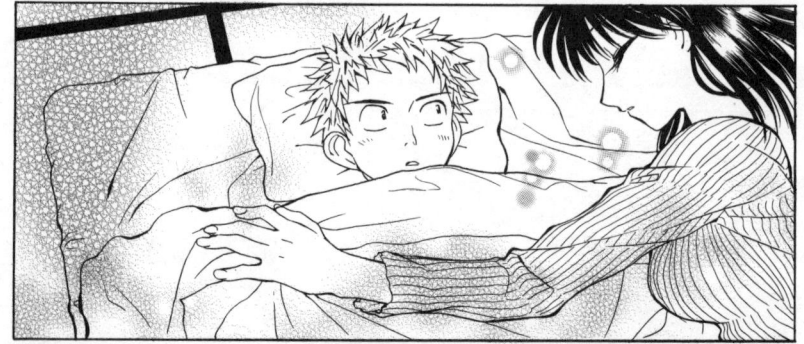

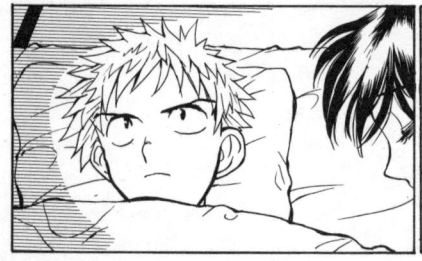

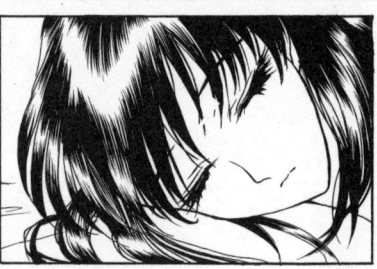

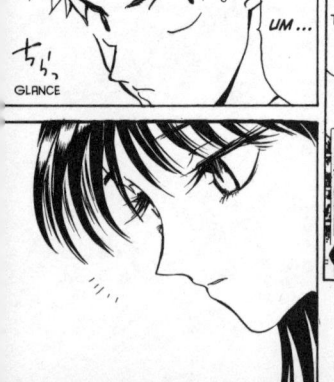

UM...

ちらっ
GLANCE

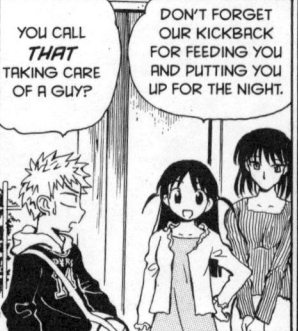

YOU CALL *THAT* TAKING CARE OF A GUY?

DON'T FORGET OUR KICKBACK FOR FEEDING YOU AND PUTTING YOU UP FOR THE NIGHT.

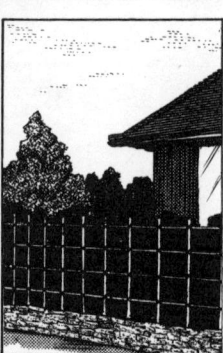

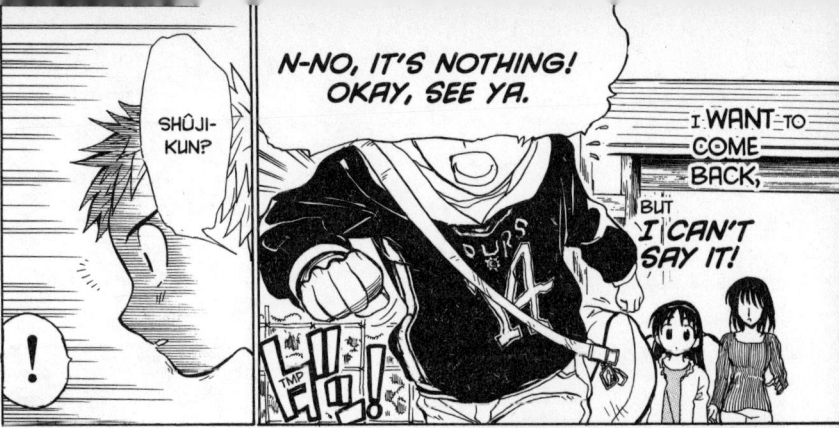

SHÛJI-KUN?

N-NO, IT'S NOTHING! OKAY, SEE YA.

I WANT TO COME BACK,

BUT I CAN'T SAY IT!

!

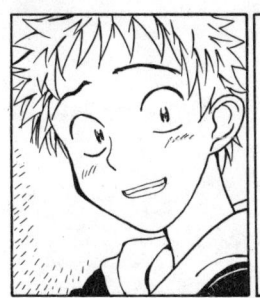

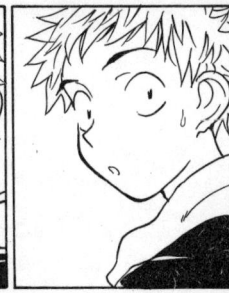

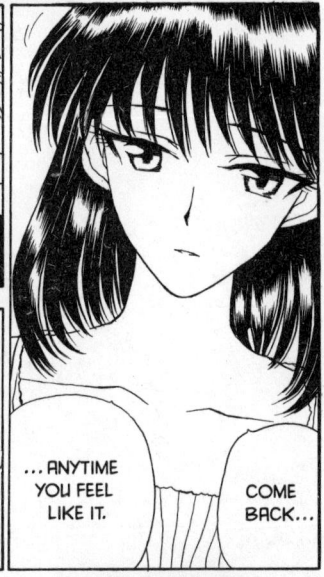

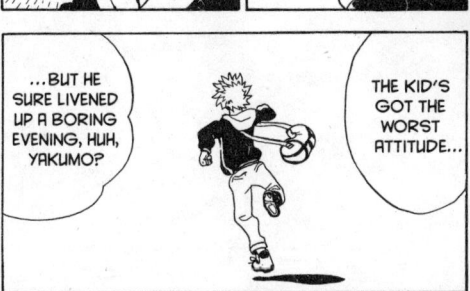

...BUT HE SURE LIVENED UP A BORING EVENING, HUH, YAKUMO?

THE KID'S GOT THE WORST ATTITUDE...

...ANYTIME YOU FEEL LIKE IT.

COME BACK...

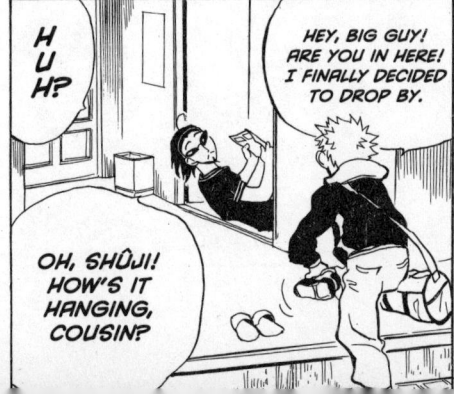

H U H?

HEY, BIG GUY! ARE YOU IN HERE! I FINALLY DECIDED TO DROP BY.

OH, SHÛJI! HOW'S IT HANGING, COUSIN?

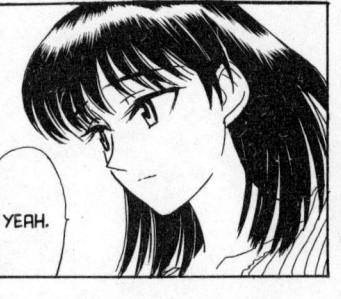

YEAH.

♭02........Fin.

To be continued in Volume 2

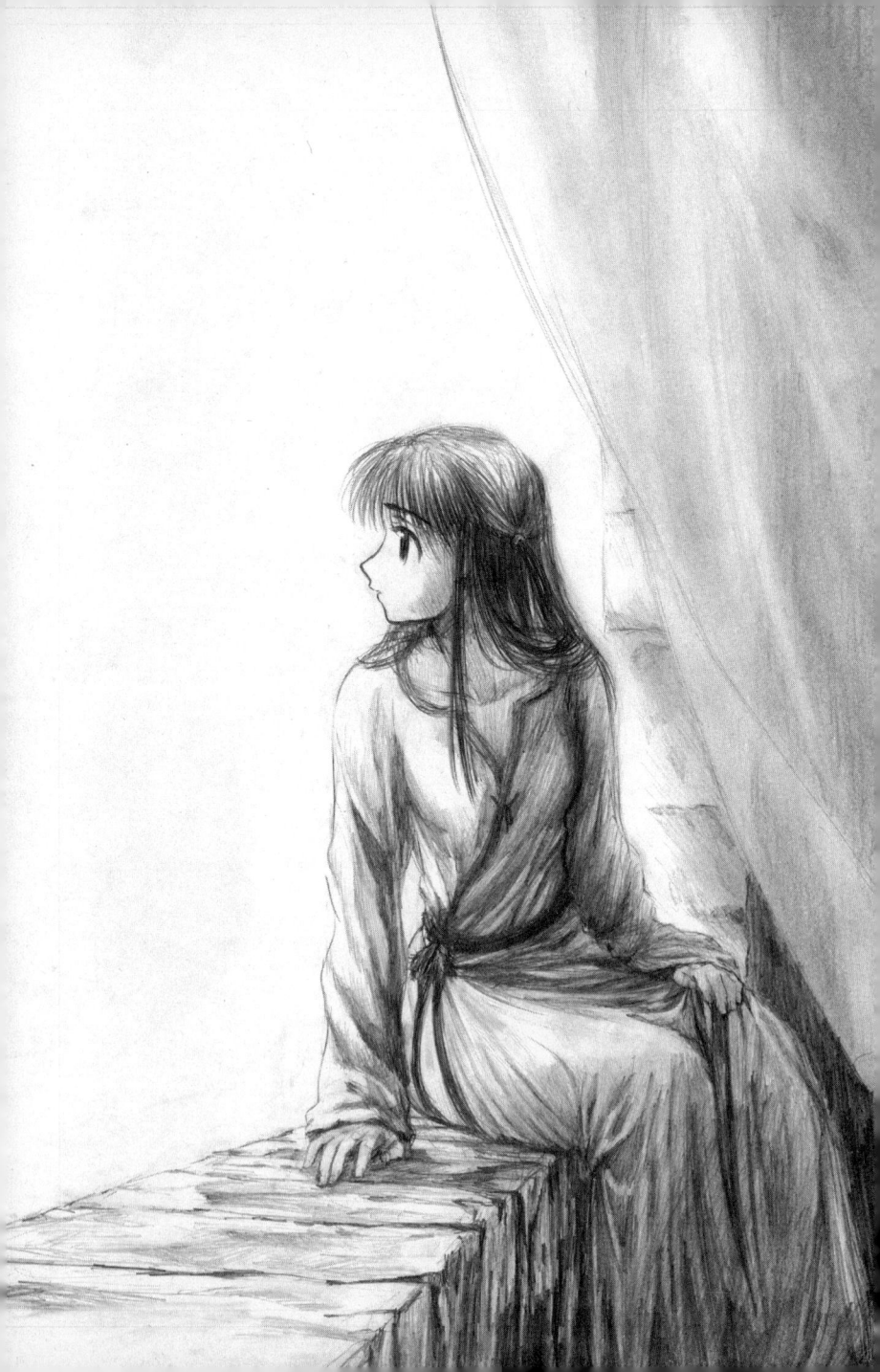

About the Creator

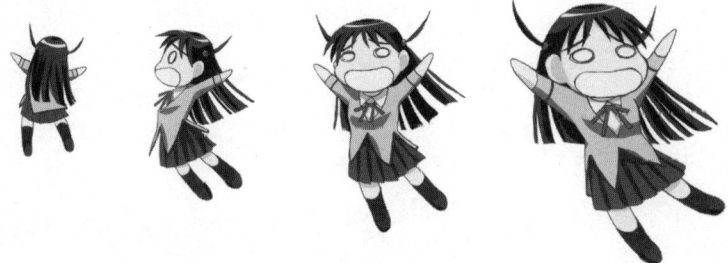

Jin Kobayashi was born in Tokyo. *School Rumble* is his first manga series. He has answered these questions from his fans.

What is your hobby?
Basketball

Which manga inspired you to become a creator?
Dragon Ball

Which character in your manga do you like best?
Kenji Harima

What type of manga do you want to create in the future?
Action

Name one book, piece of music, or movie you like.
The Indiana Jones series

Translation Notes

Japanese is a tricky language for most Westerners, and translation is often more art than science. For your edification and reading pleasure, here are notes on some of the places where we could have gone in a different direction in our translation of the work, or where a Japanese cultural reference is used.

Family or Personal Names

Most students in a Japanese classroom are identified by their family names, for example, Karasuma-kun. Even a close friend may use the last name, such as when Mikoto addresses Tenma, but you'll find that most people in a friendly relationship will use personal names.

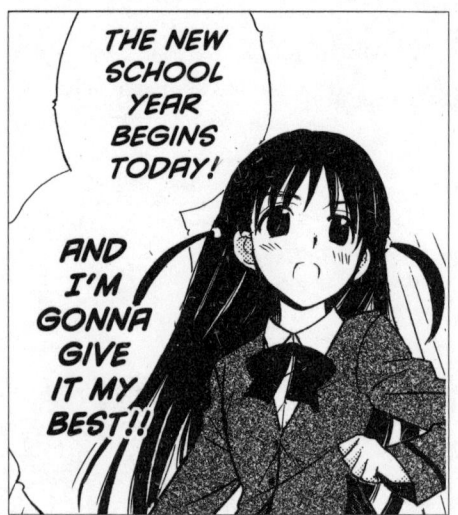

Page 5, Second-Year High School Student

Japanese high schools are arranged a little differently than most American high schools. Grade school is grades 1–6; middle school is grades 7–9; and high school is grades 10–12. Since Tenma is in her second year of high school, she is the same age as juniors in American high schools.

Page 5, New School Year

Unlike American schools, which typically start the academic year in August or September, the Japanese school year begins in early April.

Page 6, How to Pronounce *Tsukamoto*

Many language teachers will tell you that in Japanese every syllable is pronounced. That is not entirely true; some vowel sounds nearly vanish. In the *tsu* sound of *Tsukamoto*, the *u* sound is hardly heard, so to sound more accurate, one should pronounce the name as if there were no *u* sound: Tskamoto.

Page 6, Ôji

Just a little Jin Kobayashi pun. Using different kanji, the pronunciation of Karasuma-kun's personal name, *Ôji*, also means prince.

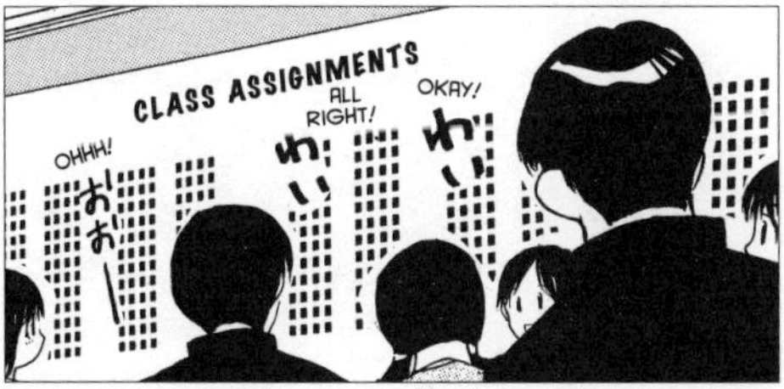
CLASS ASSIGNMENTS
OKAY!
ALL RIGHT!
OHHH!

Page 6, New Class Assignments

Every new class year, homeroom assignments are posted on the school bulletin board, as is the case in American schools, but in Japan the stakes are higher. In Japanese schools, the students typically stay in the same room and the teachers move from class to class, so the students who are in your homeroom are the students you will see all day, every day, for nearly every class for the rest of the year.

Pages 11 and 12, Can't Write

In Japan, admitting that you love a person (*kokuhaku*) is almost a formalized ritual. One can leave a love letter in the shoe locker (see note), or just come out and say it. In Japanese one of the ways of saying it is, "*Watashi wa, anata ga suki desu.*" Or simply, "*Suki desu.*" The

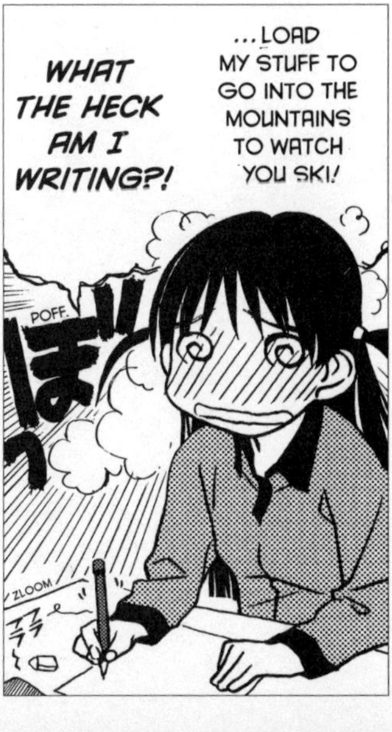
...LOAD MY STUFF TO GO INTO THE MOUNTAINS TO WATCH YOU SKI!
WHAT THE HECK AM I WRITING?!
POFF.
ZLOOM

usual word for love/like/having a crush is *suki*. There are other words, of course, but this is the one Tenma cannot seem to say. The Japanese words that came out of her pen were: *sukii*, to go skiiing; *sukippu*, skipping; *sukiyaki*, a kind of food; *suki ga nai*, to have good defenses; *sukiru-appu*, to improve your skills; and *sukinshippu*, skinship, or building a parental relationship with an infant through touch. The translation tried to take the first two letters of the word *love* and match the Japanese meanings as closely as possible. Still, as in the original, the words get further and further away from the one Tenma wants to write.

Page 13, Love Letters in the Shoe Locker

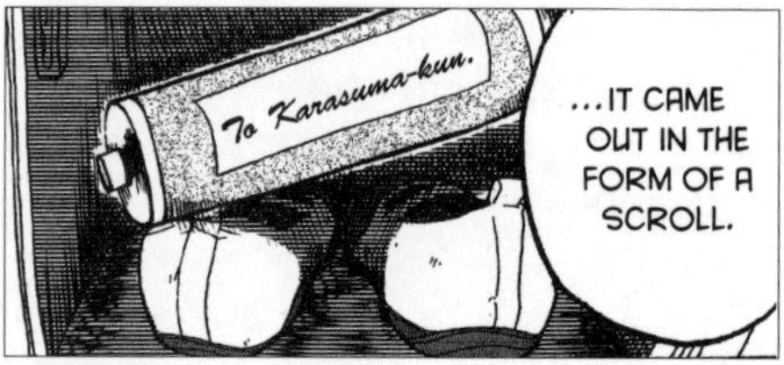
To Karasuma-kun.
...IT CAME OUT IN THE FORM OF A SCROLL.

Leaving a love letter in a student's shoe locker is a longtime tradition in stories about school-age love (and probably has plenty of precedent in reality, but most likely not to the extent you find in romances). The shoe locker is one of the places where a student in love can be sure that the object of his or her affection will go at the start and end of each school day, so it is a favorite place to leave notes and especially love letters.

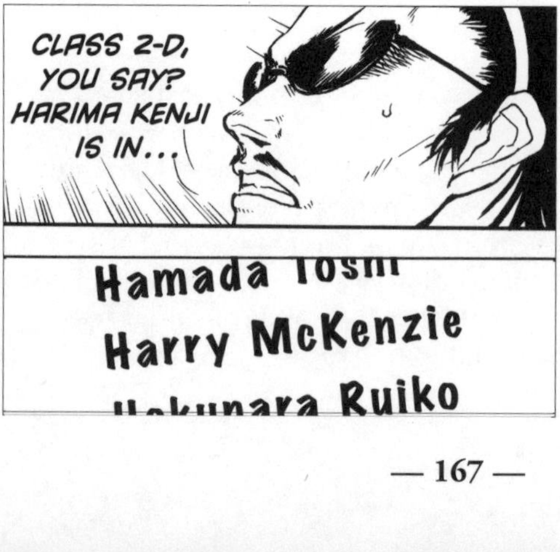
CLASS 2-D, YOU SAY? HARIMA KENJI IS IN...
Harry McKenzie

Page 20, Harry McKenzie

The Japanese pronunciation of the name Harry McKenzie sounds almost exactly the same as the name Harima Kenji.

Page 34, Sonko

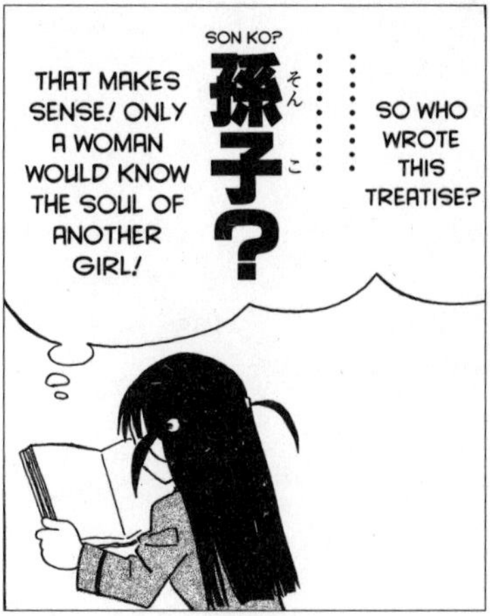
SO WHO WROTE THIS TREATISE?
SON KO?
孫子?
そん こ
THAT MAKES SENSE! ONLY A WOMAN WOULD KNOW THE SOUL OF ANOTHER GIRL!

The second kanji in Sun Tsu's name is also pronounced *ko* by the Japanese, and that same character can be found in many popular girls names such as Junko, Kyoko, Keiko, Yûko, Tomoko, etc. In fact, in post-war Japan it was the fashion to name female children with a name ending in *ko*. (This fashion has changed in the past ten to twenty years.) So when Tenma looks at the kanji for the name Sun Tsu (usually pronounced *Sonshi*, in Japan), she automatically thinks the book was written by Sonko, a woman.

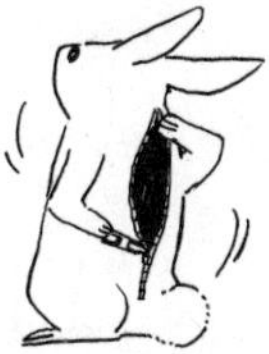

Page 36, Take Off Like a Hare

In Japanese this appeared as the kanji compound (two or more kanji put together to form a single word) *datto*, made up of the kanji for *undress* and *rabbit*. Since *datto* is not a very commonly used word in Japan, it wouldn't be unusual for a junior in high school to be unfamiliar with it.
Note: Sun Tsu does talk about running away like a rabbit, under certain circumstances.

Page 37, Beloved

The kanji that Tenma wanted Karasuma-kun to read for her was one that is pronounced *suki*, a homophone for the Japanese word for love, but this kanji means an opening in one's defenses. She wants to hear him say "I love you" to her, even if it's a trick. Since there are no good homophones for love that can be found in Sun Tsu's *Art of War*, I chose to make it a pronunciation of *beloved*, which is found in a section of *The Art of War* that advised generals to treat their soldiers like their own beloved children in order to foster loyalty.

Fortunately, *beloved* also sounds like an endearment an old-school boyfriend might use.

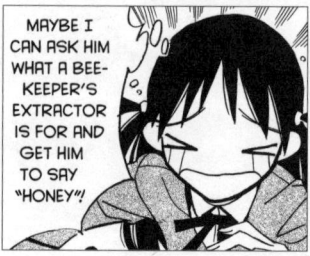

MAYBE I CAN ASK HIM WHAT A BEE-KEEPER'S EXTRACTOR IS FOR AND GET HIM TO SAY "HONEY"!

Page 38, Honey Extractor

There's another word pronounced the same as *love* in Japanese (*suki*) that means plow. So in the same vein, my mission was to find a word that would be an endearment (*honey*) but that would also have something to do with a tool that might be found on a farm.

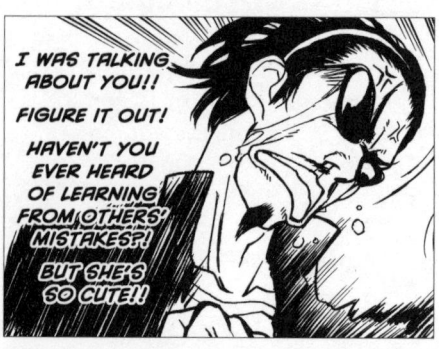

I WAS TALKING ABOUT YOU!! FIGURE IT OUT! HAVEN'T YOU EVER HEARD OF LEARNING FROM OTHERS' MISTAKES?! BUT SHE'S SO CUTE!!

Page 43, Learn from Others' Mistakes

The old Japanese proverb that Kenji used is one that translates to, "Instead of accusing others of bad behavior, learn from it and behave well yourself."

Page 45, Shampoos in the Morning

Most baths in Japanese households are taken at night. But there is a group of people who wash their hair in the morning, and these are given the name of *asashanha*.

Page 52, Wrote the Kanji Wrong

The left side of the final kanji character is incorrect. Tennôji wrote it with a radical indicating *man* rather than with the proper radical, which means left side.

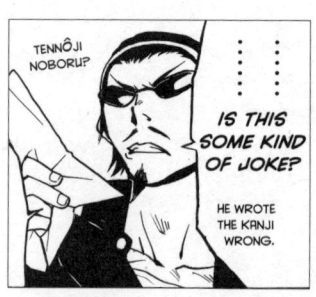

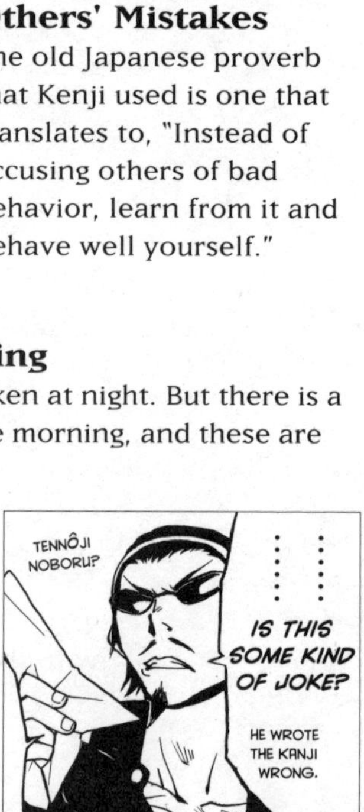

TENNÔJI NOBORU? · · · IS THIS SOME KIND OF JOKE? HE WROTE THE KANJI WRONG.

Page 62, Mama-chari

ちりん
ちりん
CHING
CHING

These are what used to be called women's bicycles in the U.S. One-speed, or three-speed at best, a distinctive basket, and a traditional low-bar frame make up the standard bike ridden by housewives all over Japan. The name, *mama-chari*, comes from *mama* (mother) and the onomatopoeic sound of a bicycle bell, *charin charin*.

Yagami-saka Hill on the way to school...

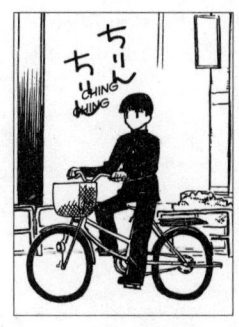

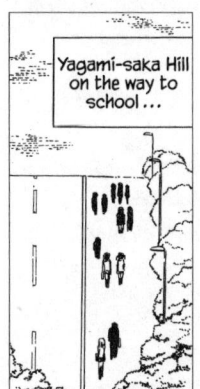

Page 63, Yagami-saka/Shisshin-saka

The kanji for arrow, *ya*, differs from the kanji for loss, *shitsu*, only by the elevation of the top horizontal line, so they are easily mistaken for each other. The author is giving the audience a clue that half-British Eri is still having a few problems with her kanji.

Page 76, Measurements Check

BE NICE TO ME!
BOW

A measurements check or physical checkup (*shintai-sokutei*) is conducted at the beginning of the school year to record the physical condition of each student. Height, weight, sitting height, and chest circumference are some of things that may be checked. These checks are started in the first grade and data is kept until the twelfth grade. Many schools also have monthly checkups for height and weight only, administered by the teachers.

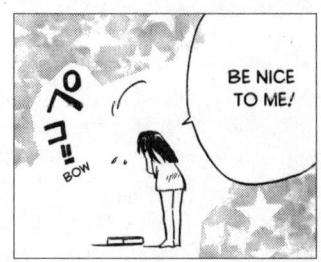

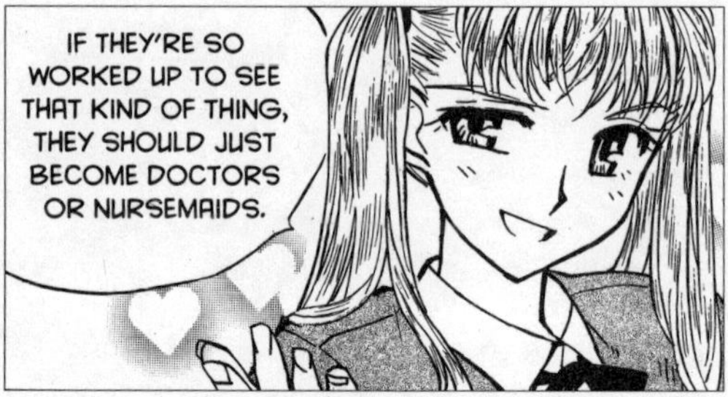
IF THEY'RE SO WORKED UP TO SEE THAT KIND OF THING, THEY SHOULD JUST BECOME DOCTORS OR NURSEMAIDS.

Page 78, Nursemaids

The Japanese word that Eri said was *kangofu*, the most common Japanese word for nurse. But since the *fu* part means woman or wife, and there is an ever-increasing number of male nurses, a more politically correct word has come along, *kangoshi*, which does not specify gender.

Page 82, What in the World Is Gunpura?

Here's the answer to Mikoto's question. The *pura* part is a shortening of *purasuchikku*, which means plastic and refers to plastic models. *Gun* is short for Gundam (from the famous giant-robot TV franchise, "Mobile Suit Gundam"). So Akira's hobby is putting together the complex, high-quality, snap-together Gundam plastic model kits that are so popular in Japan.

Page 90, Ukiyo-e

Floating World drawings are generally found in intricate wood-block prints that were created starting late in the Edo Period (1603–1867) of Japan. They include stylized, impressionistic pictures based on Kabuki plays and the pleasure districts of Japan's largest cities such as Edo (Tokyo) and Kyoto.

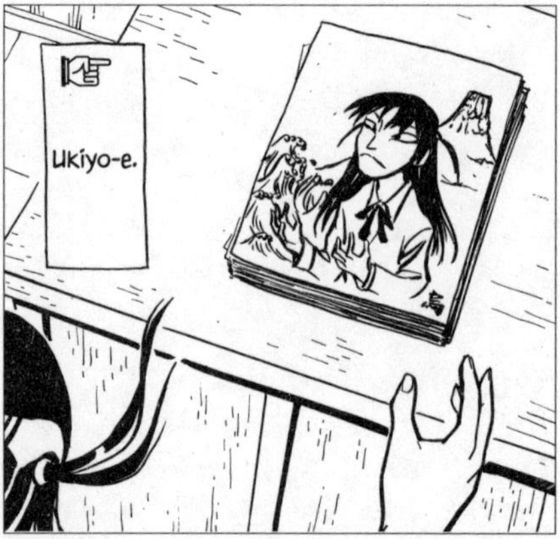
Ukiyo-e.

Page 93, Buns

One of the quick snacks in Japan is prepackaged buns that the Japanese call by the same word they use for bread, *pan*. They are usually purchased in bakeries and grocery stores, but prepackaged *pan* can also be found in vending machines and other convenient locations. Most contain fillings such as curry, barbecued pork, sweet bean paste, and other varieties. Like chips or candy bars from vending machines in America, *pan* is an inexpensive snack that quite often substitutes for a meal.

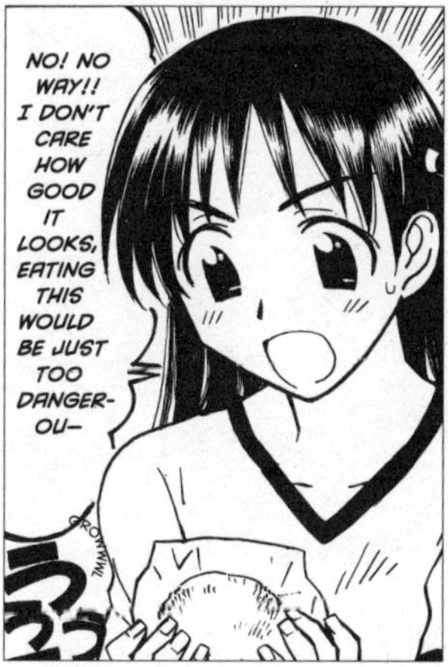
NO! NO WAY!! I DON'T CARE HOW GOOD IT LOOKS, EATING THIS WOULD BE JUST TOO DANGER-OU–

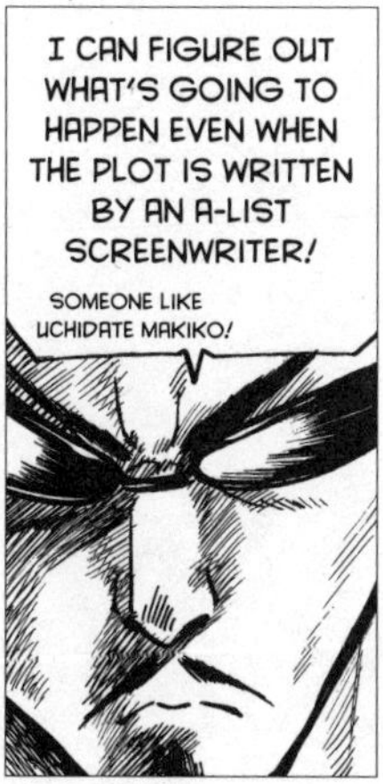
I CAN FIGURE OUT WHAT'S GOING TO HAPPEN EVEN WHEN THE PLOT IS WRITTEN BY AN A-LIST SCREENWRITER!
SOMEONE LIKE UCHIDATE MAKIKO!

Page 100, Uchidate Makiko

Uchidate Makiko is a prolific female writer of books and movies most famous for her TV dramas—eleven-episode stories, usually romantic, featuring plots that have twists and turns and, as with most television, aren't too challenging to the average viewer. (There are exceptional dramas out there, of course.)

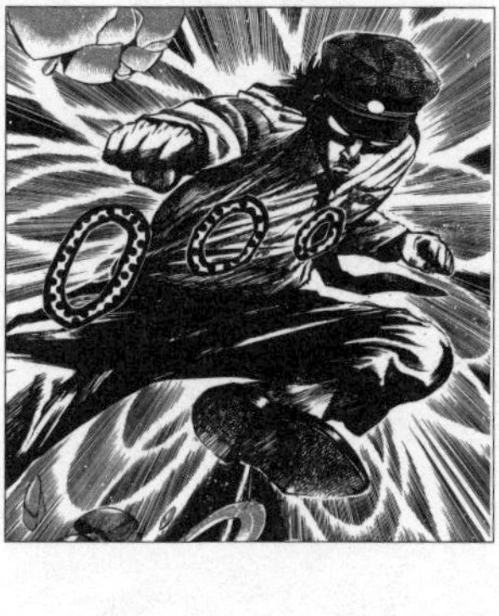

Page 103, Hurricane Kick

In this case, Hurricane is spelled Hariken, and it's made up of two kanji, one being the first character in Harima's name and the second meaning fist.

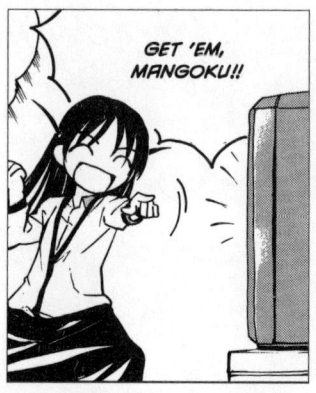

GET 'EM, MANGOKU!!

Page 109 Three to Get Killed!

Sanbiki ga Kiru! (Three for the Kill!) is an immensely popular *jidai-geki* (Warring States or Edo Period drama) that starred the handsome Yakusho Kôji as the swordsman Sengoku. Sengoku's two companions are Tono-sama and Tako (*tono* means lord, and *tako* can mean octopus). In *School Rumble*, Tenma's favorite *jidai-geki*, *Sanbiki ga Kirareru!* (Three to Get Killed!), stars the handsome Yakushamaru Kôji (*yakusha* means actor) as the swordsman Mangoku (*sen* means 1,000, and *man* means 10,000). Mangoku's two companions are Ue-sama and Ika (*ue* means above, and *ika* can mean both below and eel).

Page 111, Boss Coffee

With its stylish jet-black can emblazoned with the image of an authoritative-looking man smoking a pipe and the name Boss in big, bold letters, there's no doubt that Suntory's Boss canned coffee is aimed at a male demographic.

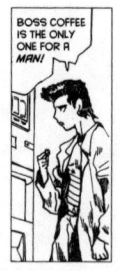

BOSS COFFEE IS THE ONLY ONE FOR A MAN!

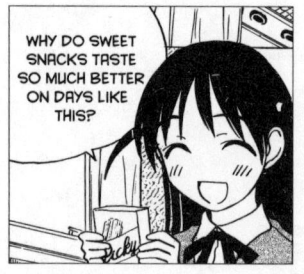

WHY DO SWEET SNACKS TASTE SO MUCH BETTER ON DAYS LIKE THIS?

Page 117, Picky Sticks

The Picky Sticks in Tenma's world are the Picky Sticks in ours. A favorite snack in Japan, and the almost-official Japanese snack food of otaku everywhere. They are thin, crunchy sticks of sweet bread covered in chocolate or other flavors.

Page 118, Old Maid

HA あははは HA HA AH
EH P!
RRRRN オオー!!
ガヤ ガヤ
KA-TUMP
KA-TUMP
I SURE AM!

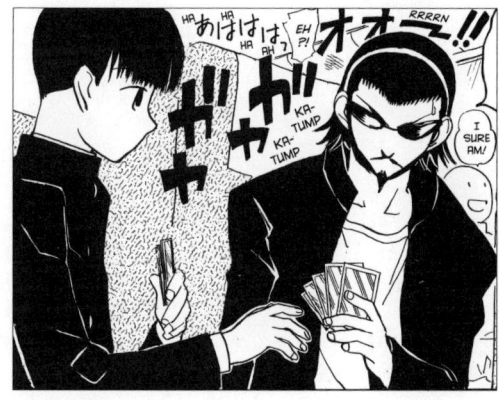

The game Karasuma and Harima are playing, *Babanuki* (which literally translates to Pulling Out Grandma), is basically Old Maid. Players take turns selecting a card from their opponent's hand, trying to make pairs and hoping not to choose the single joker in the deck. The loser is the person who winds up with the joker at the end of the game.

Page 123, Torimaru

The kanji for *Karasu* (raven or crow) differs from the kanji for *tori* (bird) by only one line. And the kanji for *ma* in Karasuma-kun's name is usually read *maru*. So thinking Karasuma-kun's name is Torimaru would be an easy mistake to make, especially for someone who doesn't pay much attention in kanji class.

Page 124, The Rainy Season and Romance

In Japan, it rains nearly every day in the month of June. This rainy season is called *tsuyu*, and it is a good idea to keep an umbrella handy. However, a couple walking home under a single umbrella is

SHAAAAAA

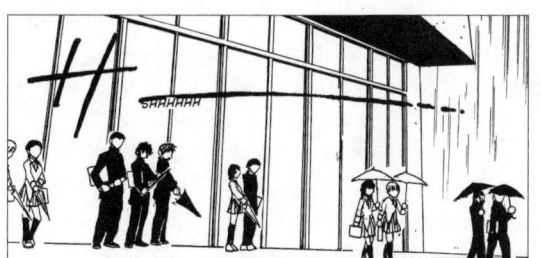

the symbol for love in Japan. Like having two names in a heart in North America, two names under a stylized triangle (supposed to represent an

umbrella) means that the two people named are in love. The reason for this is because the Japanese are traditionally shy of physical intimacy in public, and two people can share a more intimate closeness under an umbrella than would normally be allowed.

Page 125, Konnyaku

Konnyaku is a traditional Japanese jelly-like health food made from a kind of potato called Konnyaku potato, containing calcium hydroxide extracted from eggshells.

Page 130, Rain Gear

The Japanese word for rain gear is *kappa*. But *kappa* is also a water sprite. Since there are no words for water sprite that also mean rain gear in English, this translation lets Karasuma-kun's oddness speak for itself.

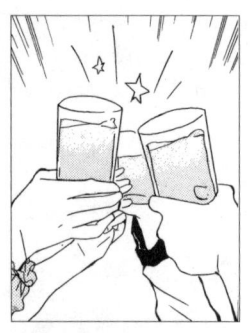

Page 133, Kampai!

Alternatively spelled *Kanpai*, this toast literally means empty glass, but for all intents and purposes, its direct translation would be the English "Cheers!"

Page 142, Bug

I THOUGHT FOR SURE YOU HAD CAUGHT THE BUG!

Another pun. Tenma says, "I thought it was love," but she uses *koi*, another Japanese word for love. As anyone who owns a fish pond knows, *koi* can also mean those huge goldfish-like carp. So Yakumo's reply is, "Koi? No, it's a cat."

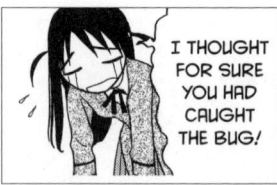

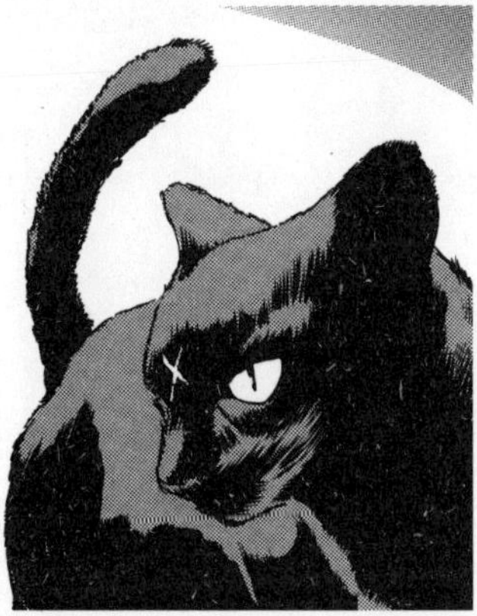

Page 145, The Cat Returns
Both the Studio Ghibli film and original manga by Hiiragi Aoi, *The Cat Returns*, are based on an old Japanese fairy tale titled *Neko no Ongaeshi* (The Cat Returns the Favor), about a cat who magically pays back a human for saving its life.

Page 151, Banana Daifuku Cakes
Banana daifuku is a *mochi* (rice paste) cake filled with sweet bean paste and a small chunk of banana.

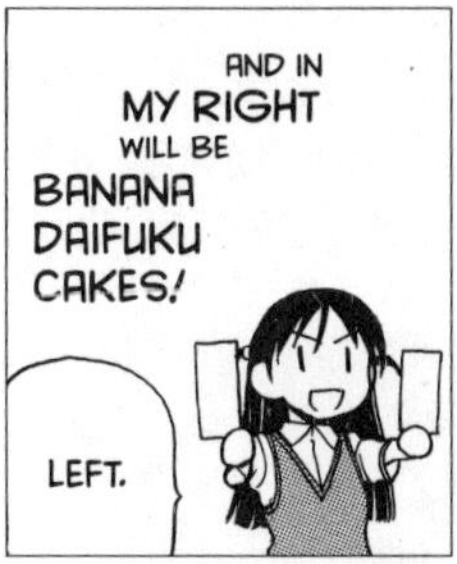
AND IN MY RIGHT WILL BE BANANA DAIFUKU CAKES!
LEFT.

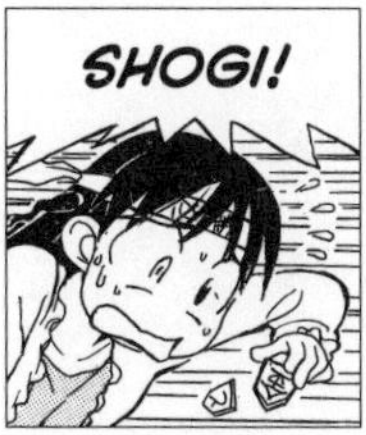
SHOGI!

Page 158, Shogi
Often called Japanese chess, shogi is a game with twenty pieces per player set on a nine-by-nine board. The object of the game is, as in chess, to capture the opponent's king.

Page 160, Yakumo-nee-chan
It is common for small children to call young (or young-looking) strangers "big brother" or "big sister." Shûji is using this form of address for Yakumo because he'd like a closer relationship with her, but it also reinforces in him that she is older and pretty much out of his league.

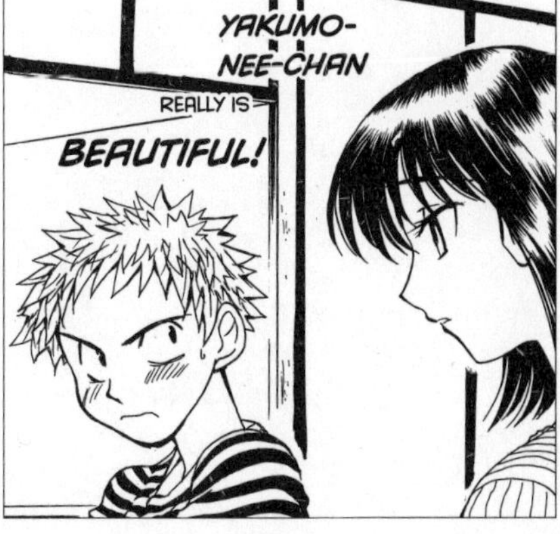
YAKUMO-NEE-CHAN
REALLY IS
BEAUTIFUL!

Preview of Volume 2

We're pleased to present you with a preview of *School Rumble*, Volume 2. On sale in English now!

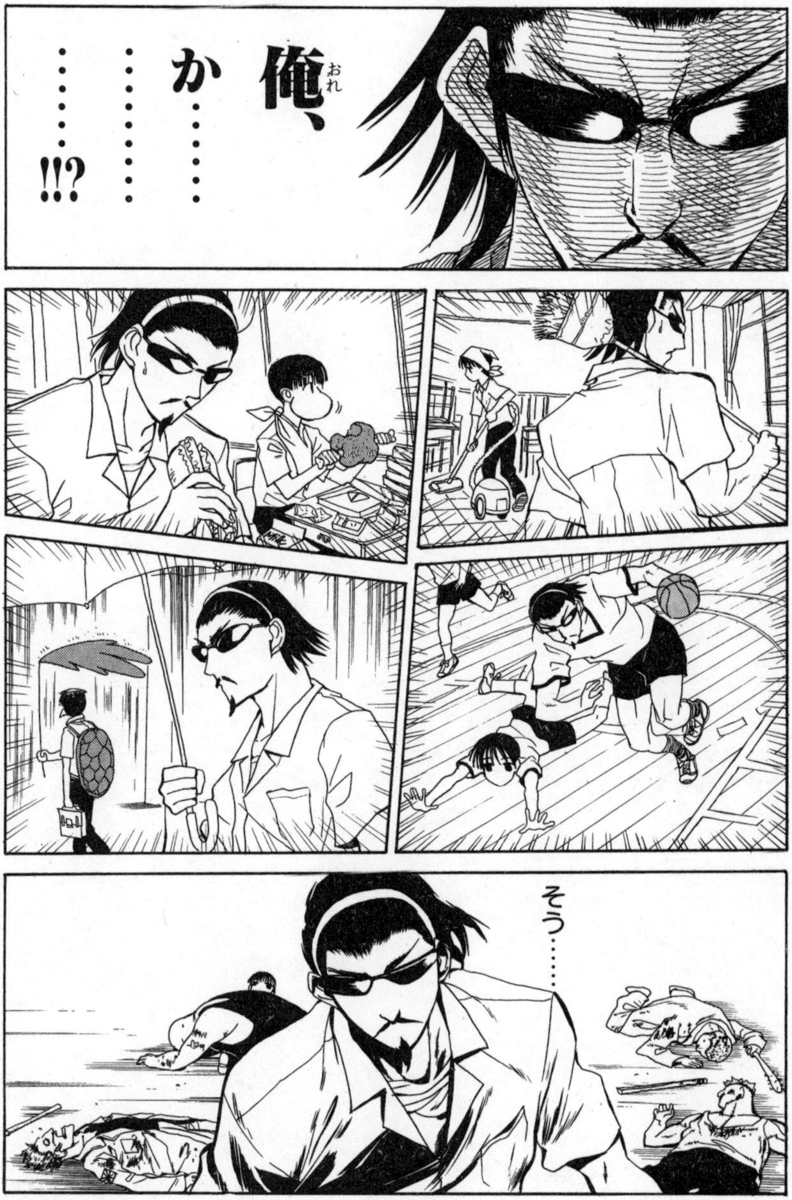

俺、か………………!!?
そう……

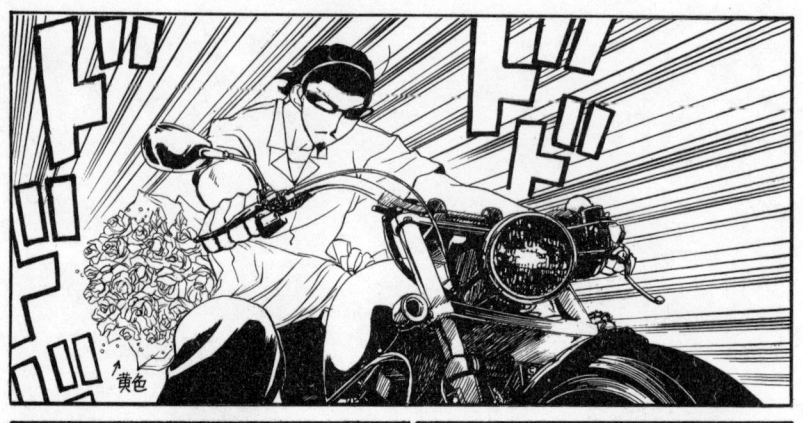

黄色

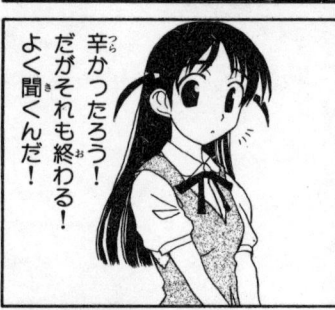

辛かったろう！
だがそれも終わる！
よく聞くんだ！

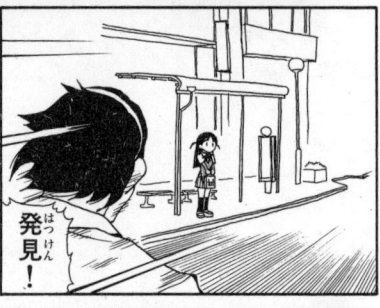

発見！

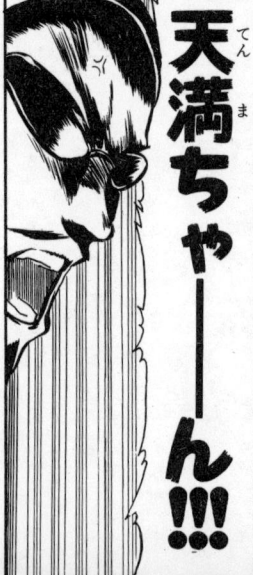

天満ちゃーーん!!!

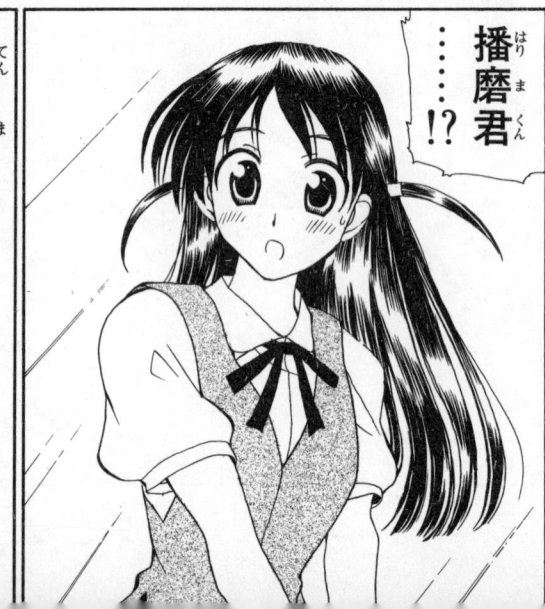

播磨君
……!?

好・・・
あぶな・・・
で
播磨拳児全治十日
なんだっけな〜〜
ナンかすげー良いことがあった気が……
その日の記憶不鮮明
サングラスとりなよ
しかし君ほど運の悪い男も珍しいな…
播磨君お見舞いに来たよー
OH!? ナゼ!? ラッキー!!

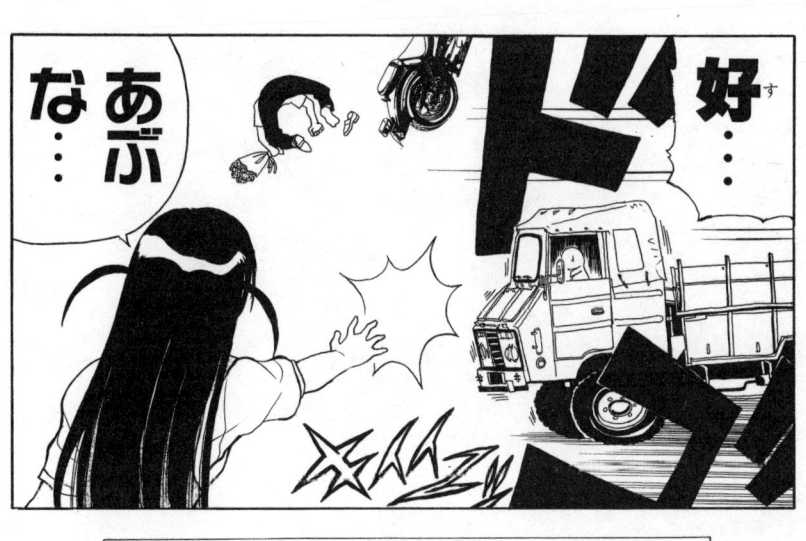

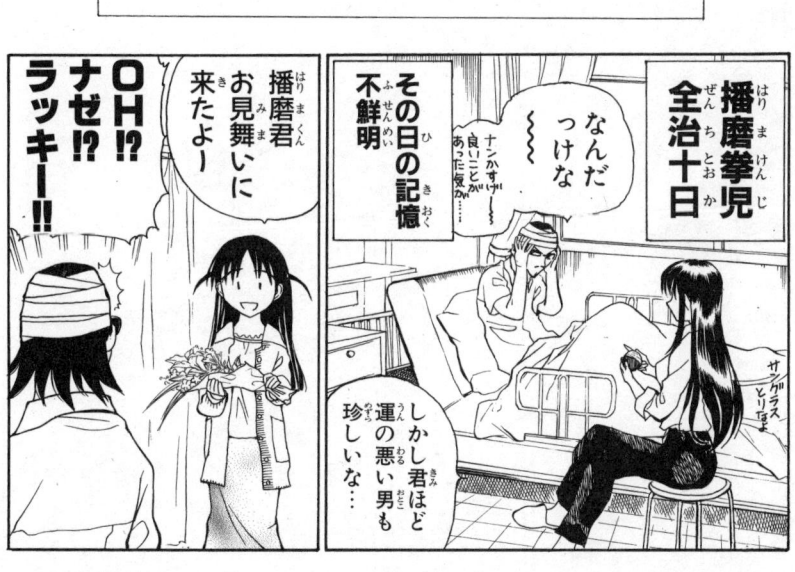

■今鳥恭介■

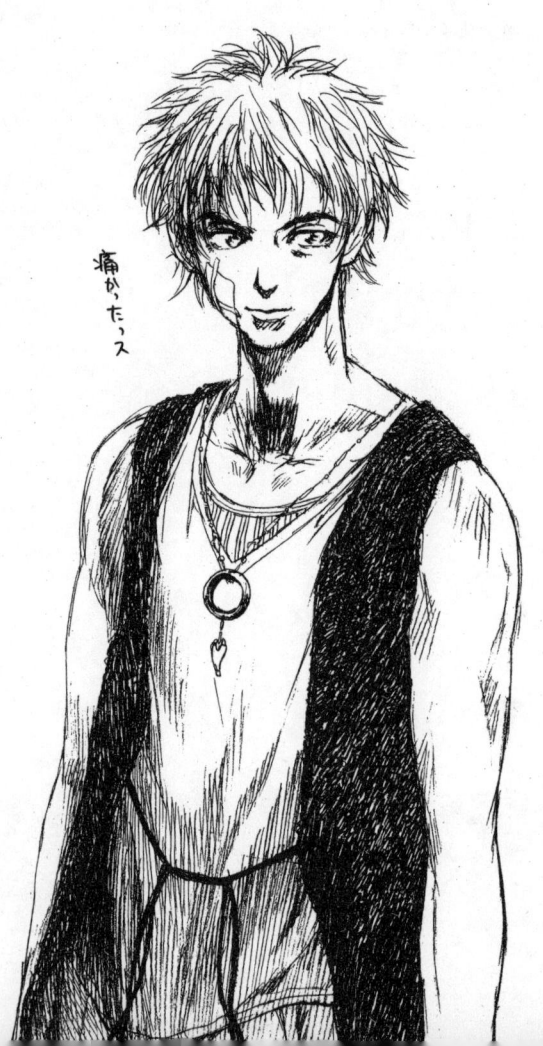

痛かったっス

FREE
wallpapers
icons
previews
downloads
competitions
visit
www.tanoshimi.tv
tanoshimi

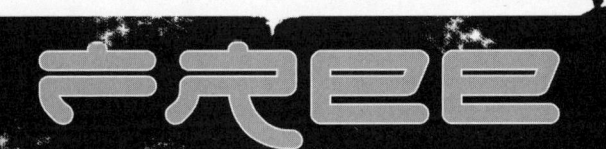

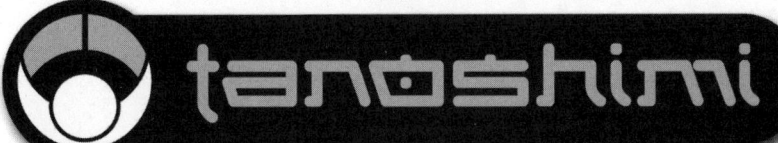

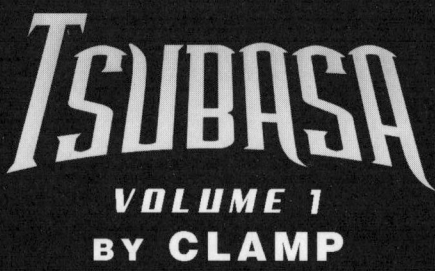

TSUBASA
VOLUME 1
BY CLAMP

SAKURA AND SYAORAN RETURN!

But they're not the people you know. Sakura is the princess of Clow—and possessor of a mysterious, misunderstood power that promises to change the world. Syaoran is her childhood friend and leader of the archaeological dig that took his father's life. They reside in an alternate reality . . . where whatever you least expect can happen—and does. When Sakura ventures to the dig site to declare her love for Syaoran, a puzzling symbol is uncovered—which triggers a remarkable quest. Now Syaoran embarks upon a desperate journey through other worlds—all in the name of saving Sakura.

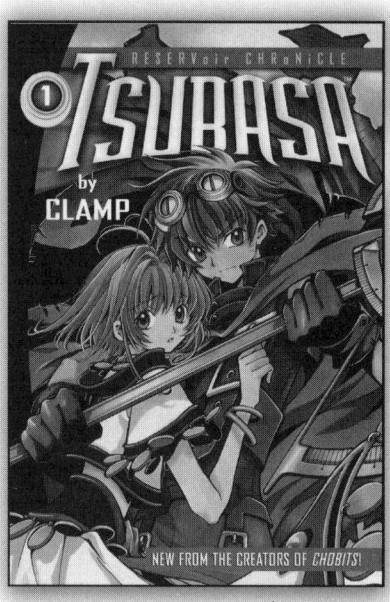

Ages: 13+

Includes special extras after the story!

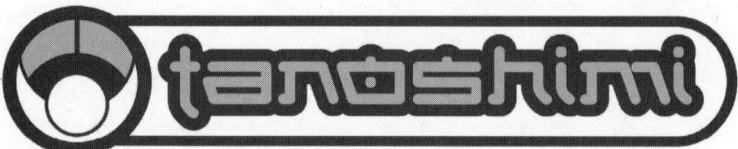

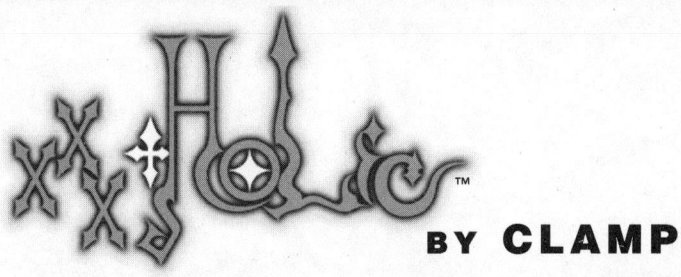

BY CLAMP

Watanuki Kimihiro is haunted by visions. When he finds himself irresistibly drawn into a shop owned by Yūko, a mysterious witch, he is offered the chance to rid himself of the spirits that plague him. He accepts, but soon realizes that he's just been tricked into working for the shop to pay off the cost of Yūko's services! But this isn't any ordinary kind of shop . . . In this shop, Yūko grants wishes to those in need. But they must have the strength of will not only to truly understand their need, but to give up something incredibly precious in return.

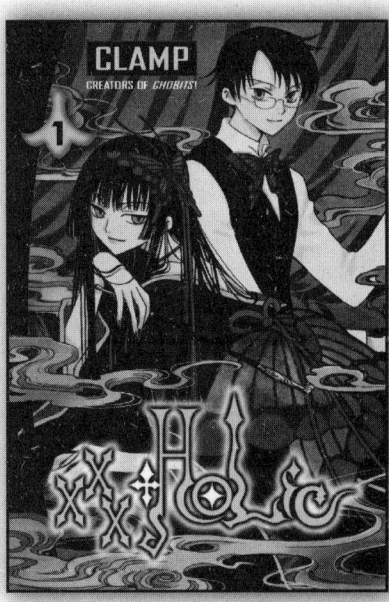

Ages: 13+

Special extras in each volume! Read them all!

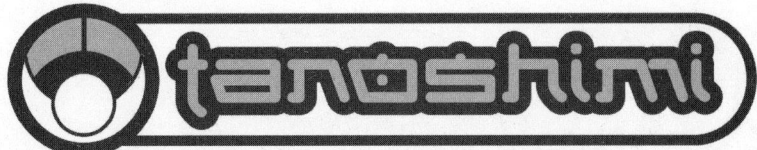

Guru Guru Pon-Chan

RUFF RUFF LIFE

Ponta is a Labrador retriever puppy, the Koizumi family's pet. She's full of energy and usually up to some kind of mischief. But when Grandpa Koizumi, an amateur inventor, creates the Guru Guru Bone, Ponta's curiosity causes trouble. She nibbles the bone—and turns into a human girl!

Surprised but undaunted, Ponta ventures out of the house and meets Mirai Iwaki, the most popular boy at school. When Mirai saves her from a speeding car, Ponta changes back into her puppy self. Yet much has changed for Ponta during her short adventure as a human. Her heart races and her face flushes when she thinks of Mirai now. She's in love! Using the power of the Guru Guru Bone, Ponta switches back and forth from dog to girl—but can she win Mirai's affections?

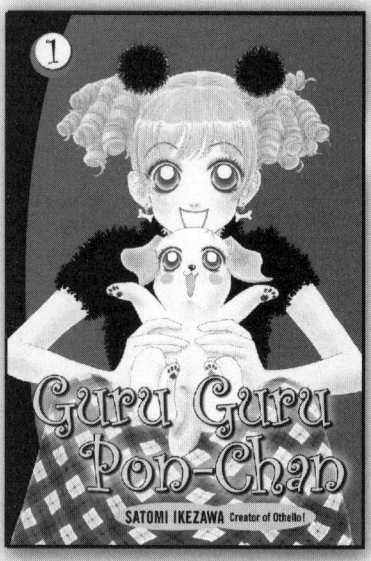

Ages: 13+

Winner of the Kodansha Manga of the Year Award!

Includes special extras after the story!

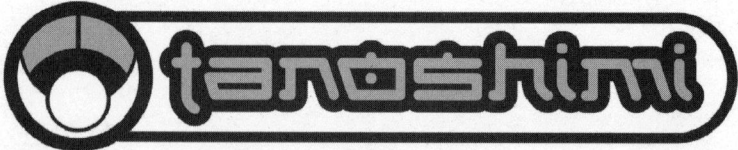

STOP!!
YOU'RE GOING THE WRONG WAY!
MANGA IS A COMPLETELY DIFFERENT TYPE OF READING EXPERIENCE.
TO START AT THE BEGINNING, GO TO THE END!
THAT'S RIGHT! AUTHENTIC MANGA IS READ THE TRADITIONAL JAPANESE WAY—FROM RIGHT TO LEFT. EXACTLY THE OPPOSITE OF HOW ENGLISH BOOKS ARE READ. IT'S EASY TO FOLLOW: JUST GO TO THE OTHER END OF THE BOOK, AND READ EACH PAGE—AND EACH PANEL—FROM THE RIGHT SIDE TO THE LEFT SIDE, STARTING AT THE TOP RIGHT. NOW YOU'RE EXPERIENCING MANGA AS IT WAS MEANT TO BE.

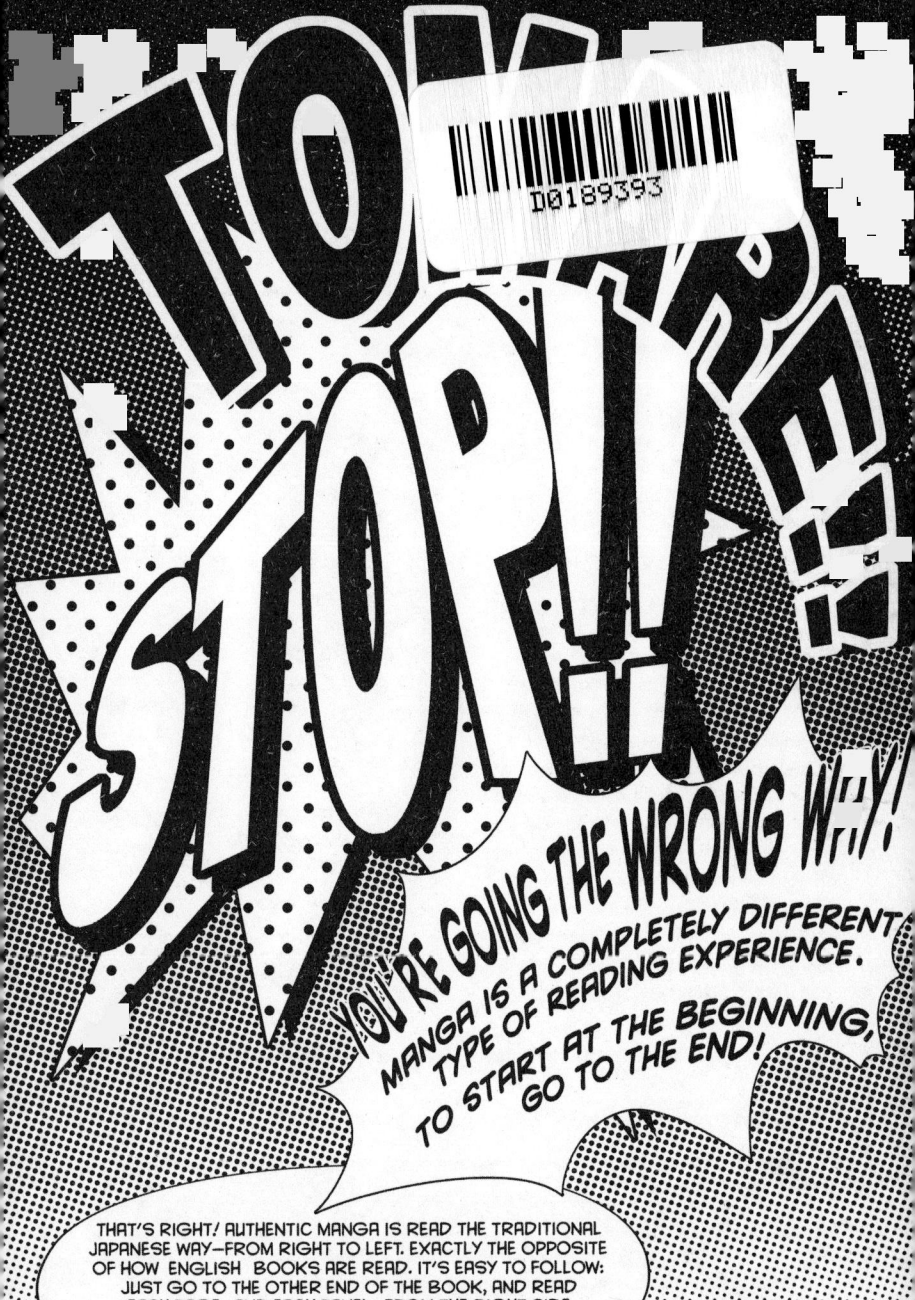